D1554170

DATE DUE

This book examines how the South Pacific was represented by explorers, missionaries, travellers, writers and artists between 1767 and 1914. It draws on history, literature, art history and anthropology in its study of different, often conflicting colonial discourses of the Pacific. It engages with colonial discourse and post-colonial theory, criticizing both for their failure to acknowledge the historical specificity of colonial discourses and cultural encounters, and for continuing to see indigenous cultures in essentially passive or reactive terms. It offers a detailed and grounded 'reading back' of these colonial discourses into the metropolitan centres which gave rise to them, while resisting the idea that all representations of other cultures are merely self-representations. Among its themes are the persistent myth-making around the figure of Cook; the western obsession with Polynesian sexuality, tattooing, cannibalism and leprosy; the Pacific as a theatre for adventure, and as a setting for Europe's displaced fears of its own cultural extinction.

REPRESENTING THE SOUTH PACIFIC

REPRESENTING THE
SOUTH PACIFIC

Colonial discourse from Cook to Gauguin

ROD EDMOND

University of Kent at Canterbury

CAMBRIDGE
UNIVERSITY PRESS

...TE OF THE UNIVERSITY OF CAMBRIDGE
...t, Cambridge CB2 1RP, United Kingdom

...NIVERSITY PRESS
The Edinburgh Building, Cambridge CB2 2RU, United Kingdom
40 West 20th Street, New York, NY 10011-4211, USA
10 Stamford Road, Oakleigh, Melbourne 3166, Australia

© Cambridge University Press 1997

First published 1997

Printed in the United Kingdom at the University Press, Cambridge

Typeset in Monotype Baskerville 11/12½pt

A catalogue record for this book is available from the British Library

Library of Congress cataloguing in publication data

Edmond, Rod.
Representing the South Pacific: colonial discourse from Cook to
Gauguin / Rod Edmond.
p. cm.
Includes index
ISBN 0 521 55054 8 (hardback)
1. Oceania – Relations – Europe. 2. Europe – Relations – Oceania.
3. Oceania – Colonization. I. Title.
DU68.E85E36 1997
303.48'29504–dc21
97–1845 CIP

ISBN 0 521 55054 8 hardback

To my parents, Rae and Don Edmond

Contents

Illustrations

Acknowledgements

Grateful acknowledgement is made to The Leverhulme Trust for the award of a Research Fellowship in 1995–96 which allowed me to complete this book. My very warm thanks go to Isobel Armstrong and Jonathan Lamb for supporting my application to the Trust, and for their interest and encouragement over several years.

I also wish to thank the librarians of the New Zealand and Pacific Room at Auckland University, the British Library, Rhodes House Library, Oxford, and the School of African and Oriental Studies Library, London, for their valuable assistance.

Closer to home, I would like to thank the University of Kent at Canterbury for a sabbatical term which enabled me to get this book started; Angela Faunch of the University of Kent's Templeman Library for the speed and ingenuity with which she retrieved obscure titles through library interloan; Jim Styles of the Library's Photographic Unit for the excellence of his reproductions; and Miles Banbery of the University's Computing Laboratory for his help and patience.

I also wish to thank several present and former colleagues in the School of English and the Centre for Colonial and Post-Colonial Research at Kent who have read and commented on parts of this book, or otherwise helped to bring it into being: David Ellis, Abdulrazak Gurnah, Lyn Innes, Jan Montefiore and Nigel Rigby.

Among many others who have provided help and encouragement, in person or by example, I would particularly like to mention Judith Binney, Z. Brooke, Murray Edmond, C. Karembeu, J. Lomu, Bronwen Nicholson and Glyn Williams.

I am grateful to Petra and Kirsty Cunningham for allowing me to reproduce engravings from their undated folio edition of illustrations from Cook's last voyage.

Particular thanks also to Josie Dixon and the production team at Cambridge University Press; to Sue Phillpott for her painstaking copy-editing; to Stephanie Rudgard-Redsell for the precision of her indexing.

Closest to home, I must thank Sarah, Cassius, Daisy and Jo for travelling with me.

CHAPTER 1

Introduction

'it is half the planet: this half-globe,
  this bulging
Eyeball of water, arched over to Asia,
Australia and white Antarctica: those are the eyelids that
  never close; this is the staring unsleeping
Eye of the earth . . .'

(Robinson Jeffers, 'The Eye')

The most banal yet awesome fact about the Pacific is its size. This vast ocean with its scattered pinprick islands has raised questions of scale, proportion and relation whenever it has been contemplated. From an outside perspective the islands of Oceania are almost submerged in the immensity of their surroundings (indeed Pacific islands have come and gone), their sea-locked inhabitants marooned on coral or volcanic tips of land. The Pacific, as opposed to its rim, is conceived as being more or less empty, the hole in the doughnut.

The inside perspective must always have been different. It is unlikely that Pacific peoples ever thought of themselves as inhabiting somewhere small, or that the disproportions of scale so striking to outsiders would have impressed them in the same way. In 1769 Tupaia, a priest from the Tahitian group of islands, drew Cook a map of his world. Taking its centre at Tahiti, the map showed seventy-four islands scattered across a large oceanic area measuring about three thousand miles from east to west and a thousand miles from north to south. The islands were arranged in concentric circles based on sailing times from the map's centre rather than on linear distance.[1]

It is also unlikely that Pacific islanders shared the continental distinction between land and sea. Both were, and are, their territory. Pacific peoples, the Tongan writer Epeli Hau'ofa insists, are

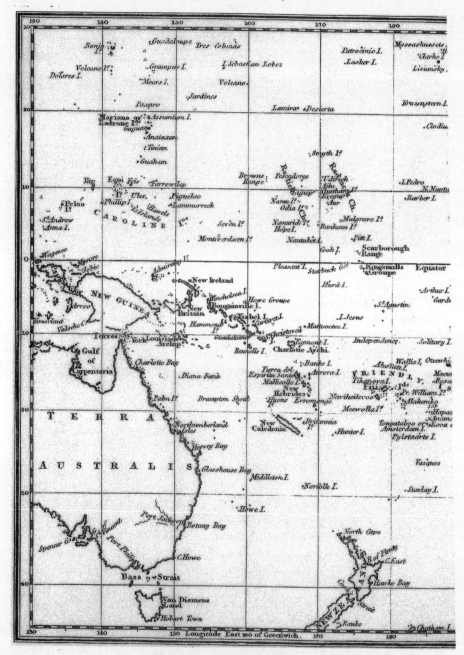

1 European map of Polynesia, 1830.

170 160 150 140 130

Maria Laxara I.

nker I.

Allen I.
:Gardner I.
: Necker I.
Birds I.
Niihau Tauai SANDWICH
Taura Oahu Morokai
Maui I.
Hawaii

Gasper I.

Cooper I.

Mallooin I.

Johnson I.
Wake I.

Coral R.

Ann I.

Manuel Rodriguez

Palmyras I.
Washington I.
Fanning I. Low I.
Christmas I.

Washington I.

Marcus I.

Balvoat I.
I.

Sarah
Starbuck I.

rie I.
Clarence I. Francis I.
I. of Danger

Penrhyn I.

Marquesas
Nuahiva
Rooapoa Ohivaoa

Caroline I.

Flint I.

Navigators Is
Ohaloah
Toomanuah
Oloo
ren I.
Palmerston I.
Savage I.
a or Rotterdam I.
Middleburg I. Rarotoa or
Rarotonga

Swarrow I.

Scilly I.
Society I.
Boradora
Raiatea
Rorooa
Huahine
Tahite
Georgian
I.
Maatea

Ohia Taokia Disappointment I.
Palliser Carlshoff I.
Chain I.
Rarreva
Dangl
Serles I.
Whitsunday I.

Aitutake
Harvey Ids
Maiti
Mouiai I. Burutu I.
Rimatara
Tubuai
Raivavai or
High I.

Gloecester I. Margaret I.
Osnaburg I.

Carysfort I.
Hood I.
Gambier I.
Crescent I.
Oeno

Four Gowns
Rapa

St. Juan Baptista

Duc̃es
Pitcairns I.
Elizabeth

Group of Is.

POLYNESIA.

2 Tupaia's chart, centred on Tahiti (Otaheite), 1769.

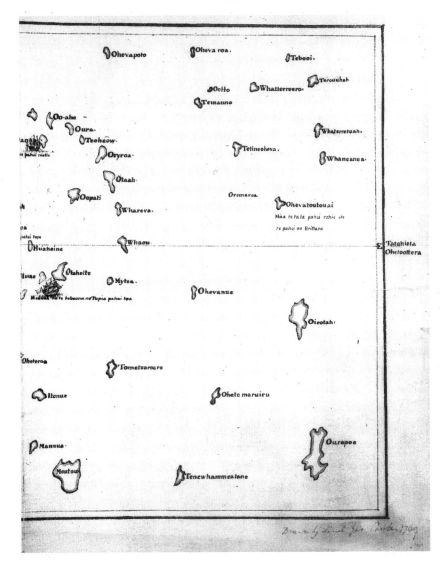

ocean dwellers inhabiting a 'sea of islands'. Derek Walcott has spoken similarly of the Caribbean. Maori, J. G. A. Pocock has argued, are as much *tangata waka* (people of the ship) as *tangata whenua* (people of the land), their histories shaped by voyaging.[2] Historically the Pacific was a large world in which people and cultures mingled unhindered by the kinds of boundary erected by the colonial powers in the nineteenth century. This sense of oceanic community, Hau'ofa argues, was never entirely lost and is being recreated in our own time in the form of new Pacific diasporas.[3]

The coral reef, with its wide, often shallow, warm, calm interior, can be seen as a physical expression of the blurred margin of sea and land in the Oceanic world. The boundaries of islands are porous and shifting, advancing and retreating each day with the tide. Sea and land become interchangeable. Micronesian seafarers, for example, inverted the western conception of a navigational environment by thinking of their canoes as stationary, with the islands moving towards and past them.[4] Such differing conceptions of the world, and their interaction, are a major theme of this book.

That so much of the planet should have remained uncharted until two hundred years ago invited speculation from early times. The Pacific was, and in a debased sense remains, a place of dreams. The earliest of these was geographic. For Pomponius Mela in the first century and Ptolemy in the second, both proponents of the theory of a spherical earth, a continental landmass in the southern hemisphere was necessary to balance the known landmasses of the north and maintain equilibrium. Their theories were the basis of Renaissance geographical thought, and of the persistence of the idea of *Terra australis incognita*, the unknown southern land, which was elaborated in the eighteenth century by de Brosse in France, Callander in Scotland and Dalrymple in England.[5] It was not until Cook's second voyage (1772–5) that the theory of the southern continent was dispelled by travelling south, as Cook wrote, 'as far as I think it possible for man to go'.[6] With the Antarctic circle established as the southern boundary of the Pacific, *Terra australis incognita* then broke up into the many small and few large islands of the southern Pacific. By the end of the eighteenth century the positional geography of the Pacific, with its associated acts of naming and possession (New Ireland, New Britain, New

Caledonia, New Hebrides and so on), was more or less established. However a whole new set of questions had been raised, of culture rather than of geography.

Cook's editor and biographer J. C. Beaglehole described the European discovery of Tahiti by Wallis in 1767 as being 'of the utmost significance ... for the whole history of the western mind'.[7] One can point out the inadequacy of a concept like 'the western mind', and emphasize the very different significance of the visit for the Tahitians (many of whom were killed by Wallis' guns), without dismissing the claim as hyperbolic. From this moment western representations of the Pacific were to form important chapters in the history of the Enlightenment and Romanticism, of nineteenth-century Christianity, science and social theory, of modern painting, anthropology and popular culture.

There was, during the eighteenth century, a paradigm shift in the way in which the native inhabitants of new worlds came to be understood and described. This is implicit in Anthony Pagden's *European Encounters with the New World* and has been spelled out by Nicholas Thomas in *Colonialism's Culture*. Renaissance perceptions of difference between discoverers and natives were religious rather than racial or national. There was what Thomas terms a 'vacancy of otherness',[8] a lack of singular character or physique accorded to the other. By the eighteenth century, however, this religiously framed colonialism was being replaced by natural history as the basis for constructing otherness. Human variety came to be seen as analogous to the differences between animal species. J. R. Forster, scientist on Cook's second voyage, exemplifies this point. One of the main sections of his *Observations made during a Voyage round the World* (1778) was titled 'the VARIETIES of the HUMAN SPECIES, relative to COLOUR, SIZE, FORM, HABIT, and NATURAL TURN OF MIND in the NATIVES of the SOUTH-SEA ISLES'.[9] Thomas suggests that this shift is more fundamental in the history of 'othering' than the distinction commonly made in Pacific historiography between the benevolence of eighteenth-century descriptions and the increasing racism of nineteenth-century representation. Whether noble or ignoble, the savage came to be understood in terms of naturalized typification and essentialized difference.[10] The later eighteenth-century voyages of Bougainville, Cook and others coincided with this new kind of interest in primitive cultures, and

the published accounts of their Pacific voyages and the specimens, including human ones, they returned with contributed
hugely to this interest.

Accompanying this shift was the attempt to represent and
understand the geographical distances between different peoples
in terms of time. The new worlds of the Atlantic and the Pacific
came to be seen as embryonic civilizations; hence the recurring
analogies between ancient Mediterranean and modern American
and Pacific worlds. As Pagden has argued, from the beginning of
the eighteenth century it became a commonplace that distances
between people in space could be expressed as distances in time.[11]
First Amerindians, and later Pacific islanders, were placed in a particular temporal relation to Europe establishing, in Pagden's term,
commensurability, that is, a principle of attachment which made
possible the recognition of others though constituted primarily in
terms of difference.[12]

In the case of the Pacific this must also have helped to bring fear
of its incalculable space under control. Mapping and the classification of human species on evolutionary lines were mutually reinforcing. In the same decade that Cook was giving shape and
meaning to western apprehensions of the Pacific, Blumenbach was
classifying human races as Linnaeus had other life forms.[13] Of
course the argument from natural history produced different,
even contradictory applications. As long as species were thought
to be fixed it encouraged an essentialist view of primitive human
life forms which helped breed nineteenth-century racial science.
But there was also a looser application which continued to see
primitive societies as evolving towards more complex forms, and
this was reinforced by Darwin's rebuttal of the fixity of species.
Both versions obviously provided a basis for racial differentiation,
understood in either essentialist or evolutionary terms. It was, for
example, the same J. R. Forster who constructed two Pacific races,
eastern and western, which formed the basis of the distinction
between Polynesians and Melanesians which was to be elaborated
in terms of contrasting evolutionary ranking in the next century.[14]
Race, however, was not the only basis of such hierarchies. In Pacific
discourse, at least, the treatment of women was seen as another
crucial indicator of relative social advancement. This axiom of the
Scottish Enlightenment was to be a key element in missionary
writing, and provided a gender as well as a racial basis for the kinds

of differentiation established between Pacific peoples during the nineteenth century.[15]

The conventional account of European contact and response in the Pacific is familiar. Bougainville announced the discovery of Tahiti as Nouvelle Cythère, and Diderot, in his *Supplément au Voyage de Bougainville*, turned the natural wisdom of his Tahitian sage Orou against the civilized barbarity of contemporary French society. This typification of the peaceful, beautiful, sensual, self-sufficient and naturally wise Polynesian stands at the head of a long tradition of using the South Pacific to write what Pagden has called 'counter-histories of civility'.[16] Cook was less classical, and the beginnings of different national traditions in representing the Pacific are apparent in his more sober reports and in his concern to defend the Tahitians from the imputation of lasciviousness.[17] Nevertheless, English readers were given broadly the same picture and soon had access to French accounts; Forster, for example, translated Bougainville's *A Voyage round the World* into English as early as 1772.

The fall from grace began with the killing of Cook in Hawai'i in 1779, an event foreshadowed by the killing of Marion du Fresne in New Zealand seven years earlier. If the mutiny on the *Bounty* in 1789 was essentially a European event, a distant echo of revolution much closer to home, it also showed the dangerously seductive and anarchic appeal of South Sea islands. Even so, when the London Missionary Society was established in 1795 it chose Tahiti as its first field of operation, having consulted Bligh among others, and established that prospects were more favourable in the South Pacific than in other possible theatres. But from the turn of the century, the account goes, this idyllic contrast to capitalist Europe was increasingly represented as an unredeemed world requiring salvation by missionary and trader. Abhorrent social practices such as cannibalism, infanticide and tattooing were emphasized; the sexualization of Polynesian cultures persisted but was now moralized rather than celebrated; the hospitality of these islands was discovered to stop short of the ready acceptance of Christianity and the European work ethic.

By the middle of the nineteenth century, however, western traders and missionaries had done their best, which was now often seen as their worst. This was the so-called Bibles-and-muskets phase. Traders and whalers depleted the islands of their natural resources, corrupting their inhabitants with guns and alcohol in the process. And as the material culture of South Sea islanders was stripped, the missionaries transformed their lifeways. The more heavily an island was colonized, the more demoralized it became. Native populations declined steadily, often sharply. It was widely assumed, sometimes to be mourned and sometimes welcomed, that Pacific peoples would soon be extinguished.

This far from parodic summary is based on the kinds of simplified antitheses and clear-cut periodization common in both Pacific historiography and colonial discourse studies. In the former, until recently, the fatal-impact thesis has been dominant. This emphasized the fragility and rapid disintegration of Pacific societies when faced with European power, goods and values. It took different forms. Such impact could be represented as beneficent or harmful, depending on whether one was defending or criticizing the civilizing mission of colonialism. But on the scale of the impact itself, imperialists and their critics agreed: indigenous cultures were more or less obliterated. Recently, Pacific historians and anthropologists have emphasized the resilience and continuity of Pacific societies in the colonial period. Far from being wiped out, they adapted and survived, often conceding less than contemporary missionary accounts, for example, were prepared to admit. Historians of the fatal-impact school have read their western sources too uncritically, mistaking the intention for the effect.

A similar debate has been going on within colonial discourse studies. The founding text of this new discipline, Edward Said's *Orientalism,* is now routinely reprimanded for having discussed the European representation of others in terms which denied them autonomy or agency. Against this, the agency of colonized peoples has been asserted, although often in terms which by emphasizing mimicry and subtly pleasing modifications of European practices tend to define indigenous cultures reactively, still leaving them as constituted by the colonizing power. An apparent impasse between these two positions, one emphasizing the power of the colonizer, the other the resistance of the colonized, has been neatly summarized by Henry Louis Gates Jr:

You can empower discursively the native, and open yourself to charges of downplaying the epistemic (and literal) violence of colonialism; or play up the absolute nature of colonial domination, and be open to charges of negating the subjectivity and agency of the colonized, thus textually replicating the repressive operations of colonialism.[18]

There seems to be no way of escaping this impasse at the level of pure theory. It needs to be addressed in specific historical and colonial situations. Large questions about the changing nature of colonialism through time and about its dispersed and differential impact are at issue, and there is no single global answer to these.

Robert Young has recently asked if there can be 'a general theoretical matrix that is able to provide an all-encompassing framework for the analysis of each singular colonial instance'. He seems to think there can. 'At a certain level, most forms of colonialism are, after all, in the final analysis, colonialism, the rule by force of a people by an external power.'[19] This is a tautology qualified out of existence. And if on the one hand it is too general to be wrong or helpful, on the other it makes colonialism synonymous with conquest and reinstates the sharp polarity of self and other which elsewhere he dismisses as inadequate. In Young's discussion, geographical and historical particularity become irritating obstructions to the task of grand theory. Critics such as Parry and Ahmad, who have argued that colonial discourse analysis has suffered from a lack of historical materialist enquiry, are guilty of 'a form of category mistake'. Colonial discourse analysis, Young argues, does not seek to exclude or replace other forms of analysis, of which there are many, but to provide a framework for this other work by emphasizing the textuality of colonialism and the inevitable continuity between our ways of thinking about colonialism and the phenomenon itself.[20] This is too casual and untheorized. If colonial discourse analysis is to provide such a framework it must be brought into a relation of mutual critique with this other work. The academic division (and hierarchy) of labour implied by Young's charge of a category mistake widens the gulf described by Nicholas Thomas as:

the Scylla of mindlessly particular conventional colonial history, which fails to move beyond the perceptions of whichever administrators or missionaries are being documented, and the Charybdis of colonial discourse theory, which totalizes a hegemonic global ideology, neither much tainted by its conditions of production nor transformed by the pragmatics of colonial encounters and struggles.[21]

It is the immodest aim of this book to try and close such gaps, but only in terms of one particular region. While I hope that the attempt will have implications for other regions and other times, global questions are neither asked nor answered. There is no attempt to construct another general theory. It is time for colonial discourse studies to be historicized in more than theory. If some of what immediately follows seems too obvious to need saying, I can only add that it is often forgotten when the flattening juggernaut of colonial discourse analysis begins to roll.

Colonialism was never a unitary formation. For much of the nineteenth century there was considerable resistance in Britain, for example, to the acquisition of colonies. And as far as the Pacific was concerned, governments were mainly indifferent. It was the target of particular interest groups such as missionaries and traders, but without their presence the interest of western governments would have been negligible. The annexation of New Zealand in 1840 was a reluctant response to pressure from missionary and settlement groups. The French protectorate established over Tahiti in 1842 was the unauthorized action of a naval commander. Britain established a protectorate over Fiji in 1874 mainly because of pressure from the governments of its two established settler colonies in the region, Australia and New Zealand. It was only at the end of the nineteenth century, with growing German and United States influence in the region, the promised opening of the Panama Canal, and in the larger context of high imperialist rivalry, that the annexation of island groups became widespread.

The history of European presence in the Pacific is not necessarily coterminous with the history of colonialism in the region. In particular, we need to distinguish between early and later phases of contact. The inequality and subordination typical of contact in the late nineteenth century were not inevitably present in earlier exchanges between Europeans and Pacific islanders. Bougainville and Cook were not looking for colonies of settlement, and this conditioned their approach and response to indigenous populations. Traders and missionaries, on the other hand, engaged Pacific islanders in colonial relationships by attempting to impose western terms of trade and belief. Neither of these groups was especially interested in appropriating land, although missionaries clearly needed bases from which to operate. Western settlement in the Pacific was slow and uneven, and many islands, Tonga for example, escaped it altogether. Hawaii was the earliest to be settled, often with the active encouragement of the Hawaiian royal family. But in southern parts of the Pacific there was little forcible dispossession, except, and glaringly, in the British settler colonies of Australia and New Zealand. There was a very limited coincidence of interest and attitude between the different colonizing groups in the Pacific. Traders and missionaries were the bane of each other's lives and viewed native populations rather differently. Missionaries needed to believe in their convertibility. The essentializing attitudes to race which hardened during the nineteenth century, and came to influence colonial policy as well as the day-to-day attitudes of administrators and settlers, no doubt influenced missionary behaviour but could never entirely replace an alternative, and older, concept of native peoples as redeemable. The singular importance of the missionaries is perhaps the most distinctive feature of the colonization of the Pacific, with implications for European attitudes and policies as well as for native lifeways.

Just as it is mistaken to assume some identity of interest, even ultimately, in the category of Europe, the self, or, indeed, any single imperial power, it is also misleading to homogenize different Pacific societies, or assume consensus within any one of them. Many Pacific cultures were intensely hierarchical, and further complicated by vertical lines of division between, for example, priestly and chiefly castes. Contact with Europeans affected these groups differently. Furthermore, this was not their first or only contact with an outside world. Pacific peoples were not marooned. They were travellers well used to meeting and receiving strangers. The most important external influences on Fiji in the eighteenth and early nineteenth centuries, for instance, came from intensified contact with Tonga.[22] Of course the European landfalls of the late eighteenth century were different from those made by other Pacific peoples, but it is reductive to assume that power relations were always one-sided. Tahitians and Marquesans often swam out to meet the ships, clambering aboard before they had anchored and breaching that solemn encounter of first meeting on the beach so frequently represented by writers and painters as pregnant with beginnings. These counter-explorers were often native women who sometimes extended this tensile zone of contact much further by travelling on the strangers' ships to other islands.[23]

For many decades after contact, exchange relationships between the two sides were often controlled by those who held

power in native societies. It is reductive to assume that all contact
was inevitably contaminating, that the natural resources taken by
western strangers always involved depletion, and that imports were
uncontrolled by indigenous cultures and were bound to be
anomic in their effects. Many of the things sought by traders –
sandalwood, for example – were not much used or prized by
Pacific islanders. The imputed fatal attraction of western goods for
indigenous Pacific populations is a version of the fatal-impact
argument. It must often have been the case that both sides of a
transaction thought they had come away with a bargain and, in
their own terms, would have been right to think so.

The important general point is that Pacific societies were colonized slowly and unevenly, and never entirely succumbed to
western goods, values and practices which inevitably were modified when they crossed the beach. Even those goods and practices
which were welcomed or irresistible became something different
in their new cultural context. As Thomas points out, the uses to
which commodities are put are not inscribed. Material objects
mutate as they are exchanged.[24] Some were assimilated; others
were simply ignored. Ahmad's point that although colonialism is
a key moment in the history of a colonized people it neither constitutes nor reconstitutes the whole of their culture is relevant
here.[25] Native cultures did not begin, or begin again, with
European contact. A much longer history had gone into their
making and some of their practices remained more or less unaffected by the arrival of the colonizer. There was continuity as well
as discontinuity across the rupture caused by the arrival of western
others. Although the small-scale nature of most Pacific societies
might appear to have left them particularly vulnerable to
European influence, it also made it possible to control and regu-
late the impact and incorporation of people and things from
outside.

This is not to deny the overall imbalance of power within which
contact occurred, and the damage which resulted. Most appalling
was the depopulation of the islands. But even here discriminations
need to be made. In particular, any discussion of depopulation
must be aware of the insistent and ubiquitous nineteenth-century
narrative of the inevitable extinction of Pacific populations, which
by the end of the century had become a colonialist mantra. There
was an overdetermined European cultural investment in this myth

of the dying Polynesian. It legitimated many different kinds of incursion into the Pacific, from imperialist dispossession to romantic or primitivist appropriation. Ultimately, I think, it can be understood in classic Saidean terms as a discourse about the west's fear of its own extinction. This and other ideas sketched out in these introductory pages will be developed in later chapters.

A few words about the book's terms of reference and its shape. Its time span covers the period from the late 1760s, when reports of Tahiti and other South Pacific islands were brought back to Europe by French and British explorers, until, roughly, the First World War. This latter date is more arbitrary, but the defeat of Germany led to a significant redrawing of the imperial map of the Pacific and to a new pattern of post-war colonial administration and mandateship.

Its geographical span is more problematic. Roughly, and anachronistically, it is the Polynesian triangle, a vast area stretching from Hawaii in the north, to New Zealand in the south-west, and Easter Island in the east. This is an anachronism for two reasons. First, the category of Polynesia did not exist when Bougainville and Cook sailed into the region: it is a nineteenth-century colonial construct. And second, as such it is an unacceptable category heavily implicated in the hierarchies of race produced by Pacific colonial discourse. It has carried this baggage into our own time and gathered some questionable new political meanings as well. In particular, it has become associated with some forms of cultural nationalism of an essentialist kind based on the claim of original possession. This threatens the status of Indian, Chinese and other more recently arrived Pacific populations, and is sharply at odds with Epeli Hau'ofa's ancient and modern conception of Oceania as a place of restless mobility, criss-crossing lines of migration and settlement, and cross-cultural mixing. Even so, Hau'ofa continues to use the term while acknowledging its undesirability and suggesting its replacement by the inclusive name of Oceania. This is a measure of the problem. We cannot suddenly disengage from earlier classifications and mappings, and perhaps it is better to understand and criticize the past in its own terms than attempt to cleanse it through verbal hygiene. Oceania itself, though a more neutral and inclusive term, is nevertheless another colonial construct. In the meantime Polynesia remains useful as well as objectionable, denoting as it does that part of Oceania which most interested the European travellers and writers of the late eighteenth and nineteenth centuries. I shall use the term while trying to remember its historical and ideological provenance.

There are further problems of nomenclature and boundaries. Until the end of the eighteenth century the Pacific was more commonly known as the South Sea. By the middle of the nineteenth century this latter term was obsolescent, except when used adjectivally for romantic or picturesque purposes. Spate explains this shift mainly in terms of geography and trade. As exploration of the Ocean extended northwards and trade followed in its wake, with Honolulu becoming an important centre of commerce, the name became inappropriate. He also suggests that it reflected a changing mental view of Oceania with western interest now concentrated on the islands themselves rather than the sea surrounding them.[26] Crossing the beach had made necessary a new term. My own employment of these different appellations reflects this changing usage but will also be influenced by the requirements of style.

Throughout the book European and western are used interchangeably. The former acknowledges that Europe spilled beyond its boundaries but is geographically inaccurate when applied to United States or Australian writers, for example. The latter depends for its reference and meaning on another geographically imprecise but widely accepted cultural and ideological divide between rich and poor, colonizer and colonized, metropolitan and post-colonial. This, in turn, is complicated by intra-European meanings of east and west, not wholly disarticulated from other east/west divides, which seem to be passing rapidly into history but retain some resonance. This terminological imprecision reflects not only the changing map of an unravelling post-colonial and post-Cold War world, but also the fluid and contested nature of our cultural and intellectual categories. With nowhere to stand outside of this process I can only make clear the senses in which I use the terms I employ.

Chapter 2 deals with the death of Cook, contemporary representations of that event, and the proliferating versions of the Great Explorer which continue to be narrated. At the end of the twentieth century Cook is more than ever a contested figure. His role in

Australia's bicentenary was as disputed as that of Columbus in America's quincentenary. Indeed, Pagden has traced an analogous refashioning of Columbus in the history of narratives of discovery of the first New World.[27] Conflicting interpretations of Cook's death have led to one of the most ferocious academic debates of recent times. I discuss the argument between Marshall Sahlins and Gananath Obeyesekere at some length, not primarily to enjoy the smell of grapeshot (although that is a secondary pleasure) but rather because it dramatizes many of the issues this book is concerned with. If the death of Cook resulted in the construction of several of the great narratives of modern imperialism, how is it to be narrated for a post-colonial era? Obeyesekere's and Sahlins' mutual accusations of Eurocentricity, supported by formidable scholarship and laced with vitriol, speak from the heart of our own time.

Chapter 3 deals with different versions of beachcombing, the act of repudiating western civilization by jumping ship, crossing the beach and attempting to join an island culture. It starts with the most famous mass example of this practice, the mutiny on the *Bounty*, and examines several early nineteenth-century literary versions of this enduring western myth. The most famous Pacific beachcomber was Herman Melville and the second half of this chapter examines *Typee*, the semi-fictional narrative of his stay on the Marquesas and a most sophisticated example of the beachcomber genre. In it Melville explored the limits as well as the pleasures of crossing the beach, discovered the impossibility of ever becoming a fully reciprocating member of the Marquesan world, and dramatized problems of cultural encounter, perception and representation familiar to contemporary anthropologists and colonial discourse analysts alike.

In attempting to cut the ties with their home culture beachcombers were obliged to treat their island hosts with courtesy, and to respect local practices. Missionaries, on the other hand, were emissaries rather than refugees from the civilized world, answerable to Europe for the success or failure of their task of conversion. Indigenous values and beliefs were to be replaced with their own. The first cohort sent to Tahiti by the London Missionary Society in 1797 arrived with no criteria for understanding the world they confronted. At first they were wholly unsuccessful: more missionaries succumbed to Tahitian lifeways than there were Tahitians converted. The home correspondence from these missionaries provides fascinating evidence of the alienation and bewilderment they experienced. In the end they prospered, and two widely-read missionary texts from this field, William Ellis' *Polynesian Researches* (1829) and John Williams' *Narrative of Missionary Enterprises* (1837), spread the news of this success. Ellis' book, furthermore, is also of great ethnological importance, full of careful descriptions of those native practices and beliefs which he is committed to extirpate. And Williams' text, for all its triumphalism, betrays many signs of the discomfort experienced by someone forced to confront the relativity of his own culture. Chapter 4 will examine these two works in detail, and compare them with the rather different narratives of home correspondence secreted in the London Missionary Society archive.

Although by the mid-nineteenth century a great deal was known about the South Pacific it remained remote and inaccessible, an inviting space for writers of fiction to fill and exploit. Chapter 5 looks closely at two examples of the use of the Pacific as a theatre for dreams of empire and adventure. It also attempts to read them back into the mid-century British culture from which they derived. Harriet Martineau's didactic fiction *Dawn Island* (1845) is another conversion narrative, the gospel in this case being that of free trade. Written for the Anti-Corn Law League, it is best understood in terms of the politics of free trade and empire of that time. It is also an interesting attempt to view a Pacific culture dispassionately according to the social-scientific theory of observation that Martineau had developed in her non-fictional writing. The Pacific was also a common setting for the boys' adventure story which flourished in the second half of the century. Many British readers' first images of the Pacific were, and are, supplied by Ballantyne's *The Coral Island* (1858). This most widely read of all Pacific texts will be discussed in relation to missionary values on the one hand, and imperial ideology on the other. Ballantyne's attempt to reconcile these sometimes conflicting value systems will be discussed in relation to larger contradictions within the formation of nineteenth-century British capitalism and imperialism.

If *The Coral Island* is the Pacific's best-known western text, then Robert Louis Stevenson is its most celebrated literary figure. Chapter 6 begins with Stevenson's travel writing in the Pacific, concentrating on how he uses, examines and moves away from many of the by now familiar tropes and conventions of representation which by the end of the century constituted a Pacific discourse, with travellers and writers often merely pressing the keys. Stevenson's Pacific fiction is of two main kinds. One explores the corrupting effect of colonialism on its western agents: 'The Beach of Falesá' (1892) is still insufficiently recognized and discussed as a prototype of Conrad's *Heart of Darkness*. The other kind, almost ignored, is his adaptation of traditional Polynesian forms to produce tales of the modern Pacific from an indigenous point of view, and with Polynesian readers also in mind. 'The Isle of Voices' and 'The Bottle Imp' (1892) look both ways in their attempt to construct a multicultural readership, and anticipate the post-colonial Pacific literature in English which has emerged in the late twentieth century.

The language of disease and corruption in Stevenson's Pacific fiction intensifies in the Pacific writing of Jack London (chapter 7). Like Stevenson he visited the Hawaiian leper colony on Molokai; London, however, used this experience to produce a series of intense, obsessive stories in which leprosy is a figure for both the damaging effects of colonialism and European fears of contamination by sexually appealing Polynesian bodies. In his travel book *The Cruise of the Snark* (1911), and his stories set in the Melanesian islands, London replicated the racial hierarchies found in much western nineteenth-century Pacific writing. If Polynesians are now leprous they were once beautiful; Melanesians are intrinsically repellent. His late Pacific stories, however, which return to a Hawaiian setting, show a new interest in the possibilities of cultural retrieval from the Hawaiian past, and his non-fictional writing of this period sheds much of its earlier racism in an optimistic contemplation of the rich mix of twentieth-century Hawaiian culture.

Chapter 8 deals with French representations of the Pacific. The sharp delineation of distinct national traditions in colonial discourse can result in yet further kinds of homogenization. Nevertheless, there are general features which distinguish much French writing about the Pacific from British and North American representation. For more than half a century after Bougainville's voyage the main French investment in Oceania was philosophical. Enlightenment and Romantic myths of *le bon sauvage* and Nouvelle Cythère were predominantly, though not exclusively, French constructions. The South Sea became the testing ground for ideas of the natural. Even when Maori seemed to prove the philosophers wrong by killing Marion du Fresne the idealization of Polynesian cultures continued, often to the annoyance of French explorers who visited Oceania. One fascinating attempt to pit the philosophers against the explorers and produce a nuanced picture of South Sea cultures was made by Dumont d'Urville in *Les Zélandais: Histoire Australienne*, written in the 1820s (which makes it the first New Zealand novel) but not published until 1992. From the mid-nineteenth century France had a naval and administrative presence in the South Pacific. Literary representation, however, exoticized the region, self-indulgently to the point of narcissism in Pierre Loti's *Le Mariage de Loti* (1880). In Loti's hands elegiac treatment of the Pacific reached its apogee: Polynesia dies slowly and beautifully to satisfy the decadent nostalgia of a European romantic. Gauguin, although influenced by Loti, and perhaps the best-known proponent of the fatal-impact argument, developed an altogether more complicated relation with Pacific island cultures. Both the older tradition of Gauguin criticism which assigned him a leading role in an unproblematized European primitivist tradition, and more recent feminist and post-colonial critique which sees his work (or more commonly, and justifiably, his life) as complicit with sexual and colonial exploitation, have been reductive. Concentrating mainly on his writing, I shall argue that Gauguin's work is more self-conscious, conflictual and ironic than either of these traditions has allowed. This chapter, which covers the time span of the whole book, will also be retrospective and summarizing.

It will be clear that my primary interest is in *European* representation. I have attempted, however, to ground these representations in the home cultures from which they derived, to read them back into the sponsoring institutions, publishing history and other cultural contexts in which, and for which, they were produced. Indigenous points of view are not forgotten but they are often out of reach. There is a shortage of sources that represent such points of view, and I have had limited access to those sources that do exist. No doubt if this book had been written in Hawaii it would have been rather different. There are real dangers here. To concentrate on the conventions through which a culture was textualized while ignoring the actuality of what was represented is to risk a second-order repetition of the images, typologies and projections under scrutiny. And there are particular dangers of this when writing about the Pacific. At least as important as the silencing of native voices by the colonizing powers, agencies and their apologists, has been the silencing of Pacific cultures by those intent on valorizing them. As the editors of *Voyages and Beaches: Europe and the Pacific 1769–1840* have written, the Pacific's 'mythic value lies in its silence and in the unfathomable enigmas proposed by its mute-ness'.[28] European primitivists and fatal-impact historians alike have exploited this muteness for their own profit. It is, of course, the Pacific version of the orientalist constitution of authority on the basis of the other's absence.

Nevertheless, many of the texts examined in this book do tell us something about indigenous lifeways and points of view. The attempt to describe another culture is never simply an act of appropriation, nor are images of the other merely versions of the self-image of the observer. The contemporary reification of other-ness reproduces the sharp 'us and them' opposition of colonial discourse itself, and simplifies the complex transactions and migrations of the history of colonialism. Furthermore, the problem of understanding and describing otherness is not pecu-liar to the colonial period and will not disappear with it.[29] Although I am primarily interested in the ways in which Europeans represented the Pacific, and how in constituting the cultures of which they spoke they reconstituted their own, this is not to deny them more objective significance as well. Ellis' *Polynesian Researches* is an indispensable source of inevitably tainted knowledge about early nineteenth-century Tahiti; without it we would know much less about that culture. The ethnographic value of his book is not cancelled by its contrary impulse to expunge Tahitian culture. The fact that western cultures in the colonial period have partly con-stituted themselves through the ideological construction of others does not mean that all such constructions have no more than reflexive value. By developing inventories of tropes and narrative strategies common to such texts colonial discourse analysis has sometimes encouraged this view, while bleaching such writing of its variety and singularity.

Originally I had thought of compensating for the relative absence of historical indigenous viewpoints by ending with a discussion of the emergence of a contemporary Pacific literature in English since the early 1970s. The idea was first to show how Europeans had represented Pacific islanders, and then how Pacific islanders were now representing themselves. This proved altogether too neat, and ran the risk of implying that contemporary Pacific literature was basically a response to western representations. That recurring construction of the determining colonizer and the reactive indigene would once more have been repeated. Many simplifications would have followed. Writers such as Albert Wendt and Epeli Hau'ofa have acknowledged the important influence on their work of African and Caribbean post-colonial writers, for example. Both have also been positively influenced by canonical western writers, including those who wrote about the Pacific. As the dying narrator of Wendt's Samoan novel *Leaves of the Banyan Tree* (1979), who wishes to become a second Tusitala, remarks: 'If my novel is as good as Stevenson's *Treasure Island,* I will be satisfied.' Wendt and Hau'ofa also draw fruitfully on indigenous story-telling traditions. They and others have, of course, responded to the kinds of representation discussed in this book, but they also come from outside, and range well beyond, the limits of European discourse. The writing-back model can easily become the literary sequel to the fatal-impact thesis. Contemporary Pacific literature in English is not an historical appendage and deserves independent treatment. I shall return to it briefly in the epilogue.

CHAPTER 2

Killing the god: the afterlife of Cook's death

'A schooner captain had told him [Tembinok of Apemama]
of Captain Cook; the king was much interested in the story;
and turned for more information . . . to the Bible in the
Gilbert Island version . . . Paul he found, and Festus, and
Alexander the copper-smith: no word of Cook. The inference
was obvious: the explorer was a myth.'
(R. L. Stevenson, *In the South Seas*, part 4, ch. 4)

Captain Cook was killed at Kealakekua Bay on the island of Hawai'i
on 14 February 1779. News of his death reached England almost
a year later, having travelled overland from Kamchatka in the
Arctic circle of the Pacific to London where it was received on 11
January.[1] *The Gentleman's Magazine* for that month carried Captain
Clerke's report that Cook and four mariners had been killed 'in
an affray with a numerous and tumultuous body of the natives'. It
went on to compare him with Magellan, killed by natives in the
Philippine Islands in 1521, but also drew a contrast which was to
be repeated in written and other representations of Cook from
that time on:

in this he [Magellan] widely differed from our great countryman, that he
was the aggressor, in endeavouring to extort tribute for his master the
King of Spain; but Captain Cook was on the defensive, and in this, as a
voyager, was almost singular, that he never knowingly injured, but always
studied to benefit the savages whom he visited. Thus at Otaheite, where
he was best known, he was looked upon as a kind of tutelar deity.[2]

From this moment Cook's death was mythologized. It became
the founding event of colonial Pacific history, that beginning
which, as Peter Hulme has argued in the North American context,
is necessary if the European presence is to be justified and its
usurping violence disavowed or suppressed.[3] In Europe the death
of Cook became the Pacific's original sin, its Fall for which

Polynesians must atone. Of course the representation and mythol-
ogizing of his death were more complex than this, taking different
forms and being translated into several, sometimes competing,
narratives of imperialism. In this chapter I am concerned with the
production and circulation of these narratives and their images,
particularly in the years immediately following Cook's death when
the subject was a matter of intense interest and speculation. This
also involved the production of counter-myths, mainly evangelical
in origin, which were later to become entangled with so-called
native Hawaiian histories of the death of Cook.

By the nineteenth century these myths had consolidated and
become less active. The centenary of Cook's death was virtually
ignored by the Royal Geographical Society; imperial interest lay
elsewhere, in central Asia and Africa.[4] In the twentieth century,
however, Cook was resurrected, particularly in the white settlements of Australia and New Zealand which adopted him as the
founding father of their Anglo-Saxon nationhood. Returned to
life, Cook has been killed again in a variety of new ways. This is particularly true of recent years as post-colonial theory and colonial
discourse analysis have spread like an antibody through the disciplines of history, anthropology, literature and cultural studies. In
particular, the death of Cook has been brought to life by the
contest between Sahlins and Obeyesekere over how to narrate this
event in a post-colonial age peculiarly sensitive to the charge of
Eurocentricity. The chapter as a whole, therefore, tracks the multiple identities of Cook since his death. It explores how this great
floating signifier has been used to inaugurate different European
and Pacific histories. And it examines how Cook's death was, and
has become again, a classic example of how narratives of cultural
encounter and imperialism are constructed, reproduced and contested.

Cook had first sighted the Hawaiian group in January 1778,
making brief landings at the northern islands of Kauai and Niihau.
When his sailors went ashore at Kauai one of the natives was shot
dead. Coming ashore later, Cook found that the natives prostrated
themselves in front of him. The ships then headed north in search
of the Northwest Passage, the goal of Cook's third voyage, only
returning to the Hawaiian group in November. The island of
Hawai'i was sighted in early December. Cook kept off-shore for six

weeks, trading with native boats as he circled the island, finally anchoring in Kealakekua Bay in mid-January. The reception was tumultuous and for the next fortnight or so the ships enjoyed hospitality lavish even by Polynesian standards. On the day he arrived Cook went through an elaborate ceremony with the priests at their shore-side *heiau* or temple. The Hawai'ian commoners, encouraged by their priests, fell flat on their faces chanting 'Orono' whenever Cook came ashore. Although the supply of provisions continued undiminished the Hawai'ians became anxious to know when the ships would leave and seemed pleased when they departed on 4 February. They were back in a week. *Resolution* broke its foremast in a storm and returned to have it repaired.

This time the reception was very different. The bay was under *tapu* (taboo) and although the priests renewed their hospitality the King, Kalani'opu'u, was less welcoming. The Hawai'ians did not seem to understand why the ships had returned. Theft and obstruction were more frequent than before and there were several skirmishes between the Hawai'ians and Cook's men on the afternoon of 13 February. That night *Discovery*'s cutter was taken. Next morning Cook went ashore with a group of marines to make Kalani'opu'u his hostage for the return of the cutter. This had been his customary response to serious theft throughout his three voyages, although the show of force was unusual. At first the King agreed to accompany Cook but on reaching the shore one of his wives, and then several chiefs, pleaded with him not to go. As a large crowd gathered, news arrived that a chief had been shot dead by one of Cook's officers while trying to leave the bay. The crowd pressed in, Cook was challenged, he fired and the confrontation erupted into violence. When it ended, Cook, four marines and seventeen Hawai'ians were dead.

Almost ever since Cook's death there has been general agreement that when he came ashore at Kealakekua Bay the Hawai'ians treated him as if he were a god. It has come to be believed that they thought of him as their year god Lono, the bringer of peace and fertility, whose advent begins the annual rite of Makahiki. Cook's editor and biographer J. C. Beaglehole accepted this, as have most modern scholars. Marshall Sahlins, in particular, has argued the case with sophistication and in detail, applying it specifically to the moment of Cook's death. How did this story of his apotheosis come about? It began to develop almost immediately after the news of his death reached England, and certainly before the next European vessel visited the Hawaiian group in 1786. We need to go back to those years immediately following Cook's death to uncover its genesis.

One of the earliest responses to Cook's death was Anna Seward's 'Elegy on Captain Cook'. Published in 1780 just a few months after his death became known, it quickly went through three editions and a fourth followed the publication of the official journal of the third voyage in 1784. Cook is a 'new Columbus' but a 'mild hero', one whose goddess is 'BENEVOLENCE'. This 'dove of human-kind' is also godlike. He 'pours new wonders on th'uncultured shore', and in lines that recall the description of the final days of creation in *Paradise Lost* he coaxes 'antarctic Zealand's drear domain' into life. In the wake of Cook birds sing, bulls roar and 'lo! the stately horse . . . thunders o'er the plain'. His second visit to Tahiti makes clear the benefits of his first:

> See! chasten'd love in softer glances flows,
> See! with new fires parental duty glows.

but now Cook is dead and this 'smiling Eden of the southern wave' has fallen from grace. Like Orpheus he has been killed by those to whom he brought 'Fair Arts and Virtues', although whereas the Thracians were content merely to 'tear his quiv'ring limbs', the Hawai'ian 'on his limbs the lust of hunger feeds!'

Although killed in Hawai'i Cook is mourned in Tahiti, and thus begins a familiar distinction within European representations of the Pacific. He is also mourned by that 'Ill-fated Matron' Mrs Cook, whose husband's 'bones now whiten an accursed shore!' There was to be a European as well as a Hawai'ian cult of Cook's bones. These bones whiten from exposure but they are also poten-tially redemptive, a patch of light at the heart of darkness. Most of all, however, he is mourned by the nation which sent him across the world on his charitable mission. And it is as Britannia's hero, still attended by BENEVOLENCE, that he makes his last voyage to where 'angels choir him while he waits for THEE'.

This elegy was widely admired. Samwell, surgeon on *Discovery* and the liveliest of the journal writers on Cook's last voyage, rewarded Seward with some South Sea curios.[5] *The Gentleman's Magazine* roundly praised it and made much of the imagined Tahitian reaction to Cook's death: 'How the account of his immature death must affect those friendly people'.[6] In the following year it carried a poem 'To Miss Seward' from a Mr Haley thanking her for being the comforter of the nation.[7] The reasons for this are clear. Seward's elegy is a more developed version of that first obituary in *The Gentleman's Magazine*. It propagates a myth of 'anti-conquest' which Mary Louise Pratt has argued is characteristic of eighteenth- and nineteenth-century narratives of imperialism. By this she means representations which secure the innocence of the European appropriator at the very moment of taking possession. Such 'strategies of innocence are constituted in relation to older imperial rhetorics of conquest associated with the absolutist era'. The main protagonist of this anti-conquest narrative she terms the 'seeing-man', the figure whose imperial eye passively looks out and possesses.[8] Seward's Cook conforms closely to this type.

Helen Maria Williams' 'The Morai: An Ode', published in *Poems* (1786) and as an appendix in Kippis' *Narrative of the Voyages Round the World Performed by Captain James Cook* (1788), is Anna Seward's 'Elegy' revisited. The picture of Cook's death is entirely conventional: 'His blood a savage shore bedew'd.' The mourning figure of Mrs Cook reappears, and so too does the predictable immortalization of Cook by 'Albion' and the 'Muse of History'. Its new element is a contrast between Cook's benevolence and the enormities of the African slave traders. Cook was also enlisted in Hannah More's anti-slavery poem 'The Black Slave Trade' (1788) in which slave traders are the modern equivalents of Cortés and Columbus, Cook's antithesis:

> Had these possess'd, O Cook! thy gentle mind,
> Thy love of arts, thy love of human kind;
> Had these pursued thy mild and liberal plan
> DISCOVERERS had not been a curse to man!

Cook was often eulogized by women poets in the years following his death. He became, in certain respects, a feminized hero, and this, along with his martyrdom, facilitated the often implied comparison with Christ. A radical refashioning of the traditional image of the explorer was taking place.

There were variations on this theme of 'Mild Cook, by savage fury robb'd of breath' within the anti-conquest narrative of his life and death. William Cowper's celebration of Cook, 'Charity', written in mid-1781 and published in *Poems* in 1782, though

mourning Cook's death made his life its moral centre. It emphasized Cook's belief in the common origin of humankind; with him
'the rights of man' and 'The tender argument of kindred blood'
were articles of faith. He would not 'endure that any should con-
troul / His free-born brethren of the southern pole', and in this
he is utterly different from earlier explorers:

> While Cook is loved for savage lives he saved,
> See Cortes odious for a world enslaved.

By 1784 however, after reading the official account of Cook's
death, Cowper's view of him underwent a sea change. He now
believed that Cook had been punished for idolatry:

God is a jealous God, and at Owhyhee the poor man was content to be
worshipped. From that moment, the remarkable interposition of
Providence in his favour was converted into an opposition that thwarted
all his purposes . . . We know from truth itself that the death of Herod was
for a similar offence . . . Besides, though a stock or stone may be worshipped blameless, a baptized man may not. He knows he does, and, by
suffering such honours to be paid him, incurs the guilt of sacrilege.[9]

The entirely conventional comparisons Seward had made with
Orpheus or Christ have now become literal and sacrilegious. This
embryonic counter-myth was to become a common missionary
view of Cook during the nineteenth century, particularly among
the United States missionaries in Hawaii where it fed into native
accounts of his death.

Cowper's neo-primitivist sympathy for the natural life is with-
drawn in *The Task* (1785). Its opening section celebrates 'civil life',
that state when 'man, by nature fierce, has laid aside / His fierce-
ness'. Those living beyond the pale of civil society include gypsies
('Self-banish'd from society'), savages, and the inhabitants of 'the
favour'd isles / So lately found', who:

> Can boast but little virtue; and inert
> Through plenty, lose in morals what they gain
> In manners – victims of luxurious ease.

Although civilization will now turn its back on these contented
victims of indolence, this at least will protect them from 'navigators uninform'd as they'. The reference to Cook is unmistakable,
and reinforced by the figure of Omai, whom Cook had taken to
Britain and returned to Tahiti, abandoned on the beach and
lonely for Britain:

Methinks I see thee straying on the beach,
And asking of the surge that bathes thy foot
If ever it has wash'd our distant shore

Cowper, an avid reader of the accounts of Cook's voyages,[10] fundamentally revised his view of the explorer after reading the account of his death, and helped to initiate one of the most powerful of the counter-myths of Cook. He must also have helped to circulate the idea of Cook's deification.

It is difficult to know how widespread was the idea of Cook's divinity before the publication of the official account of the voyage in 1784. The Admiralty made great efforts to ensure its publication was not pre-empted; all personal records of the voyage remained classified material until the official account had appeared. Nevertheless, this secrecy was breached. The first journal to be published appeared anonymously (it was by Rickman, one of Cook's officers) in 1781, and claimed that the Hawai'ians worshipped Cook as a deity. Rickman's journal quickly went through two editions in London, as well as a pirated one in Dublin, and was widely reviewed.[11] *The Gentleman's Magazine*, for example, ran an extended review over two months in the course of which it described how Cook had been paid 'the same honours that are paid to the great E-a-thua-ah-nu-eh, or good spirit, cloathing him in the same mantle, and assigning him a place of worship, which the sailors called *Cook's Altar*'.[12] Rickman's god is not called Lono, nor is the identification of Cook with an Hawai'ian god absolute, but it is easy to see how the myth was forming. The other significant journal account to be published before 1784 was by Ledyard, an American who had been a marine with Cook. This appeared in the United States in 1783 and according to Beaglehole much of it was a copy of Rickman's. It repeated the story of Cook's divinity but was also hostile to Cook and helped inaugurate 'the bad press he traditionally had for many decades in Hawaii'.[13] Already a distinct United States version of the man was beginning to emerge.

A Voyage to the Pacific Ocean, published in three volumes by the Admiralty in 1784, was designed to secure Cook a place in the pantheon of European immortals. It was published by the King's bookseller and was planned to appear on the opening day of Parliament. In the event the publication date was held over until the King's birthday. Every effort was made to ensure a publication exceptional in content and form, especially in the printing of the plates. A committee selected the drawings and charts for repro-duction. Webber, the official artist on Cook's third voyage, pre-pared reduced drawings from his originals for the engravers, and most of the plates were gathered in a separate folio atlas which accompanied the three quarto volumes. The total production cost of £4,000 was met wholly by the Admiralty. It was one of the earli-est, most lavish examples of the state subsidizing publication of its discoveries.[14] And to complete this assertion of national strength and identity through the launching of Cook as a national hero and prototype of the modern scientific explorer, the volumes were inscribed to the memory of 'The ablest and most renowned Navigator this or any other country hath produced'. The first edition, priced at four and a half guineas, sold out in three days, and purchasers were offering ten guineas for a copy. Two further editions appeared in 1785 along with a French translation.[15]

The publication of these volumes was a major event. As well as clearing the way for other accounts such as Samwell's *Narrative of the Death of Captain James Cook* (1786), it also encouraged the trans-lation of the death of Cook into other, more popular, cultural forms. The most spectacular of these was the pantomime *Omai: or a Trip round the World* staged at the Theatre Royal, Covent Garden, at Christmas 1785. It was a box office hit, had fifty performances during the 1785 season, one of them by royal command, and was repeated the following year and again in 1788.[16] Staging it was a safe bet. The official account of Cook's last voyage had created wide public interest and there had been copious extracts in periodicals and newspapers. *The Gentleman's Magazine*, for example, reviewed it over four months in the second half of 1784, concentrating on two main events: the return of Omai to Tahiti, and the death of Cook. The pantomime brought these together. Joppien has described it as 'a stage-edition of Captain Cook's voyages',[17] and although it was a travesty of the journals this is clearly how it was received. *Omai* must have given wider currency to the idea that Cook had been deified by the Hawai'ians. In this respect its finale was particularly significant. Omai has returned to Otaheite with his British bride Londina and been enthroned as king.[18] Native ambassadors from the fifteen Pacific countries visited by Cook come to witness the coronation. A British sea captain presents Omai with a gift from George III, a sword ('A

British sword is proof against the world in arms'), and then addresses the assembled natives:

CAPTAIN: Ally of joy! Owhyee's fatal shore
            Brave Cook, your great Orono is no more.
CHORUS OF
INDIANS: Mourn, Owhyee's fatal shore
            For Cook, our great Orono, is no more[19]

An enormous painting, *The Apotheosis of Captain Cook being Crowned by Britannia and Fame,* is then lowered as the English captain sings of Cook's immortality, of how 'He *came* and he *saw* not to conquer but save', and of how the gathered chiefs can 'prove [their] humanity' by mourning his death. Cook, the bearer of peace and civilization, is presented as a double god, both a Hawai'ian divinity and one of History's immortals.

In *Omai*, as in Seward's 'Elegy', Hawai'i is the site of Cook's death but Tahiti is the place where he is mourned. The two locations are sharply distinguished, establishing difference within Polynesian culture and allowing something to be rescued from the sacrilege of his death. Tahiti functions as the Pacific's mitigation. In *Omai* the chiefs assembled in Tahiti prove their humanity by mourning Cook. In Seward's 'Elegy' it is Tahiti's queen Oberea (Purea) and 'mild Omiah' (Omai) who lament his death. In Helen Maria Williams' 'The Morai: An Ode', Cook's funeral procession is imagined making its way to a marae on Otaheite. His body has somehow been spirited from Hawai'i to Tahiti for burial.

Tahiti had a special place in the European history of the South Pacific as Bougainville's Nouvelle Cythère and Cook's other home. There had been contention over its representation. Cook had defended the islanders from the myths of exoticism composed by classically educated French explorers and emphasized their social virtues rather than their innocent sensuality.[20] Nevertheless, Tahiti's image was benign, and it was a Tahitian whom Cook had brought to England to be shown the best that civilization could offer and then returned to his native island. In the 1780s Omai's role as an ambassador between the two countries, representing each culture to the other, was being mythologized. In *The Task* Cowper imagined him as a figure of pathos strung out between two worlds, unable to return to either. In the pantomime, on the other hand, this Tahitian commoner whom Cook did not regard very highly was transformed into the King of Tahiti and ratified by the British. In a sense he has become Cook's heir. In the aftermath of Cook's death and the fall from grace of the Pacific region Tahiti was allowed to retain some of its prelapsarian character, now supplemented by the figure of Omai as a signifier of British influence.

Peter Hulme has noted a similar binary encoding of fierce cannibal and noble savage in European representations of the Caribbean, expressed in the opposition of Carib and Arawak.[21] This recurring dualism is widespread in western writing about the Pacific. Cook's Journals frequently encode such a contrast. Darwin used it in his recurring contrast between Tahitians and Maori.[22] We shall see it operating in Melville's *Typee* in Tommo's repeated question of 'Happar or Typee?' It is the basis of the distinction between Polynesian and Melanesian and persists in a work such as Jules Verne's *The Floating Island* (1895) and on into the twentieth century. In the eighteenth and nineteenth centuries it was commonly established in terms of anthropophagy. In the particular instance of Cook, however, the issue of cannibalism was less prominent than the Tahitian capacity to understand the nature of his greatness and to mourn his death. It is patently a myth of incorporation, splitting the other and absorbing the Tahitian part of it, however provisionally, to the self.

The visual had a different value and function from the written in representations of Cook's death, and more generally in narrating voyages of exploration. Visual representations were arresting and easily circulated. The huge investment in the engravings for the companion atlas to the account of the third voyage shows that the Admiralty understood their importance. Significant tableaux could be constructed and symbolic attitudes struck. Such representation allowed colonial encounters to be fixed and aestheticized more easily than in written narratives. It was certainly crucial to Cook's European apotheosis. The enormous allegorical painting of Cook, Britannia and Fame suspended above the scene of his death which formed a backdrop to the finale of *Omai* was, for instance, soon published as an etching.[23]

The earliest and most famous of the visual representations of Cook's death was by John Webber. Painted in 1779 and published as an engraving three years later, *The Death of Captain Cook* was used to publicize the forthcoming official volumes and their accompa-

3 *The Apotheosis of Captain Cook,* etching of the backdrop painting to the pantomime *Omai*, first performed in 1785.

nying engravings. It was issued by print-sellers in England and France and was much sought after. In fact it was not included in the 1784 atlas, presumably because it had already been published, but seems to have been separately available as a single image for purchasers of the volumes.[24] There is no evidence that Webber actually saw Cook's death, and although his painting clearly owes

4 William Hodges, *The Landing at Erramanga*, 1777, engraving.

5 John Webber, *The Death of Captain Cook*, 1782, engraving.

6 Johan Zoffany, *Death of Cook*, 1789–97, oil.

something to eye-witness accounts it is a history piece, sternly
described by Beaglehole as having 'no great evidential value'.[25] For
this very reason it is of great interest because it played a crucial role
in the posthumous construction of the death.

   The Death of Captain Cook is the most developed example of those
images of cultural encounter that the art of Cook's voyages had put
into circulation, the end of a sequence which had begun with
Buchan's and Hodges' landing paintings and engravings and culminated in Webber's paintings of the arrival and welcome at
Kealakekua Bay which formed the largest single subject of the
1784 folio atlas. Landing scenes have great resonance, and
Webber's emphasize Cook being welcomed as the enlightened
messenger of peace and civilization.[26] By contrast, Hodges' *The
Landing at Erramanga* (painted 1776, engraved for the Journal of
Cook's second voyage, 1777) shows Cook's men and the islanders
in violent confrontation. Webber's *The Death of Captain Cook* suggests Hodges' Eromanga painting in setting and composition, with
Cook highlighted as the only pacific figure in the frame. The
legend beneath the engraving spelled this out: 'The Death of

Captain Cook. In February 1779 by the murdering Dagger of a Barbarian at Carakakooa, in one of the Sandwich Isles. He having there become a Victim to his own Humanity'.[27] In death, as in life, Cook embodies peace and civilization, and the familiar topos of the European confronting the native on a Pacific beach is given a new and exalted significance.

Bernard Smith has argued that the key to the painting is Cook's enigmatic gesture to the boat from which the crew are firing into the crowd: 'Is Cook waving to Williamson to stop firing and pull in so that he can escape, or is he commanding him to stop firing at the natives? The ambiguity is sufficiently strong to support a reading of Cook as martyr-hero willing to sacrifice his life rather than command the death of his native friends.'[28] I see less ambiguity in this painting than Smith suggests. The gesture is one of 'hold' rather than 'help'. There is no suggestion that the men in the boat might come to Cook's rescue. They are firing into the crowd further down the beach and Cook is intervening to prevent this, unaware that he is about to be struck down. He is waving, not drowning.

The lack of ambiguity in Webber's picture was replicated by King in his official account. He describes how Cook called to the men to cease firing and come in: 'this humanity perhaps provd fatal to him, the Natives on the fyring of the boats had fallen back a little, but seeing it cease presst on again in great Numbers'. Beaglehole remarks dryly: 'The story thus told has become classical . . . we may doubt whether any single shout could have been heard above the uproar; and the men in the pinnace had to stop firing to pull in'.[29] Classical indeed, and in circulation well before 1784. Webber's painting, I suspect, is the closest we can get to the origin of this story. Once again unofficial versions were helping to write the 1784 account. John Cleveley's painting of the 1780s, published as an aquatint in 1788, repeats this narrative. There is the same pacific arm gesture, and a puff of musket fire provides Cook with a halo at the moment of his death.[30] These paintings by Webber and Cleveley became the foundation texts for the innumerable illustrations of Cook's death that appeared in accounts of his life and voyages during the nineteenth century.

Smith describes Webber's painting as being in a plain style, and certainly in comparison with the other most famous visual rendering of Cook's death, Zoffany's *Death of Cook* (1789–97), it was.

Zoffany's neo-classical oil presents the confrontation at Kealakekua Bay as a timeless epic scene in which all the participants share a common dignity. It echoes Benjamin West's *Death of Wolfe* (1771) in suggesting parallels between contemporary and classical heroes, and stands apart from other contemporary paintings and engravings of Cook's death in having no sense of colonial encounter about it. Instead, it is gladiatorial. Webber's plain style, on the other hand, became the dominant method of representing Cook. Smith has argued that we can see in this a redefinition of the explorer from military to bourgeois hero, the ideal type of a new secular, expansionist, commercial order based wherever possible on peace.[31] This is persuasive and has parallels in the refashioning of the figure of the explorer already discussed in several poems. It does, however, exaggerate the documentary motive and method of Webber's painting, which is a history piece drawing on the classical figurative tradition. As it has recently been described, *The Death of Captain Cook* is the culmination of Webber's depiction of the classical ideal 'in which friezelike slender figures suggest a nobility of demeanour and Cook is celebrated as a martyred hero'.[32] One effect of this is to render the Hawai'ians less savage than the cannibals of Anna Seward's poem. Though less gladiatorial and more culturally particular than Zoffany's, Webber's Hawai'ians are also frozen in epic postures and this ensures the dignity of the whole tableau without which Cook's apotheosis would be diminished.

Smith's contrast between heroes ancient and modern is helpful but it underplays the significance of Christian iconography in literary and visual representations of Cook. In retrospect the age might look secular as well as expansionist. Cook himself was a latitudinarian in religious matters. But, as we have seen, Cook as a kind of thirteenth disciple embodying the Christian virtues of charity and benevolence, and respecting the common origin of all humankind, is an important element in his posthumous reconstruction in the 1780s. In this respect, Webber's and Cleveley's paintings are closer to Anna Seward or Hannah More than might at first seem.

Apart from the official account of 1784, the most important volume to be published on Cook during the 1780s was A. Kippis' a *Narrative of the Voyages Round the World Performed by Captain James Cook* (1788). This was to be the last substantial researched biography for more than one hundred years.[33] It had twelve illustrations by Webber, with his *Death of Captain Cook* as the frontispiece, and was dedicated to George III whose 'patronage and bounty' had enabled Cook 'to execute those vast undertakings, and to make those extraordinary discoveries which have contributed so much to the reputation of the British Empire'. The account of Cook's death is taken directly from Samwell. Kippis is muted on the subject of Cook's deification. He remarks that the ceremonies which greeted him 'seemed to fall little short of adoration' (p. 327), but the only ceremony he specifies is that of exchanging names, a widespread Polynesian practice. 'Orono' is described in a footnote as 'a title of high honour, which had been bestowed on Captain Cook' (p. 329). No other reference is made to it. This is striking in a work which otherwise is hagiography. It draws together all the terms of approbation we have seen circulating in the discourse on Cook in the 1780s. The list of his personal virtues includes wisdom, inventiveness, application, perseverance, fortitude, rationality, self-possession and simplicity of manners. The only negative quality admitted is an occasional hastiness of temper. Like the poets and the painters, Kippis stresses Cook's humanity. This posed more problems for a historian narrating the events of his voyages than it did for a painter able to freeze the moment of his death. On the third voyage particularly, Cook was often vindictive. Nevertheless, we are assured that he was always concerned to improve the lives of the islanders, that he overlooked many of their offences which others would have punished, and was always most concerned when forced into 'acts of severity' (p. 351). The standard contrast with the conquerors of Mexico and Peru is made. Cook's design was to civilize the world and meliorate its condition. His voyages were 'not to enlarge private dominion, but to promote general knowledge' (p. 365).

Kippis has an Enlightenment interest in the scientific and human knowledge that accrued from Cook's voyages. The 'untrodden ground' of the Pacific islands offers the possibility of a controlled experiment in the study of human nature. Untouched by other cultures, 'unformed by science, and unimproved by education' (pp. 360–1), the region is a social laboratory. Also in true Enlightenment fashion, he is conscious and proud of the European dimension of Cook's achievement. He refers to Michael Angelo Gianetti's eulogy on Cook delivered to the

Florentine Academy, and quotes from M. l'Abbé Lisle's encomium on Cook in his poem 'Les Jardins' (pp. 366–7) which *The Gentleman's Magazine* had published in December 1783. On the other hand, Kippis anticipates the missionary campaign which was to commence in Tahiti just eight years later and dominate the history of the European presence in the South Pacific throughout the nineteenth century:

Perhaps our late voyages may be the means appointed by Providence of spreading . . . the blessings of civilization among the numerous tribes of the South Pacific . . . Nothing can more essentially contribute to this great end than a wise and rational introduction of the Christian religion; an introduction of it in its genuine simplicity, as holding out the worship of one God, inculcating the purest morality, and promising eternal life as the reward of obedience. (p. 366)

By the end of the 1780s, therefore, two distinct myths of Cook had evolved. One was that he had been deified by the Hawai'ians; the other placed him in Europe's pantheon of immortals. These were mutually sustaining and quickly became inseparable. Most striking is the European need for a godly Cook. There has been intense controversy as to whether or not the Hawai'ians regarded Cook as a god, but in sceptical Britain there was little doubt of his divinity. The European myth of Cook had begun in his lifetime and it ramified after his death. It was, as we have seen, composed of different, often contradictory elements, but by the 1790s most of its components were in place. One of these was the comparison with figures from classical or Christian myth, sacrificial gods or religious martyrs such as Orpheus and Christ. Cook, this parallel implied, was a modern European martyr-hero of comparable stature. Another was to define Cook against the violence and cruelty of the explorers of the early modern period. Columbus and Cortés were the anti-types of this British, almost feminized hero of patience, sympathy and self-control. A third element was the representation of Cook as an embodiment of the liberal, humane values of the Enlightenment, a defender of the rights of man and an enemy of slavery. This could be given a Christian inflexion, or spun to allow Cook to appear as the harbinger of a modern expansionist, commercial and scientific Europe, Bernard Smith's bourgeois hero. Enlightenment idealism, entrepreneurial individualism and Christian values overlapped in a variety of configurations.

This summary must also take account of the anti-Cook myths

which were developing, not only within evangelical Christianity
but also within that primitivist strand of Enlightenment thought
which was always potentially hostile to European colonization.
Diderot's *Supplément au Voyage de Bougainville*, though written in
1772, was not published until 1796, but George Forster's
apprehension was well known:

If the knowledge of a few individuals can only be acquired at such a price
as the happiness of nations, it were better for the discoverers and the discovered, that the South Seas had still remained unknown to Europe and
its restless inhabitants.[34]

This was to become a sustaining myth and charter for many traveller-writers in the Pacific during the nineteenth century.

Any summary of the decade is likely to give too static and delin-
eated a picture. There was widespread debate during the 1780s
about the nature and meaning of Cook's death. Cowper's attitude,
as we have seen, changed as more became known. Rationalists and
evangelicals, colonialists and anti-colonialists, the authors of
formal odes and the producers of pantomime, were all constructing their own myths of Cook, and the lines between them were not
always clearly drawn. Kippis is an example of how Enlightenment
liberalism could co-exist with evangelical Christian moralizing. In
time these myths hardened, but in the years immediately following his death the myth-making around Cook was an active, many-
sided process.

By the nineteenth century the various myths of Cook had firmed
up and broken free of the history which, in the 1780s, was still con-
straining them. In the decade following his death sheer historical
curiosity – what *had* happened? – complicated the making of
myths. By the nineteenth century the myths were no longer being
interrogated; history had been put into myth-balls. Debate about
the death of Cook shifted to Hawaii, where the subject was contentious throughout the century.

Cook nevertheless remained a significant presence in nineteenth-century British culture. He was presented as a role model
to generations of Victorian schoolboys, particularly the younger
sons of large middle-class Victorian families who had to leave
home to better themselves.[35] Cheap and abridged accounts of his
voyages were published throughout the century and helped

launch Kingston, Ballantyne and others of the coral island school.
I also keep glimpsing Cook in Dickens. A picture of the death of
Cook appears in at least two of his novels: in Mrs Whimple's river-
side house in *Great Expectations*, where one might expect it, and
more surprisingly on the wall of Esther's and Ada's sitting room in
Bleak House. Here it is alongside a picture of a Chinese tea ceremony, which perhaps suggests some kind of orientalism at work
(Esther will be steadily busy while 'orientals' are either sedentary
or violent). Cook appears in the opening of that most restless of
Dickens' novels, *Little Dorrit*, as a type of the traveller, and the
Pacific features elsewhere in the novel as an ironic reference point
for Mrs Merdle's mock-primitivism, and as providing an analogy,
in its taboo system, for the strictness of the English Sunday. Those
'ugly South Sea gods in the British Museum' are, by Dickens' time,
at hand to be used in commenting on Victorian culture. Similarly,
coral reefs enable Dickens to make his point about 'telescopic phil-
anthropy', as Jo in *Bleak House* sits on the doorstep of the Society
for the Propagation of the Gospel in Foreign Parts, dying of
neglect, and with 'no idea, poor wretch, of the spiritual destitution
of a coral reef in the Pacific, or what it costs to look up the precious
souls among the cocoa-nuts and breadfruit' (chapter 16).

The North American equivalent of Dickens' SPGFP, the
American Board of Commissioners for Foreign Missions, was
deeply implicated in Hawaiian accounts of Cook's death. Their
first party of missionaries to Hawaii arrived in 1820 to find that the
tapu system had just been abandoned, and with it virtually the
whole of the native religion. This cleared the way for the missionaries, whose position was consolidated by the conversion of the
Hawaiian royal family in the mid-1820s.[36] As the hostility of the
Hawaiian mission towards Cook was to have such an important
bearing on his reputation it is worth looking at in more detail.

The first missionary on Hawaii to write about Cook was William
Ellis, whose *Polynesian Researches* will be examined in the next
chapter. Although Ellis joined the American mission to Hawaii he
was English, on secondment from the London Missionary Society
station at Tahiti. Unlike his American colleagues', Ellis' attitude to
Cook is relatively benign. As recorded in his *Narrative of a Tour
Through Hawaii* (1827), he walks over the rocks where Cook fell
and visits the cave where his body was taken and filleted. He recon-
structs Cook's death from conversations with natives who claim to

have been present at the time, or to have known someone who was, and concludes that King's account is basically correct. He quotes, as if directly, from native sources: 'After he was dead, we all wailed. His bones were separated – the flesh was scraped off and burnt, as was the practice in regard to our own chiefs when they died. We thought he was the god Rono, worshipped him as such, and after his death reverenced his bones.'[37] The Cook-Lono identification is taken for granted although there is some inconsistency between the first sentence which attributes chiefly status to Cook, and the second in which he is a god. More interesting, however, is the way Ellis casts this in direct speech as if he is reporting verbatim. This is a common device, particularly in missionary accounts of the Pacific, designed to render the text authentic and allow the writer to put some unlikely-sounding speeches into the mouths of native informants.

Other scenes in Ellis' *Narrative* need to be approached with a similar sense of their careful literary construction. One of these is his account of looking over the plates in an edition of Cook's *Voyages* with a group of Hawaiian chiefs: 'They were greatly affected with the print which represented his death, and inquired if I knew the names of those who were slain on that occasion. I perceived Karaimoku more than once wipe the tears from his eyes, while conversing about this melancholy event' (p. 118). The account continues, again in direct speech, with the chiefs enquiring if the missionaries had kept away from Hawaii for so long because of Cook's death. The scene is beguiling. Was ever a man more wept over than Cook? Might Karaimoku be mourning for his own dead? Is he weeping for Ellis' benefit? Did he really weep at all? The scene has been carefully constructed to draw a sharp contrast between the savage practices of the pre-conversion era and the Christian compassion of the spiritually redeemed.

Cook's part in his own death is hardly commented upon. Ellis presents him more or less as an innocent victim. He is, for example, definite that Cook tried to stop the firing but could not make himself heard. And although Ellis acknowledges 'an overruling Providence', for him this would be true of any event, and he laments the 'untimely end' of a man who contributed so much to the advancement of science and commerce and to 'the missionary in his errand of mercy to the unenlightened heathen at the ends of the earth' (p. 123).

There was a sharp national division between the evangelical missions in the Pacific over Cook. Ellis' fellow-missionary in Tahiti, the Englishman John Williams, also wrote of Cook with admiration.[38] The Americans, on the other hand, thought that Cook had been punished by God for conspiring with idolatry. James Jackson Jarves' *History of the Hawaiian or Sandwich Islands* (1843) is the mildest of these accounts. Jarves, a member of the American Oriental Society, was not a missionary but he writes from the point of view of the ABCFM.[39] Cook wittingly accepted the 'heathen farce' of his adoration. Jarves, however, also gets him on the opposite count of showing disrespect for Hawaiian religious customs: 'Cook manifested as little respect for the religion in the mythology of which he figured so conspicuously, as scruples in violating the divine precepts of his own.'[40] This refers to a controversial incident involving the destruction of a fence and some carved figures from the *heiau*. British accounts claim that Cook was given permission to do this; Ledyard's, however, sees it as a direct cause of his death. Here, as elsewhere, Jarves draws on Ledyard, feeling correctly that King's narrative is always concerned to exonerate Cook from blame. All the same, it's a bit rich – missionaries had been making bonfires of Polynesian idols for thirty years before Jarves was writing. Other twists are necessary if Cook is to be placed as Jarves wishes. In order to condemn Cook further the Hawai'ians are represented as trusting, exploited innocents. A main cause of conflict in Kealakekua Bay is said to be the sexual jealousy of the Hawai'ian men, which moralizes the tensions in a manner congenial to the missionary account. But they are also savages, and so in the aftermath of Cook's death the mask drops and 'the worst features of savage nature' become visible: 'All reverence for Lono being now terminated, the natives appeared in their true character' (p. 132).

Jarves is very conscious of writing a revisionist account: 'It is an unpleasant task to disturb the ashes of one whom a nation reveres; but truth demands that justice should be dispensed equally to the savage, as to the civilized man' (p. 118). This sense of writing from the point of view of the native is used by others as well, and will be returned to below. Jarves also makes a sanguinary addition to the corpus of stories of what happened to the bits and pieces of Cook. He quotes from the Hawaiian history *Mooolelo Hawaii*: 'The heart was eaten by some children, who had mistaken it for that of a dog;

their names were Kupa, Mohoole, and Kaiwikokoole' (p. 128). From god to dog; demythologization could not be more complete.

Hiram Bingham's *A Residence of Twenty-One Years in the Sandwich Islands* (1847) gives a full-blooded account of the missionary case against Cook. Bingham was the unofficial leader of the first party of American missionaries to Hawaii, remaining there until 1840. Like Jarves, he claims to tell the story from the Hawai'ian point of view. Cook and his men are repeatedly referred to as 'the foreigners'; the Hawai'ians, in their confrontation with the marines, are 'dauntless men': all the heroism is theirs. Cook himself fails to reciprocate Hawai'ian generosity, is proud, sacrilegious, and sets back the cause of Christianity and civilization almost fifty years. Like Herod (Cowper had also made this comparison), Cook allowed himself to be idolized and therefore 'died by the visitation of God', a more particular Providence than Ellis'.

How vain, rebellious, and at the same time contemptible, for a worm to presume to receive religious homage and sacrifices from the stupid and polluted worshippers of demons and of the vilest visible objects of creation, and to teach them by precept and example to violate the plainest commands or rules of duty from Heaven – to encourage self-indulgence, revenge, injustice, and disgusting lewdness as the business of the highest order of beings known to them, without one note of remonstrance on account of the dishonour cast on the Almighty Creator![41]

This passage self-evidently contradicts any claim to be written from a Hawai'ian point of view, but the claim itself is worth closer attention. It derives from the congruence between missionary accounts of Cook's visit to Kealakekua Bay and those of the native compilation *Mooolelo Hawaii* which has often been regarded as an authentic native history. In fact it was produced during the 1830s by native scholars at the Lahainaluna seminary, a missionary establishment. Obeyesekere has drawn attention to the history and method of this project. It was the brainchild of one of the missionaries, Rev. Sheldon Dibble, who sent scholars out to collect information from old inhabitants. He collated their findings, reconciled discrepancies and, in his own words, 'endeavoured to make one connected and true account'. It is therefore a work of many hands, North American as well as Hawaiian. Obeyesekere argues that in relation to Cook *Mooolelo Hawaii* is a myth charter for evangelical Christianity, with Cook-Lono a symbol of the idolatry the missions wanted to expunge from Hawaii. This is not to dismiss *Mooolelo Hawaii* out of hand but to suggest that whenever it deals with Cook it gets locked into the missionary agenda.[42] And it demonstrates that when Bingham and Jarves claim to be recounting the native point of view they are in fact narrating a story they have helped to shape. Spate has made a similar point about missionary accounts of Cook as an idolator and fornicator contaminating another Hawaiian account, Samuel Kamakau's 1867 vernacular history.[43]

Melville, no friend of missionaries, observed that when it came to Cook Polynesians would always pander to a European audience. In *Omoo* Tommo meets a Tahitian who claims to have met Cook. When Tommo points out that Cook was dead before the Tahitian was born, the man then says he was speaking of his father. Tommo observes:

It is a curious fact, that all these people, young and old, will tell you that they have enjoyed the honour of a personal acquaintance with the great navigator; and if you listen to them, they will go on and tell anecdotes without end. This springs from nothing but their great desire to please; well knowing that a more agreeable topic for a white man could not be selected.[44]

Presumably the scholars of Lahainaluna, aware of their teachers' hostility to Cook, were not immune from a similar desire to please. Melville also contributed to the flourishing discourse of Cook's remains. In *Typee* Tommo tells the story of an old chief from Mowee (Maui) who claimed to have eaten Cook's big toe, was taken to court for making such an outrageous claim, and was cleared because it could not be refuted.[45]

Melville makes no mention of the Cook-Lono identification. Mark Twain, visiting Kealakekua Bay twenty years later in 1866, accepts it but contests the missionary argument that Cook's death was a consequence of his idolatry. Instead, it was a legitimate response to his treatment of the islanders: 'Plain unvarnished history takes the romance out of Captain Cook's assassination, and renders a deliberate verdict of justifiable homicide. Wherever he went among the Islands, he was cordially received and welcomed by the inhabitants, and his ships lavishly supplied with all manner of food. He returned these kindnesses with insult and ill-treatment.'[46] Twain's is a secular version of the missionary account, with Cook more like Cortés than Herod. He also embellishes the story of Cook's heart accidentally being eaten by three children with the information that one of these children lived in Honolulu until recently. Twain, too, has met someone who knew someone. Liberally inclined nineteenth-century traveller-writers were often not admirers of Cook. Stevenson, arguing that Polynesian promiscuity had increased since European contact, was in no doubt that the Hawaiian account of Cook was 'entirely fair'.[47] In this case he must be referring to the widely circulated story, found in Bingham for example, that Cook had sexual intercourse with a young woman given to him by her high-ranking mother to secure the safety of her people from British threats of violence.

As well as being secularized, the American missionary account of Cook also found its way back into British evangelical writing. W. H. G. Kingston's *Captain Cook, His Life, Voyages and Discoveries* (1871) was one of more than 160 books by this best-selling author; twenty of them had Pacific settings.[48] Kingston concedes the American missionary case. Cook must have been aware that in co-operating with 'the mummery' of his apotheosis 'he was encouraging heathen idolatry and hero-worship in its grossest forms'.[49] Cook was a secular hero, a martyr for science rather than God (p. 319). But there is a good deal left for Kingston to reclaim. Cook was also responsible for 'the founding of two nations of the Anglo-Saxon race'. Thanks to him Australia and New Zealand have become important parts of the British Empire, home to thousands of British and European immigrants, centres of civilization, and in times to come 'of evangelical truth and saving faith' (pp. 119–20).[50]

This myth of Cook's founding role has been supremely important in the creation of a national and cultural identity for Australia and New Zealand in the twentieth century. It has not, however, gone unchallenged. The missionary case against Cook spread, and in 1930 a former state premier of New South Wales, Sir Joseph Carruthers, wrote a book in defence of Cook whose memory, he claimed, had been 'besmirched by narrow minded men'. The place where Cook first landed in Australia was 'sacred soil to the people of Australia and to the people of the race which produced such a man as Captain Cook'.[51] Landings inaugurate an island nation's history. Cook is here the keystone of the imperial connection between white Australians and the British. It is no surprise, therefore, that anti-Cook sentiment had also been strong among the republican circles which formed in the late nineteenth

century.[52] Although Cook had very little contact with Aboriginal
people, and that relatively peaceful, some native Australian
accounts see him very differently:

Now, when he started to knock [kill] my people up in the Sydney, that
means he started to clean [eradicate] my people. Because Captain Cook
came very cheeky, you know. He don't ask, make sure, or quieten them,
you know, [to] make it right. And when that Captain Cook started, and
shooting from Sydney right up, right up to Darwin Harbour, all over
Australia, see? That's wrong. That Captain Cook did wrong. He should
tell them, ask them fair go whether – whether that Captain Cook listen to
my people. You know?

Deborah Bird Rose points out that although this account is at odds
with western knowledge of Cook's visit it tells instead of the relations between Europeans and Aborigines.[53] Cook comes to signify
the oppression and violence suffered by the Aboriginal people
after the arrival of the white settlers. It is a similar process to the
myth-imaging of Cook that I have been tracing in the west, in
which Cook substitutes for wider historical movements.

In New Zealand historiography the classic native account of
Cook is that told by Te Horeta Te Taniwha and recorded by an
unknown European in 1852. Te Horeta claimed to have been a
small child when Cook visited Whitianga on the east coast of the
North Island in 1769. This is his account of Cook:

There was one who was the supreme man on that ship. We could tell by
his noble conduct and demeanour that he was their lord. Some of the
foreigners spoke a great deal, but this man did not say very much: he
merely took our garments in his hands and touched our clubs and spears,
and the feathers that we wore in our hair. He was a very good man: he
came up to us children and patted our cheeks and gently touched our
heads while he spoke in a quiet voice. Perhaps he was talking to us: but
we could understand nothing at all.[54]

It is unlikely this is how he actually saw Cook eighty-three years
earlier. The iconography is unmistakably Christian. Cook is Jesus
come to New Zealand to redeem its inhabitants: 'suffer the little
children' is the sub-text of this account. And Te Horeta was a very
little child indeed. The contrast with the Australian Aboriginal
account is striking. An entirely different myth model is at work,
though one familiar enough from European accounts of first
contact in other parts of the world. Obeyesekere and the New
Zealand historian David Mackay argue that the benign Maori

version reflects the better race relations of New Zealand compared with Australia.[55] However, it is just as likely that the much closer contact between Maori and Pakeha in New Zealand meant that Maori accounts were assimilated to European ones earlier and more thoroughly than in Australia. As we have seen in the case of *Mooolelo Hawaii*, native accounts were inevitably modified by European transcription, and the difference between these Maori and Aboriginal versions of Cook probably has more to do with the transmission of sources than the different history of race relations in the two countries. After all, the history of settlement in New Zealand was hardly peaceable.

Rather like the eighteenth-century British state, twentieth-century Commonwealth governments of New Zealand and Australia have invested heavily in Cook in their construction of a national identity. Beaglehole's monumental scholarship received extraordinary institutional and state support in New Zealand, while Joppien and Smith's lavish three-volume edition *The Art of Captain Cook's Voyages* enjoyed similar backing in Australia. In late eighteenth-century Britain the investment in Cook was an expansionist assertion of power, including that of knowledge, against European rivals. For New Zealand and Australia in the mid- and late twentieth century it has had more to do with fixing a national identity by establishing a point of origin, a founding moment for a national history at a time when imperial ties were loosening and the relation with Britain was being redefined. The figure of Cook preserved the link with Britain while ratifying the growing independence of those 'Anglo-Saxon nations' he had founded.

In contemporary Pacific writing in English Cook has also become a figure of fun. A short story by the wonderfully inventive Tongan writer Epeli Hau'ofa opens with a fantastic history of Cook's chamber pot, much loved and sat upon by the great navigator, who was relieved of it by islanders. Thereafter it became the kava drinking bowl of the island's chief, and, when he had given up his own impotent brew for sailors' rum, the receptacle in which the chief's concubine prepared tea for the island's first white missionary. In a neat reversal of normal European naming practice the island is known to Polynesians as Chamber Island. This tall tale of Cook's pot neatly encapsulates the history of early contact and satirizes reverent western narratives of his voyages.[56]

This chapter has followed in the wake of the multiple identities

7 John Webber, *An Offering before Captain Cook, in the Sandwich Islands*, 1784, engraving.

of Cook since his death. These have included Cook as a Hawaiian god, Christian hero and apostate, as a national, European and imperial hero, a bourgeois, scientific and anti-slavery hero, a boys' adventure hero, a common man's hero, a woman writer's hero, a founding hero, an oppressor of Aborigines and so on; the list is not exhaustive. All of these identities are categorical. Since at least the moment of his death he has become a floating signifier who does not exist apart from these and other representations. This is not to reduce history to textuality but, rather, to insist on the textuality of history. Cook once existed, and his life can be described in different ways. While he lived, however, there were limits to the number of different ways he could be described. From the moment of his death at Kealakekua Bay these limits were washed away. His body was dismembered; its flesh was removed from its bones and some of this flesh was returned to the British; the bones were distributed among the Hawaiian chiefs and priests; the future King of Hawaii, Kamehameha, was said to have received Cook's hair,[57] and stories of his remains proliferated. In a similar way his identity fragmented, bits and pieces of him were claimed by governments, missionaries and native populations, among others, and used metonymically. In a sense, Cook himself was colonized.

Modern scholarship is inevitably caught up in the proliferation of myths around Cook even as it claims to be 'written against these mythic imaginings'.[58] There is no place to stand outside of this process. New Cooks keep appearing over the horizon. For Paul Carter, Cook is an early type of the phenomenologist, preoccupied with the particular, attentive to the claims of locality and the limits of observation, an exponent of 'the travelling mode of knowledge' inscribed in maps and 'the open-ended form of the journal'.[59] This Cook is perhaps not as different from Beaglehole's as Carter's discourse suggests. Carter, in fact, is out of joint with the times in proposing Cook as a hero. More common is a revisionist view of him from some kind of post-colonial perspective.[60] And the matter of his death itself has once more become a *cause célèbre*. The final section of this chapter will examine the argument between Sahlins and Obeyesekere over whether or not the Hawai'ians thought Cook was a god.

In several books and a series of articles Marshall Sahlins has argued that Cook's arrival on Hawai'i in January 1779 coincided with the

Makahiki festival, a ritual celebration in which the war god Ku was
supplanted by the god of peace and fertility, Lono, followed eventually by a ritual counter-attack resulting in Ku's reinstatement and
Lono's exile.[61] Cook's arrival, Sahlins argued, was understood by
the Hawai'ians as a real parallel to the Makahiki ritual, and he was
taken as a figuration of Lono. After a stay of almost three weeks,
during which Cook was honoured as never before on a Pacific
island, he departed just as the Makahiki festival was concluding. In
other words, he made a perfect ritual exit. But this concordance
between Cook's actions and the Makahiki ritual calendar was
broken by his forced return a few days later because of a damaged
mast. Now, Sahlins argued, he was out of phase with the Hawai'ian
ritual cycle and his death followed almost inevitably.

Sahlins' case was widely accepted until 1992 when Gananath
Obeyesekere, in *The Apotheosis of Captain Cook*, blew a post-colonial
whistle. Sahlins' theory, he claimed, was just a further stage in the
western mytho-biography of Cook and part of a long European
tradition that native populations saw white men as gods. He
argued that the Hawai'ians were perfectly capable of dis-
tinguishing a British sea captain from one of their gods; he questioned whether there was actually a Makahiki festival going on at
the time; he argued that the ceremony Cook underwent on
landing was one for installing high chiefs, not gods, and that it was
only after his death that he acquired divine status: what actually
happened was not pre-mortem apotheosis but post-mortem
deification. Cook's apotheosis was a European myth fed back into
native accounts of his visit by American missionaries.

Sahlins, in *How 'Natives' Think: About Captain Cook, for Example*
(1995), has replied that far from rescuing the natives from the slur
of primitive gullibility, Obeyesekere has colonized and silenced
them by imposing norms of bourgeois European rationality on
Hawai'ian culture. His 'self-proclaimed defence of "preliterate
people who cannot speak for themselves" is imperialist hegemony
masquerading as subaltern resistance'.[62] Sahlins and Obeyesekere,
therefore, mirror each other almost perfectly. Each claims insider
privilege, Sahlins as a Pacific expert, Obeyesekere as a native Sri
Lankan able to speak for other colonized peoples; each accuses
the other of unloading their preconceptions on the other; most
glaring is the mutual accusation of Eurocentricity.

Sahlins mounts a convincing theoretical reply to the charge that he is augmenting and dignifying the western myth of Cook's apotheosis. He does this in terms of a comparative discussion of how Polynesian and other Pacific cultures assimilated strangers within their own categories of being. Although this sometimes involved making gods of Europeans, he argues, there was nothing abject about this. Rather, it was a means of bringing the European under indigenous forms of ritual and exchange, and can be seen as cultural appropriation on native terms rather than a humiliating submission to western superiority (p. 181). Nor was this assimilation of the strange to the familiar necessarily inflexible or static. Indigenous categories of being were often adjusted to take account of contradictions at the empirical level. In several places Sahlins provides elegant and subtle formulations of the place of cultural structures in historic events, as here for example:

> while they [cultural structures] invariably do find a place in the ordering of history, this does not mean that the order so effected is compulsory, prescribed in advance, or achieved without benefit of conscious subjects. The logic of any given response to a historical situation is never the only one possible and rarely the only one available . . . It follows that the event is culturally constructed . . . [but] . . . to say that an event is culturally described is not to say it is culturally prescribed. To conflate the cultural structuration of events with the necessity of one particular ordering is abusive, leaving the realist interpretation based on universal sensory capacities as the only analytic alternative. (p. 251)

Sahlins feels that his account of Cook's death has been reductively conflated in the manner described above. He also feels that the terms in which Obeyesekere denies the Cook-Lono identification leave his antagonist in the universal realist position of assuming that all people think and react in roughly the same way. This, he argues, is no more than an historically and culturally specific empiricism derived from Hobbes and Locke. The passage as a whole seems to open up a space outside the closed, antithetically symmetrical structure of the argument between the two.

This is not borne out in practice, however. Sahlins' narrative of Cook's death remains vulnerable to Obeyesekere's charge that his representation of mythical thinking is too inflexibly based on a 'rigid interpretation of symbolic forms'.[63] Sahlins repeats the account he gave in *Islands of History* and continues to downplay the historical event. He argues that when Cook went ashore early on the morning of 14 February to take the Hawai'ian King hostage, he reversed the climactic confrontation of the Makahiki festival. Rather than the canoe of Lono being set adrift, Lono had gone ashore with the intention of taking the King to sea. This ritual inversion provoked the crisis and led to Cook's death which was, in part at least, a ritual demise. Every action described that morning is interpreted in terms of this structure. For example, the offerings of pigs and red tapa cloth pressed on Cook as he made his way to where the King was staying are seen as yet more evidence of Cook's divinity. Sahlins has repeatedly made the point that such offerings are proof of his identification with Lono. And yet the *history* of that morning is that an angry Cook came ashore with a party of armed marines who had been ordered to put ball rather than shot into their muskets. Although the Hawai'ians would not have known about the ammunition, it must, so to speak, have been written all over Cook's face. And their offerings were, for once, brushed aside.

Sahlins' sense of what was abnormal that morning is the ritual inversion of Cook-Lono coming ashore out of phase with the Makahiki festival. Cook's editor and biographer Beaglehole has a different understanding of what was abnormal: 'He [Cook] had decided on the abnormal – that is, on an immediate descent on the village, with the marines at his back, and marines armed as if for battle.' He cites King, Cook's lieutenant: 'things carried on in a quite different manner from formerly'.[64] This historical sense of the abnormal keeps disappearing from Sahlins' account. To suggest that the inhabitants of Kealakekua Bay were intimidated, even frightened, by this early-morning invasion is not to impose European norms on differently minded natives. The gifts might well have been propitiatory. It becomes a flat and static narrative if such detail is always reduced to yet more evidence of Cook's imputed divinity. Sahlins can see Cook only as Lono, and everything therefore falls into that frame. There is no allowance for singularity; it is all form and structure. In the end the whole event becomes a still photo, the anthropologist's equivalent of all those paintings of the death of Cook. On the other hand, if all the evidence of his divinity is denied it becomes, as Sahlins charges, a monocultural explanation, and yet another still photo. Somehow we need to try and see the event as a kind of photomontage, or a moving picture shot from different angles.

It is not clear that on the morning of his death Cook was still regarded by most Hawai'ians as an embodiment of Lono. Sahlins has, I think, established that when he first anchored in Kealakekua Bay after his prolonged circling of the island he was taken as such by the thousands of Hawai'ians gathered to welcome him, or at least that they had been instructed to do so by their priests. He has also established that there was a posthumous cult of Cook's bones amounting to deification, although this was unlikely to have been instantaneous. It is not clear, however, that the Hawai'ians in the immediate aftermath of Cook's death believed they had killed Lono.

There was likely to have been categorical confusion over exactly *who* they had killed. As Cook had become more familiar to the Hawai'ians, particularly in the period between his forced return and his death, their sense of his divinity seems to have been dissolving. Sahlins explains the different reactions of the priests and chiefs to the return of the ships (the priests were welcoming, the chiefs suspicious) in terms of the rituals of Makahiki, and makes short work of Obeyesekere's case that resentment was provoked by anxieties about food supply. But the rash of petty theft, and the decline in respect shown by commoners, is typical of the Polynesian response to the British elsewhere in the Pacific, where Cook had not been deified. Bougainville at Tahiti in 1768, and Marion du Fresne in New Zealand several years later, were both subject to anxious questioning about the length of their stay. Prolonged visits seriously disturbed the customary life of the inhabitants. Anxiety can be explained without recourse to either supposed food shortages or Makahiki rituals. Beaglehole wonders if the forced return with a damaged ship lowered the esteem in which the British had been held. He also wonders, again following King, whether familiarity had bred contempt.[65] Sahlins would disallow such questions as imposing European rationality on people who thought differently, but the treatment of Cook on the afternoon before his death suggests he was no longer held in awe.

The events of that afternoon were a curtain-raiser for the confrontation of the following morning. A shore party getting water was obstructed; tongs from the *Discovery* were stolen, and in the chase to recover them a chief was assaulted and an angry confrontation ensued; Cook himself, with a marine, was sent miles inland on a wild-goose chase by local natives who followed him, laughing and jeering. Sahlins' attempt to explain this incident is weak:

Inserted by Obeyesekere to show that Captain Cook was hardly being treated as a god, these incidents could only demonstrate such by our standards of divinity. The argument ignores the specificity of the status of Cook-Lono as a royal adversary at this moment and the ambivalent dispositions of the chiefs. Indeed Maui-the-trickster is a paradigmatic Hawai'ian figure of defiance of the god in favor of humanity. (p. 236)

Sahlins' repeated charge of applying inappropriate standards of divinity is here left unbolstered by any alternative explanation. Would the ambivalent disposition of the chiefs have been understood by the commoners? If so, how did this ambivalence translate into their mockery of a god? And what is the connection between Maui and the Hawai'ians who misled Cook? Surely this is a non sequitur. Unless the incident can be explained in terms compatible with Cook's divinity the whole structural explanation of his death next morning becomes difficult to sustain.

Sahlins' structuralism also has difficulty accommodating the violence in the relations between the British and the Hawai'ians. The sporadic outbursts of minor violence on the eve of Cook's death have just been noted. On the morning of his death, before going ashore to take Kalani'opu'u hostage, he gave orders to seal the bay, and some of the *Discovery*'s guns were fired at canoes to send them back to shore. *Resolution*'s cutter was sent after a large sailing canoe already making out of the bay and this led to the shooting of a chief, news of which reached the crowd gathered on the beach and was perhaps instrumental in converting their fear into confrontation. The fight on the beach left not only Cook dead, but four marines and seventeen Hawai'ians. Very soon after Cook's death *Discovery* fired into a crowd of Hawai'ians gathered where the mast was being repaired. There were further incidents in the next couple of days, including a cannon attack in which many Hawai'ians were killed and the priests' village was fired; British shore boats returned to their ships with two Hawai'ian heads stuck on the bows. Beaglehole's account of this last attack is brief and muted. Obeyesekere's post-colonial perspective makes more of it; it is an explicit part of his agenda to highlight the revenge of Cook's ships on the native population. Sahlins ignores it. His structuralist reading of Cook's death has little space for the violence and power imbalance of the encounter, and his account of the contact between British and Hawai'ians becomes aestheticized and, consequently, depoliticized. One of his very few references to violence comes in the course of an interesting passage on how the European understanding of first contact is not necessarily commensurate with native histories. Nor, he continues, is the native experience and understanding of violence:

> Nor did the 'violence' of the European intrusion always mean what we (by common sense) think. Huli history reminds us that such violence has neither self-evident meaning nor patent historical significance. The Huli did not lay their deaths on White men because the killers were not White men. So nothing can be taken for granted or deduced a priori, even from the Horror. Not without the indigenous understandings of what happened, why, and who was concerned – which may well turn out to be cosmic questions. Nothing here could have been deduced directly or transparently from our own moral sentiments. (p. 188)

The Huli are New Guinea Highlanders, and 'the Horror' refers to the terrible violence of two gold prospectors who crossed their territory in 1934. Although their carnage exceeded anything known in local battles it is ascribed by the Huli not to white men but to *dama* (spirits). Like Cook, these prospectors were a 'historical metaphor of a mythical reality' (p. 187).

This kind of argument dovetails too neatly with imperialist apologetics to be used with anything other than great caution. What Sahlins in practice ignores, although there is no doubt he could handle this with aplomb on the theoretical level, is that colonial violence has its own structures which lock on to native ones and frequently overwhelm them. Violence in colonial settings is never simply an unfortunate accident or a necessary means of self-defence, a mere blot on the landscape. It is systemic; integral to the process of contact and settlement. As Greg Dening has written of early culture contact in the Marquesas: 'There was violence in the Outsiders' presumed right to possess the Land; there was violence in the assumption of cultural superiority; violence in the prejudices, violence in the goodwill to make savages civilized and Christian; violence in the realpolitik of empire and progress.'[66] Cook had neither the missionaries' zeal for conversion nor the traders' greed, but his visit to Hawai'i was enacted within the same broad structures of colonial contact. Violence was the foreshortened cultural lesson, the ultimate social control to which recourse was made when the attempt to control others by peaceable means broke down. This, it seems to me, is what happened on the beach that morning. Violence, which was implicit in every encounter

Cook had with Pacific peoples, and had been simmering in the days immediately before his death, erupted and overwhelmed the social rituals which until then had more or less regulated relations between the British and the Hawai'ians. This was true for both sides. The difference between them, of course, was firepower, which, as Cook well knew, was what made his landfalls possible. After all, what is happening when natives call westerners gods? It is a way of explaining the greater manifest powers of the stranger. Violence, or its threat, is integral to this process.

My point is to try and resuscitate Sahlins' account by breathing history back into the narrative. The moment of Cook's death cannot be explained wholly in terms of native categories of understanding which remain essentially undisturbed by the irruption of the British into the Hawaiian world. Again Greg Dening puts it well: 'The historical reality of traditional societies is locked together for the rest of time with the historical reality of the intruders who saw them, changed them, destroyed them. There is no history beyond the frontier, free of the contact that makes it.'[67] As he goes on: 'To know the native one must know the intruder.' Sahlins is not much concerned with the intruder, which is odd given his theoretical interest in the dialectics of cultural encounter. He ignores the European end of the question of Cook's divinity, whereas an important part of Obeyesekere's argument is the interaction between Cook's European apotheosis and his Hawai'ian status. To accept that he was initially identified with Lono, and that this identification was reinstated some time after his death, is not to deny the long history of a myth of white gods which has served European interests. Cook's death must also be understood in these terms, and Obeyesekere has suggested ways in which his European apotheosis might have interacted with indigenous versions of his divinity. Events at Kealakekua Bay certainly recharged the myth of white gods which subsequent western visitors then brought back with them to Hawai'i. In the decade or so after Cook's death the story of his divinity was slowly inflated by Europeans. An analogous, though probably more rapid, inflation seems also to have taken place in Hawai'i. The interaction of these two processes remains an essential part of the story. It is a more complicated matter than seeing either Europeans (Obeyesekere) or Hawaiians (Sahlins) as prisoners of their own myths.

Sahlins and Obeyesekere also tend to assume that all Hawai'ians thought the same thing. Both would find this remark irritating. At various points in their writing they make general concessions about possible differences of understanding between chiefs and priests, elites and commoners, men and women, young and old, and so on. Sahlins is again fluent on these matters: 'For it need not be supposed that all Hawaiians were equally convinced that Cook was Lono, or, more precisely, that his being "Lono" meant the same thing to everyone' (p. 65). The concession in the first part of this sentence is rather heavily qualified by the second. But again: 'the social differences of opinion which are apparent in the historical documents can hardly exhaust the inde-terminacies and perplexities, let alone the disagreements, that in all likelihood marked the initial Hawaiian understandings of Cook' (p. 66). When, however, it comes to detailed examination of what happened and why, these caveats are forgotten. Thus, if the sight of Cook's blood disturbed the belief that he was Lono this is either a nineteenth-century invention, or else it means that 'the Hawaiians must have believed [it] up to that moment' (p. 110). All those perplexities and disagreements have dis-appeared.

There is an underlying argument in Sahlins that the identifica-tion of Cook with Lono firmed up as the ruling castes engaged the people in the service of their interpretation. The *history* of Cook's stay, however, suggests that the identification loosened as the ships became more familiar. And who believed what? Were the commoners more sceptical than their superiors? Was the elite manipulating the people for its own ends? What was really going on in the minds of Hawai'ian commoners as they were obliged to fall on their faces whenever Cook passed? Was it religious awe, or was it resigned acceptance of a barely understood ritual which they were compelled to undergo? What is the relation between this obeisance and the taunting of Cook on the eve of his death? These questions may be unanswerable, but their very unanswerability should make those who venture to write about 'how "natives" think' proceed with more caution.

Spivak's discussion of her now famous question 'Can the sub-altern speak?' is relevant. She argues that the diametrically opposed positions on the subject of widow sacrifice (sati) in India (summarized in the colonialist sentence, 'white men are saving

brown women from brown men', and the nativist one 'the women
wanted to die') foreclose heterogeneity and even work to legitimate each other. These 'dialectically interlocking sentences'
involve a 'violent shuttling' which becomes the displaced figuration of the subaltern, denying her any position to speak from.[68]
Something similar is happening in the Sahlins/Obeyesekere
dispute. The sentence 'natives often regarded Europeans as gods'
is contradicted by another, 'Europeans like to think natives regard
them as gods.' Both sentences are concerned with chiefs, priests
and officers. Subaltern voices (Hawai'ian commoners or British
sailors) are muffled or inaudible, ignored in the process of
imperialist subject-constitution which, in Spivak's terms, is at stake
in this debate. We cannot fill the silence of others with speech of
our own but these silences need to be acknowledged, along with
the fact that our understanding is therefore often blocked or
incomplete. Sahlins turns a quotation from Certeau against
Obeyesekere, rebuking him once more for substituting European
rationality for Hawaiian culture, but it is equally relevant to his
own work:

In the text of the ethnographic project . . . are irreducible details (sounds,
'words', singularities) insinuated as faults in the discourse of comprehension, so that the travel narrative presents the kind of organization that
Freud posited in ordinary language: a system in which indices of an
unconscious, that other of conscience, emerge in lapses or witticisms.
The history of voyages would especially lend itself to this analysis by toler-
ating or privileging as an 'event' that which makes an exception to the
interpretive codes. (p. 118)

It is the exclusion of singularity and exception, the failure to
acknowledge different points of view and the sounds of silence
which mar Sahlins' and Obeyesekere's arguments and turn them
into mirror images of each other.

Sahlins' attempt to narrate the death of Cook from the point of
view of Hawai'ian ideas and practices cannot simply be dismissed
in terms of a post-colonial theory which condemns all putative otherness as a form of orientalism. Apart from the self-defeating (and
self-aggrandizing) nature of this position, Obeyesekere's critique
of Sahlins highlights the danger when doing this of stepping into
the very trap he is busy pointing out to his adversary. On the other
hand, Sahlins' view from the shore seeks always to contain the singular within the expected, and in doing so produces a staged

account of Cook's landfall at Kealakekua Bay which ritualizes its violence and sanitizes its effects.

The matter of Cook's death has been more contentious at some times and in some places than in others. In the decade following the event Britain was the main site of interest. An important element in this was the confident mood of Britain following the Seven Years War, which had left France badly weakened. Cook was represented as a modern explorer, a suitable emissary for the enlightened, expansionist mercantile culture he represented. His death provided this world with the martyr it needed to dignify its mission. As we have seen, however, this ideological reformulation of the explorer was a contested matter whose contradictions were never reconcilable. The representation of Cook as an anti-conquest hero, the 'seeing-man' whose autoptic gaze, to borrow Pagden's term,[69] calmly possessed whatever it saw, was contradicted by accounts of Cook firing villages and punishing and shooting their inhabitants. Enlightenment liberalism, entrepreneurial individualism and Christian ethics strained against each other. The most unstable element in this uneasy compound was also the most important – that is, Cook's apotheosis. Although native adoration of the European stranger confirmed the superiority of his own world while denigrating that of the savage, it also made the explorer complicit in superstition and idolatry. Furthermore, it raised the fear which shadowed most later writing about the Pacific of cultural regression, of going native.

It was this, rather than Cook's mild heroism, which was central to the next significant phase of contention about the death of Cook. Evangelical Christianity was bound to be sensitive to any hint of sacrilege, and missionaries in the field were peculiarly alert to the danger of being decivilized. The antipathy towards Cook felt by the missionaries on Hawaii, therefore, was an overdetermined phenomenon, also fed by incipient rivalry between British and United States governments in the Pacific. The specific matter of Cook's death was less important to the settler colonies of New Zealand and Australia than the myth of his founding role. Nevertheless, his martyrdom enhanced this role and lent it a religious aura.

Viewed in this perspective, what is the significance of the contemporary debate around Cook's death? Although more

circumscribed than earlier manifestations, it is reductive merely
to dismiss the Sahlins/Obeyesekere controversy as an academic
dog-fight (or god-fight). It is also a cultural encounter of a
post-modern kind, with the very ground on which the antagonists
stand a matter of dispute. Obeyesekere claims to speak from the
perspective of the colonized and accuses Sahlins of practising a
neo-colonialist anthropology. Sahlins disputes the position
Obeyesekere stakes out for himself and claims to be speaking from
a more authentic native point of view. Both try to position themselves on the beach, looking out to sea, as the European ships sail
in. The effort itself has not, until recently, commonly been made
though its inherent dangers are too apparent for self-congratula-
tion. Each antagonist, in effect, tries to cast the other as Cook.
Sahlins becomes the proto-imperialist that Obeyesekere takes
Cook to have been; Obeyesekere becomes the European realist
that Sahlins assumes Cook was. The death of Cook becomes, by
symmetrical displacement, the death of an academic opponent.
The gladiatorial aspect of this contest can be ignored. Far more
significant are the different kinds of attempt at coming to terms
with a colonial past and breaking free of the mind-sets which legit-
imized it. The death of Cook has become a particular focus of this
attempt which cannot be other than fraught and protracted. The
examination of an old colonial encounter has resulted in a new
culture war within the western academy, but one with implications
wherever the pressure of the colonial past and present is felt. As a
result, and in the meantime, it has become necessary to keep on
killing Cook.

CHAPTER 3

Mutineers and beachcombers

Six months in a leaky boat

(Split Enz)

The violent death of Cook undermined prelapsarian myths of the Pacific but reinforced that essential line, at once fundamental and fragile, dividing civilization from savagery. In killing the great navigator the islanders could be seen as having conformed or reverted to type; such actions were in character. To turn one's back on civilization, however, was inexplicable and scandalous. White savages were immeasurably more reprehensible than black or brown ones because they chose to throw off the restraints of civilization. Native backsliding, as we shall see in the next chapter, frustrated the missionaries but was to be expected. Opting for savagery, however, turned accepted categories inside out and hierarchies on their head.

The type of the white savage in Pacific writing was the beachcomber, that anomalous figure who jumped ship, was shipwrecked or escaped from a convict settlement and crossed the beach to become a participating member of an island culture. Unlike the sailors or traders who merely visited and therefore remained strangers, beachcombers settled and were accepted. This acceptance depended, in large measure, on conforming to the social pattern of their hosts. Many beachcombers, already alienated from their home cultures, were prepared to try. As a result they were detested by the official representatives of European culture in the South Pacific. As early as 1801, at the request of the missionaries, the governor of Port Jackson attempted to have them removed from Tahiti and many were driven to remoter islands in the region.[1] It is clear why missionaries should have seen beachcombers as an obstacle to their task of conversion, but the intolerance and hostility directed at them went deeper. Beachcombers represented a 'heart of darkness' vision of regression which haunted those Europeans who lived on the islands. They also fascinated a home culture safely distanced from this threat but nevertheless unsettled by it, as the return and trial of the *Bounty* mutineers was to show.

In popular imagination, then and since, the mutiny on the *Bounty* was a mass act of beachcombing. Bligh himself was the original authority for such an explanation:

I can only conjecture that they have Idealy assured themselves of a more happy life among the Otaheitans than they could possibly have in England, which joined to some Female connections has most likely been the leading cause of the whole business . . . what a temptation it is to such wretches when they find it in their power however illegally it can be got at, to fix themselves in the most of plenty in the finest Island in the World where they need not labour, and where the alurements of disipation are more than equal to anything that can be conceived.[2]

To the mutineers this was mere self-exculpation. They denied Tahiti was the cause and blamed Bligh's conduct as captain, another self-exculpatory explanation. Bligh's provocations are beyond doubt, and Tahiti might not have been sufficient cause, but its allure for sailors is well attested.

Something like mutiny was said to have been brewing on that most exemplary of Pacific voyages, Cook's first. Beaglehole dismisses the alleged plot, described in a letter from Matra (a midshipman on the *Endeavour*) to Banks in 1790, as the exaggerated sum of a number of unrelated and trivial incidents; and certainly Matra's letter was prompted by the *Bounty* mutiny. Beaglehole does, however, concede it likely that plans for remaining in Tahiti would have been mooted as sailors scraped and painted the ship in preparation for putting to sea again.[3] Men who simply jumped ship, like the two who deserted shortly before *Endeavour*'s departure, were almost invariably caught and returned. Something more concerted was usually necessary if sailors were to become beachcombers. J. R. Forster, comparing the different situations of a sailor on board *Resolution* and a Tahitian on his island, felt unable to blame the former,

if he attempt to rid himself of the numberless discomforts of a voyage round the world, and prefer an easy life, free from cares, in the happiest climate in the world . . . The most favourable prospects of future success in England . . . could never be so flattering to his senses as the lowly hope of living like the meanest Tahitian.[4]

Forster's contrast between ship and beach is central to this chapter, which begins with the *Bounty* mutiny itself and some of the literature it prompted. Its underlying question is why, in Dening's words, 'these unimportant affairs on an unimportant ship in an unimportant place'[5] should have prompted so much myth-making then and since. The *philosophes* thought they had discovered true nobility in the Polynesians but had not chosen to live with them and share their culture. This was precisely what mutineers and beachcombers attempted. For them the eye of the Pacific became a looking-glass through which they stepped, thereby unsettling the order of the world from which they came. It was easier, though, to escape the world they knew than fully to join another. The later part of this chapter will discuss Melville's *Typee* as an account of the final impossibility of the beachcomber quest.

The *Bounty* story itself has a treble plot. The first involves the mutiny, the return to Tahiti, and Fletcher Christian's quest for a vanishing island on which to settle. The second is Bligh's stubborn small-boat voyage across the Pacific and the subsequent attempt to bring the mutineers home to Britain for trial. The third is the settlement on Pitcairn of the rump of the mutineers, and the discovery of its ordered and devout community two decades later; this 'paradise regained' narrative was especially significant in nineteenth-century versions of the *Bounty* story. Twentieth-century versions, particularly in film, emphasize the first plot. For Dening's question to be answered all three need to be kept in mind. A detailed account of the whole story is unnecessary.[6] Instead, I shall isolate certain features common to it and other beachcombing narratives, in particular sexuality and tattooing, and the politics of mutiny and going native. First, however, more about the contrasting zones of ship and beach, particularly as they affected the *Bounty*.

Bligh had sailed with Cook on his last voyage and took him as a role model. He imitated Cook's attention to detail, his concern with the health of the crew, and his efforts to establish cordial relations with native chiefs. But where Cook commanded Bligh nagged, and his determination to run a tight ship became obsessive and neurotic. In his relations with officers and sailors he betrayed many of the weaknesses characteristic of leaders with an insecure sense of their own authority. In dealings with Polynesians, however, he was less prone to violence than Cook. Of course he made fewer landfalls, but in view of the celluloid demonization of Bligh it is worth insisting that he was not a particularly violent man. He was, for example, a lighter flogger than Cook, and Kennedy argues that his rules of conduct for relations with South Pacific islanders were more lenient than Cook's.[7]

The first of these rules was that news of Cook's death should be withheld from the islanders. This was to avoid the risk of undermining European authority, but it also suggests a deeper psychological dependence on Cook as a father figure. Other British captains and officers were more relaxed about divulging news of his death and, in fact, the Tahitians already knew of it. From their point of view it mattered little whether Cook was alive or dead. His influence remained crucial in their management of relations with visiting ships. When the *Bounty* first anchored in Matavai Bay the local chief Pomare sent a framed portrait of Cook, painted for him by Webber, as a symbol of friendship.[8] It had become customary for the Tahitians to take this painting to each ship that called and ask the captain to sign a message on the back. Dening associates it with other sacred treasure which by the late eighteenth century had become indispensable to any claim of paramountcy, and describes how another British captain confirmed Cook's death by presenting the Tahitians with a print of Zoffany's painting of the event.[9] This growing Tahitian museum of European contact mocked Bligh's first rule. Even in the Pacific news travelled fast, and his belief that the *Bounty*'s mission would be more difficult if Cook were known to be dead underestimated the afterlife of his former commander and the performative flexibility of representations of his death.

The *philosophes'* contrast between European constraints and Polynesian freedoms must actually have been experienced by the sailors who went ashore at Tahiti. Every aspect of life on board was measured and rationed and almost every move involved some ritual of boundary maintenance. The hierarchies of shipboard life reflected but also exaggerated those of the home culture; British culture at sea was almost a parody of that on land. On the *Bounty* all these characteristic features of shipboard life existed in heightened form. It was too small for its task of transporting breadfruit seedlings from the Pacific to the Caribbean. The adaptations needed to carry this out encroached on the space of officers as well as sailors and must have contributed to the speed with which relations between Bligh and his officers deteriorated. The *Bounty* was an overcrowded hive, and like all such hives eventually it had to be divided.

There was not much Bligh could do about the lack of physical space, but at sea he deprived his men of mental space as well. Diet and personal hygiene had been a concern of Cook's, too, but Bligh's intrusion into the personal space of all those who sailed under him was experienced as invasion. He stormed boundaries rather than adjusting them. Nowhere is this more apparent than in his insistence that the sailors should be cheerful. To this end he had recruited Michael Byrne, a half-blind Irish fiddler, to provide music for dancing. When several of the crew refused to dance he cut their grog ration. Nothing could better illustrate the contrast between ship and beach than the compulsory jollity of Bligh's dancing sessions and the voluntary pleasures of Matavai Bay.[10]

For all crew in the Pacific, but particularly for those on the *Bounty*, the beach must have represented freedom, excess and plenitude, nature rather than culture as they understood it. Managing the relations between these zones of ship and beach was always difficult. This was not simply a matter of worlds in conflict. The freedoms of the beach were also a reward for the discipline of the ship and an essential part of its maintenance. Prolonged relaxation of the discipline, boundaries and hierarchies of the ship, however, must have made their eventual reimposition more difficult. Bligh remained in Matavai Bay for five months during which time, it has been suggested, he abandoned control of the company.[11] He was busy securing breadfruit, and was sometimes unwell, but it was too long to stay in one place. It allowed time for relations between the crew and the Tahitians to cohere, and alternative patterns and rhythms of life to be established.

Most sailors going ashore on South Pacific islands saw the beach as a trading zone where food, sex and other necessities could be obtained. They kept a cultural distance. To remain at anchor for five months, however, meant that some of the men would, in effect, become beachcombers rather than sailors. By the time Bligh finally sailed from Tahiti a number of his crew and officers had been tattooed in the Tahitian fashion and had established permanent relationships with Tahitian women. Fletcher Christian's famous remark on the eve of the *Bounty* mutiny, 'I am in Hell', could have been wrung from a sense of being pulled between two cultures as well as from the despair he felt at Bligh's treatment. His fellow-mutineers, with their equally famous cry of 'Huzzah for Otaheiti', seem to have felt no such division.

It was this cry as much as the mutiny itself which caused scandal. A group of British men, led by one from an ancient gentry family, had chosen to turn their backs on civilization. Much of the public interest at the eventual trial of those captured mutineers who survived the wreck of the *Pandora* on the journey home centred on Peter Heywood, sixteen years old when he had embarked as a midshipman on the *Bounty*, and son of another prominent gentry family with connections in the higher levels of the Navy. When the *Pandora* had arrived at Matavai Bay to arrest the mutineers left on Tahiti (Fletcher Christian and his band were already on Pitcairn), Heywood, convinced he had played no active part in the mutiny, gave himself up. In a letter to his mother he described rowing out to the *Pandora* with his messmate George Stewart, much to the confusion of its crew: 'being dressed in the country manner, tanned as brown as themselves, and I tattooed like them in the most curious manner, I do not in the least wonder at their taking us for natives'.[12] Dening suggests how he must have appeared to the officers of the *Pandora* as he sailed out to them: 'He was so innocent that he could not see how offensive his figure was . . . He stood on the canoe, wrapped in a barkcloth *maro*, tanned and tattooed, 'gone native' and virtually indistinguishable from them, deviant to system and rule.'[13]

Such reversion was tantamount to guilt. No doubt this would have been confirmed if one of the earliest European poems written in the South Pacific, penned by Heywood while living among the Tahitians in 1790, had been produced at his trial. 'A Dream' reflects on some of those paradoxes of cultural difference which in some form or another troubled most visitors to the South Seas. Of Tahiti he wrote:

> Sure friendships there, and gratitude and love
> Such as ne'er reigns in European blood
> In these degen'rate Days, tho' from above
> We precepts have and know what's right and good
> And tho' we're taught by laws of God and Men

> How few there are who practice what they know.
> Yet they from Nature's dictates use each man
> As they could wish to them all Men should do.[14]

Although found guilty, Heywood was granted a royal pardon and within six years had become a captain. The best efforts of the naval establishment were spent on reclaiming this young midshipman for the European culture whose degeneration he had mused upon in Tahiti. Heywood was also the hero of Sir John Barrow's redemptive account of the mutiny and its aftermath, *The Eventful History of the Mutiny . . . of H.M.S. Bounty* (1831), supported by Heywood's loyal and forlorn sister whose dreadful verse punctuated Barrow's history. Dead within a year of her brother's acquittal, Nessie Heywood's apparent sacrifice completed and justified his redemption.

It hardly needs to be said that in Tahiti Europe found its heterosexual other. However it was moralized, there was no doubt that the colourful centre of the eye of the Pacific, the gaze that emanated from Tahiti, was feminine. Bligh's explanation of the mutiny, for instance, depended on this assumption. The beach was understood as a border for sexual exchange across which European sailors sought Polynesian women. Hawkesworth's *Voyages* (1773) told stories of erotic pleasure on Tahiti which caused scandal and delight, and were inflamed by the parodists and pamphleteers who elaborated his accounts of Banks' sexual adventures and mishaps.[15] Banks, as Roy Porter has put it, journalized himself as the first South Seas rake[16] and Pacific voyaging became a version of the eighteenth-century grand tour, offering more exotic sexual initiation than was commonly found in southern Europe. This was a class-specific version of a more general stereotype of the Pacific as a heterosexual paradise.

But male homosexuality was also common in Polynesian cultures. It took different forms, varying from the transvestism or social effeminacy of the Tahitian *mahu* to the undifferentiated identities of the *tayo* and the Hawaiian *aikane*.[17] Sexual exchange across the beach must also have taken a variety of forms. Hard evidence is scant, but it is clear that young sailors and officers were desired by native men. Lieutenant King seems to have been so at Kealakekua Bay, and it would be surprising if Heywood had not been similarly appreciated. There is no way of knowing how this desire was met. Lee Wallace concludes that on the evidence of

Cook's Journals the European male body was conscious of being visible to Hawaiian male desire and does not seem to have squirmed under that scrutiny. Under the Articles of War sodomy was a hanging offence, another glaring contrast between ship and beach. Prosecutions and conviction for this offence, however, were infrequent, a fact difficult to interpret. Did this mean that sodomy was uncommon, or ignored? I imagine this varied according to the particular captain, ship and beach. More than this it seems impossible to know, but it needs to be remembered that the heterosexual aura around the Polynesian world was a European projection and that the homosexuality of Polynesian cultures had its own allure.

Heywood's letter describing how he rowed out to the *Pandora* also included an explanation of why he was tattooed:

> I was tattooed, not to gratify my own desire, but theirs; for it was my constant endeavour to acquiesce in any little custom which I thought would be agreeable to them . . . provided I gained by it their friendship and esteem . . . The more a man or woman there is tattooed, the more they are respected; and a person having none of these marks is looked upon as bearing an unworthy badge of disgrace, and considered as a mere outcast of society.[18]

A number of the *Bounty*'s crew had been tattooed before the mutiny occurred. Dening suggests that it became the badge of a voyage to Polynesia,[19] the eighteenth-century equivalent of buying a t-shirt. It became an important site of cultural exchange, one of the most significant examples of two-way traffic across the beach as designs from each culture were incorporated into the other.[20] Contemporary western tattooing originates from this encounter between Tahitians and Europeans, and tattooing in western cultures soon became a subcultural marker of marginalized individuals and groups.[21] Although Banks' tattoo added to the frisson of his erotic exploits the practice soon became associated with lower-class white savagery. Rev. Robert Thomson, for example, wrote of seamen on the Marquesas that they differed only in colour from 'their fellow savages; they are tattooed as much as the natives – run as naked – live as loose, and are more openly insultingly vile in our presence than even the natives'.[22] After the *Bounty* therefore, perhaps earlier, a tattoo was far more than a souvenir. Unlike a t-shirt it could neither be taken off nor left behind.

We also need to consider what tattooing meant in Polynesian cultures. Tattooing modified the body to reconstruct individual identity according to the requirements of the social milieu. Within Polynesian cultures the marks it made on the skin were secondary to the proof it offered of socially salient transactions having taken place. It was not, as most nineteenth-century western observers considered, a form of graphic art but a ritual.[23] When Europeans were tattooed by Polynesians, therefore, it must have meant very different things to the two sets of participants. From the Polynesian point of view tattooing involved a reinforcement of the skin, often as a protection against threats to the body from gods and other supernatural forces, and was intimately connected with rituals of rebirth and maturation.[24] It always involved a closer integration with the social group. From a European point of view, however, this refashioning of the body surface implied a repudiation of western culture. It had, therefore, an opposite significance, being a rejection of the civilized body and a highly visible move towards assimilation into so-called savage culture. Or at least, if not consciously registered in this way by the tattooed subject, this was how it came to be regarded by the European observer.

But there were similarities as well. Tattooing in Polynesian cultures was intimately associated with sexuality, there being both general analogies and specific connections between tattooing and defloration. Gell, following Anzieu, argues that tattooing always involves an intrinsically sexualized kind of bodily looking in which the gaze of the onlooker is congruent with that of the seducer.[25] As usual the missionaries were on to something when they saw tattooing as an incitement to vice and lewdness. These sexual associations are present in western as well as other cultures and were, as we shall see, exploited by Melville in his representation of different forms of sexuality in *Typee*.

The *Bounty* mutineers brought back to England for trial were one particular focus of the fascinated horror with which the tattooed body came to be regarded in the west. Heywood, who seems less innocent than Dening suggests when writing to his mother of merely acquiescing in 'any little custom', was described by Bligh as 'very much tattowed and on the Right leg is tattowed the Three Legs of Man as that coin is'. Another, Morrison, neatly illustrated the dialogue of forms involved in the meeting of the Polynesian tattooer with the western body by having the Order of the Garter tattooed round his thigh.[26] This was relatively discreet compared with the facial tattooing characteristic of more devolved

Polynesian cultures such as the Marquesan and Maori. A French beachcomber, Cabri, who had lived with the Taipi on the Marquesas and was tattooed from head to foot, supported himself on returning to Europe by exhibiting his body.[27] Moana (or Temoana), principal chief of Nukuhiva at the time of French annexation in 1842, had also exhibited himself around English ports in between serving on whaling vessels.[28] This absorption of the savage tattooed body into the popular culture of early nineteenth-century Britain is yet another example of its multiple valencies.

The *Bounty* affair also had explicit and immediate political implications, raising questions about the political ordering of civil society. Its coincidence with the French Revolution was simply that, but when news of the mutiny reached Britain late in 1789 it must have added to the alarm of that year. Old regimes were crumbling and the spread of radical political ideas was generating anxiety among the upper classes. Even defenders of the established order were concerned at its failure to govern responsibly. Jane Austen's admiration for the Navy is well known, and for her the ship, the country house and the state were analogous institutions requiring similar kinds of leadership and organization. Mr Knightley's benevolent paternalism was the model, rather than the absenteeism of Sir Thomas Bertram, perhaps tending recently imported breadfruit trees from Tahiti on his Caribbean estate.

Ships are a microcosm of the political order, and however spontaneous the mutiny might have been it was received in Britain as an act against constituted authority, welcomed by some but anathema to the ruling classes. Dening points out that the Navy's determination to hunt down the mutineers and bring them back to Britain for trial indicates how political the *Bounty* mutiny really was. He also shows how European politics were spilling over into the Pacific. In June 1791 the tricolor was first raised in the region, on the northern Marquesas by the captain of a French vessel who named this group 'The Islands of Revolution'.[29]

Byron wrote 'The Island' at the beginning of 1823 while still working on *Don Juan*. It is based on the *Bounty* mutiny and the subsequent fate of the mutineers on Tahiti, although the setting has been shifted to Toobonai (Tubai). Byron drew on Bligh's own

Narrative (1790) for the mutiny itself, but the events on the island he describes are imaginary. He did not use any of the subsequent material about the recapture of the mutineers on Tahiti, the wreck of the *Pandora*, or the settlement on Pitcairn. He did, however, as the 'Advertisement' to the poem announces, draw on one of the most famous Pacific beachcomber narratives, William Mariner's *Account of the Natives of the Tonga Islands* (1817).

The politics of rebellion in 'The Island' are conservative. Clearly there is no connection in Byron's mind between the *Bounty* mutineers and the Greek insurgents he was shortly to set out to join. Bligh is 'The gallant chief' (I, ii), mutiny is 'the black deed' (I, viii), the *Bounty* without its captain is 'a moral wreck' (I, vii), and the island the mutineers regain is a 'guilt-won paradise' (III, ii). Although the poem's sympathies are a little more evenly distributed than this suggests, the fundamental wrongness of the mutiny is insisted on to the end: 'Their life was shame, their epitaph was guilt' (IV, xi).

The island, on the other hand, is the moral centre of the poem. The sailors' desire to return is endorsed although the means they adopt is condemned. Toobonai is not the seductively deceptive land of the lotus-eaters, nor are its women sirens. It has an educative and civilizing influence, with republicanism as part of its appeal; it is 'the equal land without a lord' (I, ii). Although the island has provoked the mutiny it can also redeem it. By returning there the unruly sons of Europe will be tamed by love and become what 'Europe's discipline' has failed to make them, civilized (II, xi). In the meeting of the old world with the new the advantage is entirely with the latter. Europe is tainted with 'The sordor of civilization' without having abandoned the savagery 'which man's fall hath fix'd' (II, iv). The European is therefore doubly degraded. The Polynesian, by contrast, seems only lightly touched by original sin. Pre-contact Toobonai was not quite Paradise. The songs at the opening of the second canto, reworked from a prose translation in Mariner, tell of past battles and impending war with Fiji but their gentle melancholy hardly impinges on 'the harmony of times / Before the winds blew Europe o'er these climes' (II, iv).

In describing the island, Byron draws on, develops and bequeaths most of the tropes and stereotypes of the Enlightenment and Romantic tradition of representing the South Pacific. It is like a particularly well-stocked supermarket, with everything within reach and packaged for the consumer's convenience:

> The cava feast, the yam, the cocoa's root,
> Which bears at once the cup, and milk, and fruit;
> The bread-tree, which, without the ploughshare, yields
> The unreap'd harvest of unfurrow'd fields,
> And bakes its unadulterated loaves
> Without a furnace in unpurchased groves,
> And flings off famine from its fertile breast,
> A priceless market for the gathering guest. (II, xi)

No labour is involved. The land does not need to be worked; the food needs no preparation; the bread comes sliced and wrapped, and the shopping is free as well as easy: this is 'The goldless age, where gold disturbs no dreams' (I, x). In the absence of labour, time becomes irrelevant. The young lovers' days on the happy shore are unpunctuated by the clock:

> Their hour-glass was the sea-sand, and the tide,
> Like her smooth billow, saw their moments glide;
> Their clock the sun, in his unbounded tow'r;
> They reckon'd not, whose day was but an hour. (II, xv)

This picture of the South Pacific as a world without time became a nineteenth-century commonplace and persists in popular accounts of Polynesian cultures today. The Romantic tradition invested heavily in it yet, as we shall see in Melville, also came to find it a source of unease. In Byron's poem, however, it is wholly admired.

The island is also markedly feminine. Gender was one of the most obvious and telling means of fixing the differences between Europeans and others. There is a long tradition of representing primitive cultures as feminine and child-like, with civilization as masculine and patriarchal. In Byron, and more generally within the Romantic tradition of South Pacific representation, Polynesian culture is coded feminine in quite particular ways. It is a culture of the body, of bathing and oiling and languid ease. The female Polynesian body becomes synonymous with a coral island paradise, and the beach Europe's imagined space of sexual freedom. Neuha is at the head of a tradition of nineteenth-century Polynesian heroines who function in this way. She is the songstress who inhabits 'the cave / Of some soft savage' (I, ii) for which the sailors mutiny at the opening of the poem. In a fairly obvious sense she *is* the cave. Like many of her successors in other Romantic texts she is associated with water and bathing. The cave, the rock pool or the lake hidden in tropical foliage often feature in these texts as a European male fantasy world of erotic water play. Neuha is 'In growth a woman, though in years a child' (II, vii). From the publication of Hawkesworth's *Voyages* there had been fascination in Europe with the early age of puberty in Polynesian females, and this became another recurring feature of the nineteenth-century tradition I am sketching.

Like Melville's Fayaway and her later successors, Neuha has lightish-coloured skin:

> for through her tropic cheek
> The blush would make its way, and all but speak:
> The sun-born blood suffused her neck, and threw
> O'er her clear nut-brown skin a lucid hue,
> Like coral reddening through the darken'd wave,
> Which draws the diver to the crimson cave. (II, vii)

The ability to blush, apart from being represented as sexy, is important in the colour register separating Polynesians from darker races. Polynesian colouring placed them outside the conventions of representation for black peoples, and new kinds of contrast and comparison were developed. Southern Europeans were a common point of comparison, and the ability to blush enabled further distinctions and discriminations to be made within that leaky umbrella category of the other. 'A rosy tint upon a rich and mantling olive' is an entirely typical example of this process whereby the female Polynesian body was simultaneously sexualized and categorized.

Neuha, in other words, *is* the island. She is what draws the sailors back. She embodies its innocence, its life and its redemptive energy, and offers an alternative bounty for the guilty mutineers. In this she is twinned with the poem's romantic hero, Torquil, 'the blue-eyed northern child . . . of the Hebrides' (II, viii). It has been suggested that the original for Torquil was George Stewart, who married the daughter of a Tahitian chief and was drowned in the wreck of the *Pandora*.[30] But Stewart, who became Fletcher Christian's lieutenant, was too involved in the mutiny for such an innocent role and, if an original there must be, Peter Heywood better fits the bill. Neuha and Torquil are 'Both children of the isles' (II, xii). Byron's poem privileges islands. Whether Pacific or Hebridean, they are detached from mainland cultures and therefore uncontaminated by civilization. They are also the source of song and legend. Neuha is a songstress and the poem expresses a preference for song ('untaught melodies') over writing ('our accomplish'd art / Of verse') (II, v) as part of its privileging of the primitive and the exotic. Torquil's childhood has been 'Nursed by the legends of his land's romance' (II, viii), which have taught him hope and endurance and prepared him to be the fit auditor of Neuha's legend, her 'olden tale of love' (IV, ix), at the end of the poem. Elsewhere Byron had expressed a feeling of Celtic affinity with the orient, and in 'The Island' he extends this to the South Seas, anticipating a comparison that Stevenson was to develop at the end of the century. Torquil is 'free as ocean's spray' (II, ix) but the island habitat of his childhood means he is also 'tempest-born in body and in mind' (II, viii). But with Neuha on 'the happy shores' (I, x) of Toobonai he is calmed:

> His heart was tamed to that voluptuous state,
> At once Elysian and effeminate. (II, xiii)

His idyll, however, must be broken. The crime of mutiny remains unpunished and the poem's version of the *Pandora* arrives to capture the mutineers.

The men are hunted down, killed or captured, except for Christian, of whom more soon, and Torquil who is saved by Neuha. The rescue of Torquil concentrates the imagery of caves and diving which is scattered throughout the poem. As we have already seen the cave is the heart of light, the source of song and feminine beauty which calls the sailors back to the island. But it is also a 'thirsty cave' (II, vi) which needs to be refreshed. This comes from the sea, urged by the wind, but also from the diver who is drawn to this submarine world of 'the crimson cave' (II, vii). At the poem's climax Neuha rescues Torquil from his pursuers by diving into a protected cave whose only entrance is many feet below the surface. Torquil plunges after her, following the 'streak of light behind her heel / Which struck and flash'd like an amphibious steel' (IV, vi), and surfaces in an enclosed cave vaulted and gloomy like a cathedral. Neuha, however, has prepared a pleasure dome:

For food the cocoa-nut, the yam, the bread
Born of the fruit; for board the plantain spread
With its broad leaf, or turtle-shell which bore
A banquet in the flesh it cover'd o'er;
The gourd with water recent from the rill,
The ripe banana from the mellow hill;
A pine-torch to keep undying light,
And she herself, as beautiful as night,
To fling her shadowy spirit o'er the scene
And make their subterranean world serene. (IV, viii)

This is Nature's 'chapel of the seas' (IV, vii), fugitive, erotic, and scene of the legend of a young chief who used it to shelter the woman he loved from a threat to her life, which Neuha now recounts. This tale of symbolic death and rebirth echoes that of Neuha and Torquil except that the gender roles have been reversed. In Byron's poem the cave is thoroughly feminized and it is therefore Neuha who saves Torquil, purges his guilt and redeems him. The captured mutineers are returned to civilization and its disciplines on a 'floating dungeon' (IV, xv) while Torquil and Neuha enjoy their sunken paradise. Innocence is regained by something more sustaining than a royal pardon.

Byron's source for the cave is Mariner, whose vivid description he follows in detail.[31] Like Torquil's, Mariner's dive is guided by the light reflected from the heels of the Tongan he follows; the cavern is like a Gothic vault; there one of the company tells the same story which Neuha repeats to Torquil. The striking difference, however, is that Byron has feminized and heterosexualized his version. In Mariner the Tongan King, Finow (Finau), and his male companions retreat to the cave to drink kava. It is a male club, reminiscent of the Taboo Groves in *Typee*, and the story of the young lovers is told to an exclusively male audience. The point, however, is the same: 'How happy were they in this solitary retreat! tyrannic power now no longer reached them: shut out from the world and all its cares and perplexities; – secure from all the eventful changes attending upon greatness, cruelty, and ambition; – themselves were the only powers they served, and they were infinitely delighted with this simple form of government.'[32] The idyll of the cave, the underwater fantasy of Byron's poem, is an eroticized retreat from both the politics of mutiny and the warrior society recorded by Mariner. When Neuha and Torquil resurface they emerge into an idealized pre-contact world:

Again their own shore rises on the view,
No more polluted with a hostile hue;
No sullen ship lay bristling o'er the foam,
A floating dungeon: – all was hope and home! (IV, xv)

The politics of the poem have by now become incoherent. The mutineers have been captured and justice will be done, as justice must. However, the polluted source of that justice, Europe, has vanished from the scene leaving one of its renegades free to enjoy the 'peace and pleasure . . . As only yet the infant world displays' (IV, xv). Only islands can perform such magic.

One of the main ways in which 'The Island' manages this sleight of hand, condemning the mutiny while idealizing one of its perpetrators, is by sidelining its leader. Fletcher Christian is neither hero nor villain, indeed he is curiously absent until late in the poem when his death is used to counterpoint Torquil's rebirth. He appears briefly in Canto I as a haunted Byronic figure, unnamed but recognizable by his famous line, 'I am in hell! in hell!' (I, viii). There is no place for him in the idyll of Canto II, and it is only during the flight from those come to recapture the mutineers that he is given any dramatic status. In focus for the first time, Christian is represented as a doomed existential figure whose 'worst wound was within' (III, iv), an 'extinct volcano' who declares:

For me, my lot is what I sought; to be,
In life or death, the fearless and the free. (III, vi)

Whereas Torquil and Neuha are associated with water and vegetation, Christian's terrain is rock. Trapped on a crag, he demonstrates the futility of mutiny by firing a button from his vest when his ammunition has gone and then leaping to his death shaking his fist at the world (IV, xii). The contrast with Torquil is stark, and he too becomes part of Torquil's redemption. Christian is used to demonstrate the self-destructive despair inherent in rebellion, and his inability to find peace on the island exonerates the 'happy shore', and therefore Torquil, from any lasting complicity in the mutiny. He also becomes the prototype of the guilt-wracked European male adrift on the Pacific, cut loose from home yet unable to find another, mocked by the contrast between the paradise he has lost and the hell he inhabits.

Fletcher Christian was not hunted down. He took the *Bounty* with eight other mutineers, six Polynesian men (from Tubai, Tahiti and Raiatea), twelve Tahitian women and a baby to Pitcairn, a remote uninhabited island only two miles by one in size, which Carteret had sighted in 1767. The island was shared out among the nine mutineers, none of the Polynesians receiving any land. One woman was allocated to each of the Europeans and the remaining three were given to the Polynesian men. An initial rebellion by the Polynesian men resulted in the execution of its two leaders. Another, several years later, brought about the death of five of the mutineers, including Christian. A chain of killings followed and, after further deaths from suicide, accident and natural causes, by the turn of the nineteenth century only one of the mutineers survived. This was John Adams, now the sole adult male in a community of nine Polynesian women, an eleven-year-old Polynesian girl, and twenty-three children who had been born on the island. To complete this gruesome actuarial account, Dening has calculated that 86 per cent of the founding male population of Pitcairn were individually murdered.[33] Adams then underwent a religious conversion and proceeded to reorganize life on Pitcairn along lines that the missionaries on Tahiti were by now struggling to achieve. When the settlement was accidentally discovered by an American vessel, the *Topaz*, in 1808 it was a God-fearing, Sabbath-observing, Bible-reading community presided over by a benevolent patriarch.

The first literary response to news of the discovery of the Pitcairn settlement was Mary Russell Mitford's volume *Christina, The Maid of the South Seas* (1811), a very long poem in four cantos. It tells a story of reconstruction and settlement redeeming the mutiny and creating peace and order from carnage. The paradise regained by Torquil at the end of 'The Island' is erotic, personal and in tension with the paradise lost by Christian and the threat of British justice. The paradise retrieved on Pitcairn in Mitford's poem, however, is chaste, social and secure.[34] There is no evidence that Byron had read her poem, and the similarities in their characterization of Christian probably derived from the difficulty liberals experienced in reconciling condemnation of the mutiny with admiration for some of the principles Christian seemed to embody.[35] Mitford's 'Advertisement' highlighted this problem: 'Irresistibly attracted by the character of the gallant and amiable Christian, she yet distrusted the partiality, which might have led her to extenuate his crime; and if she has erred, it has been on the side of authority.' Like Byron, Mitford eased this dilemma by giving the central role to someone else. In both poems there is a displacement of Christian in order to contain the troubling sympathies he provoked. In *Christina* he is dead, figuring as a remembered character in its retrospective account of the mutiny.

Mitford also offers more specific exoneration. Christian was compelled to mutiny because Iddeah, the native woman he had lived with, was pregnant, her child would be killed by the Arioi (a Tahitian cult whose members were not permitted to reproduce) and Bligh had refused to allow her to escape on the *Bounty*. It was not sex and the good life that drew Christian back to Tahiti but a threat to the unborn child. Mutiny was his last resort in the face of Tahitian infanticide. This introduction of a domestic theme allows Christian to be represented as legally guilty but morally justified. His guilt-wracked existence following the mutiny underlines this: thereafter, 'on his brow of care / He wore the livery of despair' (II, xxxii). The child he goes back to save dies. Mad with grief, and haunted by Bligh's 'pale form', when he learns that Iddeah is again pregnant he jumps from the cliffs of Pitcairn in the hope that by atoning for Bligh's assumed death he will save the life of his second child:

> Vain was all help; – the sudden shock
> Scatter'd his brains upon the rock. (III, xxi)

These memorable lines also wipe the slate clean. Having mutinied to save the life of his first child, Christian now dies to save the life of his second, Christina.

Mitford's poem elaborates a myth of settlement based upon a patriotic love of home and the English countryside. It opens with a storm at sea and a celebration of British manliness:

> A Briton calmly pac'd the deck;
> Can storms the British spirit check?
> That spirit which still higher soars,
> As tyrant threats, or cannon roars! (I, ii)

It is 1811 and Britain is at war with France. Between each mountainous wave the ship is momentarily 'Becalm'd and tranquil, as the lake / That smiles by Derwent's woody brake' (I, iii). This is the first of many such moments in the poem when the peaceful certainties of the English countryside are invoked. This particular reference also recalls the landscape of Christian's childhood and his association with Wordsworth.[36] The storm subsides and land is sighted. But this is no ordinary South Pacific paradise. Instead of 'hut or rude morai' the watchers see:

> garden trim, and cottage wall:
> Cots, such as Thames' mild waters lave,
> Or shine in Avon's mirror wave;
> Where English peasants feel the power
> Of evening's sweet domestic hour;
> Where wearied veterans cease to roam;
> Where comfort cries, 'here is my home!' (i, xi)

They have discovered England in the South Seas. Their first view of human life, a young couple decked with flowers and bearing fruit, confirms this. They are dressed like natives,

> But not a trace of Indian feature
> Appear'd in either glorious creature:
> For his warm blood as brightly glow'd
> As if in British veins it flow'd;
> And she – the roses of her cheek
> Might shame the dawn's refulgent streak. (i, xiii)

The sailor who sees them through his glass is Henry, of England's finest stock. Fitzallan, the gentrified Jack Adams of Mitford's poem, homesick for England, revives at the sight of Henry's yellow locks and blue eyes, while the touch of an 'English hand' sends thrills through his English blood (ii, ii).

The poem establishes an important contrast between Tahiti and Pitcairn which is central to its attempt to create some corner of the South Pacific which is for ever England. Christian and those mutineers for whom 'higher duties called' (ii, xxxiii) were impelled to depart the casual hedonism and violence of Tahitian culture. They were a minority among the 'rebel crew'. As for the rest:

> In luxury and vice they trod,
> Woman their idol, sense their God.
> Few were there wise. Well was it time
> To quit this soft voluptuous clime. (ii, xxxiv)

The *Bounty's* crew, therefore, divided for the second time, a virtuous minority going off to found an English settlement, the reprobates left behind in vicious sloth. With *Paradise Lost* echoing loudly, Christian, Fitzallan and other redeemable mutineers establish a small replica of the mother country in the South Pacific which will eventually be readmitted to the English diaspora. (It remains to this day a British crown colony.)

The Pitcairn settlers must *work* to create this new world, their labour adding value to the project. Mitford shows them digging for Britain:

> Soon felt the vale the British spade;
> Soon rose the cottage in the shade. (III, xvi)

Natural plenitude is unnatural; work is needed to justify harvest:

> By natural toil win nature's wealth,
> Food, raiment, cheerfulness and health. (III, xvi)

Only Christian fails to settle, but his death redeems the whole community: he dies that it might live. Thus Henry arrives to discover a new Eden offering a third chance. Europe is tainted (Mitford makes the conventional Romantic contrast between the state of nature and civilization), Tahiti has failed to meet the promise of its first reports, but Pitcairn can be different from either of these. It will be predominantly European but remote from the accumulated historical guilt of that continent. Paradise is being rewon.

Christina and Henry secure it. Christina is fitted to do so by her name, her beauty, and above all by her filial and domestic virtues. When first seen she is draped over her mother's tomb uttering 'a daughter's woe to heaven' (I, xxxviii); it is the anniversary of her mother's death. Christina, however, is her mother's opposite. Whereas Iddeah is (a little) like Kurtz's savage woman, Christina embodies the domestic ideal. She blushes, her eye is lowered, her foot is slender, and she possesses the 'holy charm . . . [of] modesty' (II, xlii). If her role in the settlement and reconstruction of Pitcairn is to replace Iddeah's savagery with English domesticity, Henry's is to bring English genes untainted by the *Bounty* mutiny. Together they will atone for the sins of the parents. Traces of Tahitian grace and beauty will survive in the succeeding generations but the stock will be predominantly English, as will the setting. One small part of the Pacific will have been colonized and redeemed.

A final element in *Christina* is worth noting. The volume has 132 pages of notes supporting 177 pages of verse. These include long passages from Bligh's account of the mutiny, the journal of Cook's last voyage, Bougainville, Hawkesworth, a *Quarterly Review* article on the discovery of the Pitcairn settlement and so on. This amounts to far more than the mere acknowledgement of sources and is a feature of other nineteenth-century imaginative literature about the Pacific. Whereas facts in eighteenth-century travel fiction typically form a seamless part of the text, in the nineteenth century they separate out from romance to become weighty ballast in the form of notes. Why should ethnographic and other factual material have been more difficult to integrate in nineteenth-century fictive travel writing about the Pacific than it had been in the eighteenth? There is, of course, a long tradition of confusion, both deliberate and accidental, between travel writing and the romance or the novel. Associated with this is the problem of authority and authenticity. We shall see in a moment how this issue dominated the reception of Melville's first work about the South Seas. The elaborate and repeated cross-referencing of the same few canonical texts in Pacific writing suggests anxiety around the question. One response to this was to textualize the South Pacific, to fill its vast 'empty' space by making it dense, known and increasingly familiar. In doing so, citing became an important supplement to writing.

In July 1842 Herman Melville jumped ship at Nukuhiva in the Marquesas. He escaped inland with another member of the crew of the whaling vessel the *Acushnet* and spent three to four weeks in the Typee valley.[37] He left the Marquesas on another ship a month after his desertion and spent the next two years working his passage around the Pacific. The experience of these years was the basis of Melville's early writing. His first book, *Typee*, was completed within a year of his return to the United States and appeared early in 1846. Melville presented it as an autobiographical narrative, but even before it appeared its authenticity had been questioned by its London publisher John Murray. Several reviewers on both sides of the Atlantic were equally sceptical.

These criticisms were silenced, however, when Melville's companion came forward and testified to its accuracy. Richard Tobias Greene had become separated from Melville in the Typee valley and had been tricked into leaving the Marquesas, and his unfinished story was a prominent loose end in Melville's narrative. 'The Story of Toby', now that it was available, appeared as an appendix to all later editions of *Typee*. John Murray even brought it out as a separate pamphlet. This persuaded most readers that

Typee was literally accurate and it was not until the publication of Charles Roberts Anderson's *Melville in the South Seas* in 1939 that its fictive and intertextual elements were established. Melville's stay among the Typee had been no more than three to four weeks, not four months as the book had stated. His ethnography of the Typee and other details of the Marquesas drew heavily on the accounts of earlier visitors which he read subsequent to his own stay. By the time that Melville was travelling and writing the South Seas were already extensively textualized. *Typee* is an elaborate blend of fact and fiction, authenticity and romance, which needs to be read within and against this already complex discursive tradition.[38]

It is, broadly speaking, within that Enlightenment and Romantic tradition which imaginatively appropriated the South Pacific in order to construct its case against the ignobility of civilization. Melville's brief against civilization is, however, more consistently pursued in *Omoo*, the sequel to *Typee*, where he seeks to expose the harm done by missionaries, traders and the colonizing powers in Tahiti. This damage had hardly begun on the Marquesas at the time of Melville's stay, and not at all in the valley of the Typee. In *Typee* he is more concerned with the attempt to escape one's own culture and enter another, with crossing the beach and living on the other side. For all that it is based on only a few weeks' experience *Typee* is a beachcomber narrative, though a highly sophisticated one. It asks: how do you approach and enter another culture? how do you read something new? how do you describe something which has not been represented before? how well can you ever know another culture? In his eventual failure to enter and understand, to abandon his culture of origin and feel at home elsewhere, to cross back over the beach and depart without violence, Melville's persona Tommo marks the beginning of the end of a quest which Bougainville had inaugurated three quarters of a century earlier. It continued, of course, and persists today, but after *Typee* its force had begun to weaken. By pushing this Enlightenment and Romantic tradition further and more critically than it had ever been taken *Typee* began to expose and dispel its illusions.

Typee, like the *Bounty* mutiny, begins with the desire to go ashore, to escape the discipline of the ship for the imagined freedom of the beach. Conditions on board are ripe for mutiny, but the crew is too divided for this and so Tommo decides to steal away. Nevertheless, mutiny hovers around the opening of *Typee* and technically occurs in *Omoo*, though with comic rather than serious consequences. Those who go ashore are called 'liberty-men' but the beach at Nukuhiva is crowded and not a place of liberty at all. Seven vessels of the French Navy are anchored in the harbour and there are soldiers encamped ashore. Tommo then must cross this less than happy shore and go inland in search of the happy valley. He has already had an intimation of such a place when visiting the bay of Tior and wandering into its valley: 'an immense arbour disclosing its vista to the eye, whilst as I advanced it insensibly widened into the loveliest vale eye ever beheld'.[39]

It is here too that we have the first emblematic confrontation of civilization and savagery, a cultural encounter which Tommo observes and which anticipates his own first encounter with the Typee chief some chapters later. It involves a meeting between the Rear-Admiral of the French fleet Dupetit-Thouars, decked out in all the paraphernalia of his rank, and the ancient chief of Tior who, apart from a loin-cloth, 'appeared in all the nakedness of nature' (p. 66). In Tommo's account of this meeting the advantage is entirely with the native chief and he wonders, rhetorically and rather predictably, which is the happier of the two. The confrontation and the musings it prompts are entirely conventional. They are, however, to come under some pressure when Tommo finds himself in a parallel situation but without the reassurance of the despised French armed forces.

From the start, therefore, freedom is elusive. Mutiny is ruled out, the beach is occupied, and escape is difficult. Within a few minutes of crossing the beach Tommo and Toby are trapped in a mass of tall reeds as tough and stubborn as 'rods of steel' (p. 77). The only way through is by throwing themselves on to the reeds which spring back into place when the pressure of their bodies is removed, closing in on them from behind. And then suddenly they are out of the thicket. This sets the pattern for their journey. It is made through a contradictory landscape in which nothing is as it seems. At close quarters Paradise proves to be a place of promise and obstruction, safety and danger, shelter and exposure, sunlight and shadow, plenty and starvation, health and sickness, freedom and captivity. Everything is deceptive, uncertain or double-faced. When the thirsting Toby discovers a clear stream he loathes its waters: 'Had the apples of Sodom turned to ashes in my mouth, I could not have felt a more startling revulsion' (p. 96). It is a landscape of Paradise and hell, of fruit and snakes. When Tommo and Toby finally break through into the promised valley they run to the fruit trees. They have not eaten for days. The fruit, however, is decayed; its rind has been opened by birds and most of its flesh has been eaten. Those 'apples of Sodom' are recalled. But this impression of a fallen world is immediately contradicted by the first sight of its inhabitants:

They were a boy and a girl, slender and graceful, and completely naked, with the exception of a slight girdle of bark, from which depended at opposite points two of the russet leaves of the bread-fruit tree. An arm of the boy, half screened from sight by her wild tresses, was thrown about the neck of the girl, while with the other he held one of her hands in his. (pp. 112–13)

This is more than 'A Peep at Polynesian Life', Melville's subtitle to *Typee*: it is a glimpse of Adam and Eve, an anticipation of Gauguin's Tahiti. It also seems to answer the most urgent question that has shadowed their journey: is the valley Happar or Typee?

At the heart of the mythic landscape which Melville constructs out of the mountains and valleys of Nukuhiva are the contrasting settlements of the Happar and the Typee, the former peaceful and hospitable, the latter fierce and cannibalistic. The two valleys in which they dwell are adjacent, and as Tommo and Toby make their difficult descent into the paradisal valley that they have seen from the mountain peaks they seem to face the alternatives of being feasted or eaten. Happar or Typee? The question is nervously repeated, and although the Edenic tableau which greets them suggests Happar, their meeting with the elders of the tribe is unsettling:

One of them in particular, who appeared to be the highest in rank, placed himself directly facing me, looking at me with a rigidity of aspect under which I absolutely quailed. He never once opened his lips, but maintained his severe expression of countenance, without turning his face aside for a single moment. Never before had I been subjected to so strange and steady a glance; it revealed nothing of the mind of the savage, but it appeared to be reading my own. (p. 116)

This recalls and revises the earlier encounter between the French admiral and the old chief. Tommo no longer gazes from a safe distance and draws complacently edifying morals. He is now subject to the Polynesian gaze and feels his mind emptied by it. The chief then asks the question that has been filling Tommo's mind – Typee or Happar? Tommo answers correctly – the Typee would not want to be confused with their enemy – but from his point of view it is the wrong answer. This is not the happy valley they have sought. And yet in many ways it proves to be, as neither Typee nor Happar conform to their reputation. Toby is later wounded by a Happar raiding party and Tommo lives in blissful ease among the Typee. The sharp antithesis of Happar and Typee, like that larger opposition of civilization and savage, is complicated. Tommo finds himself living in a Happee valley.

Tommo's life with the Typee, however, is one of idyllic captivity. He is welcomed and made much of but not allowed to leave. Another paradox emerges. Tommo has escaped from captivity into captivity, a pattern which is repeated in *Omoo* when, after escaping back across the beach to a new ship, he finds himself once more subject to arbitrary power and is forced to join a mutiny in order to get ashore at Tahiti, which lands him back in captivity. Tommo's account of his stay with the Typee is a captivity narrative, though of an odd kind. Life there conforms to most of the archetypes of the romantic dream of islands. It is a world untouched by civilization, without work or time or seasons, in which 'a day is the history of a life' (p. 210). It is also an erotic paradise with a miniature lake where the young women bathe and frolic with Tommo, and which seems to expand when he and his particular favourite, Fayaway, go boating. In the most flagrant scene of this kind Fayaway becomes the masthead, her unwound tapa robe the sail, and Tommo steers with the paddle as they glide across the lake, Fayaway's long brown hair streaming in the gentle breeze.[40]

This highlights the apparent contradiction at the centre of the text. If civilization is rebarbative, and the savage culture of the Typee so pleasurable, why does Tommo wish to escape? Insofar as *Typee* is a captivity narrative it is at odds with its own thesis that civilization is not worth the candle. An obvious response to this problem is that Tommo wants to escape because he fears for his life. Why do the Typee look after him so well but refuse to let him go? Are they feeding him out of hospitality or are they fattening him up? Like most other things in this text the cannibal theme is treated ambivalently to provide humour as much as tension. When the native doctor pulverizes Tommo's injured leg he leaves it in the

condition of a rump steak ready for cooking (p. 127). The Hansel
and Gretel theme of fattening the victim is playful as well as
serious, teasing the European readers' fascinated horror with
cannibalism. Its treatment darkens in the final sections when
Tommo discovers that the tapa-wrapped packages hanging from
the roof under which he sleeps contain heads, one of them
European. This realization of the savagery hovering over him is
then intensified by his glimpse of what he assumes are the remains
of a cannibal feast: 'my eyes fell upon the disordered members of
a human skeleton, the bones still fresh with moisture, and with par-
ticles of flesh clinging to them' (p. 316).

This propels the captivity narrative forward to its climactic
moment of escape, but does not condemn the Typee culture
whose appeal the rest of the text has worked so hard to establish.
Indeed, a defence of cannibalism has already been mounted in
one of those extended passages on civilization and its discontents
which recur in both *Typee* and *Omoo*. In this case the practice of
eating one's enemies slain in battle is compared favourably with
European torture, execution and other kinds of civilized ferocity
(pp. 18off.). And in terms of the book's thesis there is no question
that the savage state of the Typee is preferable to western civilization. If the one is not wholly immune from evil, the other is
defined by it. The fear of cannibalism is essential to the captivity
narrative but it is not the sole unambiguous cause of Tommo's
desire to escape. In fact, it is never established that the Typee really
are cannibals. As Neil Rennie points out, Tommo's evidence is
obtained while in an 'unhappy frame of mind' in which his
'imagination ran riot'. This leaves unresolved whether cannibalism is a Marquesan practice or the product of Tommo's, and the
western observer's, frame of mind.[41]

There are other, deeper reasons for Tommo's escape. *Typee* is a
quest narrative that fails to find what it seeks. Tommo discovers an
emptiness at the heart of Paradise; the happy valley ultimately dis-
appoints. Towards the end of a string of mainly ethnographic
chapters, during which time the captivity narrative is suspended,
he describes the vivid colouring of the birds of the valley. This riot
of colour, however, is soundless: 'the spell of dumbness is upon
them all – there is not a single warbler in the valley!' (p. 290). The
dumb beauty of the birdlife oppresses Tommo with melancholy:
he has discovered the heart of silence. This silence is associated

with other elements of Typee life which he finds attractive but melancholy. How do you live in a world where 'a day is the history of a life'? What are the implications, both personal and cultural, of unlimited ease? (Melville is at one with all those other commentators on Polynesian cultures who insist that the islanders never work.) Earlier in the ethnographic chapters Tommo describes the vast stone terraces, almost overgrown, which he takes to be the work 'of an extinct and forgotten race' (p. 217). As he muses on time's ruins he contrasts the vigorous achievements of the past with the enervated culture he now sees. This is not his standard contrast between the states of civilization and nature, but between the natural state of the present-day Typee and some antecedent *civilization* from which it represents a decline.

From this perspective the happy valley is not an alternative realm against which civilization can be measured but rather a former civilization approaching extinction. Marquesan society is presented as static and lacking the energy to reproduce itself. This feeling is much stronger in *Omoo*, where outside influences are seen as responsible for what Melville considers will be the inevitable extinction of Tahitian culture: 'Years ago brought to a stand, where all that is corrupt in barbarism and civilization unite, to the exclusion of the virtues of either state; like other uncivilized beings, brought into contact with Europeans, they must here remain stationary until utterly extinct.'[42] Thus Melville's law, which he also sees operating in Hawaii.[43] Among the Typee, however, who have yet to experience the mongrelizing effects of European contact, there is a more profound decline at work from within. It is appropriate for such a paradoxical text that the causes of this inner decay should be the very things that Melville most admires about Typee culture and which he uses to criticize the west. Polynesian culture is too laid back to defend itself against the epidemic of civilization.

It need hardly be said that Tommo's discovery of silence and nullity is self-discovery rather than an insight into Typee culture. *Typee* challenges its own romanticism and dissolves the dream of a better place in which to make one's home. Better it might be, but home never; the beach cannot really be crossed. The appeal of Marquesan culture is almost exclusively aesthetic and sensual. Tommo describes it mainly in terms of nature and food, and these terms are extended to its inhabitants. Fayaway laughing has a mouth like a cleft arta with its milk-white seeds embedded in red, juicy pulp (p. 134). Marnoo, her male equivalent in beauty, has an intricate tattoo of the artu tree on his back, so that a rear view 'might have suggested the idea of a spreading vine tacked against a garden wall' (p. 194). Young Marquesan women are like climbing plants, decorative, sweet-smelling, and forever winding themselves around Tommo.

In the ethnographic chapters Tommo attempts a more systematic and detailed account of Typee life, but in doing so implicitly refutes the notion that one can know another culture by observation, reason and inference. His account of Typee religion, for example, ends with the disclaimer, 'I saw everything, but could comprehend nothing' (p. 244). This is unusually frank. More typically he assumes an understanding which the text elsewhere fails to support. Sometimes, as when the chief Mehevi tries to explain the taboo system or the Feast of the Calabashes, he remains cheerfully but defiantly ignorant. There are whole areas of Typee life, particularly to do with the sacred, which he fails utterly to comprehend.

Tommo cannot speak of what he fails to understand. There are other aspects of Typee life however which, though understood, are unspeakable. Caleb Cain has drawn attention to the recurring trope of preterition in writing about the Pacific. William Ellis, for example, ostentatiously draws 'the veil of oblivion' over that unspeakable part of the Polynesian character which the epistle to the Romans described so faithfully and distressingly.[44] Cain argues that the unspeakable practice of cannibalism, about which western texts on the Pacific are so loquacious, is used by Melville to speak of the even more unutterable practice of homosexuality, about which such texts are mainly silent. Both practices involve a particular attention to the body of the desired and are caught in a similar double bind of fascination and horror.[45]

The Taboo Groves, scene 'of many a horrid rite' (p. 140) and an exclusively male preserve in which the elders gather to lounge, eat, smoke and sleep, are one particular focus of this association in *Typee*. The first description of the Taboo Groves also includes a vivid account of Marquesan tattooing which is used to intensify the repugnance Tommo experiences at the scene. The combined effects of time and tattooing have 'obliterated every trace of humanity' from the old men. Tattooing has turned their bodies green, their skin has 'a frightful scaly appearance', their flesh hangs in 'huge folds', and they appear 'to have lost the use of their lower limbs altogether' (pp. 142–3). Tommo is appalled by this scene of satiated torpor. Here, and elsewhere in the text, tattooing is the third term of a cluster linking cannibalism and sexuality.

The attempt at a calm, objective, dispassionate description of native lifeways in the ethnographic chapters breaks down entirely when Tommo himself is threatened with being tattooed. The sight of a tattooist at work alarms him, and when the man turns his attention to the blank white canvas of his European skin he runs for what feels like his life: 'Horrified at the bare thought of being rendered hideous for life . . . I struggled to get away' (pp. 292–3). The scene is partly comic – the tattooist pursues Tommo back to his dwelling – but it also marks the point at which Tommo once and for all opts for civilization. At the beginning of *Omoo*, while the vessel which rescues him is still sailing in the Marquesas group, Tommo meets an English beachcomber tattooed Marquesan style with a broad blue band stretching across his face from ear to ear, and, for good measure, with the figure of a shark on his forehead. Tommo regards him with horror. The man is 'a renegado from Christendom and humanity', his mark worse than Cain's;[46] he is, of course, an image of what Tommo has just escaped.

Tattooing, however, can attract as well as repel. In the figure of Marnoo, for instance, it is associated with a very different treatment of homoeroticism. Marnoo is a Polynesian Apollo, with a 'matchless symmetry of form', curling ringlets and a cheek of 'feminine softness' unblemished by tattooing. The rest of his body, however, is 'drawn all over with fanciful figures'. In particular, his back is decorated with the slender shaft and graceful branches of the beautiful artu tree. This is set off by his only costume, a 'slight girdle of white tappa, scarcely two inches in width, but hanging before and behind in spreading tassles' (pp. 193–4). Nigel Rigby has pointed out the close similarity between Marnoo's name and the word *mahu* used to describe the Marquesan and Tahitian figure associated with transvestism and the assumption of female roles and styles.[47] When at first snubbed by Marnoo, Tommo likens his feelings to those of 'the belle of the season . . . cut in a place of public resort by some supercilious exquisite' (p. 195). Marnoo is, in every sense, a transgressive figure, free to cross sexual, tribal and cultural boundaries (he has shipped on whalers). He is also a figure of sheer fantasy whose body markings bear no relation to any ethnographic accounts of Marquesan tattooing, unlike other descriptions of tattooing in *Typee* which are consistent with such accounts.[48]

Tattooing also figures in the representation of Marnoo's fantasized counterpart and heterosexual opposite, Fayaway. Although Tommo regards tattooing as a 'hideous blemish', his description of Fayaway's tattoos is eroticized. In particular he notes three 'minute dots' decorating each lip and discernible only in close-up (pp. 134–5).[49] Suggs has described how the tattooing of young Marquesan girls was associated with their entry into active heterosexual relations and was performed on anatomical parts of sexual importance, including the lips. This culminated in an elaborate ceremony for adolescent girls involving the inspection of both tattooing and genitalia. Gell has also noted the equivalence of mouth and genital tattooing in other Polynesian cultures.[50] However we explain Melville's understanding of such practices, his description of Fayaway seems to utilize this displaced genital tattooing in creating a heterosexual eroticism to set against Marnoo's homosexual allure.

As with so much else in this text, the representation of sexuality through cannibalism and tattooing keeps doubling. In the Taboo Groves, tattooing is associated with repellent, decaying, male homosexual bodies; in Marnoo, however, this is reversed. The attractive pole of this opposition between forms of tattooing then doubles again into heterosexual and homosexual alternatives (or complementarities), with the heterosexual as represented by Fayaway dominant, but the homosexual in the form of Marnoo remaining palpably attractive.

In the end Tommo's escape is instinctive rather than reasoned. While living with the Typee he has sensed, if not understood, that culture is more than the structures, values and lifeways of a people. It is also what engages an individual's emotions and loyalties, binding him to others. The things which have attracted him to Typee culture are superficial, and shadowing these is the unspeakable, itself both appealing and appalling. The curious subtitle Melville gave to *Typee*, 'A Peep at Polynesian Life', is entirely appropriate. Tommo is neither equipped nor able to have more than a peep. The word itself has become infantilized but Melville uses it seriously, though not without irony. When he is trapped in the reeds at the beginning of his escape Tommo discerns 'a peep of daylight' (p. 78) which leads him out of the thicket but soon into another. This is very like his experience of Typee culture. Those moments in chapter 32 when Tommo first has 'a glimpse of three human heads', and then a 'slight glimpse' of the skeleton he assumes has been cannibalized, are the most graphic examples of the peeping by which he gets his fleeting, often furtive, impressions of Typee life. The knowledge derived from peeping will be voyeuristic or inadvertent, uncertain or unreliable.

The deeper initiation that tattooing represents is neither desired nor fully possible. To be tattooed is not to become Marquesan but to cease to be western. Or, at least, it is to become confined to those marginal groups, with little stake in their society, for whom tattooing in western cultures has provided an alternative social matrix.[51] Tommo's horror at the prospect of being tattooed is usually understood as a recoil from becoming a savage, but it can also be read as anxiety about being declassed. Early in *Typee* the tattooing on the face of Tommo's minder, Kory-Kory, has been described in intricate detail, the triple hooping reminding Tommo of someone gazing out from behind the grated bars of a prison window (p. 131). This suggests not only Tommo's own captivity (Kory-Kory is jailer as well as friend, another example of the doubling which is such a feature of *Typee*) but the divide which keeps the two worlds of the novel apart. For all the rebarbativeness of western civilization and the seductiveness of the Typee world, Tommo is unable to cross from one into the other. In the end he cannot deny the experience of his own culture and remain content with mere physical repletion, which is the closest he will get to native life. Nor can he accept the disturbing undertones of Marquesan life which he can hear, as it were, off stage. He returns to what he knows and dislikes, having run away from a world he has enjoyed but failed to know and accept.

And his break with this world is final. The violence he must resort to in securing his escape ensures this. As one of the pursuing Typee chiefs tries to seize the oars of the boat, Tommo hits out with the boat-hook: 'It struck him just below the throat, and forced him downwards. I had no time to repeat the blow, but I saw him rise to the surface in the wake of the boat, and never shall I forget the ferocious expression of his countenance' (p. 332). This is sometimes read as the moment when Tommo discovers the savage in himself, but in fact it marks his return to civilization. The tattooed and the untattooed face stare at each other from their different worlds. This is the last of several encounters scattered through the book when gazes meet and separate worlds are confirmed. The contrast between this final encounter and the meeting at Tior of the French admiral and the old chief is striking. Tommo's attempt to cross the beach and look out on the world with Polynesian eyes has failed, and with this failure the Enlightenment and Romantic construct of the noble savage and the protean westerner has broken down. The last scene on the beach as Tommo makes his escape is one of hesitation, confusion and misunderstanding recalling similar moments in the early history of contact in the Pacific. Like Kalani'opu'u, Tommo is compelled to sit upon the beach. Like Cook he is left at the water's edge waiting for the boat to pull in and rescue him. Like many other visitors he is unable to cross back over the beach without resorting to violence, after which there can be no return. The two worlds of the ship and the beach remain locked in opposition.

There is nothing liberating about Tommo's release. Once again he escapes from captivity into captivity. *Omoo* opens with his arrival on board the *Julia*, whose crew has just rescued him. He is immediately depressed by what he finds and nostalgic for what he has left. The disorder and casual violence of the *Julia* contrast with the peaceful self-regulating culture of the Typee. No one has died in the valley during his stay, but the *Julia* is a ship of death. When it reaches Tahiti the crew is forced into mutiny in order to get ashore, and the cycle begins again. Tommo's release from his idyllic captivity, therefore, in no way mitigates the case against civilization. On the contrary, it is confirmed by the debasement of Polynesian culture Tommo finds in Tahiti. However, the discovery of *Typee* is that those who come from the modern industrial capitalist world cannot escape its culture and conditioning. To jump ship or mutiny is self-defeating. The Romantic quest is an illusion.

There is another way of addressing the apparent contradiction between the demands of a captivity narrative with its logic of escape, and the thesis of the work that the primitive world is preferable to the civilized. Until now I have discussed *Typee* as if it has a single narrative voice. In fact it has two main voices. The first of these, Tommo's, recounts the experiences of the text. The other reflects on those experiences, extracting their meanings and

weighing their significance. In its preference for Polynesian lifeways this latter voice is often at odds with Tommo's repeated desire
to escape. Tommo's voice carries the captivity narrative. It is
immersed in that narrative, a rather ingenuous voice, often jaunty
and sometimes fearful. Although well disposed to the Typee and
relishing the pleasures of the valley, it frequently expresses a com-
monsense western condescension at the strange customs and
incomprehensible language of this amusing but capricious tribe.
This voice is full of commonplaces about savage peoples. The
other voice carries the thesis and therefore challenges many of
these commonplaces. It is the moralizing voice of the critic of
civilization, mordant and distanced. The interaction of these two
voices is similar to that of Esther Summerson and the third-person
narrator in *Bleak House*, although *Typee* does not formally separate
the two in the manner of Dickens' novel.

As Tommo first sails into Nukuhiva harbour he stares fearfully
at the valley of the Typee while one of his shipmates regales him
with accounts of the treachery and ferocity of its inhabitants. He is
filled with 'a particular and most unqualified repugnance' (p. 61).
Within two pages, however, we are given a passionate defence of
the Typee. Their savagery is a response to western atrocities: 'Thus
it is that they whom we denominate "savages" are made to deserve
the title' (p. 63). And again: 'in all the case of outrages committed
by Polynesians, Europeans have . . . been the aggressors, and . . .
the cruel and bloodthirsty disposition of some of these islanders is
mainly to be ascribed to the influence of such examples' (p. 64).
This voice and point of view are quite distinct from Tommo's,
which often falls back into western stereotypes of the savage: 'But
what dependence could be placed upon the fickle passions which
sway the bosom of a savage? His inconstancy and treachery are
proverbial' (p. 122). It is precisely this proverbial wisdom that the
other voice is there to challenge.

One more example will suffice. Tommo's failure to understand
the meaning of the Feast of the Calabashes prompts the kind of
frustrated impatience commonly associated with the English
abroad. He remarks, for example, that for all the good it achieved,
'the whole savage orchestra might with great advantage to its own
members and the company in general, have ceased the prodigious
uproar they were making', and the natives' attempt to explain the
significance of the feast is dismissed as 'a mass of outlandish

gibberish and gesticulation' (p. 233). The next page, however, the opening of the following chapter, is spoken by an entirely different voice concerned to defend the Feast of the Calabashes from the lurid descriptions of Polynesian religious ceremonies found in missionary accounts. This is the voice of cultural relativism arguing not only against the bigotry of the missionaries but also against the philistine impatience of Tommo's own account. And this chapter concludes with a deadpan Swiftean pastiche of missionary talk:

In truth, I regard the Typees as a back-slidden generation. They are sunk in religious sloth, and require a spiritual revival. A long prosperity of bread-fruit and coconuts has rendered them remiss in the performance of their higher obligations. The wood-rot malady is spreading among the idols – the fruit upon their altars is becoming offensive – the temples themselves need rethatching – the tattooed clergy are altogether too light-hearted and lazy – and their flocks are going astray. (p. 246)

The brilliant irony of this passage, and the love of paradox characteristic of this voice, are quite beyond anything in Tommo's registers.

A rigorously detailed analysis of the narration of *Typee* might find this account oversimplified.[52] The whole work flicks in and out of different kinds of narration and modes of description, and the two main voices are not always as distinct as I have suggested. In the ethnographic chapters, particularly, they are sometimes blurred. The existence and dialogue of these two voices, however, are undeniable, and can be understood in terms of the failed mission of *Typee*. The philosophical voice speaks with the authority of an Enlightenment and Romantic tradition of criticizing modern European civilization by reference to a primitive culture seen as representing a state of nature. This is the stay-at-home voice mounting the case against civilization. Tommo's, on the other hand, is the travelling empirical voice which puts these ideas under pressure and is unable, finally, to confirm them. The critique of western civilization offered by the philosophical voice stands, but its investment in primitivism is also exposed. In this way *Typee* is able to challenge its own romanticism.

It is not, however, able to escape the impasse it reaches between an unacceptable civilized world and an unattainable primitive one. This is because it remains caught within the organizing categories of colonial discourse. The text continues to use the binary constructions of civilized and savage, culture and nature: it merely reverses them. The oppositions themselves remain in place. This means there are fixed limits to how far the commonplaces of Tommo's voice can be challenged. The Typee continue to inhabit the realm of nature, not culture. It is simply that nature is preferred to culture. This renders them highly vulnerable to any contact from outside their valley. They are admired primarily for what they are not, and defined almost wholly against European norms and practices.

The logical consequence of this is to suggest that the Typee world will be extinguished by any prolonged exposure to its European antithesis. Lacking an identity independent of its western other, Typee culture will be driven out by a kind of Gresham's law of colonialism. It is not granted the ability to respond to change, to absorb new influences, and to be modified in the process without at the same time losing the defining identity Melville attributes to it. Like most other European travellers and writers in the Pacific Melville has found one unspoiled island, different from all the rest, on to which he can project his own desires and ideals. The Marquesas are untouched though threatened. Tahiti and Hawaii are shop-soiled and their value will continue to decline as contact increases. These cultures will disappear first, but eventually Typee culture will also be extinguished. Melville's inversion of one set of commonplaces of colonial discourse in the Pacific means that he is unable, finally, to conceive the possibility of a hybrid culture of the kind Stevenson was to glimpse.

The happy island of the *Bounty* mutineers or the Pitcairn reconstructionists has, in Melville, become the more remote and fugitive happy valley. The beach is now occupied and therefore contaminated. Access to the valley is difficult and its promise remains, tantalizingly but inevitably, out of reach. Europeans, finally, cannot dwell there on the same terms as its inhabitants.

CHAPTER 4

Missionary endeavours

The founders of the London Missionary Society (LMS), set up in 1795, had read Cook, spoken with Bligh, and decided that Tahiti was the most promising part of 'the heathen world' for a mission. The only anticipated difficulties were 'such as may arise from the fascination of beauty, and the seduction of appetite'.[1] Two years later eighteen missionaries, 'Godly men who understood mechanic arts', landed on Tahiti.[2] Very few were ordained ministers; most were artisans – carpenters, bricklayers, weavers, tailors and the like. Gunson describes this group of 'godly mechanics' as an artificial class separated from their fellow-artisans and home culture by their dogmatic beliefs and strict way of life. They brought with them, therefore, a particularly rigid version of their own culture which they tried to impose on their native hosts. Many had undergone some kind of conversion experience, and their missionary impulse was fed by a desire to reproduce this experience in the lives of others.[3] The urge to convert also clearly involved a projection of their own deep sense of original depravity on to the heathen islanders. Nevertheless, the earliest missionaries landed on Tahiti in a spirit of optimism and brotherhood. The South Pacific was seen as a distinct kind of field marked out by its hospitality and imputed receptivity to the Christian message. Those who had chosen and instructed the first missionaries relied on secular accounts of the region, and the newly arrived missionaries were to complain that they had been misled about what to expect. Certainly, they arrived with few criteria to understand what they met.

The early years of the mission were disastrous for the LMS and a matter of almost complete indifference to the Tahitians. By 1800 a number of missionaries had shipped out for New South Wales and several had gone native, among them John Cock; only five remained. A new cohort arrived in 1801, including John Davies, a Welsh school-teacher, who was to write a history of the early mission to Tahiti. His gloomy chronicle of the following years is one of much labour, no fruit, and neglect by the Society which had sent them out. It was six years before he received any communications from London. His complaints of LMS neglect and failure to understand the conditions in which the missionaries were working are a constant feature of letters from the Tahitian mission throughout its history. This example is chosen almost at random: 'Our state & circumstances are not known. We have to purchase all our food & often with clothes from our backs. We want regular fixed salaries for our support . . . I expect as I have the dropsy that I shall leave a young family unprovided for, therefore Sir please to send us word what will be done for them & by whom.'[4]

Anxiety about 'the seduction of appetite' also haunted these early years. The instructions issued to Davies and his band warned them of their 'corrupt inclinations . . . [and] Carnal Lusts': 'Avoid to the utmost every temptation of the Native Women. Let no brother live separately from all the rest, and if any one sleeps alone, let it be in a house that is prohibited to the Women.'[5] In Britain it was women who fell; in Tahiti it was missionaries. This rhetoric of fear pervaded the missionaries' own writing, as in this letter from Davies to the LMS Directors: 'Let it be remembered, that we stand in a slippery place, that we are assaulted by temptations and trials, which few but ourselves experience . . . darkness and perplexity attend our path of duty.'[6] In this, at least, the LMS responded to the missionaries' needs. Four young women were sent out by the Directors as suitable partners for the single missionaries. Port Jackson was the market place and three marriages followed. Within a year of arriving on Tahiti two of these women had died, and thus began a grisly round in which as missionary wives died, usually in childbirth, their widowers would return to New South Wales for a replacement. Although child-care was a prime reason for this, the missionaries had also fully internalized the idea that it was better to marry than to burn.

The missionaries aligned themselves with the Pomares from the beginning, mistaking them for monarchs and ascribing to them more sovereign power than they actually had.[7] By 1808, after several years of conflict on the islands, Pomare's power was temporarily eclipsed and most of the missionaries, fearing for their safety, withdrew to Port Jackson. They returned in 1811 in changed political circumstances and for the first time began to make headway. Pomare's defeats might have weakened his belief in the efficacy of his own gods. Certainly, he had long realized that the missionaries were a potential source of European goods and therefore a means of consolidating and extending his power. In 1812 he announced his conversion to Christianity, other conversions followed, and a conclusive victory over his rivals at the battle of Fei Pi in 1815 resulted in a more or less unified kingship. It also handed the missionaries an ascendancy in Tahitian affairs which was to last until the arrival of the French in the mid-1830s. In effect, Pomare's victory in 1815 made the LMS a kind of established church. It also enabled the missionaries to influence many other aspects of social and political life and gave them power out of all proportion to their numbers. During the 1820s they consolidated their position as teachers, law-givers and traders. Christianity spread to all the Tahitian islands and beyond. Auxiliary societies of the LMS were established on many of the converted islands which paid tribute, in the form of oil, hogs and the proceeds of trading, to the Society in London.[8]

During the years of its ascendancy the LMS mission in Tahiti was divided between an old guard, most of which dated back to 1797 or 1801, and a new wave of missionaries which had arrived in 1817, almost doubling the size of the mission. Although the Windward Islands, Tahiti and Eimeo (Moorea), had at least nominally been Christianized, little headway had been made on the Leeward Islands of Huahine, Raiatea and Borabora. Among the new arrivals were several with the energy and ambition to extend the existing field. In particular there was William Ellis, who arrived with a printing press, and John Williams whose evangelizing zeal was to extend beyond Tahiti to the Raratongan group, Samoa and eventually the New Hebrides (now Vanuatu), where he met his death and became Britain's second Pacific martyr-hero. Their accounts of the Tahitian mission will be considered in detail in the next section of this chapter.

Within a year most of the new arrivals had moved to the Leeward Islands; Ellis went to Huahine, Williams and L. E. Threlkeld to Raiatea, J. M. Orsmond to Borabora. This was resisted by some of the older missionaries who particularly disapproved of the removal of Ellis' printing press from the Windward group.[9] Their resentment was exacerbated by the report of an LMS deputation sent out in 1821 to inspect the mission which singled out the Leeward stations for especial praise. This prompted bitter letters back to London from the older missionaries and led to a break-down in relations between the established and new missions.[10] Davies was vitriolic about the deputation and personally abusive in his account of the work of the new missionaries.[11] His bitterness also sprang from accusations of sexual misconduct with native women which the new missionaries had made against him. The older missionaries on Tahiti defended Davies while their Leeward brethren wrote scandalized letters to London repeating the allega-tions, including one that 'Mr. D. has been with Pomare's wife.'[12] Davies wrote a twelve-page letter to London insisting, 'I am no *adulterer*, no *fornicator*, no abettor of *immorality*', and ascribing the charges to '*envy, jealousy, malice* and *revenge*', singling out Mrs Williams for particular attack.[13]

The whole affair was bitter and prolonged. The correspondence about it reveals the close mutual scrutiny under which the mission-aries lived, and makes clear the possibilities for projecting one's own fears and guilt on to others. There is evidence of a kind of moral panic among the arrivals of 1817. A joint letter from Williams and Threlkeld just as the Davies affair was beginning complains of the 'abominable customs' of the natives, the super-ficiality of their conversion, and ends with a hastily scrawled post-script by Threlkeld deploring the day he came to the islands:

such are the abominations in these Islands and such are the oppositions of one and another and such is the confusion that exists among us that it is no disgrace not to belong to this society and do implore the Directors to change my station. I regret that ever I left . . . to come to this place of furious strife envy and every evil work.[14]

Punctuation, like morality, has collapsed. Another letter from these two warned that it was 'highly imprudent for *any Single Man* to remain longer than can be avoided in these Scenes of Lasciviousness'.[15] Davies would not have been the first LMS mis-sionary to have sexual relations with a Tahitian, but there is a strong element of displaced panic in the response of the new mis-sionaries. Merely to have survived on the islands for so long would have required the older missionaries to develop some sense of cul-tural relativism. Threlkeld and Williams entirely lacked this, and, whatever the truth of the case, their denunciation of Davies was the response of dogmatic Christians in a state of severe culture shock. Later cohorts of missionaries arriving in Tahiti were to respond similarly.

The missionary fear of degeneration focussed particularly on their children. Threlkeld wrote to London that all his wife's efforts were needed in the home 'unless we choose to degenerate and become Heathen savages ourselves',[16] and Williams wondered how his children could hope to grow up as religious and civilized beings in such a setting: 'they will naturally degenerate intermix & marry with the natives & become outcasts from Society, & useless beings at least.' He pointed to the example of the daughter of one of the older missionaries who had been 'degraded to the lowest degree'.[17] From the missionaries' point of view these fears were not groundless. Their children knew only the culture they saw around them and lacked the defence systems of their parents. No doubt they came to have an easier relation with Tahitian ways than with the distorted version of British culture represented by their parents. Sexuality was the obvious concern. Orsmond, a jaundiced but experienced observer, put it this way:

If our children, by the turgency of their breasts, shew signs of puberty, it is immediately asked who was her men [*sic*], or was it the father. For it is maintained that no one can menstruate till she has been ruptured by coition. By 7 or 9 years of age all are ruptured. They say, 'Oh let them alone, they are only children, and will grow the faster for it.'[18]

The main concern for their sons was tattooing, descriptions of which in missionary writing are frequently sexualized. Many of the boys, and some of the girls, were inscribed with this visible and permanent mark of savagery.[19]

Bad relations with LMS headquarters in London remained a constant feature of life in the Tahitian mission field. The older missionaries bore deep grudges and the younger ones soon developed them. In 1819 the usually taciturn Ellis wrote a nine-page letter replying to accusations of extravagant purchases for his own 'ease and gratification'. A year later Williams was answering similar charges. In 1822 the visiting LMS Deputation received a formally worded but strongly felt letter from all the new missionaries complaining about the lack of confidence they felt in the support of the London office.[20] For the older missionaries nothing ever

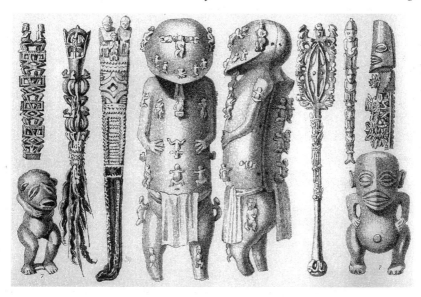

8 Illustration showing South Sea idols, from William Ellis, *Polynesian Researches*, 1830.

changed. Henry Nott's request for home leave after twenty years in the field was made conditional on reducing the expenses of his voyage. His reply expressed the hurt and frustration that every missionary in the field experienced at some time: 'What is a person in such circumstances to do to lessen expences? I leave this question to your own consciences and to God.'[21]

This opening sketch of the early history of the LMS on Tahiti has concentrated on relations within the mission and with London. The next section will examine two very influential missionary texts from the Tahitian field, William Ellis' *Polynesian Researches* (1829) and John Williams' *Narrative of Missionary Enterprises* (1837). These titles neatly capture the divided impulse within missionary thought and writing which this section will explore. Both tell of the high years of the mission to Tahiti and are silent about its divisions. Correspondence from the field to LMS headquarters in London, however, tells a different story. The third section of this chapter will compare these competing accounts, consider the extent to which the missionary aim of conversion actually succeeded, and theorize the colonial entanglement of this encounter. It is not my

9 Frontispiece to John Williams, *Missionary Enterprises*, 1838.

intention in examining these missionary texts to labour either
their prejudices or my indignation at their presumption. Nor, in
comparing the published texts with the correspondence, will the
letters necessarily be regarded as more truthful. Both are equally
forms of representation, constructed to achieve certain kinds of
effect and aimed at particular readers. My intention is to interpret
these sources and their surrounding history in order to understand better the nature of contact, exchange, adaptation, subordination and resistance which characterized the encounter of
missionaries and Tahitians in the first forty years of the nineteenth
century.

The influence of William Ellis' *Polynesian Researches* on nineteenth-
century writing about the Pacific is comparable to that of Cook
and Bougainville in the later eighteenth century. Southey wrote in
the *Quarterly*: 'A more interesting book we have never perused.'[22]
Darwin acknowledged it as one of the main sources of his understanding of Polynesian cultures and defended its account against

other writers who had attacked the missions.[23] Melville was another who saw the Pacific partly through the eyes of Ellis, and in the mid-1840s the young Wilkie Collins based his first, still unpublished, novel 'Iolani; or Tahiti as It Was' on *Polynesian Researches*.[24] Sixty years later it was the primary source of Victor Segalen's Tahitian novel *Les Immémoriaux* (1907). Ellis' text did much to revise the widely held view of missionaries as ignorant and narrow-minded, and became probably the most important source of information about Polynesian cultures in the first half of the nineteenth century. As its title suggests, *Polynesian Researches* is different from most other missionary writing in being distinctively ethnographic and not conspicuously aimed at a missionary-supporting readership. In this it has some of the characteristics of what Mary Louise Pratt has termed 'anti-conquest narratives', which underwrote colonial appropriation while rejecting the rhetoric of conquest and subjugation.

These narratives were part of the process by which modern imperialism sought to redefine itself in civilizing and reciprocal terms. Pratt sees them as taking two apparently different but, in fact, closely related forms. First, there was the narrative of scientific neutrality, the classificatory project of eighteenth-century natural science which became extended to ethnography. The other was that of sentimental travel writing, narratives of human reciprocity of which the transracial colonial romance was the archetype. These apparently different narratives both offered a discursive space in which Europeans could detach themselves from the unequal and exploitative nature of colonial relationships. They also complemented each other in that the language of sensibility offered an alternative, humanized way of describing colonial subjects who had already been classified and fixed in place. Together, Pratt argues, they functioned as legitimating ideologies for the harsh realities of colonial appropriation.[25]

Polynesian Researches uses both of these narrative forms. Its two volumes are full of detailed ethnographic accounts in an apparently neutral language of scientific observation. These passages work very much as Pratt describes. They naturalize the presence and authority of the European observer. They fix Tahitian culture in a timeless present so that particular episodes are not seen as events in time, perhaps as a response to the observer, but as expressions of inherent traits and customs. Such descriptions produce colonial subjects for a European audience by seeing everything in terms of the differences or similarities between the native culture and the observer's own. This enables the observer to create order out of chaos by placing the native culture in what Pratt terms 'the Euro-colonial discursive order'.[26] In similar manner Aijaz Ahmad has argued that by assembling 'a monstrous machinery of descriptions' colonizing discourses were able to classify and ideologically master colonial subjects while concealing this behind a mass of facts.[27] Greg Dening has even claimed that there is no more untrustworthy source than the *formal* descriptions by observers of the cultures they confront.[28] Much of this can be conceded without dismissing such writing out of hand. While set-piece accounts of the life and customs of other peoples need to be read with the same suspicion accorded other kinds of description, the ethnographic sections of *Polynesian Researches* are infinitely more valuable than the blatant essentializing and denigration of some of its other parts. I am more interested in contextualizing this style of writing in relation to other kinds of account than in situating it unproblematically within some global and impervious colonialist logic of description.

Polynesian Researches also inscribes the human-centred, interactive narrative typical of the sentimental mode. Ellis' arrival in Tahiti is a good example which, like most arrival scenes, represents a myth of beginnings. The first Tahitian Ellis meets comes on board for breakfast. He says grace before eating, to the amusement of the officers, whose genial scorn is regarded by the Tahitian with compassion. Ellis finds this scene 'the most pleasing sight I had yet beheld' (I, p. 59).[29] In it, Ellis lines up with the converted savage against the civilized but irreligious British officers. It is an ideal tableau, a text for the sermon Ellis wishes to preach to his western audience, expressing the writer's desired relation with the native population he has come to convert. As with many such scenes, its historical accuracy is less important than its mythical truth. Although things will never be as perfect again, this sentimental narrative shapes Ellis' text. Structurally, the missionary is akin to the European lover of the transracial romance. He brings the love of God rather than man, but like his secular equivalent he teaches the fickle, inconstant Polynesian the lesson of devotion, redeems him through love and civilizes him. Or rather, this is the ideal narrative of reciprocity which *Polynesian Researches* keeps trying to establish.

It is, however, a much more divided text than this. It cannot allegorize away the palpable difficulties the mission confronted, and although it does employ narratives which conceal the reality of colonial relationships it has no wish to disguise the effort to transform native culture. This would be to deny the whole purpose of the mission. On another level, then, *Polynesian Researches* is not an anti-conquest narrative at all. It tells of Christian soldiers battling with the forces of Satan, of the holy battle of Fei Pi, of victory and conversion, and employs a much older providential narrative going back through Bunyan to the Bible. And, of course, there are many Christian readers, a potential source of funds for the mission, who want to hear this story. Telling it, however, was not straightforward, as this strangely hybrid and fissured text demonstrates.

The recurring deep structure of *Polynesian Researches* is an alternation between science and sermon, between neutral description and vehement denunciation of Tahitian lifeways, between the Tahitians as redeemable and irredeemable, between the divinely guaranteed success of the mission and its overwhelmingly difficult task. Christopher Herbert has explained these violent alternations in terms of two competing models for understanding native life. The first is that Polynesian culture was characterized by ungoverned human desire, the absence of social control, and by an all-pervading anomie: that it was, in effect, cultureless. This was the model the missionaries brought with them; their writ, he says, 'was to produce allegories of natural depravity'. The other, competing model derived from their slow realization that Polynesians inhabited a world of meanings, an organized ensemble of customs and institutions; in other words, that they possessed a culture. The minutely detailed ethnographic descriptions of *Polynesian Researches* are a sign of this alternative paradigm, and an attempt to solve the interpretive riddle of Tahitian lifeways. This alternative model of understanding was, crucially, a consequence of the missionaries learning the Tahitian language; the linguistic paradigm became a metonym for the culture as a whole.[30]

This argument is helpful in understanding the divisions found in Ellis' text and other missionary writing, although the sequence Herbert outlines is disputable. LMS missionaries did not necessarily *arrive* with a natural-depravity model in mind. The South Seas had been chosen precisely because they were thought to be different from other primitive regions. As late as 1840 one of the long-term missionaries was writing back to London complaining at the misleading expectations implanted in new recruits: 'You make them believe . . . they are going to heaven; and when they arrive, instead of heaven, they find black men and fiends and barbarized missionaries, and even the devil himself not cast out.'[31] Depravity was as much a discovery as an 'originating proposition', an experiential response to cultural difference. The textuality of these conflicting discourses should also be emphasized. Ellis would have been familiar with ethnographic description in the work of earlier Pacific explorers. There were home models as well in the work of early nineteenth-century social investigators. Ellis experienced Tahiti in the light of these narratives as well as in terms of some putative missionary writ; hence the competing generic models which shape his text, the clash of discourses and their complex interaction.

It is time for some examples, although no one example can quite demonstrate how the oscillation between science and sermon creates the basic rhythm of the text. The first is commonplace and entirely characteristic. Ellis concludes a long, detailed, informative chapter on native plants and food production with a moralizing passage on the Tahitian's strange indifference to God in the midst of such plenty. Indeed, and this is a point often made by evangelicals in the Pacific, God's benevolence seems to have fostered a strange insensibility to his benefits among those who enjoy them (I, p. 379). Are God and nature, then, at strife? Why should unredeemed man enjoy such favour? These questions trouble several of the set-piece passages of natural description, often in sublime mode, which are scattered through the text. They also raise the issue of work, a matter on which no European text on the South Pacific is ever silent. *Polynesian Researches* speaks for them all when it declares, 'The indolence of the South Sea Islanders has long been proverbial', although attitudes to this 'fact' varied. For Melville or Gauguin it was their particular attraction, whereas for Ellis it was 'one of the most formidable barriers to their receiving our instructions, imbibing the spirit and exhibiting the moral influence of religion, and advancing in civilization' (I, p. 450). In fact Ellis' own text provides ample evidence of the Tahitian capacity for labour. It describes, for example, how the Tahitians build Ellis a house and a printing office, and follows this with an account of some native dwellings capable of holding two or three thousand people; one of these is 397 feet long. After seven pages of this, Ellis then reverts to the indolence stereotype and dismisses most native dwellings as 'only temporary and wretched huts, as unsightly in the midst of the beautiful landscape, as they were unwholesome and comfortless to their abject inhabitants' (I, p. 390). The dissonance between description and judgement is characteristic. There is a civil war between eye and mind going on throughout the text.

It is present again in a long section on tattooing. First, Ellis explains the missionaries' prohibition of this practice because of its connection with idolatry and other 'abominable vices'. He then proceeds, however, to a detailed description of its techniques, extends this into an aesthetics of tattooing (Tahitian tattoos have 'greater taste and elegance' than other Polynesian forms), and even to some passages on tattooing as an index of individual character (II, pp. 465–6).[32] Female tattooing practices are described with the same close interest. Then, suddenly, it becomes an 'immoral practice' again, and we are given a long account of a tattoo rebellion of young men led by the sons of local chiefs. A crusade is preached against them and the rebels are captured, tried and punished. The account ends with Ellis at his weekly service preaching on the rebellion of Absalom (II, pp. 466–77). This whole section is marked by the alternation of different kinds of narration; ethnography is framed and corrected by a Christian moral discourse, and the attempt to describe something strange is overridden by something familiar. This has been prepared for earlier when the death of the leader of this rebellion, who is the son of the King of Huahine, has been recounted (I, pp. 503–9). There it was narrated as a Victorian death-bed scene with the wronged wife, grieving father and anxious missionary all watching for signs of repentance. This familiar piece of genre painting has carried forward into the narrative, assisting it to revise the ethnographic account.

These formal dislocations express conceptual problems. Indeed, contradiction exists at the very heart of Ellis' subject, the Polynesian. How is this recently discovered savage to be described and categorized? Existing discourses of savagery, whether from classical texts or modern accounts of the Caribbean, were not adequate to the task.[33] In fact, the whole project of scientific classification required that they should be inadequate: new types required new descriptions. The main discursive problem presented by the European discovery of Polynesian cultures was how to redefine existing discourses of savagery from the Mediterranean Old World, and the Atlantic New World, to explain this new New World. Herbert, for example, gives too generalized an account of South Seas savagery, one equally applicable to the Caribbean or southern Africa. What is most interesting about western accounts of the Pacific is the attempt at a specific description which would distinguish Polynesians from other savages.

The formal dislocations of *Polynesian Researches* are a symptom of the difficulties this entailed. It opens with Alexander von Humboldt's description of the South Sea islanders as 'a mixture of perversity and meekness' living in a 'state of half-civilization' (I, p. 4). This is to be Ellis' text. Sometimes he uses it to draw parallels with the half-formed state of classical civilization. Their polytheism, for example, is compared with that of antiquity, a parallel reinforced by Ellis' belief in the common origin of all myth systems (I, p. viii). Tahitian canoes remind him of the ships in which the Argonauts sailed, and the comparison is supported by a strikingly classical-looking illustration of a Tahitian war canoe (I, pp. 168–9). More commonly, however, their state of 'half-civilization' is compared to that of childhood. Volume II opens with a long account of 'the Polynesian character'. Its defining feature is inconstancy. Like children, Polynesians are quick to learn but slow to concentrate; their interest is easily roused but hard to sustain; they have enthusiasm but no stamina:

When a boat manned with English seamen, and a canoe with natives, have started together from the shore – at their first setting out, the natives would soon leave the boat behind, but, as they became weary, they would relax their vigour; while the seamen, pulling on steadily, would . . . if the voyage occupied three or four hours . . . invariably reach their destination first. (II, p. 26)

So much for a people that had spread itself many thousands of miles over the Pacific. The comparison is between adults and children. Adult character is formed; the contradictory half-formed nature of children, on the other hand, means that all their virtues are double-edged. In this example, spontaneous enthusiasm quickly becomes defeated exhaustion. The reconceptualization of the savage as child-like was packed with implication. A whole developmental language which came to be applied to childhood during the nineteenth century was also extended to savagery. Like children, savages can grow, mature and become civilized. The other, whether child or savage, can become like us. Ellis emphasizes, for instance, the ease with which Polynesians learned to read and write and compares them favourably with Europeans in this respect. As Nicholas Thomas has pointed out, the ambivalence of the native character in missionary discourse was a prerequisite for conversion.[34] Without it there was no helping them. On the other hand, there was no certainty of it happening. The analogous processes of socialization and civilization, with their defining organic metaphors, could easily go wrong. Plants can go to seed, children turn out bad, while savages can revert. Reversion, Ellis insists, is ugly; there is nothing inherently noble about the Polynesian savage. Like children, Polynesians are strongly marked by original sin but potentially redeemable. Dr Arnold was soon to talk in very similar terms about his boys at Rugby. These complex transactions between the figure of the savage and the child result in the construction of the Polynesian as a contradictory and unstable figure who produces unease at every level of Ellis' text. A correspondingly contradictory and unstable array of narratives – scientific, sentimental, punitive – is therefore mobilized to try and contain and explain this figure.

Eventually *Polynesian Researches* attempts to reconcile these competing narratives under an overarching domestic one in which home figures as the keystone of any culture worth the name. Ellis' text describes a thorough implantation of the domestic. The home was the main site of missionary endeavour and the subject of his most rhapsodic passages. On Huahine, where Ellis was based, 'the neatly finished cottage' replaced 'the lonely and comfortless hut', in a process he compared to natural growth; civilization had taken root. Houses were grouped in villages, gardens and plantations were enclosed, and women were accorded their proper place at the centre of a newly privatized family. No longer exposed to 'that humiliating neglect to which idolatry had subjected them', they could now anchor the family, cultivate their minds, and learn bonnet-making (II, p. 120). Clothes were always a focus of missionary attention. European clothing was more seemly, it provided work for idle hands and a potential market for British manufactures (II, pp. 129–30). And to be clothed was to be in one's right mind. It is hardly surprising that, 'to use their own powerful expression', the Tahitians sometimes wondered 'whether they were the same people who had been contented to inhabit their former dwellings' (ii, pp. 79–80).

Domesticity becomes the great subject of the second volume. It is the one sure index of both Christianity and civilization, the site where these two often uneasily related ideas can be perfectly married. It is the ultimate destination of Ellis' narrative, reached after almost eleven hundred pages of vicissitude:

> domestic happiness, though formerly unknown even in name, is now sedulously cultivated, and spreads around their abodes of order and comfort, its choicest blessings. The husband and the wife, instead of promiscuously mingling with the multitude, or dwelling in the houses of their chiefs, live together in the neat little cottages reared by their own industry, and find satisfaction and comfort in each other's society. Every household virtue adorns their families; the children grow up the objects of their mutual affection, and call into exercise new solicitudes and unwonted emotions of delight. Often they appear sitting together reading the Scriptures, walking in company to the house of God, or surrounding, not indeed the family hearth . . . which in their warm climate would be no addition to their comfort, but the family board, spread with the liberal gifts of divine bounty. The father at times may also be seen nursing his little child at the door of his cottage, and the mother sitting at needlework by his side, or engaged in other domestic employments. (ii, pp. 572–3)

Of course this is sheer melodrama, a glaring example of the imposition of home values, and an expression of missionary anxieties. Within the text of *Polynesian Researches* it replies to an earlier set piece mourning the absence of domestic virtues in pre-Christian Tahitian society (i, p. 221). It therefore dramatizes the effects of conversion by rendering Tahitian culture as an ideal version of rural England, with a Pooterish explanation for the absence of a family hearth. Generically it is very similar to any number of Victorian novels which end with the restoration or reconstruction of family life after a lengthy narrative in which it has been threatened with disintegration or degradation, or been damagingly absent. It is, therefore, a version of Pratt's sentimental narrative of human reciprocity, though totally unembarrassed by the idea of conquest. It complements the ethnographic narrative, and not just by humanizing it. In bringing the sentimental to bear on the ethnographic the latter is refashioned so that a different kind of cultural description becomes possible, one which is familiar rather than strange. For this to happen, however, the corrective narrative, a version of Herbert's depravity or Pratt's conquest narrative, must also be deployed. In the same way, discipline, and sometimes punishment, became central to the task of raising and educating children in the nineteenth century. This is the rhetoric of Ellis' second volume. It does not succeed in reconciling the competing narratives and stabilizing the text. If anything, it highlights the instabilities, drawing attention to what it tries to obscure and failing to cancel the unease which the generic promiscuity of this text expresses.

Polynesian Researches ends on this domestic note, with the Ellises looking back at Huahine from the bay as they depart for Hawaii. It is 1822. They see a town of cottages, gardens, roads, schools and a chapel. The natives are clothed and in their right mind, 'wearing hats and bonnets of their own manufacture'. All are professing Christians, most can read the Bible, many are baptized. The production of coffee is about to begin (II, pp. 575–6). Christian civilization has arrived and Ellis can depart.

John Williams' *Missionary Enterprises* was published in 1837 when he and his family were back in England on furlough. Never able to rest from evangelizing, Williams turned his missionary zeal on his home culture as he toured the country lecturing, gave evidence to a parliamentary committee on British settlements overseas, addressed the Corporation of the City of London and saw Polynesian translations through the press.[35] *Missionary Enterprises* was part of this onslaught. It aimed to sell the South Seas mission at home. The book was dedicated to William IV, and copies were sent to Princess Victoria and fifty selected noblemen. The text contained a number of direct addresses to the British reading public and ended with an appeal to the sons of noblemen to value missionary above military valour and become 'soldiers of the cross' themselves. It sold quickly and was well received. The eighteen-year-old George Eliot wrote to a friend describing it as 'deeply interesting . . . [although] Mr. W. is a dissenter . . . the B[isho]p of Chester highly commended his work . . . and it has since been published by all denominations'.[36] Once again the South Seas were on the map and Williams, the son of a cockney tradesman, was fêted in a manner that recalled the treatment Omai had enjoyed fifty years earlier.

Missionary Enterprises is a different kind of text from *Polynesian Researches*, as the titles make clear. Williams writes a busier, more campaigning work directly aimed at a missionary-supporting readership. It is a conversion narrative recording his energetic pursuit of lost souls across the Pacific. It is more explicitly colonialist than Ellis', yet has moments of surprising cultural insight. Generically it is a simpler text, less divided and more transparent than *Polynesian Researches*.

Certainly it is a conquest narrative. Williams' greatest pride was to return to his base on Raiatea surrounded by confiscated idols, as in the following description: 'And as other warriors feel a pride in displaying trophies of the victories they win, we hung the rejected idols of Aitutaki to the yard-arms and other parts of the vessel, entered the harbour in triumph, sailed down to the settlement, and dropped anchor amidst the shouts and congratulations of our people' (pp. 107–8).[37] The frontispiece of *Missionary Enterprises* was an engraving of two missionary couples seated with idols strewn around them. Williams dispatched boxes of idols to London as regularly as a modern traveller would send postcards. There they were welcomed as tangible evidence of the destruction of idolatry, and displayed in the Missionary Museum rather as Williams had suspended them from the rafters of his chapel on Raiatea. On Raiatea they were then abused in addresses by native speakers. In London, far from the context which gave them meaning, they were cherished as horrible objects whose repudiation confirmed the success of the mission.[38]

Missionary Enterprises is also a kind of business report. Williams saw the capture and recovery of lost souls as a commercial enterprise. He complained of overmanning in the Tahitian station, and in a famous letter compared his activities to those of a merchant in search of pearls.[39] Williams combined the care of a double-entry book-keeper with the ambition of a merchant whose capital was souls. He also complained regularly about his 'contracted sphere', and longed for a ship with which to extend his enterprise. He wrote, again famously, of this to the LMS Directors: 'I cannot content myself within the narrow limits of a Single reef & if means is not afforded a continent to me would be infinitely preferable for there if you cannot ride you can walk but to these isolated Islands a Ship must carry you' (p. 66). In the end he built his own boat the *Messenger of Peace*, sixty feet long, eighteen feet wide, complete with a flag made by some ladies in Brighton. The prolonged account of this in *Missionary Enterprises* is pure Robinsonnade, right down to the description of constructing a pair of smith's bellows, and it became the centre-piece of his lectures in England. Not surprisingly, Williams figured in Samuel Smiles' *Self-Help* (1859) as one of the 'heroes of the gospel. . . Like the Apostles, he worked with his hands.'[40] With this boat he was able to establish missions on the Raratongan or Cook Island group (then known as the Hervey Islands) and later on the Samoan Islands (then known as the Navigators). Samoa offered a base for the push into the western Pacific that became Williams' grand plan: much of his time in England in the mid-1830s was spent raising support for the conversion of Melanesia. The aldermen of the City of London voted him £500 after he had addressed them, and with this and other money he raised he was able to buy a new ship, the *Camden*, to sail back to the Pacific. Now virtually free of LMS control, he returned to Samoa in 1838 with a shipload of missionaries and a hold full of cargo for his eldest son, John, who was to set up as a trader.

Above all, *Missionary Enterprises* is a providential narrative. Very much in the manner described by Max Weber, Williams read the world for evidence of God's favour and found it wherever he looked. He had a far more particular sense of providence than Ellis. When he almost drowned (p. 268), or was almost shot (p. 338), his survival was an expression of divine grace. Providence is the structuring principle of Williams' narrative. After an outbreak of tattooing among young Raratongans, for example, he preached an angry sermon warning 'that God would not now, as in the days of their ignorance, wink at such wickedness' (p. 383). Soon after, the island was devastated by a hurricane. Miraculously, however, Williams' ship was saved, swept inland several hundred yards where it rested undamaged in a grove of trees. Mrs Williams was less fortunate, the shock of the hurricane causing her seventh still-birth, but 'God . . . in judgement remembered mercy' and her life was spared (p. 400). The workings of providence enable Williams to thread these events together into an intelligible narrative of punishment and redemption which is the pattern of the whole work. The generic forebear of this providential pattern is *The Pilgrim's Progress*, which Williams had translated into Raratongan. *Missionary Enterprises* is rather like Bunyan's text but without the inner drama, as if it had been rewritten by Samuel Smiles.

The Pilgrim's Progress helps to hold *Missionary Enterprises* together, providing it with a generic coherence that Ellis' text lacks. It is able to do this because *Missionary Enterprises* is much less curious about native lifeways, less troubled by ethnography, and therefore gets into fewer difficulties. It even has less overt moralizing because there is not the same need to try and shut out the worrying implications of detailed ethnographic description. Williams shares with Ellis the view of Tahitians as children, but in *Missionary Enterprises* this is rarely challenged by any recognition of the complex unity of Tahitian culture implicit in ethnographic accounts. Paradoxically, this means that Williams' occasional moments of cultural insight are less conspicuously revised by any alternative narrative.

In an interesting passage towards the end of *Missionary Enterprises*, for example, he remarks on how most races, 'barbarous' as well as 'civilized', think themselves wiser than others, and that Britain itself has suffered from 'degrading representations'. From Roman times, he goes on, the English have been regarded as stupid, a view now common among South Sea islanders. Although he argues that Polynesians lack 'depth of thought', in 'quickness of perception, a tenacious memory, a thirst for knowledge . . . great precision and force in the expression of their thoughts . . . the South Sea islander does not rank below the European . . . many of them would, if they possessed equal advantages, rise to the same eminence as the literary and scientific men of our own land' (pp. 515–6). He then acknowledges the surprising complexity and sophistication of Polynesian languages: 'Polynesian dialects are remarkably rich, admit of a great variety of phraseology, abound in turns of peculiar nicety, and are spoken with strict conformity to the most precise grammatical principles' (p. 527). Examples are given of refinements beyond the scope of the English language.[41] In this passage Williams is making the kind of cultural comparisons commonly found in the Enlightenment and Romantic tradition of counter-civility. His long familiarity with Polynesian cultures must have begun to erode the stock generalizations of LMS discourse.

On the subject of language Williams had become expert; here, knowledge simply contradicted conventional prejudice. Herbert's point that learning the Tahitian language was crucial in making possible an understanding of the society as more than simply lawless and anomic is an important one. A missionary's status, among both his own kind and the native population, depended heavily on his fluency in the local language. Ellis and Williams were quicker than most to learn, and correspondence between them after Ellis had departed for Hawaii included whole paragraphs written in Tahitian.[42] It is also the case, however, that Williams was attempting to sell Polynesians to his British readers. They have almost become his product, and although criticism outweighs admiration, he is also defensively proud of the culture he has been attempting to transform. Such notes are heard less frequently in his correspondence. *Missionary Enterprises*, particularly in its later sections, was written with an eye to winning support for his plans. It grants Polynesians a dignity that his letters frequently dispute.

Williams also uses a domestic narrative, though less strategically than Ellis. This is partly a consequence of the greater restlessness of *Missionary Enterprises*. Nevertheless, Williams' description of the wholesale reorganization of Raiatean life into villages is central to the good news he reports. It is the sentimental narrative which succeeds conquest. His account of the converted native village of Arorangi, with its neatly arranged cottages and tastefully laid out gardens which contrast with the random disorder and violence of unconverted native settlements, was to have an important influence on later writing about the Pacific. Ballantyne, for example, in *The Coral Island* (1858) borrowed it almost word for word. Harriet Martineau's Pacific novel *Dawn Island* (1845) also highlighted the absence of domestic comforts and the low status of women in traditional Polynesian societies, before dramatizing the domestic reorganization of native life along lines which seem to be derived from Ellis and Williams.

This recurring domestication of the Polynesian is a complex and ambiguous matter. Thomas emphasizes that the missionary trope of the family, with the native as child emerging from a protosocial condition, and the figure of the mother (remember all those child mothers in Victorian fiction) as pivotal to this process, contrasts sharply with the essentialist understanding of racial types in secular colonialist discourse. In his study of the Western Solomons mission of the early twentieth century he found that the Solomon Islander was not constructed as a species-like entity but, rather, as a thing of parts, some to be suppressed, others to be drawn into the creation of a new Christian islander. His argument is carefully nuanced, emphasizing that this infantilization also reflected the missionaries' relation to the islanders, and that the trope of the family is one of great generality whose specific meanings could vary according to the narratives in which they were employed and the practices they inflected.[43] The co-existence of these apparently contrasting essentialist and domestic discourses also needs to be emphasized. Both are found in missionary writing from the Tahitian field, the former more commonly in correspondence, the latter in published works, but also adjacent to each other in the same text, whether book or letter. Both are available to be deployed as the situation requires; neither is discrete. The dominance of one discourse or the other is not merely opportunistic, but a result of the contradictions and uncertainties in describing and conceptualizing the subjects of their mission. Thomas explains this overlapping of essentialist and domestic discourses in terms of the contradictory colonial objectives of hierarchizing and incorporating, arguing that the trope of the family reconciled hierarchy with humanity in the short term at least.[44] This parallels my explanation of Ellis' use of the same trope to reconcile the tensions between the exclusivist basis of civilization and the universalist pretensions of Christianity. Within colonialist texts the absolutely other is often redefined as the domesticated other in the process of European self-consolidation and affirmation.

The domestic anxieties of missionary families on Tahiti must have made this an urgent matter. Spivak, in particular, has shown how in establishing a 'good society' the woman has a crucial signifying role, often as an object of protection.[45] The Tahitian woman was represented as both the centre-piece of a reconstituted Polynesian family, and as urgently in need of such protection. A useful point of reference here is Sarah Stickney Ellis' long narrative poem of the Pacific, *The Island Queen* (1846). Ellis, who wrote those numerous guides for the mothers, daughters and wives of England which did so much to codify middle-class domestic norms in the mid-nineteenth century, became William Ellis' second wife after his return to England. Her poem gives an idealized account of the LMS mission to Tahiti, much of it derived from *Polynesian Researches*, and includes an heroic sketch of the recently martyred Williams. The island queen of the title is Queen Pomare, 'a slighted wife', victim of French aggression and duplicity, and a figure of pathos abandoned by the British. By the end of the poem another island queen, Victoria, has been similarly invoked, – 'A wife – a mother – gentle queen' – one whose situation appears to contrast vividly with Pomare's. But the poem implies that Victoria and her island could also be threatened by their common enemy, France:

> Thou, only thou, couldst rend the eagle's breast,
> And tear the brooding mother from her nest.[46]

Violation of domesticity is the common figure for this threat to the two queens, nurturing mothers of their nations.

In Sarah Stickney Ellis and in Williams, however, the use of the domestic is more familiar and less busy than in *Polynesian Researches* where it has to try and bind the text rather than merely ice it. Their sweeping generalizations about Tahitian life are at one with the great organizing contrast of civilization and savagery on which most missionary and other nineteenth-century writing on the Pacific was based. William Ellis' careful particularity about Tahitian lifeways, however, repeatedly threatens this distinction by suggesting that far from needing to be rescued by civilization, the Tahitians already have one.

Missionary Enterprises ends with a ringing assertion of the dignity of missionary work. Soon, though quite inadvertently, Williams was to ensure its ennoblement. Back in Samoa he prepared for the push west into Melanesia. The *Camden* sailed for the New Hebrides and began to distribute Polynesian missionaries among the islands. In November 1839 it anchored off Eromanga, an island where Cook had been involved in bloodshed more than sixty years earlier. Williams went ashore, trouble broke out, and he failed to make it back across the beach to the waiting whaleboat. He was caught at the water's edge and clubbed to death. It was an almost parodic replay of Cook's death, and an analogous apotheosis followed. Daws describes how news of his death caused a wave of conversions in Samoa, and how in England Williams became the centre of a Protestant cult, with colour prints of his death and cheap editions of his book in great demand.[47] He became, in Samuel Smiles' phrase, 'the martyr of Erromanga'.[48] He also became Britain's second Pacific martyr-hero, one as appropriate for his period as Cook had been for the later eighteenth century. Sahlins also points to a parallel deification on Eromanga, where, it is claimed, Williams was killed because he had stumbled into the island's great annual feast, and after his death was consecrated as Nobu, the name of the Eromangans' lost creator-god.[49] Replies are invited.

If the main point of the published missionary text was to report good news, though without minimizing difficulties, letters from the field to LMS headquarters emphasized difficulties and needs, though without undermining the mission's ultimate prospect of success. Both were forms of self-fashioning. *Polynesian Researches* might veer between accounts of the Tahitians as wholly converted and as beyond redemption, but Ellis' narrative trajectory is clear. After the early years, in which those few natives who could be per-suaded to attend missionary meetings would talk and laugh through the address and make ribald comments about the mis-sionaries' intentions (i, p. 118), conversion came abruptly as one of the great 'modern evidences of Christianity'; a 'moral desert' was transformed into a 'region of order and beauty . . . the wilder-ness . . . [has] become as the garden of the Lord' (i, pp. 274–5). The redemptive narrative, with its familiar tropes of desert and garden, shapes Ellis' text. Letters lack such a pattern. They freeze a moment in time rather than arrange a succession of such moments into a coherent narrative in the manner of *Polynesian Researches*. An archive of letters, however, secretes narratives, and to read the home correspondence from Tahiti is to uncover a counter-narrative to that offered by Ellis and Williams.

There is also an intermediate category of missionary writing represented by the unpublished histories of Orsmond and Davies. Orsmond was the most acerbic and difficult of the missionaries, and the bitterness of his manuscript, written in 1849, can partly be explained by his dismissal from the LMS four years earlier. In manner and matter it is more akin to the correspondence than to the published histories of Ellis and Williams. Davies' history was written for publication but blocked by the LMS, which was anxious about 'facts which it would be advisable to expunge'.[50] A conven-tional history in form, it is marked by personal bitterness and resentment at the success of Ellis' text. In this it also has much in common with the correspondence.

The most vivid contrast between the published histories and the correspondence is the latter's despairing, often savage, denunciations of native converts. Although there are many letters to London detailing the number of converts, baptisms, congregations and souls who 'died happy', there is a constant suspicion that conversion has been no more than skin-deep, that Tahitians profess one thing and do another, and that as soon as missionary backs are turned Tahitian backs will slide. It was one thing to destroy the Tahitians' idols but quite another to 'turn their hearts from sin'. The question 'who is *truly* converted?' was cynically answered in this letter from Raiatea in 1818: 'no one is yet baptized save 2 or 3 hundred who were baptized one day at Eimeo by a Drunken Sailor. In a word they are a nation of Antinomians.'[51] Pomare himself was the most prominent and flagrant example of the Polynesian backslider, first professing belief, then sinning, then contrite. With his entourage of *mahu* (male wives) and his frequent drunkenness he was a constant embarrassment to the mission. The missionary working with Pomare on translating the Scriptures, for example, was obliged to tolerate the distracting presence of his 'detestable pander' and 'to turn his head from them to his book to avoid seeing what passes, and still get his ears shocked with what he hears'.[52]

Although the short-term effects of conversion were often dramatic, indigenous lifeways kept being reasserted. Some, like Davies, could be philosophic about this and ask how long it had taken western cultures to develop from savagery to civilization.[53] Others, like Orsmond, were to dismiss the whole mission as a failure:

Tahiti is a vortex of iniquity, the Sodom of the Pacific and gazing stock to the world, a thorn in the eyes of the just. All contradiction, licentiousness and obsequiousness. Even now we dare not suffer our children to assemble with the native tribes. Virtue is not in Tahiti; chastity is unknown save in the presence of some only of the Missionaries.[54]

From the start, Orsmond claims, the mission was the plaything of the chiefs and kings – 'a Missionary's influence away from the Chief is froth': 'The Mission cannot prosper . . . The Chief, the King have been everything, and Christ nothing. Cases of conversion we find not. Our words are idle tales.'[55]

Scepticism about the sincerity of conversion bred cynicism or paranoia among the missionaries. Orsmond's cynicism is defensive and eventually self-indulgent. More interesting are the anxiety and disturbance revealed in Williams' letters, as, for example, in his lengthy instructions to the native missionaries he left on Aitutake, in the Hervey group, in 1823. 'You have become like a City erected on a Hill,' he wrote; 'Many are the Eyes looking at you.' He then specified these eyes – his own, Threlkeld's, those of the LMS in London, of all the believers in England, the eyes of Jesus: 'Also those of the Heathen among whom you may reside. They will watch you with *Rats Eyes* – to find little crooked places in your Conduct.'[56] The paranoid resentment of this passage expresses the psychological discomfort of the missionary role in Polynesian cultures. The price of Christian truth was unceasing vigilance. The need for self-scrutiny had been obvious from the beginning, but it could not have been anticipated that the Polynesian gaze would provoke a fear of being judged and out-faced.

The correspondence also uncovers moments of casual racism which help explain the scrutiny Williams found so disturbing. There is a telling illustration of this in a letter from the missionary Platt, who was stationed on Borabora. Platt was suffering from feefee, or filariasis, a painful swelling of the extremities. Williams had already suffered this condition and been operated on by Threlkeld, who was at this moment in Sydney replacing a dead wife. Platt therefore asked Williams if he would be able to perform the operation. In a matter-of-fact way he reported Williams' equally matter-of-fact reply: 'He has returned for answer that he believes he could perform it. However he will make the experi-ment upon some of their own people first before he ventures to engage, he will then come down and try.'[57]

Missionaries were eventually forced to recognize that nothing could cross the beach unchanged. Ellis records how a native priest renamed his personal god Satan after it had been branded as such by a missionary, a term of damnation thereby becoming baptismal and sacred (1, p. 219). On Samoa, later in the century, cricket had to be prohibited soon after its introduction by the officers of a vis-iting ship because matches with two hundred a side were lasting for a month at a time, to the detriment of home, work and worship. The official historian of the London Missionary Society com-mented: 'The excitement passed beyond all reasonable control, and led to much that was distinctly heathenish.'[58]

Episodes of this sort can be read in terms of Homi Bhabha's

concept of mimicry and taken as examples of the way in which the authority of the colonizer is subversively travestied by those it targets. Mimicry, for Bhabha, is both resemblance and menace, a sign of 'spectacular resistance' in which 'the words of the master become . . . the warlike, subaltern sign of the native'.[59] Although this is an attempted corrective to the passivity of colonized cultures implied by Saidean approaches to colonial discourse, it is still primarily concerned with how the colonizer perceives the transactions of colonial encounter. It is the colonizer who experiences the partial resemblance of mimicry as menacing, and it seems to be in this that the subversion consists. Colonial discourse, underwritten by colonial power, has ways of dealing with this threat, if such it is, of partial resemblance. Ellis, for example, explained the hybrid nature of Tahitian housing and clothing as an intermediate stage in the civilizing process, indicating 'the peculiar plastic, forming state of the nation' (II, p. 124). Gendering also assisted this process of explanation. Tahitian women wore European clothing with more propriety than Tahitian men:

the only inconsistency we ever observed was that of a woman's sometimes wearing a coat or jacket belonging to her husband or brother. The men, however, were less scrupulous . . . I have seen a stocking sometimes on the leg, and sometimes on the arm, and a pair of pantaloons worn one part of the day in the proper manner, and during another part thrown over the shoulders, the arms of the wearer stretched through the legs, and the waistband buttoned round the chest. (II, pp. 125–6)

In this case gendering helps assimilate partial resemblance to a European frame; Tahitian women, like their British sisters, are instinctively more civilized than men.

I am sceptical of the claims Bhabha makes for mimicry. If we are looking for ways of restoring the agency of native subjects under colonialism there were more effectual kinds of practice and response. Mimicry is situational, tends to be individual rather than collective, and carries with it the unfortunate implication of clowning. Post-colonial readers can take pleasure in its playful post-modernism while more challenging manifestations of syncretism, resistance and the assertion of indigenous practices are elided.[60]

Is it possible to get closer to the experience of contact from the native point of view? Can we, while still dependent on missionary texts, begin to construct a history of native subjects somehow distinct from colonial descriptions of them? I have analysed the meta-narrative strategies of *Polynesian Researches* and *Missionary Enterprises*, and suggested ways in which these are designed to occlude or reconcile problems and contradictions at the heart of the missionary project. I have also used the correspondence in order to highlight some of these difficulties as they were recorded day by day rather than ordered in retrospect. I shall now examine several particular incidents described in published and unpublished missionary texts to try and get closer to the Tahitian experience of LMS colonization. This is not just to see what wonderful signs they yield, but to try and discriminate between the various responses to different kinds of intrusion.

In my first example, mimicry goes well beyond defensive or indirect subversion to become offensive and violent. The episode is recounted in *Missionary Enterprises*. A Raiatean, part of a conspiracy of young male islanders to kill Williams and rid themselves of Christianity, appeared outside the missionary's house:

He was dressed in a most fantastical manner, having his head decorated with leaves, and wearing a pair of trowsers as a jacket, his arms being passed through the legs; he wore also a red shirt instead of trowsers, his legs being passed through the arms, and the band buttoned round the waist. He came, brandishing a large carving knife, and danced before the house, crying, 'Turn out the hog, let us kill him; turn out the pig, let us cut his throat.' (pp. 130–1)

The portly Williams, failing to understand he was the pig, was only prevented by the arrival of a deacon from rushing out to confront the man. Clothes, as Ellis understood, are socially discursive and form part of a larger signifying system. Here the fantastical dress vividly expresses resistance to the new order introduced by Williams, which included the covering of native bodies with European clothing. It is different from the native styles of wearing European dress described by Ellis, which seem more an example of the pragmatic way in which European things were absorbed, tested and modified. There is nothing consciously transgressive suggested by Ellis' description, and partial resemblance creates few problems for the missionary observer. It is easily incorporated into his narrative. Even if he has missed an element of parody the paternalistic relation of missionary to native is unaffected. Ellis might even have found it reassuring that the lessons of civilization were not instantly learned. In the case of Williams' antagonist, however, parody has become violent confrontation in which existing power relations are directly challenged. Discipline must therefore follow. The conspirators were banished for four years, and the incident was used to help persuade the chiefs and people of Raiatea to adopt the code of laws which Williams and Threlkeld had been drawing up.

The second example comes from Orsmond's manuscript and concerns resistance to tithing. Orsmond and William Henry, gathering money for the local auxiliary of the LMS, were refused contributions by a whole village on Eimeo: "'We will not give it" one and all replied. I said, "Why not? Who is the author of this your resistance?" In a moment they one and all turned round their heads to the ground, spatted each one his bare bottom in our faces, crying as they did so, "We are the authors, we are the authors."'[61] This is rather different from the clothes rebellion. It is a traditional way of expressing contempt in many Polynesian societies (a Maori activist was arrested for this during a royal visit to New Zealand some years ago), rather than something improvised with materials recently introduced into their world. Being customary and communal it was much more difficult to punish. The insistence on collective responsibility and agency – 'We are the authors' – was irresistible. Orsmond immediately left the scene and Henry, much upset, soon departed the island altogether. As an assertion of the Tahitians' own culture it was more disturbing, and harder for the missionaries to confront, than the situationist response of the dressing-up incident.

The final example is from Raiatea and concerns the wife of a chief pregnant with a child fathered by another man. Williams attempted to interfere with the custom of providing large quantities of food for female chiefs during confinement, telling his congregation that it was inconsistent with Christianity 'to pay the same respect to an adultress as to a person who had been faithful to her husband'. They ignored him and countered his threat of expelling any individual preparing food for the woman by threatening a mass walk-out from his church and settlement if anyone was singled out. Williams wrote defiantly to London that 'A person who acts directly in opposition to his profession must be separated from us if ten thousand follow him', but in fact he was powerless in the face of this collective refusal.[62] This incident differs from the other two in that it is less a reaction to the missionary presence and demands, than a straightforward assertion of their way of life. In continuing to provide the food they are asserting the continuity of their own history, and refusing to become the objects of someone else's. It was much harder to prohibit this kind of customary practice than to resist the threat of violence or the refusal to pay tithes. The missionaries seem to have found it easier to introduce the new than to eliminate the traditional. From the Tahitian point of view, no doubt, the new would always be modified by assimilation; the abolition of customary practices would be experienced as sheer loss. It is hardly surprising, therefore, that the plot to kill Williams should figure in *Missionary Enterprises* while the insistence on feeding the adulterous female chief should remain unpublished in the letters. One story tells of resistance overcome, the other of resistance unmet.

The customary practice which most obsessed the missionaries, and which became the most important site of conflict with the Tahitians, was tattooing. There was a concentrated effort to prohibit this practice. The legal code established on Huahine in 1823, which was to serve as a model for many other South Pacific stations, stated: 'No person shall mark with tatau, it shall be entirely discontinued. It belongs to ancient evil customs. The man or woman that shall mark with tatau . . . shall be tried and punished.' The punishment for men was road-making, for women mat-making, and for persistent offenders 'the figures marked shall be destroyed by blacking them over'.[63] This particular aspect of a more general body discipline which the missionaries attempted to impose repeatedly failed. Tattooing rather than alcohol was the main symptom of 'backsliding' recorded in missionary correspondence. One such account of expelling some young baptized Tahitians for having tattooed themselves helps to explain why the missionaries were so against it: 'It is not only the evil of the thing itself that we exclaim against, but the many other evils that accompany it especially when the Sexes get together to mark themselves.'[64] In this account, the reversion to savagery that tattooing expresses has been heavily sexualized. In fact, for the missionaries, tattooing became a metonym for a whole culture they were trying to extirpate. This was particularly so in the Society Islands, where it was closely linked with the Arioi cult which the missionaries correctly understood to be the mainstay of pagan religion.[65] One account of native insubordination on Raiatea described tattooing as 'the Cockade' of the rebel party.[66] Tattooing, then, could do service for savagery, sexuality, paganism, republicanism or any other troubling aspect of Tahitian life. In this case, however, the missionaries had chosen to fight on ground difficult to hold. Idols could be burnt but tattooing could only be smudged; it was impossible to obliterate. It was easy for older men, already tattooed, to renounce the practice. Younger men, on the other hand, were compelled to live without it themselves while constantly seeing it displayed on the bodies of their elders. Tattooing therefore, during the period of missionary ascendancy, became the most significant site of opposition to the cultural transformation the missionaries were attempting to effect.

It might seem that these examples of overt resistance are too unambiguous to be worth mentioning. If so, it is a measure of how far the post-modern post-colonialism of Bhabha and others has turned away from agency and resistance in pursuit of its psychoanalytic shadow. In its fascination with mimicry this school has almost lost sight of those conscious and material forms of resistance which were primarily responsible for the conflict between colonizers and native populations. The concept of mimicry subtly disturbs the passivity of colonial subjects which colonial discourse theory has been prone to imply, while ignoring the continuity of native lifeways and the resistance to assimilation which have normally been among the most salient features of colonial encounter. By concentrating on how unconscious mimicry reacted in the mind of the colonizer to produce the tensions and ambiguities of colonial relationships, the passivity of so-called colonial subjects has been underwritten in a new way. The assimilation of the post-colonial to the post-modern has resulted in a dehistoricizing of colonial relationships.

It is clear that the wholesale transformation of Tahitian culture described by Ellis and Williams was exaggerated. It was always much less consensual and complete than *Polynesian Researches* and *Missionary Enterprises* claim. The disorder of missionary writing, even though its agenda was unapologetically one of religious and cultural hegemony, and the Pacific one of the main theatres of success for nineteenth-century missions, is testimony to the vigour and adaptiveness of Tahitian culture. The tensions and contradictions within, and between, different kinds of missionary writing are clear evidence of the intricate and embroiled nature of the cultural encounter between Tahitians and missionaries. There was neither fatal impact nor cultural amnesia.

This, however, is not to deny the impact of conversion. The Tahitian system of religion was intimately connected with every aspect of native life and its sudden overthrow, no matter how incomplete, produced extensive shock waves. There is an interesting letter from the older missionaries, written just before Ellis and Williams arrived at Tahiti, describing how in the aftermath of conversion they are being asked for advice in civil and political as well as in moral and religious affairs. They are uneasy with this unforeseen consequence of conversion, and describe how they have told the king and chiefs, 'that being Strangers, and come to their Country as teachers of the Word of the true God . . . we will have nothing further to do with their civil concerns, than to give them good advice'.[67] Although the phrase 'good advice' is an obvious loop-hole, the missionaries' hesitation is not disingenuous. They took very seriously the LMS policy of 'Christianity before civilization' and were uncertain how to deal with the changed circumstances of post-conversion Tahiti. The common periodization of missionary activity in the Pacific into a zealous colonizing phase in the first half of the nineteenth century and a more considered ethnographic approach in the second is dubious.[68] The early missionaries on Tahiti were more cautious than this suggests, and *Polynesian Researches* is monumental evidence of ethnographic curiosity in the early part of the century. The cohort of missionaries which arrived in 1817 had fewer qualms about their civilizing role, and paid no more than lip service to 'Christianity before civilization'. The legal codes which Ellis and Williams devised for Huahine and Raiatea, and which were then exported to other island groups, are the most obvious example of the mission stepping in to fill the civil vacuum created by the adoption of Christianity. This was preceded, however, by an initial reluctance to get involved in Caesar's work.

Davies' history offers a judicious summary of the general European impact on Tahitian life in the period of LMS supremacy. Where the advantage was obvious, as with firearms, boat-building and money, for instance, the European way was followed. Changes in land tenure and the organization of labour, however, were less welcome. Why produce cotton when cotton goods were readily available from ships for the price of a hog or a few fowls ? And he makes clear that Ellis' and Williams' vaunted domestic revolution was short-lived. Plastered houses provided insufficient ventilation and the Tahitians drifted back to their former ways of building. Tables, chairs and sofas were abandoned and the traditional practice of sitting and eating on the ground was resumed.[69]

Although there was a period in the 1820s when the LMS wielded considerable political influence, from the end of that decade there was a selective but steady drift back to older ways. In 1834, a long letter to Queen Pomare from William Ellis, now Foreign Secretary of the LMS, expressed strong concern at the lack of respect shown to the missionaries, at the neglect of Sabbath observance, and the general decline in manners.[70] The waning influence of the LMS was hastened by the arrival of new colonizing influences. The 1830s and 40s saw more frequent visits from traders, and the arrival of whalers, the French Catholic mission and the first settlers. Inadvertently the LMS presence provided a bridgehead for these rival forces, and as the missionaries became a minority of the Europeans living on the islands their influence weakened. Papeete became one of the larger and more lawless ports in the Pacific, host to seventy or eighty whaling ships each year. The effects of these arrivals on the native population are beyond the scope of this chapter, but it was the LMS as much as Tahitian culture which broke up in the new circumstances.

CHAPTER 5

Trade and adventure

'She had adventure after adventure, of course, the Pacific is
that sort of place.'

(Bill Manhire, 'Cannibals')

By mid-century the excitement generated by the European discovery of the islands of the South Pacific was dwindling. Both the
region and much of the writing about it had become missionary-
dominated, and those ideal versions of the Polynesian constructed
by Enlightenment and Romantic discourse were becoming redundant. An important factor here was the shift in attitudes to race
and empire in Britain as the ethnocentric humanitarianism of the
early nineteenth century gave way to the scientific racialism of the
mid- and late century. Events elsewhere reinforced this racialism
while deflecting attention from the Pacific. The breakdown of the
Jamaican economy following the end of slavery resulted in the
negro becoming the mid-century type of the ineducable savage,
and after Governor Eyre's brutal imposition of martial law at
Morant Bay in Jamaica in 1865, and the controversy over this in
England, the stereotyping became more vicious. The American
Civil War also concentrated attention on the black population of
North America. These events, and the Indian Mutiny of 1857,
were strongly racialized and had their effect on mid-century representations of Pacific islanders.[1]

Economically and politically the Pacific islands offered few
inducements for annexation. The region was marginal to the
economic needs of Europe and North America and had little
strategic importance until the end of the century. When territorial annexation occurred, as in the case of New Zealand in 1840,
it was less to do with Britain securing economic or political advantages than the result of pressure from colonizing companies and

missionary groups. Similarly, the French protectorates established over the Marquesas and Society Islands in 1842 were the result of French naval officers helping their Catholic missions compete with British ones rather than any French expansionist policy in the Pacific. The official French policy of *la politique des points de relâche* went no further than a recognition that trading would require a few small bases for provisioning and repairing ships. Any potential rivalry between Britain and France was sorted out in the 1847 Declaration of London, establishing a status quo in the Pacific which lasted for the next thirty years. It was based on a mutual agreement to restrict activities in this unimportant region to protecting trading and missionary interests.

The situation changed somewhat in the last quarter of the century as the Pacific acquired importance in the international economy for the first time, and rivalry between Britain, France, Germany and the United States developed. However, the increasing involvement of Britain in the region is better understood in terms of pressure from Australia and New Zealand than of the political ambitions or economic needs of the imperial centre. Britain continued to feel that the Pacific islands were not worth the cost and inconvenience of administration, but the Australian and New Zealand colonists saw matters very differently. They had significant economic, strategic and religious interests in many of the island groups and pressured Britain to play a more interventionist role in the region. The annexation of Fiji in 1874 was one consequence of this. It gave colonialism in the Pacific a distinct character. Fieldhouse has described it as one of the best examples of 'the primacy of peripheral forces and of the force of local subimperialisms in the expansion of modern colonial empires'.[2]

The relative insignificance of colonialism in the Pacific during the nineteenth century paradoxically allowed the region to figure prominently in the proliferating and complex debates on the subject of colonialism itself. Britain's half-hearted colonial presence in the Pacific and the ever-present fact of sheer distance enabled the region to play another version of the role it had filled since its European discovery: that is, an imaginary zone or dream territory on to which European concerns could be projected. In this particular case it could be used as a testing or proving ground for the different theories of colonialism circulating in mid-nineteenth-century Britain. Its very insignificance freed it for this role. As we shall see, it would have been much harder for Harriet Martineau to write *Dawn Island* if she had chosen Jamaica as her setting rather than a virgin Pacific island whose first contact with European civilization is to be a thorough course of instruction in the economic benefits and moral superiority of free trade. In such a setting there is no resistance from history itself, no prior contamination by contact with whalers, beachcombers, missionaries or settlers, no past of violence, confiscation or slavery. Dawn Island is a tabula rasa waiting to be imprinted with Martineau's version of free trade imperialism and to learn the interdependence of free trade, peace, domesticity and ethics.

Dehistoricized versions of colonial discourse studies tend to assume that colonialism was a constant, unremitting force throughout the nineteenth century. Differences between regions and periods, between rival colonial powers, and within the idea of colonialism itself get smoothed out. Historians of the British Empire, however, particularly those of several generations ago, have often claimed that the first half of the nineteenth century was a period of anti-colonialism. From the time of Adam Smith's *Wealth of Nations* (1776) and Bentham's *Emancipate Your Colonies* (1793) through to the free trade ideology of the Manchester School and the Anti-Corn Law League, it was argued, there was little enthusiasm for the acquisition of colonies. According to this account, the high period of expansion and empire was a late nineteenth-century phenomenon ushered in by Disraeli's famous Crystal Palace speech in 1872: 'since the advent of Liberalism – forty years ago – you will find there has been no effort so continuous, so subtle, supported by so much energy, and carried on with so much ability and acumen, as the efforts of Liberalism to effect the disintegration of the Empire of England'.[3]

This, however, ignores the steady expansion of Empire throughout the nineteenth century, exaggerates the influence of a vocal anti-colonialist such as Cobden, and fails to distinguish adequately the old colonial system of mercantilist restriction attacked by Adam Smith from the very different free trade colonialism which emerged in the 1830s and 40s. Whatever Adam Smith and Bentham might have argued, and whatever implications the American Declaration of Independence might seem to have had for the future acquisition of colonies, the average rate of expansion of British possessions overseas in the first half of the century was little different from that of the second.[4]

Although the heirs of Adam Smith inherited his hostility to the old mercantilist system, by the 1820s many political economists were revising his critique and developing a new economic and ideological case for colonization. This, according to Semmel, was based on a growing awareness that Britain needed undeveloped lands to which its superfluous population could be sent, its products exported and where its surplus capital could be invested. It was further argued that without a programme to extend 'the field of production' Britain faced the possibility of social revolution.[5] By the early 1830s Bentham had come to accept the case, argued most persuasively by Edward Gibbon Wakefield, for systematic colonization and a new liberal free trade conception of empire.

Root-and-branch opposition to colonies persisted, but was less widespread and influential than used to be thought. The once-held view that early-Victorian liberalism regarded colonies as 'millstones about the neck of the mother country' was not shared by many of the period's most influential liberals. Even Cobden who did, by and large, hold this view was not opposed to colonization per se, as he made clear in a Commons speech in 1843: 'He was as anxious as anyone that the English race should spread itself over the earth; and he believed that colonization, under a proper system of management, might be made as conducive to the interests of the mother country as to the emigrants themselves.'[6] Few, if any, would have disputed this belief in an Anglicizing mission, but within this broad consensus the question of colonies was vigorously debated in the second quarter of the century.

Empire, therefore, continued to expand but on rather different principles from those of the previous century. Where possible power was extended through trade and influence rather than by taking outright control of colonized territories. Adam Smith's attack on the cost of maintaining and defending colonies remained telling. Direct rule was often a last resort when informal methods had failed to secure British interests.[7] The possibility, even, of colonial self-government was contemplated. This, however, was not conceived as a dissolution or even a weakening of empire; instead, it was part of the new imperial thinking: 'By slackening the formal political bond at the appropriate time, it was possible to rely on economic dependence and mutual good-feeling to keep the colonies bound to Britain while still using them as agents for further British expansion.'[8]

There was no consensus about the speed or extent of colonial self-government. Cain and Hopkins have remarked how the frequently deployed image of Britain as the mother country whose children would eventually grow up left open the speed at which such growth might occur as well as the nature of parent-child relations in later life.[9] There is a particularly well-developed example of this parent and child analogy in Captain Marryat's Swiss Family Robinsonnade *Masterman Ready* (1841). The Seagrave family has been shipwrecked on a Pacific island, and young William has asked his father why England and other nations are so anxious to have colonies:

'Because they tend so much to the prosperity of the mother-country. In their infancy they generally are an expense to her, as they require her care; but as they advance, they are able to repay her by taking her manufactures, and returning for them their own produce, – an exchange mutually advantageous, but more so to the mother-country than to the colony, as the mother-country, assuming to herself the right of supplying all the wants of the colony, has a market for the labour of her own people without any competition. And here, my boy, you may observe what a parallel there is between a colony and the mother-country and a child and its parent. In infancy, the mother-country assists and supports the colony as an infant; as it advances and becomes vigorous, the colony returns the obligation: but the parallel does not end there. As soon as the colony has grown strong and powerful enough to take care of itself, it throws off the yoke of subjection, and declares itself independent; just as a son, who has grown up to manhood, leaves his father's house, and takes up a business to gain his own livelihood.'[10]

Marryat's liberal endorsement of long-term decolonization does not envisage hostility between parent and child. He does, however, foresee a time when England's present greatness will have been eclipsed, even perhaps by an African nation. Mr Seagrave reminds his son that the Romans once regarded the British as barbarians, and that the Moors ('quite as black as the negroes') were once the greatest and most enlightened nation of their time. Skin colour is no barrier to independence or becoming an imperial power. Marryat's liberal, historically relativist concept of empire is worth emphasizing. *Masterman Ready* was subtitled 'Written for Young People', and it quickly became a classic of its kind. Its ethos is radically different from those best-selling successors in the genre, the stories of Ballantyne and Kingston which dominated the 1860s and 70s. It is very much a work of the second quarter of the century when, as Herman Merivale recalled, there emerged a young set of colonial reformers advocating 'a reconstruction and great extension of the British dominion beyond the seas, on principles of internal self-government and commercial freedom'.[11]

Harriet Martineau's *Dawn Island* (1845) is a choice literary expression of this new liberal, informal, free trade imperialism. Martineau herself was sympathetic to Wakefield's ideas and believed in planned emigration, respect for colonial claims, and self-government when the time was ripe.[12] Although *Dawn Island* was written specifically for the Anti-Corn Law League Martineau was strongly opposed to Cobden's anti-imperialism. The spirit of her liberal imperialism is clear in her defence of Sir James Brooke, Rajah of Sarawak, who was persistently attacked by Cobden in the 1850s:

Brooke's view . . . was that Great Britain should use and extend her territorial possessions, not for the purpose of pouring in colonists to swamp the natives, but in order gradually to develop native resources, to improve native character and intelligence, and direct that improvement into the formation of a better state of society; leading back the people . . . through the stages of deterioration . . . to their ancient industry, enlightenment, and prosperity, on their way to something far higher and better still.

In this way, Martineau continued, the nineteenth century would develop 'a nobler and wiser method than was ever before used for connecting ourselves with the ends of the earth, and the outlying tribes of the human race'.[13]

Dawn Island is best read as a myth of this exalted doctrine. It takes its form from several different generic traditions. In its island setting, and as a myth of colonization, it is a Robinsonnade, but it differs from other nineteenth-century versions of this tradition (*The Swiss Family Robinson, Masterman Ready, The Coral Island*) by attempting to dramatize the experience of contact from the native point of view. *Dawn Island* presents itself as a tale of native life rather than of European settlement, and aims to put into practice the anthropological principles and techniques Martineau had outlined in *How to Observe: Morals and Manners* (1838). There she had warned against narrow or prejudiced judgements in the description of other cultures, and emphasized that the observer should remember that 'every prevalent virtue or vice is the result of the particular circumstances amidst which the society exists'.[14] *Dawn Island* also grows out of the early nineteenth-century tradition of popular educative writing. Martineau herself had contributed to this with the collections of didactic tales *Illustrations of Political Economy* (1832) which had first made her reputation, and the unarrestingly titled *Illustrations of Taxation* which followed two years later. Her *Household Education* (1849) can be read as part of this secular homiletic tradition, although it must also have been influenced by the domestic conduct books which were flooding on to the market in the 1840s. *Dawn Island* includes a distinctive domestic theme not found in other utilitarian and laissez-faire writing on colonialism.

The lifeways of Dawn Island seem to be based on Ellis' descriptions of Tahitian customs. At the opening of the story Martineau's Pacific island is facing extinction; the first chapter is titled 'Nature and Man at War'. Human sacrifice, infanticide and war threaten to make true the ancient prophecy which haunts the old priest, Miava: 'the forest tree shall grow; the coral shall spread and branch out; but man shall cease'.[15] Although the old priest is weary of war, and his adopted daughter shows some resistance to the marriage practices of her people, there is nothing within the culture strong enough to reverse this slide towards extinction. Salvation must come from over the horizon. There is a second prophecy that some day a canoe without an outrigger will arrive from another world and bring about great changes. This, of course, is the British ship which sails into the dying world of Dawn Island and redeems it with the principles of free trade.

The part of the island where the British land has been denatured by the recent war: 'all was desolate. Nothing but rank and barren vegetation overspread the scene of the late war. The voyagers turned from the bare stems of the cocoa-nut trees, and the prostrate bread-fruit trunks, and from the naked rafters where fowls had once roosted' (p. 53). They have come to an infertile anti-paradise whose people are engaged in what Brantlinger has described as 'a kind of collective suicide'.[16] More recently he has placed this in the context of the much larger nineteenth-century theme of dying races. *Dawn Island* is a fantasy of autogenocide, or blaming the victim, in which savagery itself is represented as the prime cause of the decline of native peoples. Civilization then becomes the means of arresting cultural extinction.[17] The early missionaries had argued a similar case on the basis of a supposed population decline in Tahiti between the time of Cook and their arrival. In both cases the myth justifies the presence of the colonizer. Extinction can be prevented only by western intervention, an optimistic version of the dying-race narrative which was to dominate writing about the Pacific for the rest of the nineteenth-century. More commonly it was held that when uncivilized man was touched by Europe he would melt 'as snow in sunshine';[18] Jules Verne was to describe the Polynesians as 'enervated by civilization' and slowly fading.[19] Of course these different narratives were never mutually exclusive: the autogenocide one could be used to mitigate the potential guilt of the other. Further variants will be met in later chapters.

Miava, the one inhabitant of Dawn Island with some critical purchase on his own culture, is the Europeans' point of entry into the otherwise closed world of native custom and belief. The ship's captain, noticing Miava's failing eyesight, gives the old man a pair of spectacles and his sight is instantly restored. This revelation of British magic also opens Miava's eyes to the brave new world of free trade. Practical trading lessons remain to be learnt, however. When Miava loses the spectacles his daughter steals another pair, but these do not suit his old eyes. Stolen glasses blur the vision; goods, themselves, seem able to instruct in the ethics of trading. When Miava's son-in-law steals the ship's flag the act is so transgressive that he is punished by nature itself, killed by a shark as he swims back to shore with his trophy.

As one would expect from a social scientist, Martineau understands that ideas of property and theft are culturally specific. The text acknowledges Miava's code that it is forbidden to steal from one's own kind but natural to steal from strangers. Some re-education, therefore, is necessary before Miava can grasp western codes of property and trading. But he learns quickly, assisted by the wealth of European goods the captain displays before his reawakened sight, and by Martineau's conviction that beneath all cultural difference, 'all men entertain one common conviction, that what makes people happy is good and right, and that what makes them miserable is evil and wrong'.[20] The prospect of happiness and goodness opened up by European commodities is irresistible, and a perpetual flow of trade and goodwill is promised.

Miava is led to a vision of universal peace and prosperity through free trade, and by the final chapter ('Nature and Man at Peace') his people have been saved. This intercessor between the people and their gods has been transformed into an emissary of free trade, teaching its rules and facilitating its introduction. Brantlinger puts it neatly: 'The unprogressive fetishism of the islanders is supplanted by the commodity fetishism of the British.'[21] Rebarbative native customs such as infanticide and human sacrifice are abandoned and all human life is tabooed. The missionaries have not yet come to burn the native idols, and in the meantime the gods will be offered western goods rather than Polynesian lives. The peaceful principles of free trade have made the savage practices of war and sacrifice redundant.

This outline of Martineau's narrative has involved some simplification. In line with the principles laid down in *How to Observe* she does try to understand native lifeways from a Polynesian point of view; to show, as *Dawn Island* puts it, 'the reality that there must be in any observances which so deeply involved men's passions of hope and fear' (p. 25). This goes well beyond the stock attempt at describing how the arrival of Europeans must have appeared to Polynesian islanders: the 'floating island carried along by wings', and the 'pale man-like beings' from another world (pp. 49, 52), have by the 1840s become very familiar. Much more interesting are the ethnographic curiosity of the text and its attempted sympathy with native customs. Her careful description of the rites surrounding the islanders' god Oro, for example, emphasizes that to them the god is 'not a hideous image cut in wood, but a chosen form into which the war-god descended at will' (p. 33). Cannibalism is not reviled but described as 'a divine rite permitted to valiant men' in which the spirits of the dead are transmitted to the gods (p. 33). Even the religious basis of infanticide is carefully explained. In these and other examples Martineau studiously avoids that prejudice which, as *How to Observe* had emphasized, prevents the observer from understanding what he sees.

Inevitably, however, she circulates prejudices of her own. The most striking of these is the common idea that barter was the constitutive transaction in colonial relationships, and that western commodities were so irresistible as to have the power of an inexorable historical force.[22] It has often been assumed that European goods had a fatal attraction for Pacific islanders which destroyed the integrity of their cultures. Martineau, on the other hand, sees western goods as redemptive. Both points of view simplify the complex nature of exchange relations, particularly in the early phases of contact before imperial intervention or annexation. They fail to see that western visitors were often obliged to accede to local terms of trade. They ignore the ways in which western goods were selectively absorbed according to the needs and forms of local cultures. They assume that the function and advantages of western artifacts were self-evident to others, and fail to take account of the mutability of material objects as they pass from one culture to another. And like many of the early visitors themselves, they ignore the possibility that things given out as trifles could be received as such.

In the exchange transactions of early contact it is often unclear which culture is taking the other for a ride. Cook recorded how on Tonga the eagerness of his sailors for native artifacts prompted local ridicule: 'one waggish Boy took a piece of human excrement on a stick and held it out to every one of our people he met with'.[23] The power relations of early contact were often more evenly balanced, and certainly more intricate, than the later history of colonized Pacific territories might suggest. Firearms apart, and these are certainly not in Martineau's scheme of things, Pacific societies were not inclined to absorb western goods regardless of the cost to their own culture. Nor were they inclined to trade what they most valued. For all her attempt to understand the distinctive forms and values of another culture, and her realization that the exchange of objects is always more than a merely physical process, Martineau's account of the magnetism of western goods and the irresistible superiority of free trade is rooted in the ideology of her own culture and its assumptions about primitive naivety and greed.

Her own principles of observation are also full of back doors. The great test of the morals and manners of any culture is 'the relative amount of human happiness' they permit. Although there is no universal moral sense among men, there are some influences which 'act upon the minds of all people in all countries': 'There is the same human heart everywhere; and, if the traveller has a good one himself, he will presently find this out, whatever may have been his fears at home of checks to his sympathy from difference of education, objects in life, etc.'[24]

Martineau's idea of sympathy is rescued from its potentially disturbing implications by her universalist optimism, allowing an ethnographic understanding of the complex reality of other cultures to become compatible with a belief in the supremacy of her own. If the human hearts of another culture are not beating as they should it is the duty of those who are happy to soften them. Sympathy for other lifeways might even result in a colonialist determination to supplant them.

It also means, however, that the suppression of native customs should be more tactful than the methods of the missionaries. Infanticide and war must be eliminated because they detract from human happiness, but belief in native gods can be allowed to persist. Martineau's secularist assumption seems to be that native religion will wither away as free trade grows. The cultural conversion brought about by the arrival of the British on Dawn Island is entirely secular. Infanticide is abandoned because the ship's captain persuades the islanders it is displeasing to their gods rather than abhorrent to his. It is the advent of commerce, not Christianity, which civilizes the natives. Indeed Christianity is conspicuously absent from the text, making a token appearance only in its final sentence when the departing captain describes the glow he feels at seeing how 'these children of nature were clearly destined to be carried on some way towards becoming men and Christians by my bringing Commerce to their shores' (p. 94).

Martineau's own religious background was Unitarian and she held a necessitarian belief in the working of natural law, rejecting providential intervention as morally and intellectually unacceptable. Nevertheless, until the 1840s she considered the necessitarian scheme to be underwritten by God. By the time of writing *Dawn Island*, however, her belief in God and the argument from design had been abandoned.[25] In its place emerged an evolutionary secularism grounded in the belief that political and social progress was unstoppable, and it was this which fuelled the secular but visionary optimism of *Dawn Island*. No missionary could have summoned up quite such confidence.

Dawn Island is not only a secular homily on the laws of political economy and moral progress but also a tract on domesticity. This brings it much closer to the missionary writing discussed in the previous chapter. Its opening description of the dwellings of the Dawn Islanders seems to derive from Ellis:

There was nothing in the abodes of any of the inhabitants of the island to tempt them to stay within, – no coolness, nor cleanliness, nor comfort. Holes in the roof let in the rain and mosquitos; hollows in the earthen floor held stagnant water; the long grass with which the floor was strewed was never changed, and the food and drink dropped upon it rotted and fermented. (p. 14)

This complete absence of the domestic is reinforced by an account of the low status of women, another recurring theme of missionary writing. The love plot is similarly domesticated, with a strong gender theme straight out of any Victorian courtship or wedlock narrative. Miava's daughter Idya[26] marries reluctantly and as the result of family pressure. After marriage she is burdened by the duties of her new role and repelled by the selfish demands of her husband. Like many other Victorian heroines she is rescued by the premature death of her husband, although George Eliot never resorted to a shark attack.

The ideologies of free trade and domesticity arrive together. The first European goods to be coveted are matches; Idya has spent many hours kindling and watching the fire of the oven. The ship's captain lightens Miava's and Idya's darkness: 'He had caused the shed to be lighted up with lamps . . . The unwholesome floor had also been swept out, and strewn thick with white coral sand, which seemed to glitter in the lamp light' (pp. 78–9). Once free trade has made the breach, implantation of the domestic quickly follows. Miava's and Idya's dwelling is given the aura and sanctity of the Victorian hearth, and it is this rather than Christian revelation which then challenges the customs of the islanders. The ritual murder of Idya's first-born child and the domestic tyranny of her husband are exposed as barbaric and inimical to happiness. The argument against infanticide is domestic felicity, not Christian dogma. A Victorian ideology of helpmeets is turned against Polynesian gender relations and the sexual division of labour is regendered. The captain explains how in England men get food and build houses while the women keep the houses clean, cook the food and care for the children. For the Dawn Islanders the pay-off for such a reorganization will be domestic felicity *and* the good-will of their gods. Their people will be saved.

Dawn Island, therefore, has more in common with missionary writing than either Martineau or the LMS would have cared to admit. Both conceive of the Polynesian as child-like but ready to develop into a mature, civilized being. Martineau's chapter on religion is titled 'Puerile Man and his Gods', and the captain describes his task as 'introducing the principles and incitements of civilization among a puerile people' (p. 93). We have already seen a similar conception of the Polynesian informing *Polynesian Researches*. The doctrines of Christianity and free trade are both grounded in the home. Savagery is less of a problem for Martineau than for Ellis, her necessitarian beliefs being more reassuring than Ellis' dependence on providence. Both, however, assume that to remain savage is inevitably to expire, and that civilization saves. Martineau is blither about the consequences of contact than Ellis, but both insist that contact with western civilization is essential if Polynesians are to survive. Martineau finds it much easier than Ellis to square this particular circle because hers is a dream text in which there is no resistance. Dawn Islanders need only to see western goods to be instantly persuaded of the material and ethical superiority of the culture which has produced them. Nor, in Martineau's case, is there any experiential challenge to the assumptions and mind-set of the writer. Consequently there are no impediments to constructing an unsullied myth of free trade imperialism.

The South Pacific was also the perfect setting in which new mid-century concepts of boyhood could be dramatized and elaborated. The Victorian invention of boyhood was signalled, among other things, by the emergence of the boys' adventure story in the 1840s. Rather than adult novels such as *Robinson Crusoe* or those of Fenimore Cooper being taken up by young male readers, stories begin to be written specifically for boys.[27] The difference between Marryat's *Midshipman Easy* (1836), written for adults but a success with boys, and his *Masterman Ready* (1841), written specially for boys, usefully marks this shift. By the end of the next decade public school fiction for boys had also developed, and the early classic texts of these two closely related genres were already established: Kingsley's *Westward Ho!* (1855), Ballantyne's *The Young Fur Traders* (1856) and *The Coral Island* (1858), Hughes' *Tom Brown's Schooldays* (1857) and Farrar's *Eric, or Little by Little* (1858). These and others of their kind were to provide the staple of the immensely popular boys' magazines which emerged in the 1860s and survived well into this century.

This publishing explosion was both cause and effect of the Victorian preoccupation with boyhood, which came to be perceived as a crucial stage in the growth of an English gentleman. The new manly boy comprised several rather different, even conflicting, qualities. One set of qualities emphasized physical courage, heart, pluck and guts. Boys being trained to run an empire should be fearless and daring. The adventure story expressed this spirit. On the other hand, moral responsibility was an essential part of Christian manliness and the manly boy had to learn to temper his physical vigour with the Christian virtues of restraint and piety. Ideal boyhood, as Joseph Bristow puts it, 'veered precariously between violence and virtue'.[28] This uneasy construction was held together by the ideology of chivalry as expounded by the author of *Tom Brown's Schooldays*:

the least of the muscular Christians has hold of the old chivalrous and Christian belief that a man's body is given to him to be trained and brought into subjection, and then used for the protection of the weak, the advancement of all righteous causes and the subduing of the earth which God has given to the children of men.[29]

The idealized figure of the medieval knight, staunch and heroic in battle but courteous, pure and compassionate in relations with women, children and other social inferiors, was repeatedly invoked to try and relax the tensions in the concept of the manly boy. It was also, as Jeffrey Richards has argued, deliberately promoted to produce a ruling elite for the nation and the expanding empire which would be inspired by apparently noble and selfless ideals.[30]

This ideology was forged in the reformed public school system of the mid-nineteenth century. The Rugby of Dr Arnold and Thomas Hughes was its furnace, and by the 1860s and 70s it was putting iron into the soul of the sons of the middle classes entering the new public schools. Bristow describes this process as a welding together of the gentlemanly virtues of honour, fair play, team spirit and decorum with more meritocratic bourgeois values of competition, independence and determination, and argues that it resulted in an almost classless model of the moral hero.[31] This near-classlessness is one of the most striking aspects of the new concept of boyhood. It was an inclusive ideal which all readers of boys' stories, for example, were invited to emulate. Bratton describes this genre as having a readership stretching from the ragged school to the country house, and it is clear that although the source of its values was the public school these were intended to trickle down into the expanding ranks of the administrative middle classes and their clients.[32]

There were important connections between public school and imperial adventure stories. For many, to go from public school into the imperial service was a natural progression. In *Tom Brown's Schooldays* the influence of Mrs Arnold and her drawing room is shown to nourish the Empire: 'Aye, many is the brave heart now doing its work and bearing its load . . . under the Indian sun, and in Australian towns and clearings, which looks back with fond and grateful memory to that School-house drawing room, and dates much of its highest and best training to the lessons learnt there.'[33]

The connection is even more explicit in W. H. G. Kingston's *Mark Seaworth* (1852) in which the young hero's understanding of Britain's imperial mission – that savages exist to create work for Christians, and that it is Britain's divinely ordained mission to civilize the world – is derived explicitly from the teaching of Arnold at Rugby. *Kingston's Magazine for Boys* which started in 1859 was one of the earliest of its kind and its mix of public school games, idealized accounts of England and imperial adventure brought together the main components of the ideology of the manly boy. Kingston's first editorial address looked forward to a time when his young readers would be 'battling with the realities of life under the suns of India, in the backwoods of Canada or the States, on the grassy downs of Australia, over the wide ocean, among the isles of the Pacific', and would themselves be writing accounts of their adventures for his magazine. Just as the boy is father to the man, so too the boy reader is the prototype of the imperial adventurer. The evangelical piety which informed both the public school and imperial adventure stories was also evident in Kingston's exhortation that 'the lot of all people, high and low, rich and poor, is to labour. You were not born into this world for the purpose of amusing yourselves.' *Kingston's Magazine* was clearly intended as a school magazine for the empire.[34]

From the moment of their discovery by Europeans the islands of the South Pacific provided anchorage for many different kinds of western fantasy. In the mid-nineteenth century they became the dominant setting for the emergent boys' adventure story. There was, by now, a growing Pacific archive which enabled the writers of such stories to use the region as a resonant setting for their own fantasies about the trials and triumphs of boyhood. We shall see in a moment how Ballantyne did so. In drawing on this archive adventure writers for boys were also adding to it, retextualizing the Pacific through their own narratives, projecting new fantasies on to old.

Even with such relatively simple texts this was a complex process. The reason for the absence of sexuality in this writing, for example, appears self-evident. There was no place for sexuality in the construction of the manly boy, and the emphasis on preparing the body by taming it appears to be a transparent example of sublimation. Martin Green, however, has suggested that although the authors of Robinsonnades exploited only the most edifying of the many images suggested by islands, we may suppose for some of their readers 'a margin of erotic fantasies derived from other sources'.[35] In similar manner public school fiction might well have encouraged homoerotic fantasies which the texts themselves kept strictly under wraps. More obviously, however, the Pacific came to be the prime fictional testing site and proving ground for the reconstructed manly boy of the public school-imperial axis. Ballantyne's and Kingston's Pacific stories were manuals for boys, imperialist dream texts facilitated, as I have argued, by the lack of any sustained British colonial interest in the South Pacific.

Ballantyne's *The Coral Island* is the ideal type of the nineteenth-century boys' adventure story. Unlike *Robinson Crusoe* there is no guilt about the urge to travel, nor any conflict between adventure and duty to family or society. The exuberance of its opening – 'Roving has always been, and still is, my ruling passion, the joy of my heart, the very sunshine of my existence' – is never lost; in Ballantyne's text adventure becomes a kind of duty in itself. And unlike *The Swiss Family Robinson* or *Masterman Ready* there are no parents or guardians to warn and instruct the young adventurers. They make their adventures, discovering the world as they go, and despite the work's evangelical piety 'the strongest stress falls on the fun'.[36] This must be the main reason for its enduring popularity. It went through numerous editions in the nineteenth century, has almost certainly never been out of print, and was given renewed life in *Lord of the Flies* (1954) by William Golding, who understood the potential in Ballantyne's creation of an island world without adults.

The Coral Island is also a significant text in the history of western representations of the Pacific. By making extensive use of the existing Pacific archive and translating it into the emergent form of the boy's adventure story, the work opened up the region to a vast new readership and profoundly influenced the terms in which it was seen and understood for many generations to come. Ballantyne's lens was one of the most powerful to be focussed on the Pacific.

His novel is a fruit cocktail of other writing about the Pacific which asserts the importance of reading if adventure is to be successfully negotiated. Jack, the leader of the three boys shipwrecked on the island, knows how to survive because he has been 'a great reader of books of travel and adventure' all his life.[37] In similar manner, Ralph, the narrator, is able to make his solo voyage back to the island after escaping from the pirates because he finds a copy of Cook's *Voyages* on board. In this way Ballantyne inserts his own text within a tradition which he shows to be educative and life-sustaining. Encouraged by his publishers, Nelson, to repeat the success of his first tale *The Young Fur Traders* (1856), Ballantyne read widely in their file copies. There he must have found Bowman's *The Island Home; or, the Young Cast-Aways* (1851), from which he culled a number of incidents for *The Coral Island*.[38] He also picked up and recycled South Pacific exotica. Most strikingly, he borrowed the underwater cavern from Mariner and Byron. The boys discover a submarine cave which allows them to hide from the pirates. This natural wonder, like Mariner's and Byron's, is a sanctuary to those who make the difficult dive, and is similarly compared to cathedral architecture. In Mariner and Byron, however, the underwater cave enfolds a story of threatened love, and in Byron's poem the retreat is feminized and eroticized. In *The Coral Island* women have been expelled from Ballantyne's underwater equivalent of the tree hut, and the erotic has been replaced by a typically moralizing passage about the wonder and strangeness of God's works.

Ballantyne also drew upon existing accounts of Pacific depravity. The most toe-curling scene in *The Coral Island* is when a large Fijian war-canoe is launched over the living bodies of some prisoners. Ralph hears their dying shrieks as 'the ponderous canoe passed over them, burst the eyeballs from their sockets, and sent the life's blood gushing from their mouths' (p. 216). The reader is then assured this is no fiction. Fiction or not, it certainly wasn't

Ballantyne's invention. This gruesome account had already appeared in J. E. Erskine's *Journal of a Cruise Among the Islands of the Western Pacific* (1853) as one of many examples of the cruelty of Cakobau, chief of Bau in the Fiji group.[39]

The Coral Island borrowed most extensively from Williams' *Narrative of Missionary Enterprises.* In places it is virtually Williams' book adapted for boys. Boat-building seems a natural activity for any island dweller, but when a hurricane strikes the boys' boat suffers an identical fate to Williams' on Raratonga. Just as his vessel was discovered several hundred yards inland lodged in a grove of chestnut trees,[40] so too the boys' craft is swept into some woods and found unharmed in the branches of a tree (p. 139). Williams' famous account of building the *Messenger of Peace* concluded with a story of the Raratongan King's delight at being allowed to work the bilge pumps.[41] Precisely the same story, down to the smallest details, appears in *The Coral Island* (p. 200). Indeed, it is a feature of Ballantyne's borrowings from Williams that he rarely bothers even to modify the passages he uses.

Chapter 30 of *The Coral Island* is a particularly flagrant example of this. It is important because it describes a converted native village whose peace and good order are to be contrasted with the violence and depravity of other native settlements on the island. The chapter prepares for the convergence of the adventure and conversion narratives with which the story closes. In an extended passage Ballantyne describes the neatly arranged cottages with their tastefully laid out gardens, the rows of Barringtonia trees, the footpaths and the large church with its six folding doors and windows with Venetian blinds, replicating almost word for word Williams' descriptions of Arorangi and a church on Raratonga, even down to the number of folding doors.[42] Ballantyne must have written this chapter with *Missionary Enterprises* open in front of him. The conversation of the native missionary who welcomes the boys to the village is made up almost entirely of scattered anecdotes and information from Williams. This includes the story of how a cat effected the conversion of a Raratongan chief, a natural history lesson on the three classes of Pacific islands, an account of the maltreatment of two missionaries and their wives, and a supposedly comical story about a chief wearing a lathe-turned sofa leg round his neck as an ornament.[43]

Although chapter 30 is a particularly dense example of such

borrowing, other more random instances occur throughout Ballantyne's text. There was no shortage of descriptions of bread-fruit and coconut trees to draw on, but the boys' convenient dis-covery of the candle nut tree (p. 70) – it enables them to work on their boat after dark – is described in identical terms to those in Williams.[44] Ballantyne also follows Williams' example in using 'sable' rather than 'black' to describe honourable or converted natives. In fact it became one of Ballantyne's signature notes; night is often 'spreading her sable curtain over the scene'. This is not an exhaustive list of the borrowings I have discovered, and a more thorough search might well double their number.

Ballantyne's dependence on Williams is made explicit in a much later Pacific adventure story, *Jarwin and Cuffy* (1878), in which the famous missionary guests as himself. The shipwrecked captive hero, Jarwin (Cuffy is his dog), finds himself, for reasons tedious to go into, disguised as a native and unable to reveal his true iden-tity to Williams. After a three-page account of the history of Williams' mission to Raratonga the narrative predictably takes up the building of the *Messenger of Peace*. Post-Smiles, the myth-making is complete; Williams' achievement is described as: 'one of the greatest pieces of work ever undertaken by man . . . not only because of the mechanical difficulties overcome, but because of the influence for good that the ship, when completed, had upon the natives of the Southern Seas, as well as its reflex influence in exciting admiration, emulation, and enthusiasm in other lands'.[45] The following six pages then reproduce more or less exactly Williams' own story of how he built his ship, the epic account of developing an air pump and all the subsequent labour.[46] This time, and needlessly, Ballantyne acknowledges his source.

What are we to make of these borrowings? In terms of Ballantyne's own writing career it must have been one of the habits which enabled him to write as prolifically as he did. Such borrow-ing was probably widespread among writers of boys' adventure stories using exotic locations of which they had no first-hand knowledge. Furthermore, as we have seen in the case of Melville, even those who ventured forth would draw on the writings of others. By modern standards Ballantyne's plagiarism in *The Coral Island* is startling. D. M. Thomas and Robert Stone have been in trouble for much less. If, however, this kind of borrowing was endemic to the genre then *The Coral Island* can be seen as pulling together, rather in the manner of a modern children's encyclopedia, existing knowledge about the Pacific and packaging it for young readers.

As a summary of *The Coral Island*, however, this is too anodyne. Ballantyne's text was also one of the means by which a new ideology of boyhood, the prototype of a masculinity suited for an imperial age, was disseminated. Although it depends on Williams' *Missionary Enterprises* for much of its detail and a great deal of its piety, there are many other elements not to be found in the early nineteenth-century, non-conformist, petit-bourgeois mentality of the missionary hero. Romance and chivalry are notably absent in Williams, and although there is a colonizing urge it is subordinate to the Christianizing mission. The ideological task of *The Coral Island* is to reconcile these new elements with the piety of Williams' work, to bring the bravado of boyhood into the same world as the moral earnestness of the missionary. It does this in stages. When first shipwrecked on the island, the boys demonstrate the steadfastness and resourcefulness necessary for survival. Ralph, having lost his Bible in the shipwreck, is unable to keep his promise to his mother that he will read it every morning. He is, nevertheless, able to fulfil his other promise to say his prayers regularly. Established on the island, the boys proceed to have adventures. At first these involve natural dangers such as sharks and waterspouts, and the Sabbath is carefully observed as a day of rest. Human dangers in the form of confrontations with cannibals and pirates follow, and the boys' religious observance suffers. This falling away is never laboured but is kept in view. Alone at sea with the dying pirate Bloody Bill, Ralph is unable to remember the appropriate Biblical texts for such an occasion, and comes to feel a greater sinner than Bloody Bill. It is worse to fall from grace than never to have known it. This idea is restated by the native teacher in the model Christian village and underlined by the sight of his native crew reading translated parts of the New Testament and praying. When the boys' attempt to rescue Avatea from her Tennysonian fate of an arranged marriage ends with their capture and prolonged imprisonment, Ralph once more feels the lack of a Bible and his inability to remember comforting texts.

The chums are finally saved by an English missionary, providentially blown off course on his way to Raratonga, who converts their heathen captors. As they emerge blinking from their cave they are dazzled by the sight of a tall, thin, grey-haired English gentleman with a 'frank, fearless, loving and truthful' countenance standing in front of a heap of wooden idols waiting to be torched (pp. 285–6). This gentrified missionary figure (Williams was short, stout and not at all distinguished-looking) is the deus ex machina, Golding's sea captain, who brings Christian order to the island and enables Avatea to marry her Christian Polynesian lover. Avatea and her husband return home with a native missionary for more conversion work and the boys set sail for 'dear old England' (p. 287).

The social background of the boys is lightly sketched but it is clear, nevertheless, that the authority structure on Coral Island reflects the 'natural order' of their home culture. Peterkin Gay is the youngest – he is thirteen – and his colloquialisms, which baffle the narrator, betray his lower-class origins. Appropriately he is the clown of the party, a version of the chirpy cockney. Ralph Rover, the narrator, is fifteen and comes from a long line of sea captains. He is a serious young chap 'much given to meditation' (p. 276), with an interest in marine biology. Jack Martin is the eldest, eighteen though he looks twenty, a 'tall, strapping, broad-shouldered youth' with a 'good education' (p. 22). The hierarchies of age, class and valour echo each other. Jack is 'clever and hearty and lionlike in his actions, but mild and quiet in disposition', and a natural leader (p. 22). The model is that of the public school prefect with a serious younger friend and a cheeky fag. It has been partly democratized (Peterkin would never have attended a public school) so as to appeal to a wide range of young readers, but its stereotypes and hierarchies remain intact. In many ways, not least in its locker-room banter and dormitory japes, *The Coral Island* is a public school story in a colonial setting. In similar manner, many public school stories are adventure yarns in a domestic setting, with their heroes, dormitory pirates and savages of the lower fourth.

When Jack, Ralph and Peterkin reappear in Ballantyne's *The Gorilla Hunters* (1861) this hierarchy is underlined, and the nature of the apprenticeship they have served in *The Coral Island* is made clear. Peterkin has become a great hunter and imperialist adventurer, indiscriminately 'fighting with the Caffirs and the Chinamen . . . punishing the rascally sepoys in India . . . hunting elephants in Ceylon . . . tiger-shooting in the jungles . . . harpooning whales in the polar seas, and shooting lions at the Cape'.[47] Ralph is now a naturalist of independent means collecting gorilla specimens in equatorial Africa. Jack not only leads their expedition but also persuades an African king to appoint him commander-in-chief and find suitable subordinate posts for Ralph and Peterkin. This reincarnation of the trio should be kept in mind as I look more closely at the elaboration of a 'colonial chivalric code' in *The Coral Island*.[48]

The conflictual values of this code are embodied in Jack. His natural leadership and all-round competence are first put under serious pressure in a confrontation with cannibals. The boys watch with horror as the captives of a cannibal party are murdered, roasted and eaten. Jack prevents Ralph from trying to emulate Robinson Crusoe and intervene, but when three women are dragged to the fire and an infant is wrenched from its mother's arms and hurled into the waves Jack is unable to restrain himself. He attacks the cannibal chief, wins a great victory, and restores the infant to its mother's breast. One of the women saved, younger and lighter-skinned than the others, is Avatea, who from now on will require frequent rescue. For all his magnificent courage in the face of overwhelming odds, the text registers something disturbing about the manner of Jack's victory. It describes how the cannibals are 'awestruck by the sweeping fury of Jack, who seemed to have lost his senses altogether' (p. 162), and although this might seem an excusable response to the depravity he has witnessed, Jack's tendency to go berserk is emphasized in his later confrontations with savagery, usually when rescuing Avatea.

This reflex of meeting savagery with savagery is something the native missionary counsels against. He refuses, for instance, to communicate Jack's threat to destroy the village where Avatea is being held if she is not released, advising that evil must be overcome with good. Imprisoned, Jack comes to regret 'the hastiness of . . . [his] violent temper', although he continues to distinguish between this and the attempt 'to try to succour a woman in distress' (p. 280).

The story's conclusion endorses the native missionary's advice. The boys do not rescue themselves, or anyone else for that matter, but are delivered by providence in the form of a gale and an English missionary. Waiting passively for something to happen, however, is no basis for adventure stories or the creation of empires. What is required is a marriage of the honourable school-boy code exemplified by Jack with the pious evangelism of the missionary ideal, a matching of physical and spiritual courage. The text works hard (in so far as this can be said of such a mechanical writer as Ballantyne) to distinguish these different positions and then to reconcile them. A peaceful, evangelizing, bourgeois chivalry is intended to emerge. But *The Coral Island* also demonstrates that this is a precarious construction. The most courageous and honourable of the boys, the story's paradigmatic hero, is also the most prone to go berserk. The public school ideal central to the imperial project is itself vulnerable to regressing and turning savage in colonial settings. Admittedly this is because of the outrage caused to its chivalric morality – we are still a long way from the world of Stevenson's Randall or Conrad's Kurtz – but it does raise the question which had haunted the missions of how to extirpate savagery, or even confront it, without becoming savage yourself. If the chivalric code itself is vulnerable to degeneration into mere physical violence, then the problems of grafting it on to an evangelical ideology are compounded. *The Coral Island* does not explore this problem – it is not that kind of text – but by exposing it it reveals a tension at the heart of this significant mid-century ideological formation.

The harsher, more violent *The Gorilla Hunters* has to confront it directly. It does so in an extended disquisition on 'the muff', the boy who is naturally mild and gentle. Although there is nothing wrong with this, we are hastily assured, the muff is also timid and unenthusiastic and will grow up unable to protect his wife and children. Muffs, therefore, must learn to swim, dive, wrestle, box and so on. In doing so they will become 'sensible fellows' able to defend themselves and others. But this is only with respect to the training of nerves and muscles. Men sensible in this respect can also be 'uncommonly senseless in regard to other things of far higher moment'.[49] The passage twists and turns as it endeavours to reconcile physical vigour with Christian virtue.

This idea of bourgeois chivalry can be located more precisely within the socioeconomic forces driving British colonial expansion in the nineteenth century. Cain and Hopkins contest the idea that nineteenth-century imperial expansion was primarily a consequence of industrialism. Instead, they argue, its roots were in commerce, finance and the rapid expansion of service-sector capitalism. Its heart was the City of London and it was based on 'gentlemanly' rather than industrial capital. Imperialism became one of the prime methods by which a gentlemanly elite of land-owners, bankers and City merchants which had survived the republicanism and secularism of the early nineteenth century prospered and renewed itself. Even later in the century, when free trade had destroyed the old colonial system and weakened landed power, the new economic and political structures and the imperialism that flowed from these were not dominated by manufacturers and industrialists. The City and the service sector overcame their hesitations, supported free trade and were its main beneficiaries.

They also carried into free-trading Britain many of their gentlemanly cultural values. In particular, the new public schools were used to create a gentlemanly class which combined aristocratic ideals of leadership and service with new administrative skills and techniques. This class, in turn, transmitted gentlemanly cultural norms to the lower levels of service capitalism. Although Cobden had thought that the coming of free trade would usher in the supremacy of the manufacturing and industrial classes, economic and ideological power remained with this gentlemanly class which survived all the challenges to its hegemony and renewed itself through the service sector.[50]

This gentlemanly code was aristocratic in origin, but those who subscribed to it were never a caste. It was based on status rather than birth, and status could be acquired. The code itself seemed timeless, although in fact it was in a permanent state of renewal, adapting to meet changing circumstances and to reconcile or blur resulting social tensions. Its chivalrous medievalism, for example, was a Victorian invention, a code of honour which placed duty before self-advancement and which underwrote the long educational *rite de passage* by which the status of gentleman was confirmed. Cain and Hopkins summarize this process: 'In these and many other ways, Victorian England was looking back, not merely in nostalgia but with creative intent, at the same time as its technological inventiveness was opening up new economic and geographical frontiers. As the Industrial Revolution gathered pace, so too the demand for ramparts and armour rose.'[51]

Chivalry, therefore, was one of the ways in which gentlemanly capitalism secured its hegemony. Another was the reformed and expanding public school system. This recruited from the emergent service sector and made gentlemen out of the sons of City merchants, bankers and professionals. Gentility was conferred by educating 'those who lacked property . . . in country houses set in broad acres, emphasizing individual effort within a context of communal endeavour, and instilling the values of order, duty and loyalty'.[52] In this way the landed interest secured the allies it needed and City wealth acquired the gentility it coveted. The nineteenth-century gentleman was based on a compromise, a potentially uneasy alliance between dominant and emerging sectors. It is not surprising, therefore, that the figure of the gentleman became the subject of much debate among social commentators and novelists, nor that the ambiguities and tensions of this construction should have been explored in imperial texts.

Cain and Hopkins see the imperial mission as 'the export version of the gentlemanly order':

When confronted with the challenge of new frontiers, gentlemen assumed proportions that were larger than life and at times became heroic figures. The empire was a superb arena for gentlemanly endeavour, the ultimate testing ground for the idea of responsible progress, for the battle against evil, for the performance of duty, and for the achievement of honour.[53]

Overseas expansion played a central role in maintaining property and privilege at home, and the link between the domestic and colonial elements of this strategy was the 'gentlemanly diaspora', a co-operative elite which exported the values of economic progress, differential property rights and political stability wrapped in the ideals of manly honour and duty.[54] Maintaining the gentlemanly code became one of the imperatives of colonialism, and this, in its turn, helped reinforce gentlemanly capitalism at home. The imperial gentleman was not simply a parodic reflection of his stay-at-home twin but was actively constitutive in his maintenance and elaboration.

But, as we have seen, the figure of the gentleman was constructed out of potentially unstable elements. Furthermore, while on the one hand the swelling ranks of gentlemen must have threatened to dilute the code, on the other, these *nouveaux gentilshommes* themselves became more rigidly exclusive as competition for their positions increased. This exclusivity was expressed in terms of race and class. Pride of race became a substitute for family lineage and blood. Lorimer argues that it was only in the second half of the nineteenth century that white skin became an essential quality of a gentleman.[55] Certainly, pride in the common inheritance of the Anglo-Saxon race became one of the defining characteristics of the new gentlemanly class. This reformation also required a stronger insistence on class difference; not all Anglo-Saxons were the same. In colonial settings, therefore, gentlemen conceived of themselves as civilized men in an uncivilized world; at home they were an enlightened class in a roughly equivalent kind of world.[56] This enlarged group came to be defined less by its members than by those it excluded. In similar terms, the core of Ballantyne's readership has been described as the sons of a rising class of first-generation wealth determined to defend the system which had allowed it to rise, and bring to heel the savages of those lands conquered by British tenacity.[57]

This modified concept of gentility intersected with increasing scepticism, from around the middle of the century, about the possibility of civilizing native peoples to English ways. This was both cause and effect of the scientific racialism of the latter half of the century. These currents of thought, mainly derived from the infant discipline of anthropology, fed into and were inflected by many of the social and political tensions surrounding the idea of the gentleman. Once again we see how social attitudes rooted in the domestic tensions of mid-Victorian England were projected on to the empire, and then reflected back, in a double movement whose ideological function of resolving strains within this new figure of the gentleman could never be wholly fulfilled. As Lorimer argues, it was the tensions of mid-Victorian society as much as the imperial experience itself which fostered the more developed racialism of the second half of the nineteenth century.[58]

Something more needs to be said of this racialism. When Robert Knox announced in 1850 that the key to human history lay in 'tracing human character, individual, social, national, to the all-pervading, unalterable, physical character of race',[59] he voiced what soon was to become an orthodoxy. The cultural as well as physical characteristics of peoples came to be understood as biologically determined, and race became the overarching category of human history. Although this idea was used to support different kinds of argument – Knox, though ferociously racist, thought that colonialism was a futile enterprise – it was always based on an

unquestioned belief in white supremacy.[60] This encouraged a
return to favour of the polygenist case that races had separate
origins, after half a century or so in which monogenism, the belief
in the common origin of humankind, had been the prevailing
orthodoxy. The connection between monogenism and the ethnocentric humanitarianism of the early nineteenth century, and polygenism and the scientific racism of the later period, is obvious.

Knox, an anatomist, was the leading advocate of this revived
polygenism, and it became particularly influential in the 1860s
when a faction within the Ethnological Society (itself an offshoot
from the Society for the Protection of Aborigines) broke away to
form the rival Anthropological Society of London. Founded in
1863, it publicized the ideas of Knox and his followers. Its popular
influence was considerable, although in scientific circles the polygenist theory was shortly superseded by evolutionary explanations
of the origin of races. This did not mean, however, that scientists
came to believe in racial equality. They remained convinced that
races were distinct in nature and capability, but now looked to theories of natural selection as applied to human societies for
confirmation of Anglo-Saxon superiority. This developing social
Darwinism became yet another ingredient in the stiff brew of scientific racialism which had so shaken earlier confidence in the
capacity of native peoples to become civilized.[61]

This confidence, once shared by evangelicals and philosophical
radicals alike, was in retreat by the 1860s. The example of Herman
Merivale, Professor of Political Economy at Oxford, later Under-
Secretary for India, and a cautious voice on these matters illus-
trates this. His *Lectures on Colonization and Colonies*, delivered at
Oxford at the end of the 1830s, envisage a future in which the
principles of the philosophical radicals, aided by the civilizing
work of the missionaries, will result in peaceful, well-established
colonies of settlement. Native populations will be treated justly,
and even if they prove to have only a limited capacity for civilization they can at least be partly assimilated, 'although remaining
always a subordinate race to the Whites'. Tahiti and the Sandwich
Islands are cited as prime examples of this process.[62] In his previous lecture Merivale had described the Polynesians as 'promising
subjects for experiment', comparing them favourably with the less
docile and migratory 'North American Indians'.[63] He also advo-
cated intermarriage as a means of assimilation and of overcoming

colour prejudice, noting the 'superior energy and high organization' of many 'half-blood' people.[64]

In his 1861 Appendix, however, Merivale's tone has become pessimistic. Europeans excite 'terror and hatred' almost wherever they come into contact with 'unsubdued races of inferior civilization'. Intermarriage as a means of amalgamation is utopian. Although Polynesia remains one of the few regions where 'a tolerably numerous and intelligent race . . . have been brought mainly within the limits of Christendom', even here 'a period of discouragement and relaxation' has followed early success. He also notes the unabating population decline of the Polynesians.[65]

There is little sign in Merivale of the scientific debates of the period and this suggests, I think, that science followed as much as it led opinion on the racial question. The ideas of Knox and the Anthropological Society were the extreme wing of a general shift of opinion away from the more benevolent paternalism of the earlier nineteenth century. This involved the hardening of older patterns of thought as often as it did the formulation of new, blatantly racialist stereotypes. The child/savage analogy, for example, so important in missionary writing about the Pacific, could be redefined so that the savage became a *permanent* child, incapable of growing up. The modification of old tropes was at least as important as the production of new racialist ones, demonstrating the continuity as well as the difference between older forms of paternalism and its explicitly racialist successor.[66] And lying behind this were the interwoven domestic and imperial tensions discussed above.

In Martineau and Ballantyne we find different, though not unrelated, mid-century myths of colonialism. Both writers use the Pacific as an attractively uncomplicated setting for dramatizing these different forms of colonialist ideology. Martineau's is transparently that of free trade imperialism. Ballantyne's, more complexly, is a version of the gentlemanly capitalist ethos, best described as a kind of evangelical chivalry. The unqualified optimism of Martineau's *Dawn Island* is hardly sustainable beyond the middle of the century, although a Christianized version of this optimism remains in Ballantyne's buoyant tales. It is accompanied, however, by a deepening racialism which contrasts sharply with Martineau's cultural relativism, Merivale's advocacy of mixed marriage, or Marryat's suggestion that England's greatness might one day be eclipsed by an African nation. This is apparent in *Gascoyne the Sandal-Wood Trader* (1864), the Pacific tale Ballantyne wrote following *The Coral Island*, where the Polynesians have been conspicuously negrified and supposedly jocular racist abuse is commonplace. This tendency in Ballantyne has been noted before, but is usually dated somewhat later and seen as specific to his southern African stories of the 1870s and 80s.[67] By the early to mid-1860s, however, racialism was increasingly a part of the definition of a gentleman and Ballantyne's imperial adventure stories reflect this shift.

Neither Martineau nor Ballantyne were particularly interested in the South Seas. They sought a region where their ideas about empire, and in Ballantyne's case the love of adventure, could be elaborated without too much resistance from history itself. Their choice of the Pacific might have been influenced by a persisting optimism about the region compared with more turbulent parts of the empire, but more important was the fact of distance, the sheer difficulty of actually experiencing the region, and its rich textual history. This freed it to become a space of dreams.[68]

Dreams, however, are never simple. Martineau's ethnographic approach to Polynesian culture has to be put aside if her vision of a free trade utopia is to be realized. And in Ballantyne's fictional world a number of overlapping and competing elements form a potentially unstable compound. These include the tension between physical force and moral power, between knightly honour and Christian evangelicalism, between a gentlemanly collectivist code and a bourgeois individualist one, and between Christianity and commerce. This last tension also highlights the potential clash of values between Martineau and Ballantyne. In *The Coral Island* the enlightened traders of Martineau's fiction have become 'white savages'. Trading, as Bloody Bill makes clear to Ralph, is essentially piracy, and the task of trader-pirate white savages has been eased by the missionaries having tamed native populations. Merivale also equated trading with piracy, reversing Ballantyne's cause and effect to ask how the missionaries could hope to convert and civilize when the trader had got there first, 'poisoning the savage with spirits, inoculating him with loathsome diseases, brutalizing his mind, and exciting his passions for the sake of gain'.[69] This view of trading activities in the Pacific is well based historically, but it is also ideological, expressing a distaste for trade which was an important element in the gentlemanly capitalist formation. Trade was the very heart of empire, and the assimilation of free trade ideology and practice by the gentlemanly capitalist class in the middle years of the nineteenth century had been crucial to its continuing hegemony. The gentlemanly ethos, however, with its chivalric trappings, was also deployed to camouflage the material basis of its economic power. This enabled gentlemanly capitalism to deplore the practice of trade while living off its benefits. Seen together, Martineau's and Ballantyne's texts expose another of the tensions at the centre of imperial expansion in the nineteenth century.

CHAPTER 6

Taking up with kanakas: Robert Louis Stevenson and the Pacific

The Coral Island was a favourite boyhood book of Stevenson's, and at the age of thirteen he wrote a Pacific adventure story in imitation of Ballantyne's tale.[1] Several years later he approached Ballantyne outside a church in Edinburgh and invited him home to dinner.[2] The introductory verses to *Treasure Island* celebrated his early pleasure in 'Kingston . . . [and] Ballantyne the brave', and when Ballantyne died in 1894 Stevenson wrote from Samoa in support of a memorial fund, the letter being published in many leading daily papers. His early Ballantyne-inspired enthusiasm for the Pacific had been furthered by a New Zealand visitor to the Stevenson home in 1875 whose account of the Samoan islands excited him. He began a utopian novel, *The Hair Trunk or The Ideal Commonwealth*, in which a group of friends turn their backs on civilization for the 'ideal climate, ideal inhabitants, and ideal products' of Samoa.[3] During his first visit to San Francisco in 1879–80 Stevenson met the Pacific traveller-writer Charles Warren Stoddard, who fascinated him with accounts of his travels and introduced him to the work of Melville. In 1888 he also met Mark Twain, and later that year with his wife Fanny and their extended families he sailed out of San Francisco on the *Casco* for the Marquesas.

Stevenson's own Pacific writing was the product of complex transactions between an already extensively textualized Pacific and his own distinctive experience as a traveller-writer who was to become a settler. *In the South Seas*, the posthumously published account of his travels prior to settling in Samoa, opens laconically:

For nearly ten years my health had been declining; and for some while before I set forth upon my voyage, I believed I was come to the afterpiece of life, and had only the nurse and undertaker to expect. It was suggested that I should try the South Seas; and I was not unwilling to visit like a ghost, and be carried like a bale, among scenes that had attracted me in youth and health.[4]

Stevenson entered the Pacific poised between life and death, and in Part 1 of *In the South Seas* a dying narrator confronts a Polynesian world represented in similarly terminal decline. Stevenson's first landfall, like Melville's, was the Marquesas. *In the South Seas* differs from *Typee*, however, in its pronounced use of the pathetic fallacy. The only threat to Tommo's life comes from the Typee themselves; in Stevenson's text there is a deep sympathy between the narrator and the culture he visits based on his sense of their mutual impending extinction. The long elegiac tradition of representing the Polynesian world is overdetermined in Stevenson's case by the state of his health and the myths of life and death woven through his texts.

As always, the scene of arrival – first sight and first contact – involves a myth of beginnings. Sighting Nukuhiva early on 28 July 1888 'touched a virginity of sense' (p. 12), but contact was more like molestation as the Marquesans swarmed aboard with 'no word of welcome; no show of civility' (p. 16), derisively rejecting the goods Stevenson and his company offered, filling the cabin and alarming the travellers. As usual it was the Polynesians who crossed the beach first and came out to the visitors. From a distance the vegetation and landscape had seemed European, but from closer in it was strange (p. 14). European houses, 'that patch of culture' (p. 15), had also been seen first, the native village later. The descriptions keep going in and out of focus, alternating between the familiar and the strange as the narrator struggles to assimilate the unknown to the known.

Later in the day he sits writing up his journal, which was to become *In the South Seas*. The scene has quietened although the cabin is still full of Marquesans, now cross-legged on the floor silently watching Stevenson as he writes. He describes their gaze: 'The eyes of all Polynesians are large, luminous and melting; they are like the eyes of animals and some Italians' (p. 16). This seems to tame the unruly scene which has just been described. But the next sentence Stevenson wrote, which was deleted from the newspaper serialization out of which *In the South Seas* was compiled, dispelled any such domestication: 'The Romans knew that look, and had a word for it: occuli putres, they said – eyes rancid with expression.'[5] Menikoff explains the deletion in terms of the editor's concern to present the account as a journey to Paradise, and it corresponds to difficulties Melville and other traveller-writers had with their publishers over the tone and content of South Seas books. The South Seas became a marketing category for publishers, who expected the replication of benign stereotypes rather than their dismantling.

This scene is also a classic example of the observer observed, of European discomfort under the steady gaze of the Polynesian. It recalls Tommo quailing before the expressionless stare of the Typee chief which seemed to be reading his mind while communicating nothing of its own. The emphasis is slightly different in Stevenson's case, where the gaze is accusing and corrupt. His own discomfort then modulates into a generalized despair at the impossibility of articulate communication across cultural boundaries. The crowd in his cabin are like 'furred animals, or folk born deaf, or the dwellers of some alien planet' (p. 16). But true to the pattern of rapid alternation which characterizes the opening sections of *In the South Seas*, the next chapter begins with an assertion that the 'impediment of tongues' had been greatly overestimated. It is not difficult to acquire a smattering of Polynesian languages, interpreters abound, and there is an efficient pidgin, 'Beach-la-Mar' (p. 18). Each new impression cancels the last.

Pagden's discussion of Humboldt's account of the cognitive strategies of registering the unfamiliarity of new worlds as they rise out of the ocean is relevant. The eye gives priority to what is familiar, moving from the known to the unknown, naming and understanding the latter in terms of the former and thereby taking possession of it.[6] Stevenson's perceptions follow the same pattern but the orderly sequence of the eye, as Humboldt described it, is disrupted first by the observing eye of the other, which forces Stevenson to see himself as an imperial intruder, and then by the ear which has no means of filtering the unknown or organizing the unruly.

The most striking tableau of the shifting and contradictory nature of early contact comes in the third chapter. The Stevensons are ashore in a deserted cove: 'Except for the *Casco* lying outside, and a crane or two, and the ever-busy wind and sea, the face of the world was of a prehistoric emptiness; life appeared to stand stock-still, and the sense of isolation was profound and refreshing.' This is Paradise before the Fall on an island out of time, a landscape unpeopled apart from the chosen Stevensons.

> On a sudden, the trade wind, coming in a gust over the isthmus, struck and scattered the fans of the palms above . . . and, behold! in two of the tops there sat a native, motionless as an idol and watching us, you would have said, without a wink. The next moment the tree closed, and the glimpse was gone. The discovery of human presences latent overhead in a place where we had supposed ourselves alone, the immobility of our tree-top spies, and the thought that perhaps at all hours we were similarly supervised, struck us with a chill. Talk languished on the beach. (pp. 29–30)

The native presence flicks in and out of sight, unsettling and silencing the visitors, activating the paranoia induced by the Polynesian gaze. At the start of Stevenson's voyage this, it seems, is the most that can be understood of Marquesan culture. Melville's subtitle, 'A Peep at Polynesian Life', returns to mind. The episode ends, however, with the narrator explaining that more than a year later he realized the natives were actually drawing palm-tree wine, something forbidden by law, and therefore 'were doubtless more troubled than ourselves'. The acquired confidence of the experienced traveller finally cancels the discomfort of the passage.

Lacking this confidence in the early sections of *In the South Seas*, Stevenson's most frequent method of settling the unease provoked by strangeness is through a series of parallels between Marquesan and Scottish Highlands culture. This is easily the most developed example of his strategy of assimilating the strange to the familiar. Suggested perhaps by the mountainous terrain of the Marquesas, it quickly becomes a way of understanding the 'convulsive and transitory state' of their culture: 'In both cases an alien authority enforced, the clans disarmed, the chiefs deposed, new customs introduced . . . The commercial age, in each, succeeding at a bound to an age of war abroad and patriarchal communism at home' (p. 20). More detailed, and fanciful, comparisons are made between the proscription of tattooing and that of wearing kilts, between the Marquesans' loss of their long-pig (human flesh) and the Highlanders' loss of their beef, and the dropping of medial consonants common to both languages. Stevenson finds such comparisons helpful in trying to understand the unfamiliar practices of the culture he is observing. It 'not only inclined me to view my fresh acquaintances with favour, but continually modified my judgement' (p. 21). Sharing tales of his Highland fathers also helped him to acquire the native tales he sought: 'the black bull's head of Stirling procured me the legend of Rahero' (p. 22). In this way the problem of communication which had so frustrated Stevenson on the day of his arrival is partly overcome. The psychological need to make such identifications is familiar to any traveller. Most significantly, however, it underwrote the trope of the dying Pacific which dominates the Marquesan section of *In the South Seas.*

The elegiac note is struck even as the *Casco* approaches Nukuhiva when Stevenson quotes 'the sad Tahitian proverb' Martineau had used in *Dawn Island*: 'The coral waxes, the palm grows, but man departs' (p. 14).[7] This idea of *tristes tropiques* is reinforced by associating the colonization of the Marquesas with the dispossession and death of the clans, and is figured in a wide range of ways. In an early scene the Stevensons meet an old man called Tari Coffin (Stevenson's naming habits are often bold). This 'mild, long-suffering, melancholy man' (p. 32) is an exile from Hawaii, dreaming of home as 'a place of ceaseless feasting, song, and dance' (p. 31) while living in sad tranquillity with his son, Marquesan daughter-in-law and baby grandchild. He is a familiar Stevensonian figure. The opening of *The Wrecker,* Stevenson's novel which most closely shadows *In the South Seas,* uses a similar figure – the famous tattooed white man of Tai-o-hae dreaming of 'the merry clamour of cathedral bells, the broom upon the foreland, the song of the river on the weir'[8] – as a focus for its early scene-building. Tari's grandchild becomes an image of the impending extinction of the Marquesans and their tranquil despair. Its mother, Tari's sixteen-year-old daughter-in-law, expresses the thought 'always uppermost in the Marquesan bosom': 'she began with a smiling sadness, and looking on me out of melancholy eyes, to lament the decease of her own people. "Ici pas de Kanaques," said she; and taking the baby from her breast, she held it out to me with both her hands. "Tenez – a little baby like this; then dead. All the Kanaques die. Then no more"' (p. 33).

Tari and his grandchild are the proleptic image of a doomed culture. The following chapter is actually called 'Death', and it intensifies the picture of the Marquesans passively accepting their inevitable extinction, ending with yet another underlining comparison: 'Conceive how the remnant [of the Marquesan population] huddles about the embers of the fire of life; even as old Red Indians, deserted on the march and in the snow, the kindly tribe all gone, the last flame expiring, and the night round populous with wolves' (p. 42). Placed among the clans and tribes of other apparently expiring peoples, Stevenson's rhetoric permits the Marquesans no escape. Myth is then underwritten by history in the next chapter, 'Depopulation', where the valedictory images of the previous chapters are reinforced by a sociological account of the demographic consequences of contact and settlement.

Scenes of death and extinction pervade all fifteen chapters. In 'The Story of a Plantation' (chapter 12) even the commercial enterprises of European settlement are pictured as doomed to expire, and this chapter ends with the death of a plantation as yet another emblem of the islands' fate. On Hiva-oa the process of extinction is less advanced, but this allows it to be more visible. Whereas on Nukuhiva only the elaborate stone terraces (*paepae*) on which native houses were once constructed remain, on Hiva-oa the houses are 'in the very article of dissolution . . . fallen flat along the paepae . . . poles sprawling ungainly' (p. 128). This helps to make the island 'the loveliest, and by far the most ominous and gloomy, spot on earth' (p. 126). The combination of beauty and gloom is the keynote of Stevenson's account of the Marquesas, a romantic and decadent picture of a culture which he tersely summarizes as composed of 'death, opium, and depopulation' (p. 87).

Stevenson concludes the scene of Tari and his grandchild by expanding the picture of Marquesan extinction into one of universal death: 'I saw their case as ours, death coming in like a tide, and the day already numbered when there should be no more Beretani [Britain], and no more of any race whatever, and (what oddly touched me) no more literary works and no more readers' (p. 34). This is more than a rhetorical flourish or a displaced expression of his own precarious state. The idea that the earth was dying because the sun was cooling was the particular contribution of solar physics to the many jolts administered by science to mid-nineteenth-century Britain. Developed and expounded by William Thomson (Lord Kelvin) in the late 1850s and early 1860s, it was widely discussed and accepted until the discovery of radioactivity at the beginning of the twentieth century established a source of energy for the sun.[9] One of its most important disseminators was Thomson's friend, academic colleague and business partner Fleeming Jenkin.[10] Jenkin was one of the most influential figures in Stevenson's life. The two met in 1868, soon after Jenkin had been appointed Professor of Engineering at Edinburgh University where Stevenson was a student. McLynn describes Stevenson's attitude to Jenkin and his wife as 'something like idolatry'.[11] Their relaxed free-thinking home was a sympathetic alternative to the strict and demanding Stevenson household. It was Jenkin who helped secure Stevenson's election to another free-thinking establishment, the Savile Club, which he made such use of in London[12], and when Jenkin died in 1885 Stevenson wrote a long Memoir, with an Appendix by Thomson, which introduced the collection of Jenkin's scientific and literary papers.

The links in this chain seem firm, although they are not essential to the claim that Stevenson would have been aware of, and responsive to, the idea of the death of the sun. Daniel Pick's study *Faces of Degeneration* gives *en passant* several examples of other writers in the second half of the nineteenth century who were affected by this idea.[13] The image of the expiring fire of life around which Stevenson's Red Indians huddle seems utterly conventional but can also be read as a version of Thomson's theory of the dying sun, an idea with particular resonance in a tropical zone. The equally conventional 'day already numbered' when every race will disappear also thickens in the context of Jenkin's claim that 'the rate at which the planetary system is thus dying is perfectly mensurable, if not yet perfectly measured'.[14] The larger point would be that the primitive dying race is doing service for a scientifically based and culturally reverberant anxiety about an ageing, cooling death-bound earth. These anxieties are projected on to another, less advanced culture. In turn, however, the supposedly imminent eclipse of Marquesan culture reminds Stevenson of the coming death of his own.

There is no question that by the time Stevenson arrived at the Marquesas the native culture had been seriously damaged by contact and colonization, and that its people had suffered more from illness and death than comparable island groups.[15] The contrast between the sublime landforms and the squalid social margins where European and Marquesan overlapped must have been glaring. Nevertheless, Stevenson's reading of the Marquesas drew on a long western tradition of seeing them as the most developed example of a process of extinction thought to be occurring throughout the South Pacific. The opening section of *In the South Seas* is written from within this tradition, although it has traces of the kinds of discrimination which were to challenge it as Stevenson travelled further and began to develop comparisons within the region, rather than between it and and the world he came from. He claims, for example, that the 'widespread depression and acceptance of the national end' (p. 40) of the Marquesans are distinctive among Polynesians similarly threatened. And he concedes that not all Polynesian cultures are being decimated (pp. 46–8). Nevertheless, what he writes has in part already been written for him, and it suits the trajectory of his life and the architecture of his work to represent the Marquesas so overwhelmingly in these terms. In the first part of *In the South Seas* a dying Stevenson meets a dying Pacific.

If Stevenson's entry into the Pacific is represented as a meeting with death, *In the South Seas* narrates his voyage beyond the Marquesas as a rebirth into an oceanic world capable of adaptation and survival. The move from a fecund volcanic island to a low infertile coral atoll appears to be a move from Paradise to the desert, but for Stevenson and Polynesia alike it brings the possibility of survival. For Stevenson the pressure of first contact has now eased, and with it the exhaustion brought on by what he called 'the strangenesses around us.'[16] As *In the South Seas* moves from the Marquesas to the Paumotus, and then on to the Gilberts in the western Pacific, it becomes less introspective and less inclined to sweeping generalization, more relaxed and discriminating.

This is partly a result of increasing familiarity, although the island groups he visits are very different from each other. It is also an expression of the growing independence of his writing from the tropes and conventions of the dominant late nineteenth-century western discourse of the Pacific. Some of these persist. The recurring infantilization of Pacific cultures and peoples was to remain a feature of his writing. Comparisons with the Scottish Highlands become almost reflex. And Darwinian models provided another means of explaining decline and extinction. Tembinok, King of Apemama in the Gilbert Islands, is described as 'the last tyrant, the last erect vestige of a dead society' (p. 277), and coral atolls themselves impressed Stevenson as examples of biological decadence, 'not of honest rock, but organic, part alive, part putrescent' (p. 170). Against these familiar available types of explanation and the influence of ways of thinking derived from contemporary science, there is, however, Stevenson's growing historical interest in the region and its relations with western powers and their sub-imperial clients. An early attempt at describing the effects of the informal colonial expansion he witnessed in the Pacific is found in a letter from Hawaii en route from the eastern to the western Pacific: 'The Pacific is a strange place, the nineteenth century only exists there in spots; all round, it is a no man's land of the ages, a stir-about of epochs and races, barbarisms and civilizations, virtues and crimes.'[17] At the beginning of Part 3 of *In the South Seas*, describing Butaritari in the Gilberts, the formulation is more precise:

In the last decade many changes have crept in . . . the widow no longer sleeps at night and goes abroad by day with the skull of her dead husband; and, fire-arms being introduced, the spear and the shark-tooth sword are sold for curiosities. Ten years ago all these things and practices were to be seen in use; yet ten years more, and the old society will have entirely vanished. We came in a happy moment to see its institutions still erect and . . . scarce decayed. (p. 208)

Stevenson was always fascinated by metamorphosis and this particular historical moment had a special interest for him. As he travelled by yacht and pen further into the Pacific he became increasingly alert to the mutations going on around him, as well as his own.

In the South Seas moves from travel to settlement. Its final part, 'The Gilberts – Apemama', which tells of the Stevenson party's time as guests of King Tembinok, is a prelude to settlement in Samoa. The cluster of houses built for them on a site chosen by Stevenson, which they named Equator City, anticipates the estate at Vailima. Stevenson's amused respect for the despotic patriarchy of Tembinok is apparent, and the King's household from which men were excluded, and which Stevenson compares to Samuel Richardson's circle of admiring women, also prefigures aspects of his later establishment at Vailima. This final part of *In the South Seas* is better focussed than the earlier ones. Stevenson looks more closely than before at the particularities of native lifeways and begins to experience the complexity of cross-cultural transaction from the point of view of the settler rather than the traveller. Again this anticipates his Samoan years, and particularly his involvement in the tangled political struggles between competing imperial powers and native groups which was to be the subject of *A Footnote to History* and his series of letters to *The Times*.

A Footnote to History tells of the culpability of the three colonial powers in Samoa – Britain, Germany and the United States – in fomenting civil war between rival chiefs and their supporters, and in failing to keep faith with the agreement reached at the Berlin Conference of 1889 guaranteeing the Samoan people the right to elect their own king. It also indicts German economic exploitation, describing the extensive coconut plantations of the German firm founded by Godeffroy as 'a wen that might be excised tomorrow without loss but to itself'.[18] Not a root-and-branch attack on colonialism in Samoa, it is nevertheless fiercely critical of the arrogance, ignorance and duplicity of all three powers. Stevenson's modest title is tinged with irony. Although he realized there was little prospect of 'the mass of people at home' taking much interest in Samoan affairs,[19] he was convinced of the significance of the events going on around him and thought they could be fashioned into a new kind of history:

Here is for the first time a tale of Greeks – Homeric Greeks – mingled with moderns, and all true . . . Here is for the first time since the Greeks (that I remember) the history of a handful of men, where all know each other in the eyes, and live close in a few acres, narrated at length and with the seriousness of history. Talk of the modern novel; here is a modern history.[20]

Stevenson's pessimism about the work's likely reception has been borne out, but his 'modern history' is worth closer study than space permits.

The wars themselves, an engagement between the German forces and Mataafa in 1888–9, the battle between Mataafa and Laupepa in 1893, and the rebellion of Tamasese the younger at the end of 1893, were scrappy, violent and inconclusive. Stevenson supported the cause of Mataafa, the one chief anathema to all three western powers, whom he likened to the Haitian revolutionary Toussaint L'Ouverture.[21] His scathing denunciations of the imperial powers and their officials expressed in *A Footnote to History*, nine long letters to *The Times* written over four years, and an even longer letter to the *Pall Mall Gazette* (separately published in London as a pamphlet, *War in Samoa*), put him in danger of being deported. Together they voiced a deep concern over what Stevenson called the 'progressive de-civilization of these islands' as a result of the interference and maladministration of British, German and American officials. In the war which broke out between Laupepa, who had been installed as king by the western powers, and Mataafa, Stevenson was concerned at the breakdown in the Samoans' 'own native, instinctive, and traditional standard' of warfare.[22] Another element in this 'decivilization' was the European disregard of their own standards of justice in sending Mataafa into exile on the Marshalls without trial or warning. Stevenson was angry at the injustice and alarmed at a situation in which native values seemed to be collapsing while European ones were ignored by those who represented them. He wrote movingly of Mataafa and the other chiefs exiled with him:

Taken from a mountain island, they must inhabit a narrow strip of reef sunk to the gunwale in the ocean. Sand, stone, and cocoanuts, stone, sand and pandanus, make the scenery. There is no grass. Here these men, used to the cool, bright mountain rivers of Samoa, must drink with loathing the brackish water of the coral. The food upon such islands is distressing even to the omnivorous white. To the Samoan, who has that shivering delicacy and ready disgust of the child or the rustic mountaineer, it is intolerable.[23]

Stevenson always identified with chiefs and was never less than eloquent about exile. This passage repeats the child and Highlander analogies met with so often in his Pacific writing. Mataafa, as McLynn points out, has become 'Charlie over the water'.[24]

There is no doubt that Stevenson himself was also excited by the prospect of war between Mataafa and Laupepa. He wrote to Colvin that 'war is a huge *entrainement*; there is no other temptation to be compared to it, not one', and went on to describe 'a kind of children's hour of firelight and shadow and preposterous tales . . . marches of bodies of men across the island . . . the coming on and off of different chiefs; and such a mass of ravelment and rag-tag as the devil himself could not unwind'.[25] Fanny Stevenson's diary also describes Stevenson's exhilaration, as, for example, when he returns with his cousin Graham Balfour from a visit to one of Mataafa's chiefs: 'They came back quite wild with excitement, burning to join in the fray. It is going, I see, to be a difficult task to keep Louis from losing his head altogether.'[26] The opportunity for chivalry seems to have been too much for the men in the Stevenson household. Fanny complained of being put 'in the position of the British female', and described Stevenson 'in deep sulks' because of her refusal to play the role he expected. She also described how Bazett Haggard, the British Land Commissioner in Samoa and brother of H. Rider Haggard, 'intoxicated with excitement and romantic feeling' and needing women to protect, wanted Fanny and and her daughter Belle to lie under the table while he defended his office against the attack he imagined was pending.[27] All this must have been galling for Fanny, whose prowess with a gun was well known and had once been attractive to Stevenson.[28]

Stevenson's childhood love of toy soldiers persisted into adulthood, and elaborate war games with tin soldiers were a favourite recreation at Vailima.[29] At times Stevenson responded to the conflict in Samoa as if it were merely healthy full-blooded adventure, a chance for men to show their mettle. But in *A Footnote to History* and his letters to *The Times* it is shown to be tearing Samoa apart, damaging Europe in the eyes of Samoans, and threatening the well-being and security of all those living on the islands. The history Stevenson witnessed 'under the microscope',[30] and narrated to western readers, stood firm against the romantic chivalry to which he inclined and which Ballantyne and others had established as a dominant Pacific discourse. It is ironic that Stevenson should have been rebuked by *The Times* for romancing in his reports from Samoa[31] when these reports, telling in detail of financial scandals, press censorship, and other illegal acts by the officials appointed after the Berlin Conference, were among the most down-to-earth and uncoloured pieces he ever wrote.

Stevenson's last published remarks on these matters were in his 'Address to the Chiefs on the opening of the Road of Gratitude' in October 1894, just two months before his death. This road linking Vailima with the public way down to Apia had been built by Mataafa chiefs grateful for the support Stevenson had given them during their imprisonment. In his address he told the assembled chiefs, 'there is a time to fight, and a time to dig'. The only way to defend Samoa, he continued, was 'to make roads, and gardens, and care for your trees, and sell their produce wisely . . . to occupy and use your country'. Pointing to the example of the Scottish Highlands, and the more recent one of Hawaii, he warned that if they did not occupy their own country others would. To dig rather than fight would ensure they survived the threat of extinction:

And I see that the day is come now of the great battle; of the great and the last opportunity by which it shall be decided, whether you are to pass away like these other races of which I have been speaking, or to stand fast and have your children living on and honouring your memory in the land you received of your fathers.[32]

The style is a wonderful blend of the Scottish pulpit and the Samoan *malae*. The romance of the Highlands is to be redeemed by the work ethic of the kirk; the domestic virtues of labour must replace the heroic ones of war.

The story in which many of the concerns discussed so far are most concentrated is Stevenson's novella 'The Beach of Falesá'. His letters to Colvin give a clear account of its genesis. The idea for the story 'shot through me like a bullet in one of my moments of awe, alone in that tragic jungle' on the estate at Vailima.[33] He wrote and reworked it over the next year, and by September 1891 could report his satisfaction with this 'sterling domestic fiction':

It is the first realistic South Sea story . . . everybody else who has tried, that I have seen, got carried away by the romance and ended in a kind of sugar candy sham epic . . . Now I have got the smell and look of the thing a good deal. You will know more about the South Seas after you have read my little tale, than if you had read a library.

He was, however, less confident about its reception:

But there is always the exotic question; and everything, the life, the place, the dialects – trader's talk, which is a strange conglomerate of literary expressions and English and American slang, and Beach de Mar, or native English, – the very trades and hopes and fears of the characters, are all novel and may be found unwelcome to that great, hulking, bullering whale, the public.[34]

The 'exotic question', the century-old tradition of using the South Pacific as a dream territory for western fantasies, did indeed make it difficult to accept 'the smell and look of the thing', as his subsequent problems with the serialization of the story were to prove.[35]

Like most Pacific texts 'The Beach of Falesá' opens with a landfall. Its narrator, Wiltshire, comes ashore at Falesá to run a trading station after years 'on a low island near the line, living for the most part solitary among natives'.[36] He smells the breeze of wild lime and vanilla coming off the island and feels renewed by the sight of woods and mountains. It is an archetypal South Sea opening recalling Tommo's and Stevenson's first view of the Marquesas, although being already familiar with the Pacific it is smell, rather than sight or sound, which first catches his attention. Wiltshire is a version of these and other figures who cross the beach with ideas and assumptions which the subsequent narrative will put under pressure and perhaps dispel. In the 'The Beach of Falesá', however, the story deftly travels further than its narrator. Wiltshire is an old Pacific hand. He has a clear line on kanakas – 'it's easy to find out what kanakas think. Just go back to yourself anyway round from ten to fifteen years old, and there's an average kanaka' (p. 215); and on the proper relations between Europeans and natives – 'It would be a strange thing if we came all this way and couldn't do what we pleased' (p. 184). Wiltshire is tricked by a rival trader, Case, into taking a native 'wife' who is tabooed. As a result no one will work for him, and he is forced to make his own copra, thereby experiencing some of the dependence and powerlessness felt by native people in their relations with traders and settlers. In particular he is brought up against the casual sexual exploitation of 'taking a wife'. He goes through a mock ceremony with Uma in which she receives a certificate saying that 'Uma daughter of Faavao of Falesá . . . is illegally married to Mr. John Wiltshire for one night, and Mr. John Wiltshire is at liberty to send her to hell next morning' (p. 171); Stevenson had seen such a document on Butaritari.[37] Later, as a result of the taboo and his unwilling discovery that he would rather have Uma 'than all the copra in the South Seas' (p. 189), he is properly married to her by a visiting missionary, the service this time conducted in Polynesian. The story ends with Case's defeat and a flash forward to Wiltshire, long married to Uma, worrying about the future of his daughters. The pattern is a familiar one in nineteenth-century fiction; Menikoff summarizes it as 'the education of a bigot'.[38]

Wiltshire's education, however, is far from complete. The casual unthinking racism which has characterized his language from the beginning is never more prominent than in the closing lines of the story as he worries about his daughters:

But what bothers me is the girls. They're only half castes of course; I know that as well as you do, and there's nobody thinks less of half castes than I do; but they're mine, and about all I've got; I can't reconcile my mind to their taking up with kanakas, and I'd like to know where I'm to find them whites? (p. 231)

Wiltshire has either reverted to type or else his experience has failed to change his racist beliefs. His world view, based on a late-Victorian hierarchy of races, remains intact. Although, as Katherine Bailey Linehan has argued, the narrative dramatizes the unsettling and disorienting shifts of perspective that follow Wiltshire's exclusion from the company of his fellow-traders and his close emotional engagement with Polynesian culture in the form of Uma,[39] one consequence of this disorientation is a defensive or unthinking reassertion of the racial hierarchies which the story itself has dismantled. This is what I meant by saying that the story travels further than its narrator.

It is also, I think, a subtle exercise in authorial self-exploration. Stevenson hated the arrogance of white settlers and officials, remarking bitterly of the Chief Justice and President appointed after the Berlin Conference that 'They have forgot they were in Samoa or that such a thing as Samoans existed and had eyes and some intelligence.'[40] The satire is clear, therefore, when Wiltshire asserts that having come so far he can do as he likes. But as we have seen, the analogy between Polynesians and children is a commonplace of Stevenson's non-fictional writing. By putting this sentiment in Wiltshire's mouth the satire is doubled, reflecting back on author as well as narrator, and constituting the deepest level of the story's exploration of the complexities of white racism in a colonial setting where the native population is regarded as somewhere mid-point on the scale between white supremacy and black inferiority. Some of Stevenson's own cherished categories are held at arm's length in producing his most profound account of the psychology of the colonialist in the South Pacific.

The focus of Wiltshire's story is the relationship with Uma, and it is here that Stevenson writes most consciously against the main tradition of cross-cultural romance in Pacific and other colonial texts. Mary Louise Pratt has argued that the love plots in such texts normally rewrote actual colonial relations, romantically transforming the sexual exploitation they involved and establishing the beneficent female 'nurturing native' as a key figure in this sentimental version of the anti-conquest narrative. These transracial love plots embody ideas of cultural harmony and reciprocity which mystify actual colonial relations until, typically, they break down in their denouement with the departure for home of the European male, leaving his native lover to pine and die.[41] The narrative Pratt outlines is broadly true of *Typee*, of several of the French texts to be considered in a later chapter, and any number of conventional South Sea romances. This romance plot also functions as an allegory in which a feminine Polynesian culture gives itself voluntarily to a masculine, European, colonizing one which will later abandon it on the beach, leaving it to wilt and die.

In 'The Beach of Falesá' the love plot is founded on the exploitation of the mock marriage and blasphemous certificate. The only language Wiltshire and Uma have in common is pidgin, the language of trade. It becomes, however, a reluctant romance in which Wiltshire's feelings for Uma develop against all his instincts and prejudices, and against the grain of normal colonial sexual relations. The focus is on Wiltshire; Uma's feelings remain more shadowy. At first she seems grateful for the comfort that living with Wiltshire will bring. Later, as she realizes he has been tricked but that she will not be cast off, gratitude develops into a love which remains largely unexplored. An obvious reason for the lack of access to Uma's feelings is Wiltshire's first-person narrative. Another is the pidgin she speaks. Stevenson has been criticized for the diminishing effect of pidgin in his depiction of Uma, but it is an interesting experiment in which this bastard language is put to uses it can hardly bear. Pidgins evolved in colonial settings to meet the basic needs of the colonizer. In the Pacific they were languages of trade and it is appropriate that Wiltshire's chattel-wife should speak to him in 'Beach-la-Mar'. When a pidgin becomes the native language of a new generation of children it develops into a creole, a more complex language used to express all the interactive needs of its speakers.[42] In terms of this distinction, Uma's language is pidgin struggling to become creole, as a master and slave relationship is redefined as one of reciprocity and love. Indeed, the conclusion of 'The Beach of Falesá' implies a more general creolization of the Pacific.

Another aspect of the story which removes it from the conventions of transcultural romance is that Wiltshire and Uma actually work together. Pratt notes that typically these love relationships 'unfold in some marginal or privileged space where relations of labour and property are suspended'.[43] In Pacific romances this is often the pool, lake or cave. Wiltshire, with the store that he runs tabooed and labour unobtainable, is forced to make his own copra from trees owned by Uma's mother. As he works with the two women, discovering in the process the extent to which natives water their copra to compensate for the dishonestly weighted scales of the trader, he is jeered at by Case's negro employee. The inversions in Wiltshire's situation are just about complete, and they underwrite the story's main reversal, the relationship of Wiltshire and Uma.

Most significantly, Stevenson's rewriting of the transcultural romance ends as a domestic-problem story. Wiltshire does not depart leaving a distraught Uma waving from the beach. She is not ruined, nor does she fade and die. Instead, as Wiltshire tells us, 'She's turned a powerful big woman now, and could throw a London bobby over her shoulder' (p. 231). The mere presence of those mixed-race children, whose future concerns their father, is striking. For all the sexual commerce across the beach in Pacific romances there are curiously few offspring. Their presence in 'The Beach of Falesá' suggests that the Pacific has a future, albeit a hybrid or creolized one. Unlike most nineteenth-century writing about the Pacific, including some of Stevenson's own, Polynesian culture in this story is not killed off by a more vital colonizing one. It will survive, not unchanged, and at great cost, but it nevertheless has a future in which neither European nor Polynesian will be quite the same. The beach, as a result of colonization, has become a degraded margin but not a fallen one. There is no nostalgia for some mythic golden past. The present is squalid, and the future a matter of concern, but Polynesian culture will not disappear to satisfy the rage, guilt or elegiac melancholy of western romantics.

'The Beach of Falesá' is also an adventure story in which the rivalry between the two traders, Wiltshire and Case, culminates in a bloody shoot-out in high bush at the spot where Case has set up a museum of horrors to intimidate the native population and con-solidate his power over them. The climax of the story comes when Wiltshire kills Case and destroys his box of tricks. It has been sug-gested that the 'swashbuckling romance' of its conclusion was intended to allow Stevenson to smuggle in his social criticism under cover of the kind of adventure story he had built his repu-tation on.[44] There are several objections to this. It simplifies his attitude to his reading public; it misdescribes the final, very brutal confrontation between Wiltshire and Case; and it ignores the careful interweaving of the different strands of imperial adven-ture, social criticism and domestic realism which make up the text.

'The Beach of Falesá' demystifies the imperial adventure story as thoroughly as it does the cross-cultural romance.[45] Its narrative of petty, violent trading rivalry suggests the decadence and parasitism of imperial adventure, and makes it an interesting precursor of *Heart of Darkness*. Just as it refuses the Romantic opposition between a fallen European world and a prelapsarian Pacific one, it also rejects the imperialist contrast of virile adventurer and dark continent. The violence of the fight between Wiltshire and Case is toe-curling: 'I gave him the cold steel for all I was worth. His body kicked under me like a spring sofa . . . I tried to draw the knife out to give it him again. The blood came over my hands, I remember, hot as tea' (p. 228). Wiltshire then faints from the pain in his shot-away leg, but on coming round 'the first thing I attended to was to give him the knife again half a dozen times up to the handle. I believe he was dead already; but it did him no harm and did me good' (p. 228). This is not in the service of some imperial ideal: Case must be killed if Wiltshire is to trade. The violence is between white men: 'will you please to observe,' Stevenson wrote of the story to Colvin, 'that almost all that is ugly is in the whites?' [46] In 'The Beach of Falesá' the idea of 'playing the white man' is repeatedly ironized.

A more sophisticated version of the failure to see the interrelation of imperial and domestic themes in late nineteenth-century male fiction is Elaine Showalter's *Sexual Anarchy*. She sets up an opposition between 'Queen Realism', epitomized by the fiction of George Eliot, and 'King Romance', a late nineteenth-century reaction to the dominance of the female realists by Haggard, Kipling and Stevenson who remade the high Victorian novel in masculine terms: 'in place of the heterosexual romance of courtship, manners and marriage that had been the specialty of women writers, male critics and novelists extolled the masculine and homosocial "romance" of adventure and quest, descended from Arthurian epic. Conan Doyle called Stevenson "the father of the modern masculine novel".'[47] Showalter terms this new literary genre the male quest romance. It involves an escape from the constraints of modern European civilization into some anarchic space of the primitive in quest of an imagined heart of darkness. From out of these 'Sotadic Zones' (Sir Richard Burton's term for those steamy latitudes, including the South Sea islands, where there was a minimum of sexual regulation) the male narrator tells his story to an implied male reader or to a male audience. This circulation of the quest romance between male speakers and auditors reinscribes the story of female exclusion central to the genre and the period.[48]

Insofar as this accurately describes a type of story told by Haggard, Kipling or Conrad, 'The Beach of Falesá' can actually be read against its tropes and conventions as a dismantling of the male quest romance. It features a reluctant questor, pitted against men and assisted by women. The heart of the story does not hide a truth, nor is it the imagined centre of some exotic civilization. Instead, it is a white man's trick. Although it is hidden deep in thick bush, Wiltshire's journey to Case's museum of tricks (which Uma will also make on the night of the final confrontation) is not described in terms of a sexual expedition into a primordial female body.[49] The theatricals are exposed by a reluctant questor motivated by profits and heterosexual love. And there is no mystical or symbolic experience, merely a bloody shoot-out between two small-time traders.

The relation between imperial and domestic themes in nineteenth-century writing is more complicated than Showalter allows. *Mansfield Park* and *Jane Eyre* are just two examples of the intertwining of imperial and domestic themes in the nineteenth-century realist tradition. Imperialist adventure stories often go beyond epic themes of discovery and conquest to end with settlement and domestication. And in 'The Beach of Falesá', an ironic adventure tale ends as a domestic-problem story.[50] Stevenson's Pacific writing, at least, needs to be placed more subtly within a tradition, itself complex, which it uses and undercuts.

The Wrecker might seem to conform more closely to Showalter's typology of the male quest romance. It is certainly a homosocial romance of adventure and quest. The narrator-adventurer-questor, Louden Dodd, has a series of emotionally intense relations with men, not only his alter egos Pinkerton and Carthew who dominate the first and second halves of the work respectively, but with lesser characters (Bellairs and Hadden) as well. It is an almost exclusively male world of adventurers telling and listening to stories. The virtual absence of women in this work highlights the educative (not redemptive) role played by Uma in 'The Beach of Falesá'. But adventure in *The Wrecker* is thoroughly debased and all the quests are chimerical. The treasure at the heart of this novel is opium, whose debilitating effect on the Marquesans Stevenson had deplored in *In the South Seas,* and the quantity discovered, in a scene of mayhem and carnage (chapter 15), is so small that Dodd and Pinkerton are financially ruined by their quest. Other less material kinds of quest are similarly exposed as illusory. This is a novel whose loose, meandering, improvisational structure expresses perfectly the shifting, opportunistic and illusory aspirations of its characters. In a strikingly Conradian phrase, the narrator justifies his quest for the wreck of the *Flying Scud* (whose hold contains the opium) in terms of 'the redeeming element of mystery' (chapter 10). This mystery, however, is revealed to have been another bloody shoot-out between trading rivals, with nothing redemptive about it.

Both these texts, therefore, emphasize the sheer ugliness of colonial adventuring in the Pacific. It is based on greed (there is no redeeming idea) and results in exploitation and corruption. In his journey through the Pacific Stevenson had sought adventure and contemplated becoming a trader. *The Wrecker* had been started as a means of financing the purchase of a schooner (to be called the *Northern Light*) for trading among the islands. Further experience of the Pacific trading world turned Stevenson from this idea, and adventure, too, no matter how exhilarating in prospect, proved inglorious and corrupting.

The most vivid figure of corruption anywhere in Stevenson's writing is Captain Randall, 'the father of the Beach' in 'The Beach of Falesá'. Wiltshire meets him in the back room behind Case's store:

In the back room was old Captain Randall, squatting on the floor native fashion, fat and pale, naked to the waist, gray as a badger and his eyes set with drink. His body was covered with gray hair and crawled over by flies; one was in the corner of his eye – he never heeded; and the mosquitoes hummed about the man like bees. Any clean-minded man would have had the creature out at once and buried him; and to see him, and think he was seventy, and remember he had once commanded a ship, and come ashore in his smart togs, and talked big in bars and consulates, and sat in club verandahs, turned me sick and sober. (pp. 167–8)

This is normally read as an expression of the European fear of regression in savage places, a graphic anticipation of Conrad's Kurtz. Wiltshire's description of Randall as 'that remains of man' (p. 169), and his horror at being in the same room with him, reinforces this. Randall is a nightmare image of what Wiltshire might become. *The Wrecker* and *The Ebb-Tide* have a similar interest in the degeneration of westerners in the Pacific, unlike Stevenson's travel writing which concentrates on how Pacific cultures are being contaminated by white incursion. But the visibly decomposing Randall is very specifically an image of the corruption of trade. He lives at the heart of Case's store (the station was once his), which is almost empty of stock apart from the contraband of guns and liquor. Rather like Krook in *Bleak House*, he expresses the decay and corruption at the heart of his world. He even explodes like Krook, though not spontaneously, being blown up while dynamiting fish in another image of violent and unnatural incursion.

The Ebb-Tide is Stevenson's bleakest account of Europeans in the Pacific. Islanders figure hardly at all. The opening lines set the keynote: 'Throughout the island world of the Pacific, scattered men of many European races and from almost every grade of society carry activity and disseminate disease.'[51] The story opens on a beach which mocks every western stereotype of the Edenic Pacific. It is a place of disease, full of the sound of 'men coughing, and strangling as they coughed' (p. 177): an influenza epidemic is raging on Tahiti. It is dark, cold, wet, and the only shelter for the trio of men whose story the text narrates is a deserted crumbling prison. This particular beach is Papeete, but it could be Apia, Noumea or Suva; to be 'on the beach' is by now a phrase used to describe destitute whites anywhere in the South Seas. The Pacific is diseased, and as in *Bleak House*, the disease has turned back on those responsible for it. Next morning a schooner is visible in the harbour flying a yellow flag, 'the emblem of pestilence' (p. 184), indicating smallpox. This is the boat on which the trio will escape to the hell of yet another beach, on the uncharted but ironically named New Island, where smallpox has preceded them but is nothing to the moral contamination of the place. Before they leave, one of their number, Robert Herrick, who is the moral and psychological centre of the story, writes a farewell letter to his one-time sweetheart which ridicules conventional images of the South Pacific with heavy irony: 'Think of me at the last, here, on a bright beach, the sky and sea immoderately blue, and the great breakers roaring outside on a barrier reef, where a little isle sits green with palms. I am well and strong' (p. 190).

Names are made to work hard in this story, none more so than Herrick's: 'Gather ye Rose-buds while ye may' would make a grimly ironic epigraph for *The Ebb-Tide*. Herrick is a version of the recurring Manfred figure in western writing about the Pacific. The appeal of the Pacific as a place to disappear in was obvious. It offered a refuge for damaged reputations, black sheep, remittance men and the like. But there is also a long literary tradition of it as a kind of nightmare world on which an existential anti-hero is cast adrift. This figure is not only in retreat from the western world but in search of something – his identity, or some larger sense of purpose. It is not a material quest, but in Stevenson's versions this figure gets caught up, to his disgust, in a search for treasure. As a consequence the self-disgust which marks these figures is heightened. Herrick is Stevenson's most developed version of this type, a near-relative of the superfluous hero of nineteenth-century Russian fiction who seeks death but cannot die.

Fletcher Christian with his cry of 'I am in hell' is the founding figure of this tradition; Bligh determinedly making his epic small-boat voyage back to Europe to secure justice is its anti-type. There is even a muscular version of the existential anti-hero in Ballantyne, the eponymous hero of *Gascoyne the Sandal-Wood Trader* who wrestles with his guilt and despair across the Pacific and is finally redeemed as the very model of a Protestant trader, teaching Sunday school and keeping his books meticulously on a remote 'oceanic gem, which has been reclaimed by the word of God from those regions that have been justly styled "the dark places of the earth"'.[52] *The Wrecker* is full of estranged sons, reprobate heirs, remittance men and other runaways hiding behind aliases. Its most developed example is Carthew (aka Dickson, Goddedaal and Madden), alter ego of the narrator, and representative of 'a kind of new Byronism more composed and dignified'.[53] He is a melancholy nihilist, *l'étranger* marooned in the Pacific, inadvertently caught up in the horror of the *Flying Scud* affair, and thereafter permanently exiled from his family estates. Wealthy and guilt-stricken, he is last described as the owner of a trading schooner which Dodd sails for him, these twinned characters a pair of prosperous itinerants in a Pacific world unable to offer redemption.

Herrick, in *The Ebb-Tide*, is a straitened, more desperate version of Carthew. Another Oxford-educated gentleman, though of

commercial not landed stock, forced into clerking because of his
father's business failure, he has undergone 'a long apprenticeship
in going downward' (p. 174). After drifting from job to job in
North America and breaking off contact with home, he changed
his name in San Francisco, spent his last dollar on a passage to the
South Seas and ended up on the beach at Tahiti. His companions
are Davis (alias Brown), a disgraced American sea captain, and
Huish (alias Hay, also Herrick's alias, and Tomkins), a 'wholly vile'
cockney. The trio ship out of Papeete on the *Farallone* (a fitting
name for the psychologically marooned Herrick) with a cargo of
champagne and thoughts of profit. This is a death ship on which
they re-enact the voyage of its previous captain and mate, the alle-
gorically named Wiseman and Wis[e]hart, who have lurched
drunkenly across the Pacific, contracting smallpox on one of their
carousing landfalls. Treasure gleams only to disappoint. Most of
the champagne is bottled water; the cargo is a fraud. The next, and
final, oasis is also a mirage. An uncharted island is sighted, its
lagoon reflected in an 'elusive glimmer in the sky' (p. 235): Davis
thinks of pearls. It proves to be a pattern coral island ('The beach
was excellently white, the continuous barrier of trees inimitably
green' (p. 236)) enfolding a simulacrum of rural England. Once
within the lagoon the *Farallone* is confronted by a settlement:

a substantial country farm with its attendant hamlet: a long line of sheds
and store-houses; apart . . . a deep-verandah'd dwelling house . . . a building with a belfry and some rude offer at architectural features that might
be thought to mark it out for a chapel. . . From a flagstaff at the pier-head
the red ensign of England was displayed. (pp. 238–9)

The squire of this manor, Attwater, is a model of one kind of
English colonialist: Cambridge to Herrick's Oxford, physically
impressive, langorous, dressed in exquisite white drill, carrying a
Winchester rifle.

This, however, is another beach of death. Attwater's island has
been overrun by smallpox and most of his native staff have died.
One of the store-houses is a shipwreck museum, a random collection of ghostly lumber. Attwater shows Herrick the island's graveyard – 'a field of broken stones from the bigness of a child's hand
to that of his head' (p. 253) – and quotes 'The rude forefathers of
the hamlet sleep!' This is Stevenson's elegy in a Pacific graveyard.
It is also a further stage in his intermittent musing on the political

question of power and consent. Attwater is responsible for many of the deaths. His treatment of the natives is brutal and arbitrary, and we learn that there has been an unsuccessful mutiny on the island. Attwater is a modern Prospero whose ambition, the collection of pearls, is economic rather than intellectual, and whose power is bullets rather than magic. In this he typifies the modern imperialist.

Stevenson had witnessed the arbitrary nature of imperial rule in Samoa as *The Ebb-Tide* was being written, and McLynn suggests that it expresses the destruction of his hopes for a Samoa ruled by Mataafa.[54] In fact the most naked example of absolute power Stevenson had seen in the Pacific was that exercised by Tembinok on Apemama. Part 4 of *In the South Seas* is dominated by Tembinok and Stevenson's fascination with his rule is palpable. Although his people live and work 'at the constant and the instant peril of their lives', life proceeds in an orderly and sober manner 'as in a model plantation under a model planter'. And yet as Stevenson admires 'this triumph of firm rule' he is troubled by a problem he thinks will concern western societies in the future: 'Here was a people protected from all serious misfortune, relieved of all serious anxieties, and deprived of what we call our liberty. Did they like it? and what was their sentiment towards the ruler?'[55] It was clear they did not like it at all, and Stevenson began to worry about the safety of his party in the event of Tembinok being assassinated. He nevertheless continued to admire the autocratic rule of the King of Apemama. By the time of *The Ebb-Tide*, however, and no doubt influenced by events in Samoa, absolute power has became lethal and insane. Attwater, emphasizing his ability as a marksman, compares himself to Tembinok ('There was an old king one knew in the western islands' (p. 258)), but he is Tembinok shorn of illusion and the 'model plantation under a model planter' has become a hell on earth. When the kind of power wielded by the native king is transferred to a European the result is horrifying.

Attwater himself is a misanthropist and a religious fanatic, a disturbing compound of opposites around whom a recurring pattern of blinding light (his clothes) and forbidding shade (his house) is concentrated. Stevenson's instruction to his illustrator was explicit: 'Attwater's settlement is to be entirely overshadowed everywhere by tall palms.'[56] Herrick, to whom Attwater is drawn in a familiar Stevensonian doubling, confesses his despair and self-contempt.

He is first offered God's mercy-seat ('He spread out his arms like a crucifix; his face shone with the brightness of a seraph's' (p. 255)) and then, when Herrick makes clear his atheism, upper-class rudeness ('the dark apostle had disappeared; and in his place there stood an easy, sneering gentleman, who took off his hat and bowed' (p. 256)). This confrontation on the beach between a cruel fanatic and a despairing nihilist is emblematic: *The Ebb-Tide* offers no other ground on which to stand. Everyone, in Herrick's words, is 'going to hell in their own way' (p. 276). Unable to drown himself, fighting for life even as he wishes to be rid of it, Herrick realizes, 'He must stagger on to the end with the pack of his responsibility and his disgrace' (p. 277). He is inescapably free, implacably confronted with the consequences of his actions for the duration of his life. And what better setting in which to realize the enormity of this than on a small coral island in an apparently boundless ocean with a mad patriarch and an abject penitent (Davis has been converted and Huish killed). The *Farallone* has burnt and sunk in the lagoon and Attwater's own schooner, the *Trinity Hall*, is approaching as the story closes. Herrick, one assumes, will get away, but the name of the boat on which he depends does not promise well for an Oxford man.

Placing Herrick in a tradition stretching back to Fletcher Christian suggests other parallels between *The Ebb-Tide* and the story of the *Bounty*. It is not only Stevenson's restless, morbid, déclassé hero cut off from England and drifting in hell who suggests aspects of the *Bounty* story. Attwater, the religious zealot and stern patriarch of a 'scarce-believed in' island (p. 236) whose population has been decimated, also suggests John Adams and his group on Pitcairn. The two main characters of Stevenson's story divide, just as the *Bounty* story itself does, into the escape from law and obligation on the one hand, and its restoration on the other. In *The Ebb-Tide* however, the split is exaggerated, even parodied. Herrick is Christian shorn of his radical and romantic associations, enfeebled and pathetic; Attwater's patriarchalism is an insane, fascistic version of Adams'. By deflating one figure and inflating the other, rendering both as pictures of horror, Stevenson creates the kind of impasse which *The Ebb-Tide* dramatizes at every level of its narrative.[57]

To many of his friends, Stevenson became a version of the estranged and marooned anti-hero himself. As it became clear that he would never return from Samoa, there was dismay among his closest circle. Colvin thought it meant that Stevenson would be 'lost so far as keeping the powers of his mind and doing work goes',[58] a view shared by his London friends who were never much interested in his Pacific writing. By the beginning of 1892, after a year in which his writing had been entirely on Pacific themes, their fears must have seemed confirmed. In typical manner Stevenson's close male friends blamed Fanny for this apparent retreat from the obligations of the civilized social world. Some of the disrepute of the runaway began to attach itself to Stevenson, a prime source for this being the patrician Boston historian Henry Adams who had visited Vailima at the end of 1890 and reported with distaste the scene he confronted:

A two-storey Irish shanty . . . squalor like a railroad navvy's board hut . . . a man so thin and emaciated that he looked like a bundle of sticks in a bag, with . . . dirty striped cotton pyjamas, the baggy legs tucked into coarse woollen stockings, one of which was bright brown in colour, the other a purplish dark tone . . . a woman . . . [in] the usual missionary nightgown which was no cleaner than her husband's shirt and drawers, but she omitted the stockings . . . her complexion and eyes were dark and strong, like a half-breed Mexican.[59]

Adams viewed Stevenson rather as Wiltshire had contemplated Randall, and his account reeks of the term 'white trash'. In typically Romantic and patronizingly nativist terms he ranked the Stevensons, with heavy irony, below the Samoans: 'Our visit was as full of queerities as any social experiment I can recall, and in contrast to our visits to the natives, with their ease and grace of manner, their cleanliness and generosity of housekeeping, and their physical beauty, it gave me an illuminating sense of the superiority of our civilization.'[60]

Adams, like the lawyer Utterson in *Dr Jekyll and Mr Hyde*, broke through the 'red baize door' of respectability and was appalled by the disorder of otherness and creation he discovered. Different versions of the itinerant were, of course, possible. Edmund Gosse declared Stevenson's exile to be the most 'picturesque' since Byron was in Greece, and John Addington Symonds, inverting the beachcomber myth of Stevenson, criticized him for failing to live with and like the natives.[61] These different responses derived from a similar inability to understand the nature of Stevenson's life and writing in Samoa, and a failure to comprehend that the world he inhabited there was quite as much a social world as their own.

At least Stevenson's writing on Samoan politics interested and concerned the Foreign and Colonial Offices.[62] His literary work based on or using Polynesian material found almost no audience in Britain or the United States. This was particularly true of *Ballads* (1890), as Stevenson's letters confirm,[63] but there was little enthusiasm for his Polynesian tales either. He planned two separate volumes of this writing. The first was to consist entirely of South Sea ballads, the second of South Sea tales, but in the event both projects were diluted. *Ballads* was fleshed out with several Highland legends and at least one of the poems intended for the volume, 'The House of Tembinoka', was not published until the posthumous *Songs of Travel* (1895). The volume of tales, *Island Nights Entertainments*, included 'The Beach of Falesá' against Stevenson's express wishes: 'The B. of F. is *simply not* to appear along with "The Bottle Imp", a story of totally different scope and intention, to which I have already made one fellow, and which I design for a substantive volume.'[64] This, and the long rearguard action he fought against such a volume, make it clear that his writing derived from Polynesian material and forms was attempting something quite new.

Most importantly, Stevenson was feeling his way towards a Polynesian as well as a western audience. Among the recipients of copies of *Ballads* were Ori, sub-chief of Tautira whose house the Stevensons had stayed in during their time on Tahiti, Princess Moe of Tahiti from whom Stevenson had heard the legend on which 'The Song of Rahero' is based, and the Hawaiian King.[65] For the first time in his life Stevenson also had non-western readers in mind. Such readers were more clearly in focus by the time he came to write his tales 'The Isle of Voices' and 'The Bottle Imp'. He had noted the popularity of stories in Hawaiian native-language papers and magazines,[66] and written enthusiastically about the missionary Pratt's Samoan translation of Aesop's *Fables*:

simply the best and the most literary version of the fables known to me. I suppose I should except La Fontaine, but L. F. takes a long time; these are as brief as the books of our childhood and full of wit and literary colour; and O Colvin, what a tongue it would be to write, if one only knew it – and there were only readers.[67]

'The Bottle Imp' was an attempt to find, or create, such readers. It was translated into Samoan by Rev. A. E. Claxton who published it in the missionary magazine he edited, *O le Sulu O Samoa* (The Samoan Torch), in serial form during 1891.[68] This paper had a circulation of eleven hundred and Moors claims that it would have found its way into most Samoan homes. He also quotes another missionary on the story's reception: 'it caused no great sensation – not nearly the sensation that the present publication of the Arabian Nights is causing, but a great many used to ask if it were true, for in some respects it is similar to certain Polynesian fables, all of which the islanders believe to be founded on fact'.[69] It appeared almost simultaneously, again in serial form, in the *New York Herald* and the English journal *Black and White*, and was soon translated into Hawaiian as well.[70] John Charlot has argued that in writing 'The Bottle Imp' Stevenson tried to render an impression of Polynesian languages in English. However, the translation was inexpert and according to Charlot the 'prose is more Samoan in English than in Samoan'.[71]

Stevenson was an avid collector of stories, and we have already seen how he bartered stories with his Marquesan and Tahitian hosts. He met other collectors of Polynesian stories,[72] and the Beinecke Collection at Yale has unpublished manuscripts of Tahitian songs and tales that Stevenson transcribed or translated. Two of his versions of Tahitian legends appeared in *Longman's Magazine* in 1892.[73] He also began a story in Samoan about Saxon times called *Eatuina* (Edwin).[74] But Stevenson was no antiquarian; as David Daiches said, 'For Stevenson, history was a setting for the presentation of modern problems.'[75] He was not trying to emulate his fellow-countryman Macpherson and produce a Pacific Ossian reconciling native superstition with polite learning, as the eighteenth-century cult of Ossian has been described. Macpherson constructed an integral text, an identifiable genre and an individual author out of a protean collective tradition in order to represent the Highlands to a western reading public as something heroic but vanished.[76] Stevenson, on the other hand, was fascinated by the intersection of the traditional and the modern, the Polynesian and the European, which the translation of oral tales opened up. Nor was Stevenson trying to emulate New Zealand settler writing such as Alfred Domett's *Ranolf and Amohia* (1872) and project romantic stereotypes on to a 'dying race' while using

Maori culture to help create a national distinctiveness.[77] Although colonized, Samoa was only very thinly a settler society, with little or no sense among its European residents of the need for a distinct national identity. Stevenson's use of Polynesian oral culture was much less self-conscious.

There were serious problems, however, in translating or adapting Polynesian poetry. Although it is commonly assumed that the texts of oral literature vary according to the occasion of performance, this is much less true of Polynesian poetry than of story-telling and oratory.[78] Most Pacific poetry was composed prior to performance, depended on a memorized version and involved a concept of the verbally correct text. Stevenson described 'The Song of Rahero' as a native tale 'of which I have not consciously changed a single feature'.[79] This claim, however, ignored the problem of form. Stevenson adapted the non-classical European form of the ballad, but Charlot argues that its rhythms and long line (his poem is in hexameters) are very unPolynesian, and that Pacific poetry did not narrate a story but alluded to it elliptically; a plot-centred story would be told in prose. 'The House of Tembinoka' with its malleable form, shorter lines and less insistent rhythm was much closer to the native forms Stevenson was becoming interested in. In fact it was expressly related to a native literary genre, the genealogical chant of praise, which did permit a degree of improvisation.[80]

There was greater flexibility in story-telling, however, where the narrator was permitted a more improvisational or creative role. It was here that the composition-in-performance commonly assumed to be characteristic of oral literature in general featured. The western genres of the folk tale and fable were more compatible with Pacific story-telling, and what Charlot calls the Polynesian 'thought-world', than anything in the European poetic tradition.[81] The genre of the tale worked easily and well with native materials, and overlapped with the fable which Stevenson had long been interested in and which he took up again at this time. The plot of 'The Bottle Imp', as far as Stevenson knew, was taken from an early nineteenth-century melodrama. In fact, and appropriately, the story is of Germanic folk origin.[82] 'The Isle of Voices' derived from Hawaiian tales Stevenson had heard and, like 'The Bottle Imp', amalgamated European and Polynesian forms in a manner well suited to its matter.

It is interesting to try and read these tales as colonial allegories. 'The Isle of Voices' is, like Prospero's Isle, 'full of noises . . . and sometimes voices', but in this case the voices cause fear rather than 'give delight and hurt not': 'All tongues of the earth were spoken there: the French, the Dutch, the Russian, the Tamil, the Chinese. Whatever land knew sorcery, there was some of its people whispering in Keola's ear.'[83] In both these tales magic is modern rather than traditional, and associated with material greed. In 'The Isle of Voices' the sorcery referred to is the power of 'Making dollars of sea-shells' (p. 147). The wizard of the story, Kalamake the 'wise man of Molokai', regularly visits the coral atoll of the Isle of Voices on his flying mat where he joins the many others turning sea-shells into dollars. This enables him to satisfy his taste for European goods which the steamer now regularly brings to his island. These visitors are invisible to the native inhabitants of the virtually pre-contact Isle of Voices who lack the knowledge, and the need, to perform such miracles of modern alchemy. When, eventually, they do learn the secret of how shells are converted to money and try to prevent it by cutting down the trees whose leaves bring about the transubstantiation, they are massacred by the strangers they cannot see:

the man-eaters huddled back to back, and heaved up their axes, and laid on, and screamed as they laid on, and behold! no man to contend with them! only here and there . . . an axe swinging over against them without hands; and time and again a man of the tribe would fall before it, clove in twain or burst assunder, and his soul sped howling. (p. 159)

This one-sided encounter recalls early accounts of the Polynesians' first meeting with European firepower: in both cases the source of their destruction is invisible. In similar manner, the making of dollars from sea-shells suggests western economic exploitation of the Pacific islands, here particularly in the setting of the low islands (and remembering *The Ebb-Tide*), the activity of pearl-fishing. This is supported by the tale's consistent identification of supernatural with economic power. Indeed, from the point of view of the natives of the Isle of Voices economic power is supernatural. As their visitors leave, the wealth of the island vanishes: 'these millions and millions of dollars, and all these hundreds and hundreds of persons culling them upon the beach and flying in the air higher and swifter than eagles' (p. 158). Such a reading is further encouraged by the fact that Kalamake, though 'of a pure descent', is completely white. This helps identify him with European economic power. It is as if he has been bleached by his taste for western goods and the need to have the dollars to support his habit; hence his otherwise anomalous presence on the beach of the Isle of Voices.

This reading, however, cannot be wholly sustained. The story is told from the point of view of Keola, Kalamake's idle son-in-law, who learns the wizard's secret and then tries to better him. He is a kind of sorcerer's apprentice who eventually escapes on his father-in-law's flying mat from the dire consequences of his meddling, leaving Kalamake stranded on the Isle of Voices. Against the supernatural logic of the tale, Kalamake will never be able to leave. And against the logic of the imperial allegory, the tale ends happily with Keola restored to his wife. Ultimately the story's different modes and levels fail to mesh. The fantastic, allegorical and realist elements are never resolved and the story ends in realist mode in the modern hybrid world of Hawaii with the supernatural and allegorical elements written out.

In 'The Bottle Imp', possession of the bottle of the title gives its owner whatever he wishes, but to die before selling it is to be damned. Captain Cook is a previous owner, but since his time its price has declined because the bottle must always be sold for less than it was purchased. Keawe, a young Hawaiian visiting San Francisco, is tricked into buying the bottle but then uses it to build himself a wonderful modern house on the cliffs above where the ancient kings of Hawaii are buried. He sells the bottle before discovering that he has contracted leprosy, the 'Chinese Evil', as the story calls it. He then sets out to recover the bottle, this time wittingly risking his soul for the love of Kokua, his young wife. By the time he catches up with it the price has slumped to one cent. He buys back the bottle and cures himself of the leprosy but to sell it again must travel to Tahiti where French currency, with its smaller denominations, operates. After much difficulty the bottle is finally sold to 'an old brutal Haole [European]', part of the human flotsam on the beach of Papeete that Stevenson was to use again in the opening of *The Ebb-Tide*. Convinced he is going to hell anyway, and delighted at the prospect of a never-ending supply of rum for the term of his natural life, this beachcomber makes the final purchase. Keawe and Kokua return to the peace of their Bright House.

Many features of this story are amenable to an anti-colonialist reading as well. The opening scene in which the poor Polynesian is tricked by the wealthy San Franciscan into buying the bottle is typical of later Pacific trading relations. The bottle is then carried from the capitalist world into the Pacific, spreading its economic and cultural influence as it is repeatedly bought and sold. As in 'The Isle of Voices', the magic of the bottle represents the forces of modernization. In 'The Bottle Imp' this process is irresistible and literally soul-destroying. Keawe, in tracking the bottle around Honolulu, follows a trail of new wealth through this rapidly modernizing city. The young European from whom he buys it back has used it to escape punishment for embezzlement. The man's willingness to sell his soul merely to escape the consequences of a modern business crime finally convinces Keawe to risk the same for his wife. The clash of values is quite explicit. The money lust provoked by the bottle imp is a contagion very like the leprosy Keawe has contracted. It is the western rather than the Chinese evil. The law of the bottle itself, however, defies capitalist economics. Although its use value is constant, its market value declines to the point where it becomes unsellable. The tale ends neatly, as such tales should, by reversing its opening transaction: the bottle is sold back to the westerner. This, however, upsets the imperialist allegory. In the end the allegorical meaning of the bottle has to be suspended for the romance plot – Keawe's trial of love – to be happily resolved. 'The Bottle Imp' is better integrated, though not necessarily more interesting, than 'The Isle of Voices', but neither story is finally reducible to colonial allegory.

They can, however, be understood more broadly as exploring and dramatizing the intersection of Polynesian and European worlds. The juxtaposition of the traditional and modern, within Polynesian cultures as much as between them and European ones, is insistent. Keawe's house is built on top of the burial place of the old Hawaiian kings. Kalamake hides his Bible under the cushion of the sofa before taking out the flying mat and charmed necklace which will carry him to the Isle of Voices. At the end of this story Keola and his wife consult the white missionary about the likelihood of Kalamake making his way back from the Isle of Voices. He, of course, disbelieves their story and informs the Honolulu police that they seem to have been counterfeiting money. Keola, in his turn, follows the missionary's advice and makes a contribution to the leper and missionary fund. The story ends with multiplying ironies.

These intersections are also found at the formal level. Both stories mix verisimilitude of detail – descriptions of late nineteenth-century Papeete, items of modern consumer goods and so on – in familiar realist mode, with the fantastic and the supernatural. The languages of trade and magic overlap. Western and Polynesian forms and conventions meet and collide in a kind of imitative form, an enactment of the process the stories describe. Thus seen, the untidiness of 'The Isle of Voices' can be understood partly in terms of the concussive nature of such intersections.

This mixing of forms, and the culturally hybrid texts which result, are not confined to works written with a Polynesian audience in mind. Native forms also entered and affected work clearly written for western readers. 'The Beach of Falesá', for example, is not solely Wiltshire's yarn. It includes two stories told by Uma, one about a group of bewitched young men, the other of her meeting with a spirit in the form of a pig. These are different kinds of yarn from Wiltshire's, and differently told, even if the first tale owes a good deal to the Lotus-eaters (the hero is even called Lotu) and Sirens episodes from the *Odyssey*.[84] Wiltshire's story is stubbornly, even insistently, realist. Uma's stories are fabular and come from a native world that Wiltshire needs to deny. They open up ways of seeing beyond his comprehension and offer a different register for the realism to play against. They express a native way of understanding which leaves that culture vulnerable to someone like Case, and which colonialism will eventually modify, but which 'The Beach of Falesá' includes as a counter-weight to the western yarn and its realist mode. This might help explain why Stevenson was so opposed to including 'The Bottle Imp' and 'The Isle of Voices' in the same volume as 'The Beach of Falesá'. In Wiltshire's yarn, which is very markedly a story about colonialism, the realist mode must win. In the other stories, however, realism must not be allowed to override the fantastic; the delicate balance between them is necessary for their success in dramatizing the intersection of the Polynesian with the European, and the traditional with the modern.

Stevenson's frustration at his correspondents' indifference to *faa-Samoa* (the Samoan way of life) is often apparent. His reply to Colvin's suggestion that he should write less about his 'blacks or chocolates' was terse: 'You must try to exercise a trifle of imagination, and put yourself, perhaps with an effort, into some sort of sympathy with these people, or how am I to write to you?'[85] His very last letter to Colvin developed this point: 'It is the proof of intelligence, the proof of not being a barbarian, to be able to enter into something outside of oneself, something that does not touch one's next neighbour in the city omnibus.'[86] Among the European residents of Hawaii, Tahiti and Samoa it was widely felt that Stevenson 'overestimated the Polynesian race' and let down his own side.[87] His Pacific ballads and tales are clear evidence of his serious interest in Polynesian cultures, but more significant is their attempt to look two ways and include two readerships. They try to catch in print the exchange and mixing of stories which characterized his time in every Pacific island he visited. Their main interest is not antiquarian, nor are they versions of the Romantic organicism typical of the colonialist appropriation of native cultures, although no doubt elements of both these things find their way into Stevenson's rendering of this material. In producing textual hybrids intended to be read in Scotland or Samoa he was also dramatizing the process of enculturation in the Pacific at the end of the nineteenth century. This included the colonial penetration of native cultures, but his ballads and tales are more than just allegories of this process. They are also a testament to the vitality of Polynesian cultures, assertions that these are alive and active, capable of answering back and influencing the European forms and values which will modify but not obliterate them.

The contradictions in Stevenson's position are too obvious to need labouring. They were also unavoidable. His ballads and tales were a fascinating experiment whose success or failure seems less important than the attempt itself. In many ways they anticipate the South Pacific literature in English which emerged almost a hundred years later in the 1970s and 80s. If Conrad's *Heart of Darkness* provided African novelists with a founding text against which to write back, Stevenson's tales and ballads, and his use of tales in 'The Beach of Falesá', offered Pacific writers a less antagonistic model to work on.

CHAPTER 7

Skin and bones: Jack London's diseased Pacific

The legible evidence of western diseases on blemished native bodies haunted writing about the Pacific from the early moments of contact. Wherever Cook returned he found signs of his previous landfall on the inhabitants' bodies, and all his efforts at controlling spread of 'the Venereal' were nugatory. As Captain Clerke reflected on leaving Kealakekua Bay, it was not just their commander they left behind: 'Captain Cook did take such preventive methods as I hop'd and flatter'd myself would prove effectual . . . but our Seamen are in these matters so infernal and dissolute a Crew that for the gratification of the present passion that affects them they would entail universal destruction upon the whole of the Human Species.'[1] Not only did the cycle of infection and reinfection produced by Cook's many landfalls in the course of three voyages threaten the good order of his ships, but its physical symptoms were a palpable sign of the contaminating power of European civilization. They rebuked the explorer for his intrusion and contradicted the purity of his intentions.[2]

At the heart of the European paradise of the South Pacific, therefore, a counter-discourse of the diseased Pacific began almost simultaneously. Western valorization of the Polynesian body augmented the significance of any blemish to its surface, and these blemishes were most frequently ascribed to sexual causes. In fact the worst forms of venereal disease were mainly avoided. The endemic island disease of yaws gave immunity to syphilis, whose symptoms it resembled. Cook and later visitors often confused the two. Yaws was also described by Cook as a sort of 'leprous' complaint, another significant confusion.[3] The Hawaiian islands, however, lacking yaws, had nothing to hold back syphilis. They were also, by the second half of the nineteenth century, the main centre of leprosy in the Pacific.

The native population of Hawaii fell from around a quarter of a million to about fifty thousand in the first hundred years of European contact. Many of the diseases responsible for this decline, such as smallpox, measles and venereal disease, attacked the surface of the body, and the last of these to reach the islands, leprosy, was visually the most horrifying.[4] It also carried a social and moral stigma stretching back to the Old Testament. Leprosy, or Hansen's Disease as it is now more properly called, was known in the Hawaiian islands from about 1840 and was popularly believed to have been introduced by the Chinese; hence its original native name of *mai Pake*, the Chinese disease. Although it must have arrived on European ships there were few cases of European infection, and it came to be seen as a largely native affliction. From 1865 lepers were kept in isolation at a specially created colony on the island of Molokai. At first they were simply abandoned, but from the arrival of Father Damien in 1873 the colony was slowly transformed into a well-ordered community with proper food, housing and medical care. It became a magnet for late nineteenth-century traveller-writers, and for some in Europe, a model of colonialism at its best. In the Hawaiian islands, however, it was decades before the segregation policy showed any sign of controlling the spread of leprosy. While Europeans feared that the Hawaiian people were in danger of becoming a nation of lepers, Hawaiians themselves resisted the segregation policy and were quite prepared to shelter those who contracted the disease. Many unaffected Hawaiians faced with the exile of friends or relatives even chose to live with them on Molokai as *kokua* (helpers). Medicine and disease control have often been used as an instrument of colonial authority, and native resistance to segregation was the expression of a muted but nevertheless stubborn refusal to be regulated.

This apparent indifference to the disease added to European anxieties about its transmission. Hansen's identification of the leprosy bacillus in the early 1870s established that the disease was contagious, not hereditary as had often been believed. This undermined the belief in western immunity. The apparent randomness of its incidence was also a cause of unease. Damien, who eventually contracted leprosy, had put himself at risk but the case of the North American Honolulu merchant and his wife whose three children caught it was altogether more disturbing. In such a climate, theories about the disease flourished. Diseases have often been understood as judgements on a community, and as Susan Sontag has argued, those in which the causation is mysterious offer the best possibilities as metaphors for what is felt to be socially or morally wrong.[5]

During the 1870s and 80s leprosy in Hawaii was increasingly moralized as a just punishment for a corrupt and diseased society. The root of the disease came to be seen as indigenous and was located in the promiscuous sexuality of the culture. More than half a century of missionary influence had failed to discipline Hawaiian libidos and, particularly among the Protestant establishment of Honolulu, sexuality, like leprosy, was regarded as a contagion. There was even a local scientific theory which coupled them. In the 1880s a government physician developed a theory of leprosy as a fourth stage of syphilis which was influential in Protestant circles, and lay behind the allegations of sexual impropriety made against Father Damien to which Stevenson wrote a famous reply.[6] There are, of course, notable examples within western literature of the association of leprosy with syphilis and plague: Henryson's *Testament of Cresseid* is an early example, and Somerset Maugham's fictional treatment of Gauguin, *The Moon and Sixpence* (1919), substitutes leprosy for syphilis as the painter's cause of death. Epidemics are a common figure for social disorder, and leprosy in late nineteenth-century Hawaii conforms exactly to the process described by Sontag whereby feelings about evil are first projected on to a disease, and then the disease as metaphor is projected on to the world, becoming adjectival. With its murky causality, and the lack of an effective treatment, leprosy was awash with significance. The ideological advantage of sexualizing it was obvious. By linking desire and disease the retributions of pleasure were made horrifyingly visible; exaggerating the danger of contagion made all human touch suspect and expelled desire. Following the Hawaiian loss of effective self-government in 1887 the administration of the segregation laws was tightened, and increased United States influence was represented as bringing Hawaiian culture in general, and leprosy in particular, under firmer control.

The sexualization of leprosy was a projection of deep anxieties, and the figure of the leper became a social text on which the history of contact was inscribed. It is understandable, therefore, that Father Damien should have provoked such contradictory responses. In England he became a minor cult figure, and at his death in 1889 *The Times* carried a leader in which he was used to exemplify the benefits of imperialism for non-European peoples. In Honolulu he was a far more ambiguous figure, disliked by the Protestant establishment and often viewed with suspicion by his own superiors. Damien had transgressed those social and psychological boundaries which defined and structured the world of late nineteenth-century colonizers in these islands. He bridged the worlds of European and Hawaiian, clean and unclean, saint and sinner, imperialist and native. From a distance he could be reconstructed as an ideal type of the benevolent imperialist, but he made it impossible for those actually on the beach to deny the consequences of their presence. It was this which attracted traveller-writers like Charles Warren Stoddard, Stevenson and Jack London. Damien had unselfconsciously made the crossing that they approached with fascinated apprehension.

Leprosy was also causing anxiety in the metropolitan centres. Long expelled from Europe, it now threatened to return with the spread of western imperialism. It was feared that the world-wide movement of trade and labour of the late nineteenth century would create a 'free trade in disease', and that leprosy would find its way home to Europe to avenge the colonized in a kind of bacteriological writing-back. This was a fear of the reverse invasion of the body. In the very process of taking control of native bodies the colonialist was in danger of being similarly overrun. Such mirroring has haunted modern colonialism. Books like Henry Press Wright's *Leprosy: An Imperial Danger* (1889) began to appear. And the disease had rich metaphoric possibilities not only as a way of expressing the innate corruption of indigenous cultures, but also for describing the damaging effects of imperialism itself. Derek Walcott was not the first to use 'the leprosy of empire' ('Ruins of a Great House') in this sense. It offered critics of imperialism a powerful cluster of images with which to express their disquiet.

Molokai was also a publishing opportunity. The fascinated horror with which the west responded to the renewed threat of leprosy ensured an audience for the copy provided by Pacific traveller-writers. Charles Warren Stoddard published accounts of the two visits he made to Molokai, and fictionalized the experience in a nasty little story of leprosy and homosexuality.[7] Stoddard's work was known to Stevenson, who spent a week at the colony in 1889 and wrote a lengthy account of his stay which was serialized in the New York *Sun* in 1891. His better-known piece of writing on the settlement was the famous attack on the unbelievably named Rev. Dr Hyde for his slander of Father Damien. Fanny Stevenson also used a leprosy plot in a bizarre story 'The Half-White', published in *Scribner's Magazine* in 1891. This brought together western horror of the disease, the theory of its hereditary nature, and the idea that mixed-race individuals were a bridge for its transmission in the story of a Catholic priest whose involvement with a young 'half-white' girl threatens to go beyond the pastoral. Its denouement is the discovery that the priest has leprosy and must be quarantined on Molokai; the young girl is thereby saved from the analogous segregation of the convent. The figure of the priest inevitably suggests Father Damien, and the whole story sits very oddly alongside Stevenson's angry defence of him.[8] Jack London, in his turn, made the forty-mile crossing from Honolulu to the leper colony and recorded his stay in *The Cruise of the Snark*, initially a series of articles commissioned by *Harper's*. His wife Charmian Kittredge was also to record an account of their visit in her book *Jack London and Hawai'i*. London went on to write a number of leper stories which I shall come to in a moment.

First, a brief word on Stevenson's visit. Initially he was seized with shame at being there, 'useless and a spy', his writing insufficient excuse for such 'gross intrusion'.[9] Contact with the residents overcame this feeling. When he met a woman who at first mistook him for a leper and then regretted that he wasn't, Stevenson began to realize that the inhabitants did not share his own horror at the disease and at the place. From out of their abnormal state a different norm had arisen in which patients and helpers alike 'half forget the habits of a healthy world'. And why not? Life in 'this marred and moribund community' includes love, marriage, outdoor sports and music; work is available but entirely voluntary. Molokai momentarily sounds like the last hideout of Polynesia, paradoxically untouched. Stevenson concluded, lapsing into the metaphor which leprosy always seemed to prompt, 'There are Molokai's everywhere.'[10] These uneasy attempts to bridge the worlds of the clean and the unclean were undermined, however, by the fear of infection. Leprosy threatened the very existence of the island race and, perhaps, his own: 'To our own syphilis we are inured, but the syphilis of eastern Asia slays us; and a new variety of leprosy, cultivated in the virgin soil of Polynesian races, might prove more fatal than we dream.'[11]

When Jack London and Charmian Kittredge visited the colony in 1906 they made more of Stevenson's passing emphasis on the harmony of the community on Molokai. In fact, it was more or less a condition of the visit that they present a favourable picture. Permission was granted by the Honolulu Board of Health, which managed the island, in the hope that London would write favourably of its segregation policy. His account in *The Cruise of the Snark* begins festively with a description of the sports and entertainments he witnessed on the Fourth of July, at which 'nearly a thousand lepers were laughing uproariously at the fun'.[12] Molokai is a 'democracy of affliction and alleviation' (p. 101), a thriving community of churches, assembly halls, a bandstand, a race-track, a shooting range, an athletics club and two brass bands, set in a climate even more delightful than Honolulu. Inhabitants found to be clean, and therefore free to return to their homes, are often unwilling to leave. Not only are the conditions on Molokai preferable to those in the cities of the United States or Britain: 'I have seen the Hawaiians living in the slums of Honolulu, and having seen them, I can readily understand why the lepers, brought up from the Settlement for re-examination, shouted one and all, "Back to Molokai!"' (p. 110). London develops Stevenson's idea of Molokai as the paradise that most of Hawaii has ceased to be. Far more than a sanctuary for lepers, it has become a flawed remnant of the hedonistic communities that once typified Polynesian culture. What is left of that original culture of ease is now discernible only in its abodes of disease; elsewhere it has disappeared. Seen in this way, segregation works to protect the diseased from the civilized. Charmian Kittredge's parallel account of the Fourth of July celebrations is even more explicit:

The whole was a picture of old Hawaii not to be found elsewhere in the whole territory, and certainly nowhere else in the world. For no set reproduction of the bygone customs could equal this whole-souled exhibition, costumed from simple materials by older women who remembered days of the past, carried out in the natural order of life in one of the most beautiful spots in the islands, if not on the globe.[13]

London's leprosy stories were collected in the volume *The House of Pride and Other Tales of Hawaii* (1912), although they had already appeared in magazines. In these stories London, free of any pressure to justify the segregation policy, dramatizes western horror of the disease, and also uses it as an image of the dismembering and putrefying effects of colonialism. They offer a very different picture from that painted in *The Cruise of the Snark*, and Kittredge records how the stories were resented in Hawaii and accused of losing tourist trade for the islands.[14]

In 'Good-By Jack', the eponymous hero and the narrator visit the wharf in Honolulu where a boatload of lepers is departing for Molokai.[15] Jack defends the segregation policy and expresses his belief in the virtual immunity of white men to the disease. The narrator's eye, meanwhile, is caught by a beautiful young Polynesian woman about to embark: 'pure Polynesian . . . descended from old chief stock'. She is Lucy Mokunui, 'the Hawai'ian Nightingale', a noted singer. As he watches her embark she becomes the emblem of a dying people. This is a familiar elegiac representation of Polynesian culture, implying, as in *The Cruise of the Snark*, that Molokai, though contaminated and dying, is ideal in its flawed way. Honolulu, by contrast, is no longer Polynesia at all but any western capitalist city. Jack has not seen the woman, but as the boat pulls away she cries out to him, '"Good-by Jack!"' . . . 'Never was a man overtaken by more crushing fear. He reeled . . . his face went white to the roots of his hair, and he seemed to shrink and wither away inside his clothes' (p. 119). The description of Jack Kersdale's response mimics the disease he suddenly fears he has contracted. The story ends with him driving helter-skelter to the diagnostic centre for a bacteriological test. The emblematic departure of Lucy has metamorphosed into a dramatization of western fears of leprosy. Her cry of 'Good-by Jack!' suddenly reverses the story's point of view, as its central character (who bears the name of its author) rushes off to be tested.

Jack responds to Lucy's infection as if it is a sexually transmitted disease, and the story, in making this connection, draws on the previously discussed tradition of sexualizing leprosy. This is underlined by an earlier scene on to which the horror of leprosy is displaced proleptically. Its ostensible purpose is to demonstrate Jack's courage. In it he recovers a seven-inch centipede which has fallen from the rafters into a woman's hair. The description is flesh-crawling and sexualized:

The centipede, seven inches of squirming legs, writhed and twisted and dashed itself about his hand, the body twining around the fingers and the legs digging into the skin and scratching . . . It bit him twice . . . I saw him in the surgery five minutes afterward, with Doctor Goodhue scarifying the wounds and injecting permanganate of potash. The next morning Kersdale's arm was as big as a barrel, and it was three weeks before the swelling went down. (p. 113)

Although the scene offers an apparent contrast with Jack's collapse into fear at the end of the story, its connections with the story's climax are more interesting. His hand enters the woman's hair 'as gayly as if it had been a box of salted almonds' (which sounds like one of Bessie Smith's single-entendre similes) and withdraws clutching an outsize wormy bacillus which bites. Both this and the final scene end with Jack rushing off to the doctor.

'The Sheriff of Kona' dramatizes a similarly appalled fascination with leprosy. Its hero, Lyte Gregory, is another of London's muscular culture-heroes: 'of straight American stock, but . . . built like the chieftains of old Hawaii'. His story is given by a friend, Cudworth, to the anonymous narrator many years after the events described. Gregory is discovered to have 'the mark of the beast'. In fact he is exposed by a disreputable *hapa-haole* (half-caste) who has relatives on Molokai and recognizes the signs. As with Fanny Stevenson's story, the mixed-race figure is a disturbing one in narratives of disease. In 'The Sheriff of Kona' pure stock is exposed by mixed stock, and the white superman is felled by a 'native' disease. Exiled to Molokai, Lyte is rescued by Cudworth and other friends. The leper colony, apparently, is a natural quarantine for Hawaiians but not for westerners. In a bizarre nocturnal adventure Cudworth wrestles with one of the lepers, whose face is momentarily caught by a lantern:

It was not a face – only wasted or wasting features – a living ravage, noseless, lipless, with one ear swollen and distorted, hanging down to the shoulder. I was frantic. In a clinch he hugged me close to him until that ear flapped in my face. Then I guess I went insane . . . I began striking him with my revolver . . . just as I was getting clear he fastened upon me with his teeth. The whole side of my hand was in that lipless mouth. Then I struck him with the revolver butt squarely between the eyes, and his teeth relaxed. (p. 133)

Cudworth's hand now looks 'as if it had been mangled by a dog', but he has survived the assumed, though unverified, risk period of seven years without the disease incubating. Gregory, meanwhile, lives in Shanghai (returning the disease to its 'source') where there is no segregation policy. 'The Sheriff of Kona' is an extreme

example of western fears of leprosy and terror at its failure to discriminate between races. The story's terror is concentrated in the
leper's bite, which is dramatically equivalent to the bite of the
centipede in 'Good-By Jack'. It translates into a violent urge to
invade the lepers' sanctuary, smash it up, and rescue its western
victims, thereby implementing a different kind of segregation
policy. This, of course, is entirely at odds with the idea of Molokai
as the last refuge of an original Polynesian world. Intensifying the
fear is uncertainty about the mechanics of transmission. The cause
of Gregory's infection is never made explicit. Cudworth's infection, on the other hand, seems inevitable yet does not happen.
Fear and loathing are inflamed by this unpredictability, as the story
must include the possibility of Cudworth's infection at some future
time. The tripartite separation of its conclusion, with the native
lepers on Molokai, Gregory in Shanghai, and Cudworth in the
lotus land of Kona ('Where each day is like every day, and every
day is a paradise of days'), is desperately insecure.

Another way of understanding this story is by reference to
Kristeva's notion of the 'abject body'. She argues that the maintenance of the symbolic order, which I shall take as referring to both
the individual psyche and the social system, depends on a delimita-
tion of the 'clean and proper' body. The abject body challenges
this order, attesting to its provisional nature and demonstrating
the impossibility of a clear division between the clean and the
unclean, order and disorder. This body in revolt is something the
symbolic order can neither accept nor deny. Its most horrifying
manifestation is the corpse, which is almost universally surrounded by taboos and rituals to prevent contamination of the
living. The corpse is 'a border that has encroached upon everything . . . It is death infecting life . . . something rejected from
which one does not part.'[16] The putrefying but lascivious body of
the leper also, and vividly, transgresses the boundary between life
and death. As a living corpse, decomposing while it continues to
reproduce, it is a mordant example of Kristeva's category of the
abject. The western symbolic order as it was being imposed in
Hawaii required that lepers should be expelled and quarantined.
The indigenous culture, with its different understanding of the
relation between life and death, did not share this dread and need;
hence the resistance to segregation. Anxiety about leprosy's
indifference to racial hierarchies, medical categories and the

segregation policy animate 'The Sheriff of Kona' and can be seen as a particular and graphic example of the fear of the abject body in a colonial setting.

These anxieties are also present in 'Koolau the Leper', but here the point of view is reversed. A leper band makes its last stand against deportation to Molokai in the mountain passes of Kauai. This time we are with the hunted as they are tracked down by armed native police led by 'a blue-eyed American'. The story is also very differently contextualized. It opens with a native account of the history of settlement as a story of dispossession, and leprosy as one of its consequences. The physical decay of the lepers is presented as an image of the effects of colonization on native cultures. This is made explicit by mingling descriptions of human disfigurement with those of indigenous natural beauty and memories of an earlier way of life: 'One, whose bloated ear-lobe flapped like a fan upon his shoulder, caught up a gorgeous flower of orange and scarlet and with it decorated the monstrous ear that flip-flapped with his every movement' (p. 136). Here a traditional form of decorating the body survives grotesquely. As the soldiers assemble on the beach below, these leprous remnants of a pre-contact world drink and dance until 'their brains were maggots crawling of memory and desire'. One of the women weeps perpetual tears from the 'twin pits' where her eyes have been eaten away.

The whole opening scene is a lament for a dispossessed and putrefying people. Until the arrival of the soldiers they have managed to survive, precariously, as a community. Under Koolau's leadership they have created a garden in the wild in their mountain stronghold, cultivating arrowroot, taro, melons and papaia. The soldiers storm this fallen Eden. Koolau kills them one by one as they attempt to cross the narrow ridge separating the outlaw colony from the advancing line of soldiers. The colony is then shelled from the beach. One of its number is left 'in shattered fragments', the invaders completing in an instant the otherwise slow disintegration of leprosy. Trees splinter and blossom rains down on the sheltering lepers. Shattered bodies and wrecked nature combine in a horrifying jam.

Victory belongs to 'the inevitable white man', a recurring phrase in London's writing and the title of a later Pacific story. Koolau marvels at the 'terrible will of the *haoles* [Europeans]':

Though he killed a thousand, yet would they rise like the sands of the sea and come upon him, ever more and more. They never knew when they were beaten. That was their fault and their virtue. It was where his own kind lacked. He could see, now, how the handful of the preachers of God and the preachers of Rum had conquered the land. (pp. 147–8)

Koolau alone refuses to surrender, remaining free until he no longer has fingers with which to pull the trigger of his Mauser. He then lies down to die, dreaming of his 'whole-bodied youth', the gun pressed against his body. Koolau's resistance is heroic but futile. His refusal to be exiled on Molokai merely hastens his end. Once more the leper is a figure of the inevitable extinction of the culture of the colonized. Resistance is heroic but can only accelerate the process.

This story is based on an episode from Hawaiian history which had been published in Hawaiian by John Sheldon (Kahikina Kelekona), who heard it from Koolau's wife Pi'ilani in 1906.[17] In 1893 Koolau was found to have *ma'i ho'okawale* (the separating sickness, as it had now become termed in Hawaiian), but would agree to go to Molokai only if his wife and son could accompany him. Refused permission, the three took refuge in an isolated valley on Kauai. At the first attempt to take him, Koolau shot and killed the local sheriff.[18] Soldiers were then sent in but the three escaped and some soldiers were killed. Unlike London's story, the soldiers retreated whenever one of their number was shot, and eventually gave up pursuit altogether. For two years the outlaws lived hidden in a valley until first the child, and then Koolau, died of their disease. Pi'ilani then returned to her home.

The obvious difference between the original story and London's is Pi'ilani's emphasis on leprosy as 'the separating disease'. London sees leprosy as a thing of horror in itself; Pi'ilani sees it as the cause of a worse horror, the forced separation of Koolau from his wife and child. There is no fear of contracting the disease in her story. As her son dies she puts his arms round her neck and rubs his cheek against hers. There are no physical descriptions of the course of the disease. Nothing more vivid than stomach pains and weakness in the limbs is described. Pi'ilani's attitude to leprosy seems to have been typical of native feeling. In the area where they went into hiding it was reported that 28 lepers were living among a population of 120; dishes, bedding and clothing were happily shared until disfigurement became extreme. The tragedy of

Pi'ilani's story is the attempt to strip her husband of his identity. The tragedy of London's is the erosion of the body, seen as a figure for the larger erosion of a culture. For Koolau and Pi'ilani, leprosy meant their forced removal from the world which defined them. From London's point of view, Pi'ilani's story might have seemed sentimental. Certainly his use of leprosy as a trope for colonialism is politically resonant. It leads, however, to the triumph of the 'inevitable white man' and the heroic, but futile and solitary, 'guns in the afternoon' finale of his version. Pi'ilani's narrative seems entirely personal and familial, but her emphasis on the 'separating sickness' is no less political than London's more recognizable but defeated anti-colonialist rewriting.

Leprosy can also be understood in terms of the significance of the skin and body in Polynesian culture. Skin is the boundary between the self and others, between the individual and their society. It shields the self from the world and holds in the contents of the body, mediating that traffic between inner and outer worlds which constitutes the individual's sense of selfhood. It expresses the self's inner state and registers the way in which external reality impinges on the self. In Polynesian societies the skin's functions of protection and mediation were traditionally reinforced by the almost universal practice of tattooing which added an extra layer, as it were, to its defensive integument, wrapping, sealing and defending the body against spirits and enemies.[19] Leprosy can be seen as the opposite of tattooing. If tattooing strengthens the skin then leprosy weakens it until it disintegrates. By reinforcing the skin, tattooing encloses and multiplies the person. Leprosy, on the other hand, unwraps the body, strips away its social identity, makes an outside of its inside, and anticipates death through premature decomposition.

At the time of first contact, tattooing was less significant in Hawaiian culture than it was in other Polynesian societies. Gell, following Sahlins, argues that the Hawaiian political system exhibited a precocious modernity in which tattooing became disarticulated from social reproduction and played a much less important role within the total social system. Although immediately after contact Hawaiian tattooing went through a brief efflorescence based on the incorporation of motifs and decorations seen on visiting sailors, it then declined rapidly.[20] It was as if the Hawaiian body was less well protected than other Polynesian bodies against the forces of disease and modernity which attacked its skin. I am speaking partly in metaphor as a way of unfolding the larger cultural significance of leprosy in its relation to colonialism. For Melville, in the 1840s, the rot of civilization in the South Seas was most advanced in Hawaii. London's Hawaiian stories dramatize the way in which this rot had spread to those very Polynesian bodies whose beauty had convinced Bougainville that he had discovered Nouvelle Cythère. And from the Hawaiian point of view, as expressed in Pi'ilani's story, leprosy meant the loss of social and physical identity. The abject tattooed body had been disciplined in the years following conversion to Christianity. Now the abject leprous body must be expelled. As its symptoms appeared the victims were sent into exile from the world which gave them an identity, as a prelude to the loss of physical identity which inexorably followed.

The extinction theme, as we have already seen, was almost simultaneous with the European discovery of Polynesia and had undergone a long and complex history by the time London came to deploy it. His use of an explicit medical scientific discourse was in tune with a more general tendency in the late nineteenth century to formulate social critique in terms of biological theories of decline. Daniel Pick has argued that in this period the body became regarded as a source of knowledge about society rather than simply a rhetorical figure for it, and that social degeneration was discussed as a biological and anthropological fact rather than as an ethical problem.[21] Pick emphasizes that fear of cultural degeneration was and remained a European crisis rather than simply being displaced on to the non-European world.[22] I would add that ideas of degeneration and extinction also originated in Europe's contact with other cultures and were then deflected back from east to west. While agreeing that the fear of degeneration was not expressed solely in terms of a colonial other, there was a mobile and mutually reinforcing shuttling of this fear between two originating sites. In Pacific discourse the apparent decline towards extinction of Polynesian cultures repeatedly prompted the fear of a re-enactment of this process in the west. In the later nineteenth century it was frequently expressed in terms of the infection or contamination of western bodies. In Hawaii this took the specific form of leprosy. In other parts of the Pacific London discovered different diseases.

After leaving the Hawaiian group the *Snark* made the difficult Pacific traverse to the Marquesas. As it anchored in Taiohae Bay on

Nukuhiva London glimpsed the thin trail down which Toby had escaped from the Taipi, and recorded that one of his boyhood resolutions had been fulfilled. Melville's *Typee* had fed London's early dreams of travel and adventure. Now, however, he found what he took to be a dying world. Pure-blooded Marquesans were a rarity, and the extinction of the people was delayed only by the infusion of the blood of other races: 'There are more races than there are persons, but it is a wreckage of races at best. Life faints and stumbles and gasps itself away . . . asthma, phthisis, and tuberculosis flourish as luxuriantly as the vegetation. Everywhere, from the few grass huts, arises the racking cough or exhausted groan of wasted lungs' (pp. 163–4). London journeyed inland to the valley of the Taipi, but Melville's paradise was now a wilderness and all the familiar landmarks of his text had vanished. Only a dozen 'wretched creatures' survived at the heart of paradise and they were afflicted by leprosy, elephantiasis and tuberculosis: 'Life has rotted away in this wonderful garden spot, where the climate is as delightful and healthful as any to be found in the world' (p. 169).

London's explanation for this is exclusively biological. The Taipi were too pure to survive. The white race, on the other hand, survives because it is the descendant of generations of survivors of the war with micro-organisms. Natural selection decrees that 'we who are alive are the immune, the fit – the ones best constituted to live in a world of hostile micro-organisms'. The white race, in fact, flourishes on impurity and corruption while the Marquesans, having undergone no such selection, are doomed to extinction. Their only hope would have been a much larger population with sufficient survivors to lay the foundation for a new race: 'a regenerated race, if a plunge into a festering bath of organic poison can be called regeneration'. This picture of the contaminated basis of race survival through natural selection is intensified by London's awareness of the centuries-old tradition of western representation of the Marquesans as the most physically perfect of all Pacific peoples. He cites Mendana and Cook, and then adds yet another chapter to the long western history of the imminent extinction of the Marquesans. It ends at night with London watching the moon rise over the valley of the Taipi:

The air was like balm, faintly scented with the breath of flowers. It was a magic night, deathly still, without the slightest breeze to stir the foliage; and one caught one's breath and felt the pang that is almost hurt, so exquisite was the beauty of it. Faint and far could be heard the thin thunder of the surf upon the beach. . . . Near by, a woman panted and moaned in her sleep, and all about us the dying islanders coughed in the night. (p. 174)

The elegiacs are familiar, but in London's hand they are under-written by a pronounced medicalization of the discourse of *tristes tropiques*. And the appropriate disease for the loveliest, purest, and hence most fragile of Polynesian peoples is tuberculosis, that most aestheticized and eroticized of nineteenth-century illnesses. In the case of London, however, the romanticism of tuberculosis is tainted by the pseudo-science of eugenics and the social applica-tion of Darwin's biological theories which eugenics sustained.

The juxtaposition of chapters in *The Cruise of the Snark* is less random than might seem. London's account of the dying Marquesas is followed by a tale of European regeneration. This is the story of the Nature Man who greets the *Snark* as it anchors in Papeete harbour, 'a sun-god clad in a scarlet loin-cloth' who comes over the side with gifts of fruit and honey. He was Ernest Darling, who had escaped imminent death from pneumonia and mental breakdown in his native Oregon by heading south to California, Hawaii, and finally Tahiti where he squatted in the wild above Papeete. Reversing the recent history of the Taipi, the Nature Man has regained his health, developed his body and cultivated a plantation of coconut, papaia, mango and breadfruit trees in the Tahitian brush-jungle. This simple-lifer becomes London's alter ego: 'This is the book I write,' he tells London, thumping himself on the chest. After boxing with him London is indeed able to confirm that the book Ernest Darling has written is strongly bound, quite unlike the spineless ninety-pounder given up for dead in Oregon eight years earlier.

This figure of the body as book is a recurring one in writing about the Pacific. Melville uses it repeatedly in *Typee*, particularly in relation to tattooing which, as he thinks, renders the native body as an illustrated book of life. Throughout the nineteenth century Pacific and European bodies are inscribed and reinscribed as cul-tures meet and leave their impression on each other. This book/body metaphor is particularly resonant for London. Not only is the *Snark* kept afloat by the stories and articles he writes, books thereby keeping body and soul together, but as he sails further into the Pacific his own body becomes an inventory and archive of the journey. Increasingly the marks and traces left on his body become the subject of the book he is writing.

At this stage of his journey, however, London is concerned to release a counter-discourse of European health against that of Polynesian disease and extinction. This is launched by the story of the Nature Man and continued through his meeting with a similar figure on Tahaa, another of the Tahitian islands. This is an octogenarian New Englander who more than sixty years earlier had been given only a few months to live. He too has saved his life by leaving the United States and coming to settle in the South Pacific. The patterning is insistent. We are presented with another story of European resurrection in the Pacific, and another myth of colonization in which the westerner grows strong while the Polynesian declines. But even as it is being told the narrative complicates. The old man has elephantiasis, an indigenous ailment which the Pacific inflicts on those who settle. London's counter-discourse of health, incorporating as it does a myth of colonization, is almost simultaneously undermined by the Pacific taking its revenge on the colonizer. This, in turn, prepares the way for London's voyage into the western Pacific which he is to represent as Oceania's own heart of darkness.

The introspection of London's *The Cruise of the Snark* is distinctive. Compared with earlier traveller-writers he has very little interest in native lifeways, or, in this text at least, in the effects of culture contact. His eye is as much on himself as it is on the new worlds he moves through. This had begun in Hawaii where, in trying to emulate 'the man-gods' he had seen surf-riding at Waikiki, London became so badly sunburnt that he was left unable to walk. Kittredge describes foot-long blisters running into one another all over his back and legs. It was thus burnt, peeling, and acutely conscious of his own body that he had visited Molokai. In the western Pacific this self-gaze became obsessed with the sores, ulcers and fevers which attacked his body. The later chapters of *The Cruise of the Snark* are mainly about these irruptions and the attempts to cure them. He confesses, in what must be an understatement, that the rest of the crew came to look on him as 'a sort of mild monomaniac on the question of sores and sublimate'; 'how frail and unstable is human tissue,' London concludes. His fascination with this frailty is illustrated by crew member Martin Johnson's account of how London had him take photos in the

Solomons of two victims of shark attacks, one with his leg bitten off, the other with the flesh stripped from the bone.[23]

It is also vividly apparent in his western Pacific stories included in the collection *South Sea Tales* (1911). In 'Mauki', the eponymous Melanesian hero who keeps escaping from the English company to which he is indentured is finally placed on Lord Howe Island (Ontong Java) under the control of the sadistic Max Bunster, whose main instrument of power is a mitten made of ray fish skin, traditionally used as a wood file in smoothing down canoes and paddles. The first time Bunster uses it on Mauki the skin is fetched off his back from neck to armpit; thereafter the half-healed surface is regularly 'raked raw' by sweeps from the mitten. Mauki awaits his opportunity, and when Bunster is convalescing from an attack of black-water fever takes his revenge. He begins with Bunster's face, sweeping the skin from his nose, forehead and cheeks, and then moves systematically over his body. Eventually, 'a hideous, skinless thing came out of the house and ran screaming down the beach till it fell in the sand and mowed and gibbered under the scorching sun'. Mauki follows and cuts off his head which, dried and cured, is a source of great power when he returns to his native island of Malaita. This gruesome parable of colonialism in the Solomon Islands uses the body, and in particular its cuticle, to dramatize the sadistic nature of economic exploitation in the western Pacific and the savage responses it provokes.

A closely related story from the same collection is 'Yah! Yah! Yah!'. The setting is identical: an atoll ruled over by another petty western despot. His power stems from a previous visit to the atoll by an armed trading vessel which decimated the native population by deliberately introducing measles on to the island. The story is remorseless in its exposure of the basis of western power in this part of the Pacific; as one of the native inhabitants puts it, 'White men are hell.' They are also, however, 'inevitable'; resistance merely increases the dose of terror and intimidation. There is no revenge in this story. Germ warfare attacks the very tissue of native bodies and renders them helpless.

Even the one story of cross-cultural (and same-sex) love in *South Sea Tales*, 'The Heathen', has a similar obsession with microbes, laceration and amputation. It starts on a ship of death infected with smallpox, and ends violently and sentimentally with a shark attack in which the western protagonist has the skin scraped from his arm, and his Polynesian blood-brother sacrifices, first, limbs ('Both hands were off at the wrist, the stumps spouting blood') and then his life to save the European: 'And I could see in his gaze the love that thrilled in his voice.' Whether based on love or hate, relations between westerners and Pacific islanders involve illness and injury, most frequently to the limbs and surfaces of native bodies.

This same instability of human tissue was written all over London's own body by the time he abandoned the cruise of the *Snark*.[24] Apart from the 'inevitable' Solomon sores (yaws), he succumbed to a rectal ulcer (later diagnosed as a double fistula), malaria and finally a condition which looked like leprosy and was probably psoriasis. His hands swelled, the skin peeled off in layers and his arms began to silver. He was forced to go to Sydney, where the fistula was operated on and the yaws treated with an arsenic compound which pitted his skin. The voyage of the *Snark* was over. London's skin, which had burnt and blistered in Hawaii but survived the stay on Molokai, had totally erupted. His own body had become the site on which the metaphors of disease and corruption that he had used to express the effects of western settlement were literalized. The idea of European immunity from the diseased Pacific, which the stories explore so uneasily, had completely broken down. And the infections which attacked his body and penetrated his skin were not, like leprosy, those which had come with European settlement but already there and waiting. In terms of London's own imaginative logic the Pacific, or at least its western darker heart, had taken its revenge.

In *South Sea Tales* (1911) and *The House of Pride* (1912) culture contact in the Pacific is represented as a process of mutual and inevitable infection. The subject is treated with more compassion in the latter volume, mainly because of the Polynesian settings of these stories. In London's stories Polynesian culture has been contaminated by exploration, trade and settlement; Melanesia, on the other hand, is inherently savage, feeding on itself and destroying those who enter its world. One is beautiful but dying; the other indiscriminately ferocious. London's later Hawaiian stories however, collected in *On the Makaloa Mat* (1919), have a very different emphasis. They have historical depth and a more developed indigenous point of view, and they eschew the disease metaphor in their account of cultural interaction. This lessens the fatalism of the earlier stories and allows him to explore the complexities of interaction rather than dramatize its immediate consequences. The possibilities of cultural retrieval are now weighed against the evidence of cultural dissolution. These later stories are concerned with bones rather than skin, with the skeleton of a culture rather than its flesh. Flesh is grass but bones endure. London's new metaphor enables him to explore those aspects of Hawaiian culture which have persisted or are potentially recoverable.

'The Bones of Kahekili' is set in 1880 but it tells of the 1820s, in the immediate aftermath of conversion and settlement. In this and other stories of the collection the secrets and wisdom of old men and women are restored to their traditional place in Hawaiian culture. Two old men talk of the past. One, Hardman Pool, a North American with more than half a century's residence on Hawaii, is still physically powerful and vigorous. Married to a Hawaiian of chiefly rank, and father of fourteen sons and daughters, he has inside as well as outside knowledge of the culture: 'He . . . knew them better than themselves.' The other, Kumuhana, who works for Pool, is withered and feeble. The contrast between the two men reflects the history of Hawaii in the nineteenth century. But Kumuhana has knowledge that his employer lacks. In particular he knows the truth about the bones of Kahekili, the *alii'* (high chief) whose death in 1829 both men remember. The story he tells makes clear the persistence of indigenous customs well after the arrival of the missionaries. Kumuhana himself is living evidence of this, having had his tongue tattooed from root to tip.

On the night of Kahekili's death Kumuhana was chosen as a human sacrifice (*moepuu*) to accompany the *alii'* to the other world. But the burial and sacrifice went wrong. Kumuhana was spared because of the failure to secure a second *moepuu*, and Kahekili's coffin refused to sink in the Molokai Channel because it was constructed by a ship's carpenter who made it completely watertight. The carpenter also left a plate of glass over the dead man's face so that it grinned up at the funeral party from the water, threatening them from another world. In trying to fend off the *alii'* one of the party broke the glass and the coffin finally sank. Kumuhana, alone of living Hawaiians, knows the secret of its resting-place. The story is about the dilution of native traditions.

The use of imported elements like the European coffin result in malfunction. The chiefs themselves fail to produce a second *moepuu*. Yet traditional practices persist, and traces of them, like the markings on Kumuhana's tongue, linger on into the present. And the knowledge that Kumuhana possesses is sought by the most powerful rancher on Hawaii. By combining Hawaiian wisdom with western enterprise Hardman Pool is clearly intended as an emblem of the fruitful grafting of different cultures. Another of London's supermen, he is, however, incomplete without the knowledge preserved in Kumuhana's memory.

The ancestral significance of bones and their problematic relation to modern westernized Hawaii are taken much further in 'Shin Bones'. Its main protagonist, Akuli, is placed very deliberately at the intersection of tradition and modernity. He comes from a 'heaven-boosted' line which can be traced back centuries to the highest title in Polynesia. On the other hand, he is Oxford-educated and has been an officer in the British army. These differences are reflected in his own parents. Hiwilani, his mother, collects the bones of her relatives and ancestors, keeping them in big jars in her bedroom. She has returned to the traditional beliefs of her culture. His father, Kanau, is 'modern to his finger-tips', a sceptic and businessman whose investments are flourishing because of the First World War. He also collects Hawaiian 'curios' but in the totally opposed spirit of the modern museum.

Hiwilani wants the bones of her mother and grandfather reclaimed from the secret burial place of her ancestors. This location is known only to Ahuna, an ancient retainer, who insists that the young Akuli accompany him. The act of retrieval needs a modern helper. Akuli, deep in Jules Verne, cares nothing for bones but agrees to make the journey in return for securing a promise to be sent to Oxford (the story is retrospective). They travel inland together valley by valley, Akuli seeking out the past in order to secure his future. The burial place is yet another underwater cave, that ubiquitous setting of so many Oceanic stories. This one holds all 'the Hawaiian race from the beginning of Hawaiian time'. Akuli's description of the trove to his unnamed auditor is reverently and magnificently detailed. The hitherto sceptical tone of the story changes, although the narrative continues to recall the world in which this quest is incongruously set: 'I saw one of the mamo cloaks that was superior to that finest one in the Bishop

Museum in Honolulu, and that they valued at between half a
million and a million dollars . . . it was lucky Kanau didn't know
about it.'[25]

The bones and other artifacts also tell stories. Akuli is shown a
spear-head made of the shin bone of Keola who was slain for
running away with Laulani, the beautiful wife of another man.
Akuli thinks of Tennyson's *Idyls [sic] of the King*, comparing his fore-
bears to Arthur, Lancelot and Guinevere, and contrasting both
with the tawdriness of the present. Hamlet-like, he ponders the
bones and takes the spear-head with him as a reminder 'that few
men are fortunate enough to have as much of a remnant of themselves as will compose a spear-head when they are three centuries
dead'. He also takes a shin bone of Laulani's. Together they give
him the modesty and humility upon which his life has sub-
sequently been based.

Ahuna, the custodian of *alii'* secrets, is now dead, and Akuli will
die without divulging the location of the cave or returning there.[26]
He has no children and with him the line will cease. As he remarks,
'This is the twentieth century, and we stink of gasolene.' The story
has been told as Akuli and the anonymous narrator wait in the
mountains of Lakanaiito to be picked up after their car has broken
down. In an abrupt juxtaposition characteristic of its telling, the
account of the underwater cave is interrupted by the horn of the
car sent out to recover them, a modern and ironically deflating
form of retrieval.

The cave will retain the secrets whose wider cultural significance
cannot be expressed or realized in the modern world. Akuli is their
last bearer and his act of retrieval has only personal significance.
His visit to the cave has involved, on the one hand, a recognition
that the old Hawaiian world is past, but on the other, a rejection of
the materialist secular culture of his father. This is the double
bind. To bring the bones out into the gasolene stink of the twentieth century would be to have them sold and preserved in a
museum: this is the way of his father. To leave them there is to lose
them for ever: this is the way of his mother. But although Akuli's
quest cannot restore health to his land and people it teaches him
respect for the past and a way of living in the present, even if he is
the end of the line.

The story examines the opposition of tradition and modernity,
and of Polynesia and the west, without wholly conflating these two

sets of antitheses. If Ahuna is the cultural custodian of Hawaii, he has a parallel figure in the drink-sodden Oxford-educated Howard, a Stevensonian character who has introduced Akuli to Tennyson, and travelled with him to England where he died. English and Polynesian romance remain sealed in their respective ancestral caves and the custodian of each dies. Akuli inherits from both a culture rooted in the past which cannot flourish in the modern world.

Finally Akuli is of that modern world, no matter how ruefully. As he tells his story an old Hawaiian woman is making a *lei* (a garland) to hang around the neck of her exalted visitor. This traditional act fills Akuli with horror, and he hopes to be rescued before it is finished. He particularly dislikes its smell although to his *malahini* (newly arrived) companion it is pleasantly exotic. This figure, the narrator, describes the presentation of the *lei* from the perspective of an outsider:

The old wahine had finished her lei . . . with age-withered face and labor-gnarled hands, she cringed before him and crooned a mele in his honor, and, still cringing, put the lei around his neck. It is true the hala smelled most freshly strong, yet was the act beautiful to me, and the old woman herself beautiful to me. My mind leapt into the Prince's narrative so that to Ahuna I could not help likening her. (p. 203)

This appropriately touristic account makes the old woman yet another cultural custodian, again without any purchase on the present. Akuli accepts her gift graciously but for him the ceremony is an unwelcome interruption of his story, and the comparison with Ahuna a *malahini* construction. How can it be otherwise for this 'Prince without a kingdom, his loved island long since annexed by the United States and incorporated into a territory along with the rest of the Hawaiian Islands' (p. 203)? As they are driven back to the coast he throws the *lei* into the thick vegetation by the side of the road. Although the story has explored the possibilities of cultural retrieval it does not allow Akuli to become a mediating figure between past and present. Facing two ways, he is unable to follow either; nevertheless, the present is where he must live.

Both the Londons were convinced that in writing about Polynesians they were describing a dying race. This is repeatedly obvious in their non-fictional writing, and even the new interest in the Hawaiian cultural past of the *On the Makaloa Mat* collection confirms rather than challenges this belief. The dignity of ancient wisdom is necessarily overwhelmed by modern western culture. But a new perspective began to emerge in the very last of London's Pacific writing. In 'My Hawaiian Aloha', three lengthy articles written for *The Cosmopolitan Magazine*, the distaste for 'racial inter-mixing' which often disfigures his earlier writing is transformed into an optimistic view of the Hawaiian 'melting pot' as a 'great experimental laboratory'.[27] Returning to Honolulu in 1915–16 he was struck with how the islands' 'hotch-potch of races' were flourishing. Although still obsessed with the race question, and never very happy with the numerical superiority of the Japanese, he now came to see 'this medley of all the human world' as the model of a new Pacific. He wrote enthusiastically of Alexander Hume Ford's pan-Pacific movement and its belief in a harmonious future for the different ethnic groups which had spread across the region.

This, however, was not a democratic vision. It grew out of London's admiration for the neo-feudal economic relations and social structure of modern Hawaii in which a landowning class of Europeans and Hawaiians, 'knit together by a common interest, by social equality, and, in many cases, by the closer bonds of affection and blood relationship', and assiduous in fulfilling its social and philanthropic responsibilities, controlled a 'coolie and peasant labour' workforce. It was a transracial Carlylean vision of a modern feudal civilization with an increasingly assimilated Polynesian aristocracy as part of its apex. There is little acknowledgement of the extent to which American capital underpinned the whole structure. During his last spell in Hawaii London enjoyed the company of the leisured, often absentee landlords of the large sugar plantations who were doing so well during the war years, and this influenced his account of the promising social experiment he thought Hawaii had become. But his earlier figure of the destructive 'inevitable white man' had not entirely disappeared. Acknowledging that Americans have 'looted' the Hawaiian of his islands, London continued: 'Such things be. They are morally indefensible. As facts they are irrefragable – as irrefragable as the facts that water drowns, that frost bites, and that fire incinerates' (pp. 52–3).

Although London seems to be moving towards some concept of hybridity in these late essays, he certainly does not include the western Pacific in his rich Oceanic melting pot. The idea of the savage fallen Melanesian inhabiting the dark and diseased western Pacific persists in the last stories written in 1916 and collected in *The Red One*. But even here London's Pacific heart of darkness is treated with more complexity. 'The Red One', the title story of the collection and the strangest, most ambitious of his Pacific stories, is especially interesting. Set in the Solomons, on the island of Guadalcanal, it involves an English naturalist, Bassett, who is drawn into the jungle interior of the island by an extraordinary sound emanating from its heart. The sound is described in terms which compress two main European traditions of representing the Pacific, menace and promise: 'it whimpered deadly whispers of wrath and as equally seductive whispers of delight'.[28] Bassett is drawn into a quest to discover the source of the sound and decode the 'cosmic secret' he believes it contains.

Within hours he has fallen prey to the jungle. His servant is decapitated by natives in an attack in which Bassett loses two fingers, adding yet more severed limbs to the trail left by London's Pacific stories ('The Princess' in this same collection contributes several more). Poisoned by insects and shadowed by cannibals, Bassett turns savage, shooting up villages and firing their huts. Sick, wounded and half-mad, he is drawn on by 'the wonderful sound' and eventually discovered by a young native woman, Balatta, who, in a reversed re-enactment of Banks' first meeting with Aboriginals almost a century and a half earlier, rubs the dirt off his arm to reveal 'the pristine whiteness of his skin'. Banks had rubbed the smeared skin of an aboriginal with a wet finger to discover his body colour.[29] The description of Balatta concentrates the simian imagery which is a marked feature of this story: 'A twisted and wizened complex of apish features, perforated by upturned, sky-open, Mongolian nostrils, by a mouth that sagged from a huge upper-lip and faded precipitately into a retreating chin, and by peering querulous eyes that blinked as blink the eyes of denizens of monkey-cages' (p. 972).

Balatta, in yet another version of the white god's narrative, cherishes Bassett who forces himself to have sex with her in order to discover the secret of the wonderful sound. The account of this sexual act is the most extreme example of the social Darwinist modes of description which are consistently applied to the natives in general and Balatta in particular:

He shuddered, but with averted face hid his grimaces and swallowed his gorge as he put his arm around her dirt-encrusted shoulders and felt the contact of her rancid-oily and kinky hair with his neck and chin. But he nearly screamed when she succumbed to that caress so at the very first of the courtship and mowed and gibbered and squealed little, queer, pig-like gurgly noises of delight. It was too much. And the next he did in the singular courtship was to take her down to the stream and give her a vigorous scrubbing. (pp. 978–9)

Apart from the grotesque mutation of the seductive Polynesian female, this passage expresses a fascinated horror with miscegenation in which the difference between ethnic groups is dramatized as a difference between the human – the fastidious scientist who was never much drawn to women even in England – and the animal: the native woman as sheer appetite.

Bassett, however, goes through with it, and not just in pursuit of knowledge. This scene with Balatta is a striking example of what Young has termed colonialism's 'dark fantasy', in which the white male's 'ambivalent axis of desire and repugnance' is enacted in terms which simultaneously construct the native woman as both a sexual object and deeply repellent.[30] However desperately the story attempts to establish absolute boundaries between its antitheses – European and Melanesian, man and woman, science and magic, all of which are subsumed under the fundamental opposition of civilization and savagery – it shows repeatedly and obsessively that such binaries are unsustainable. Even the names Bassett and Balatta loosely echo each other. In this 'The Red One' has much in common with London's leprosy stories. Balatta is another version of the abject body, and Bassett's relation to her is homologous with that of Cudworth and his leprous assailant in 'The Sheriff of Kona'. She will even bite Bassett later in the story, although this assault is presented more sympathetically than the attack that Cudworth experiences on Molokai. The abject body, leper or savage, always bites back; the colonial subject refuses to be contained.

The story's affirmations, therefore, are constantly shadowed by their opposite. This is particularly so in the way its evolutionary assumptions and language are challenged, and finally overwhelmed, by involution. The wonderful sound emanates from a perfect sphere two hundred feet in diameter, like a massive red pearl, resting in an enormous pit carpeted with discarded gods and the bones of human sacrifices. Bassett recalls Mendana's belief that he had found the fabled mines of King Solomon in these islands, but the story makes clear that the origins of this fabulous object are stellar. Bassett regards it as the product of 'intelligences remote and unguessable', a 'colossal portent of higher life from within the distances of the sidereal universe'. Immediately this prompts another catalogue of regression imagery as he reflects on the cosmic irony of 'this wonderful messenger' falling into such a place to be 'worshipped by ape-like, man-eating and head-hunting savages': 'It was as if God's Word had fallen into the muck-mire of the abyss underlying the bottom of hell; as if Jehovah's Commandments had been presented on carved stone to the monkeys of the monkey cage at the Zoo; as if the Sermon on the Mount had been preached in a roaring bedlam of lunatics' (p. 984).

The sound which Bassett first heard down on the coast is produced by striking the sphere with an enormous post suspended from a tripod. It is also responsive, however, to mere touch. When Bassett first strokes it the surface quickens, vibrates and whispers with a mellow sibilance which he imagines to be 'like a peal from some bell of the gods reaching earthward from across space'. Good scientist that he is, however, he must test the quality of the metal itself, and in an action as horrifying as anything else in the story he plunges his knife into the sphere: 'Instantly . . . [it] burst into a mighty whispering, sharp with protest . . . rising higher, sinking deeper, the two extremes of the registry of sound threatening to complete the circle and coalesce into the bull-mouthed thundering he had so often heard ' (p. 983). Balatta prevents him from repeating the action by sinking her teeth into his forearm down to the bone. Sacrilege is countered with violence, and Balatta's action seems the more acceptable. This is not, as in 'The Beach of Falesá', a white man's box of tricks for cowing the natives that comes under assault. Rather it is the source of native power itself, ratified, no matter how ironically, by a civilization far superior to any human culture. Bassett's attempt to penetrate the mystery of the sphere is destructively futile. The stellar culture it represents cannot be peeled back to the bone. In this 'The Red One' is similar to the later Hawaiian stories. It too attempts a form of cultural retrieval, but from space rather than time, and likewise fails.

The story ends with an escape from that body which has dogged all of London's Pacific writing. As Bassett dies he loses consciousness of his body and feels his flesh now light upon his soul. This lightness of being is experienced as a freedom from pain and dismemberment and brings with it a new clarity of mind, 'a quiet ecstasy of sheer lucidness of thought'. His last act is to be taken to hear the post strike the sphere. In return for this his head will be given to Ngurn, the devil-devil man, who smokes and cures heads in his house by the breadfruit tree. Bassett hears for the last time the wonderful sound, and sees for the first time how sound and colour are transformed into each other as the red one thunders: 'In that moment the interstices of matter were his, and the interfusings and intermating transfusings of matter and force' (p. 990). At this moment of wonder, not horror, he stretches forward his head and the razor-edged hatchet of Ngurn falls. London, as he had in one of his earliest Pacific stories, 'The Chinago', again narrates an execution from the point of view of the victim. In that early story a wrongfully convicted indentured Chinese labourer merely learns that the blade does not tickle. Bassett, on the other hand, has a double vision as the axe falls, the narrative is suspended and the story ends:

Almost, when he knew the blow had started and just ere the edge of the steel bit the flesh and nerves, it seemed that he gazed upon the serene face of the Medusa, Truth – And, simultaneous with the bite of the steel and the onrush of the dark, in a flashing instant of fancy, he saw the vision of his head turning slowly, always turning, in the devil-devil house beside the breadfruit tree. (p. 990)

This is yet another version of the deep ambivalence of western narratives about the Pacific. On the one hand, the Pacific, even London's diseased western Pacific, possesses something essential that Europe needs and lacks. On the other, it dispossesses Europeans of what they most need, their life or their culture. Bassett, having crossed the beach in search of the former, finds there is no way back.

London's Pacific writing is full of archetypal narratives of quest in which the wounds of a people (and his own, too) express a parlous cultural condition. There is a very long tradition stretching back to Philoctetes associating islands with infection and quarantine. The mysterious ailment afflicting Tommo's leg in *Typee* is an earlier nineteenth-century example of this, and London's leprosy stories are a more developed version of the same idea. There is, however, a different context in which to understand London's fascination with the body in pieces. Since the nineteenth century the idea of the fragmented or mutilated body has also been associated with a distinctively modern sense of the loss of wholeness and totality. Linda Nochlin has examined this in terms of visual representation but her analysis is equally applicable to literary texts.[31] A classic modernist example would be T. S. Eliot's 'The Love Song of J. Alfred Prufrock' in which fragments of bodies (eyes, arms, fingers, a 'pair of ragged claws', 'my head . . . brought in upon a platter') drift in and out of the poem with the disturbing irregularity of the Cheshire Cat (another head without a body). In Eliot's poem the world is also in pieces, and these oddly isolated or amputated images of the body express the cultural disintegration which high modernism diagnosed and mourned. As things fell apart, the idea of coherence and totality was displaced on to the past in a characteristic move which gave modernism its contradictorily radical-conservative character. This particular structure of feeling, like so many other defining features of modernism, had its roots in the nineteenth century. Nochlin begins her study with the generation of artists immediately following the French Revolution, in particular with Géricault, reminding us that there are times in the history of modern representation when the dismembered human body has existed not just as metaphor but as historical reality.[32] A similar point has often been made about the uneasy relation of modernism to the First World War, and it is also relevant to the history of European imperialism in the late nineteenth century, whose relation to modernism remains largely unexplored.

London's Pacific stories can, in several respects, be read as bridging texts. Nochlin, for example, demonstrates Géricault's message of castration implicit in the representation of the fragmented or wounded male body, and relates this to the loss of French political potency after the fall of Napoleon.[33] This is an obvious theme, paralleled by Koolau losing his fingers and being no longer able to work the trigger of his gun. Pick, too, has noted the frequency of 'narratives of decomposition', of both bodies and families, in late nineteenth-century European fiction. He gives the examples of Huysmans' *A Rebours* (1884), Wilde's *The Picture of*

Dorian Gray (1891) and Zola's *Rougon-Macquart* cycle. In these and other texts of the period physical decomposition becomes a figure for social degeneration, which raises in turn the prospect of cultural extinction.[34]

There are also certain stylistic features which connect London with Géricault, on one side, and with modernists ambiguously grieving the loss of wholeness and certainty, on the other. Nochlin describes Géricault's shocking combination of clinical observation and romantic melodrama.[35] It is a similar combination of science, violence and nostalgia which makes London's Pacific stories so disturbing. Géricault's still lifes of amputated heads and limbs, for example, have many analogues in London's stories. Although viewed dispassionately, as if on a dissecting table, these fragments also cry out to be reintegrated with the trunk from which they have been severed. The effect of this, one also found in London's writing, is of romantic horror. On the one hand the dismemberment is medicalized and thereby naturalized; on the other, it is a vivid sign of the violence of western politics and imperialism. Metaphorically it expresses the sense of social and psychological fragmentation that seems to mark modern experience; all that was whole is now in pieces. In this we can see one of the ways in which the Pacific is assimilated to European modernity. Gauguin, to be discussed in the next chapter, offers another.

CHAPTER 8

The French Pacific

On 5 May 1772 Marion du Fresne sailed into the Bay of Islands, on the east coast of New Zealand's North Island, to a friendly welcome. This capacious bay with its deep inlets and scattered islands had been visited by Cook's *Endeavour* in 1769, and Anne Salmond remarks that the welcome was no doubt influenced by memories of the *Endeavour*'s muskets and cannon fire, 'which made trade more tempting than attack'.[1] Regular trading followed, a masting camp was established on shore and a hospital camp for sick crew was set up on one of the islands. Both French and Maori sources agree that relations between the inhabitants and their visitors were excellent.[2]

Marion was soon convinced of the benevolence and sincerity of the local people. He was predisposed to believe this, being familiar with the myth of Tahiti as Nouvelle Cythère, and having almost certainly talked with Commerson, Bougainville's botanist, who had done most to propagate it. Some months earlier in Tasmania he had sent two of his men ashore naked to allay the fears of the Aboriginals by showing that, skin colour apart, the French were like themselves.[3] This sensible and imaginative approach to achieving rapport also marked his contact with the inhabitants of the Bay of Islands, where Marion seems to have thought he had discovered a noble version of the Tahitian *bon sauvage*.[4]

But the potential for misunderstanding, and worse, in such situations was great and a mixture of small incidents and a serious, though inadvertent, violation of *tapu* led to his death on 12 June. Salmond gives a meticulous account of the events leading up to this.[5] There are many parallels with the days preceding Cook's death, including minor skirmishes over portable property, the humiliation of a local chief, a ceremony at which Marion appears to have been installed as a chief, and tensions within the local population between different tribal groups. There were also anxieties about the length of stay. In the event Marion was lured to his death by the most powerful chief in the Bay, Te Kauri, who probably felt that the French were a threat to his local supremacy. Whereas Cook came ashore to take the Hawaiian King hostage, Marion went ashore as Te Kauri's guest on a fishing expedition. Unlike Kalani'opu'u, who responded to his wife's pleading and sat down on the beach, Marion ignored a Maori warning and the pleas of his officers to stay on board. He went ashore with sixteen other men. All of them were killed and the retribution that followed was far bloodier than at Kealakekua Bay.

Marion went blithely to his death, victim of his belief in a philosophical construct. Cook's overconfidence was of another kind, a too ready belief in the efficacy of European firepower and in his own authority. Both misconceptions, however, were fed by the respect, even reverence, with which they were treated by the local population. After being crowned with feathers and presented with a *tiki* or *mauri*, Marion had asked his more sceptical ensign Roux: 'How can you expect me to have a bad opinion of a people who show me so much friendship? As I only do good to them, so assuredly they will do me no evil.'[6] The awe with which Cook had been treated must have fed both his confidence and his anger on the morning of his death. Marion's sentimentality is more attractive than Cook's hubris, but they both derived from the European's sense of being in control and inviolable.

Marion's death had enduring significance for both Maori and French and became, as Cook's death was to be for the British, the founding event and defining moment of contact and subsequent relations. When Laplace visited the Bay of Islands in 1831 and raised fears that the French were about to take possession of New Zealand, local chiefs sent an address to William IV asking for protection from 'the tribe of Marion'. A few years later Cécille was met with suspicion and hostility in the Bay because of Maori fears that he had come to avenge Marion's death.[7] From the French point of view, the death of Marion represented a fall from grace for Polynesia. In particular, it demanded a repudiation of idealized concepts of *le sauvage – bon, beau* or *noble*. This was eloquently provided by Crozet, Marion's lieutenant, in an excoriating attack on Maori as the greatest traitors on earth:

Here then we have a picture of these primitive men, so extolled by those who do not know them, and who attribute gratuitously to them more virtues and less vices than possessed by men whom they are pleased to call artificial, because forsooth education has perfected their reason. For my part I maintain that there is amongst all the animals of creation none more ferocious and dangerous for human beings than the primitive and savage man, and I had much rather meet a lion or a tiger, because I should then know what to do, than one of these men. I speak according to my experience. Having been occupied with the art of navigation ever since my childhood, I have never been able to enjoy that happy ease which permits of those studies and contemplations by means of which philosophers improve their minds; but I have traversed the greater part of the globe, and I have seen everywhere that when reason is not assisted and perfected by good laws, or by a good education, it becomes the prey of force or treachery, equally as much so among primitive men as amongst animals, and I conclude that reason without culture is but a brutal instinct.[8]

The celebration of the natural goodness of primitive peoples by armchair philosophers was to irritate generations of French explorers. Sideswipes at Rousseau and his followers became *de rigueur* in the accounts of Pacific voyages by French navigators which followed Marion's death.

This chapter will survey French representation of the Pacific from Bougainville to Gauguin. It is impossible to cover in so short a space what has elsewhere taken most of a book. Instead, I shall concentrate on several French texts which can be bolted on to the earlier Anglo-American sections. These are of interest in themselves, will give a sense of the changes in French attitudes to Oceania, and allow for comparison and summary. A parallel between the deaths of Cook and Marion has already been sketched. Dumont d'Urville's recently unearthed novel *Les Zélandais: Histoire Australienne* will be positioned alongside beach-comber and missionary writing. Pierre Loti's *Le Mariage de Loti* and Gauguin's writing and painting will be compared with *fin de siècle* Anglo-American writing. Loti's myth-making was an important part of the tradition of representation which Stevenson and London questioned. Gauguin, who is often associated with Loti, will instead be considered as part of this critical tradition of western representation.

French and British attitudes and responses to the Pacific are often described in contrasting terms of utopianism and empiricism, or romance and realism. Such typologies should be regarded with suspicion, particularly as these terms of difference have long sustained a more general opposition between France and Britain around which the national identity of each has been constructed. Insofar as there is a contrast between French utopianism and sturdy British empiricism in representing the Pacific it is the result of different traditions of social and philosophical thought, underwritten by very different social and political histories. The *ancien régime* and the French Revolution produced radical and utopian thinking of a kind virtually unknown across the Channel. Apart from the moderate constitutional reform movements of the late eighteenth century British radicalism was itself a product of the French Revolution, and was quickly moderated and complicated by the wars with France that followed.

Similarities between French and British representations, themselves the result of mutual influence, were more significant than differences. The fabled southern continent, that dream of a European alter ego in the temperate latitudes of the southern hemisphere, was British as much as French. It is true that geographic myths about the South Pacific persisted slightly longer in France. The chimera of Gonneville and Davis Lands remained a French obsession until after Cook's second voyage. These were believed to be places of fabulous wealth, one somewhere southeast of the Cape of Good Hope, the other off the coast of Peru.[9] Confused accounts of Wallis' landing in Tahiti led to rumours that Davis Land had been discovered. Bougainville looked for it briefly in 1768, and its discovery was part of Surville's instructions when he set off the following year.[10] Cook, in his day a European as well as a British figure, dispelled these illusions.

Paradisal myths of the Pacific dated from Bougainville's visit to Tahiti in 1768 but influenced both sides of the Channel. There was a particularly receptive audience for the accounts of Bougainville and Commerson in the salons of Paris. Rousseau's *Discours* were in vogue, Bougainville had returned to Paris with a real-life specimen from the good society, and from about 1773 Diderot's *Supplément au Voyage de Bougainville* was circulating.[11] This was the most eminent of several contemporary satires contrasting the natural goodness of Tahiti with the artificiality and injustice of French society. An often-told story, this does not need rehearsing.[12] Reports of Tahiti, however, struck a similar chord in London, and Banks did quite as much as Bougainville to spread the idea of it as other, better and sexier. The mutual influence of French and British writing on the Pacific should also be emphasized. It was the elder Forster, himself German, who translated Bougainville's *Voyage Autour du Monde* into English in 1772. Hawkesworth's *Voyages* (1773), intentionally or not, was a crucial British contribution to the idea of *le bon sauvage* and within eighteen months of its publication four unauthorized editions had appeared in France.[13] The construction of contrasting French and British discourses of the Pacific ignores this cross-Channel traffic.

Whatever the reaction at home, the responses and reports of French voyagers were, like those of their British counterparts, contradictory and unstable. Bougainville's Journal included passages on the stratified nature of Tahitian society and the practice of human sacrifice which were edited out of the published *Voyage*.[14] Crozet's strong blast has already been noted. When La Pérouse landed on Tutuila in the Samoan group at the end of 1787 he began sounding like Commerson. Samoans were the happiest people in the world: 'surrounded by their wives and children, they spend their days in innocence and peace, having no other care than to train birds and to gather, without working, the fruits that grow around them'.[15] Several days later however, a party gathering water was attacked, twelve were killed and twenty wounded. In an instant Commerson became Crozet: 'their features proclaimed a ferocity . . . which Nature had doubtless stamped upon them as a warning that, despite the academies which award the crown to the paradoxes of philosophers, the almost savage man, living in anarchy, is a being more malicious than the wolves and tigers of the forest'.[16] Spate points out the allusion to the Dijon Academy's prize to Rousseau for his first *Discours*. The Polynesian was condemned as treacherous for failing to live up to the constructions of French philosophers whose mistaken idealism is even more violently repudiated. La Pérouse returned to this theme after Aboriginals had thrown spears at his men at Botany Bay: 'I am however a thousand times more angry with the philosophers who so exalt the savages than with the savages themselves.'[17] This convention of French explorer writing in the Pacific died hard. As late as 1831 Laplace, after witnessing cannibalism in the Bay of Islands, wrote mocking those 'philosophers who consider man in his wild state to be a model of innocence and goodness'.[18] This suggests that generations of voyagers remained caught within the terms of the philosophers. Repeatedly shown to be wrong, their formulations were nevertheless a benchmark to which explorer narratives returned, remaining steadfastly in place even as they were repudiated over and over again.

This instability of response needs to be underlined. Salmond, for example, contrasts the first two French explorers to visit New Zealand in terms of their reading. Surville, influenced by the harsh depictions of savages in Buffon's *Histoire Naturelle*, treated Maori accordingly. Marion, on the other hand, saw them through Rousseau-tinted spectacles.[19] In both cases their vision was distorted by an ideological lens ground in Europe. This simplifies the narrative of each landfall which Salmond otherwise recounts so scrupulously. Most voyagers were likely to hold both views. Although Surville's visit ended in violence he had landed with different intentions: 'it is always better to make one's way patiently and gently rather than through force and violence which anyway seems to me unfair towards people who are in their own home and have never thought of going to bother you in yours'.[20] Marion's attitude was unambivalent, but he was the exception which proved the rule; his fellow-officers were more sceptical, without necessarily regarding Maori as inherently vicious.

There was also less unanimity among the philosophers than is sometimes implied, and an older negative tradition of representing savages was never supplanted. Voltaire, for example, used this to satirize the utopian accounts of *le bon sauvage* which followed the European discovery of Tahiti. The Forsters, European rather than French, philosophers *and* voyagers, exemplify the ambivalence I am describing. They attacked 'Rousseau and the superficial philosophers who re-echo his maxims' while often speaking Rousseau's language themselves. Stern critics of European culture, they nevertheless had an Enlightenment respect for learning and rational enquiry which prevented them from consistently idealizing the islanders. Hedonistic inertia and social exploitation repelled them in Tahiti quite as much as it did in Europe, as in this description of a chief being fed by a woman: 'we saw a luxurious individual spending his life in sluggish inactivity, and without one benefit to society, like the privileged parasites of more civilized climates, fattening on the superfluous product of the soil, of which he robbed the labouring multitude'.[21] At the same time they were capable of extended passages of sheer rapture.

The process of representing the South Pacific was never simply one of delight followed by dismay as experience corrected first impressions. Delight, unease and dismay were there together from the beginning and were to persist throughout the nineteenth century. The reflections of Le Dez, another of Marion's officers, on the death of his commander are probably more representative than Crozet's angry vilification:

What is the real nature of these people? What judgements can we make about them, having seen them in complete conflict with themselves, their barbarousness following on the greatest gentleness? We have seen nothing but contradictions in them: although brave and bold, they fled before us; although treacherous and secretive, they are without mistrust; although vindictive, they forget or think that others forget the evil they have done.[22]

He muses on the mixture of sincerity and self-interest which characterized the Maori response to the French stay, allowing both elements to co-exist without turning one against the other as an undiluted Rousseauist or realist might. Le Dez is unusually thoughtful about the complexity of cultural encounter but he is distinctive only in his acceptance of contradiction; most journal writers at least expressed it.

The revival of French interest in the Pacific in the later part of the eighteenth century was basically a matter of geopolitics. When the Seven Years' War ended in 1763 France had been dispossessed of most of her colonial empire. Canada and India were lost, the French India Company was dissolved, and Britain's colonial power had greatly strengthened. Surville and Marion, for example, were both officers of the French India Company and their voyages were a direct result of its collapse. Cook's voyages, however, dominated the Pacific in the 1770s, establishing British influence and winning enormous prestige. French navigators were conspicuously less successful and La Pérouse's ill-fated expedition of 1785 was a lavish, state-supported attempt to emulate Cook in which Louis XVI was closely involved.[23]

There was almost no active French interest in the Pacific during the Napoleonic wars. At their end France contemplated an ocean in which Australia and Tasmania were being settled by the British, New Zealand was being drawn into the British orbit, British missionary influence was paramount in Tahiti, and the United States was beginning to develop its own claims in Hawaii and the Marquesas. The Dutch and Spanish had retained their old colonial possessions and Russian activity in the ocean was spreading.[24] Peace and economic resurgence brought renewed national and mercantile ambitions, and French voyages of exploration were resumed. Their aims now included trade and colonization as well as geography and science. By the 1830s increasing French commercial activity in the Pacific had led to calls for naval protection, the need for diplomatic representation, and thoughts of colonial expansion. As other powers extended their activities complaints about the rights and treatment of nationals were heard from traders and missionaries. Slowly the French began to establish commercial, religious and diplomatic spheres of influence across the Pacific.[25]

It was into this changing Pacific world that Dumont d'Urville sailed. Born into the minor nobility, the classically educated d'Urville made his first voyage to the Pacific in 1822 as second-in-command to Duperrey. He commanded two further voyages in the Pacific, 1826–9 and 1837–40, after which his death near Paris in a train accident in 1842 seems rather unfair. His novel *Les Zélandais: Histoire Australienne* (henceforth *The New Zealanders*) was begun on the first voyage home to France and completed after his return. It lay unpublished in the National Marine Archive in Paris until 1992.[26] According to one of his fellow-officers d'Urville was anxious that a work of fiction might detract from his scientific writing and the accounts of his voyages. This raises again the problem of fact and fiction, which is central to d'Urville's text and to so much other nineteenth-century Pacific writing.

Although *The New Zealanders* can be described as an ethnographic novel this fails to convey its extraordinary mix of style and form. D'Urville presents himself as the text's editor and translator, the story itself being the work of an unnamed stowaway who had lived among Maori and left d'Urville his 'soiled, partially obliterated, often torn' notes. D'Urville has put these into order, filled some gaps, and added notes derived mainly from the published work of explorers and missionaries. These notes make up more than a third of the whole length, forming a parallel and semi-independent text.

The stowaway narrator is credited with a classical education, which enables d'Urville to use the voice he would presumably have chosen if the narrative had been first-hand. This includes Virgilian invocations ('I am going to sing of the combats, ways and customs of a distant people' (p. 29)) and echoes of Fénelon and Rousseau among others named as his sources of inspiration. Classical epic was often thought of as an appropriate form for describing pre-Christian warrior societies, and d'Urville had been struck by the parallels between New Zealand Maori and the heroes of Troy. The notes, by contrast, are in the plain style of ethnographic and explorer writing. Thus, for example, the Virgilian opening is foot-noted with a long, sober geographical description of New Zealand ('These islands extend from the 34th to the 47th parallel; (p. 223)). This alternation between story and notes, between high talk and low fact, is one of the most distinctive features of the text. It produces many different kinds of effect. Most obviously, the his-torical accuracy of the notes is used to amplify, substantiate or correct the story. There is also more complex interplay between the two parts of the text, with the story sometimes casting doubt back upon the notes.

The device of the stowaway who has lived with Maori lends the story the credibility of first-hand experience which d'Urville's own short stay in New Zealand would not have allowed. It is a familiar authenticating device. It is also based on the real-life event of the discovery of a stowaway, an Irishman called James Burns, who had been shipwrecked and was able to give d'Urville eye-witness accounts of Maori life untouched by missionary hands. In a further complication, however, this prototype of the fictional narrator, although unnamed in the story, is frequently named as a source of ethnographic information in the notes. The story itself is full of historical personages, chiefs and missionaries, for example, who rub shoulders with fictive characters. There is also an intermedi-ate category in which a real-life original is elaborated into a com-pound figure. The story's primary hero, Moudi-Pangui, is of this kind. Derived from the historical chief Murupaenga, he becomes, as Legge puts it, 'a composite, embodying every quality and virtue which d'Urville perceived in the Maori people as a whole'.[27]

Such formal devices have a long history, just as there is a long tradition of confusion, both deliberate and accidental, between travel writing and fiction.[28] The border between factual and fic-tional voyages was permeable. Imaginary voyages often drew on real accounts of travel, while travel writers embroidered their reports. This was particularly so in the eighteenth century when maritime travel and the practice of writing were so closely related.

Novelists claimed to be telling the truth and were often believed. The Preface to *Robinson Crusoe* announced: 'The editor believes the thing to be a just history of fact; neither is there any appearance of fiction in it', and this claim was often taken at face value. Travellers, on the other hand, came to be suspected of telling lies, as we have seen in the controversy over *Typee*.

D'Urville was New Zealand's first novelist. Like Melville he faced the problem of creating a text where none had existed before, and of endowing that text with authority. Pagden has discussed this problem in relation to early writing on America.[29] Ancient models were of limited use because their authority was borrowed: d'Urville's Virgilian mode, for example, can do no more than embroider. Instead, the text appeals to the 'I' who has seen what Pagden terms the 'autoptic vision'. This voice speaks in a plain style which purports to describe the true nature of things. But the claim to authority based on a single voice is frail. The author pretends, therefore, to have found something not his own but which he has edited or translated. This gives the work the prestige of an origin independent of literary tradition, and the status of a narrative not made but found. The author is effaced, becoming a mere transcriber, and the veracity of the autoptic recorder is reinforced by this effacement. Hence *Robinson Crusoe* is announced as 'Written by Himself'. Action is distinct from narration; the author merely writes it up.[30] It was not only documentary travel fiction which exploited this relation between an armchair editor and a travelling narrator: Hawkesworth's account of the voyages of Byron, Carteret, Wallis, Cook and Banks was based on a similar relation.

There are significant differences, however, between the promiscuity of fact and fiction in the eighteenth century and their relation in nineteenth-century writing about the Pacific. Defoe wrote fictional imitations, in realist mode, of real travel books; his writing was full of authenticating devices designed to overcome disbelief, not merely suspend it. D'Urville was a traveller who wrote fiction rather than a novelist pretending to write travel books, and although he included both fact and fiction, travel and romance in his text he kept them formally and visibly apart. This, I have suggested earlier, is common in nineteenth-century Pacific texts.[31] Whereas in eighteenth-century travel fiction facts become a seamless part of the text, in nineteenth-century Pacific texts romance and fact separate out with facts providing weighty ballast, often in the form of outsize notes.

We have seen this in *Christina, The Maid of the South Seas*, in *The Island Queen*, and in *Typee* where there is a tranche of ethnographic chapters more or less distinct from the autobiographical-cum-fictive text which surrounds it. Edgar Allan Poe's *The Narrative of Arthur Gordon Pym of Nantucket* (1838) combines the most bizarre and extreme of Pacific narratives with flat, prosaic and unassimilated passages on Kerguelen's Island, the nesting of albatrosses and the history of Pacific exploration, as well as using an autoptic narrator distinct from the author. Frederick Maning's *Old New Zealand* (1862), which has interesting parallels with *The New Zealanders*, also conforms to this pattern. Jules Verne's *The Floating Island* (1895) is a particularly mechanical example of the separation of fact and fiction, with *National Geographic* type entries on each island group as it is visited. Segalen's *Les Immémoriaux* (1907) is unusual in its attempt to integrate ethnographic and historical detail with the narrative. This recurring separation of fact and fiction, history and romance, underlines the awkward accommodation of ethnographic material in nineteenth-century Pacific writing compared with the ease of its integration in eighteenth-century fictional travel writing. It can be understood as a symptom of anxiety about authority and authenticity, and as an attempt to allay that unease by self-consciously drawing upon and adding to the accumulating archive of knowledge about Oceania.

D'Urville anchored in the Bay of Islands for a fortnight in April 1824. There he met three renowned chiefs: Hongi, the famous warrior who had met and acquired arms from George IV; Te Tuhi, who had also visited England and whose brother was thought to have been implicated in the death of Marion; and Pomare, who had taken his name out of admiration for the Tahitian royal family. Marion's death shadowed French-Maori relations. There had been only one brief visit from a French vessel since 1772, and Marion was the absent guest during their two-week stay.[32]

In *The New Zealanders* Marion's death represents the point of origin from which all subsequent history of contact derives, and is the moment to which the text keeps returning. The opening description of Moudi-Pangui's *pa* (fortified village), for example, is supplemented by a two-page note from Crozet describing such a village at the time of Marion's visit. This establishes a recurring now/then pattern between story and notes. Canto 2 offers a long Maori account of the events leading to Marion's death, while the notes provide an alternative European history of the event. Although the perspectives are different, both narratives emphasize French responsibility. The Maori version blames his death on a French attack on a local *pa*; in other words, it was retaliatory. The notes make clear that this attack was a response to Marion's death, and not a cause of it. However, they also give a long description of Surville's firing of a Maori village just north of the Bay of Islands in 1769, and present this as the underlying cause of Marion's death. In other words, although the detail of the Maori history is disputed by the notes, its interpretive truth is endorsed. This is culturally as well as narratologically sophisticated, admitting the validity of different points of view according to the subject-position of the speaker.

Chongui (Hongi), significantly, was in 'his mother's womb' when Marion came to New Zealand, and he represents the evil which sprang from the visit. The lesson it taught Chongui was the futility of resisting European firepower until Maori were similarly armed. His subsequent career as a chief has been devoted to acquiring arms to resist European encroachment and to subjugate other tribes. He is the text's embodiment of the 'consequences of injustice, arbitrary power and violation of human rights among . . . people who know neither moral nor civil restraint' (p. 277). Responsibility for him lies as much with the French as with the New Zealanders.

Marion's death, however, is represented as having brought good as well as evil. According to the story (there is no historical foundation for this and the notes suddenly dry up), one man in Marion's party escaped death and lived among Maori under the protection of a powerful chief. Named Balgueras (Pakeha), he married the chief's daughter and established such a reputation for wisdom and virtue that the young Moudi stayed with him and 'received Pakeha's lessons just as a plant, desiccated by the sun's rays, draws in life-giving dewdrops' (p. 91). In this way European influence enters the bloodstream of Maori culture, civilizing it from within rather than disciplining it from the barrel of a gun or with a missionary's Bible. Moudi eventually returns to his people with the intention of having them renounce cannibalism, polygamy and the practice of *tapu*. He is the harbinger of a reconstructed Maori culture based on European principles of peace, love and industry. Pitted against him is Chongui, embodiment of a warrior culture made more terrible by the introduction of European weapons. And it is not merely the seeds of Balgueras' wisdom which germinate in New Zealand soil. His half-European daughter is forced to marry Chongui, and their son Taniwa eventually falls under Moudi's tutelage and marries his daughter. In this way, too, a perfect marriage of European and Maori qualities is suggested.

Like Satan in *Paradise Lost*, Chongui is the most interesting figure in *The New Zealanders*, his allegorical role complicated by his psychological complexity, his cultural and political intelligence, and by an undertow of sympathy which pulls the text off its didactic course. His susceptibility to love, first for his wife, then for his son, is in accord with the novel's Enlightenment optimism that behind the tattoo beats a human heart. Even the cruellest of savages experiences those feelings which animate the whole human race. When Chongui weeps at his son's departure for Port Jackson, the eventual civilization of New Zealand seems assured.

More interestingly, Chongui becomes associated with Napoleon, an identification which unsettles the confidence in European values upon which the novel's civilizing message is based. The use of Napoleon as a point of reference for the Maori war party is first made by Te Tuhi who, we learn from the notes, actually met Napoleon on St Helena en route to England. When Chongui, in turn, visits England, St Helena is the one landfall between Port Jackson and England. Napoleon is now dead but Chongui admires this 'intrepid and noble warrior' (p. 165), much preferring him to the peaceable English King, George IV. One element in this is Chongui's contempt for hereditary kingship. He is scornful of the Tahitian system in which rights of birth have absolute precedence in determining leadership, and in England he discovers the same. Napoleon, however, like Chongui, has earned his right to lead.

On the face of it the identification of Chongui with Napoleon merely reinforces the Chongui/Moudi contrast. Both represent war and the destruction of their people. But this reading back into recent European history as a way of explaining the turbulent nature of New Zealand society in its early days of European contact elevates Chongui as much as it damns him. Napoleon was an ambiguous figure, even a tragic hero. D'Urville visited St Helena on his way home, as he was writing the novel, and the officers made a pilgrimage to Napoleon's house and tomb. One of them recorded the dismay they felt at the neglect of the house. Pilgrimages to this sacred place became a feature of later French voyages returning from the Pacific.[33]

A similar kind of ambiguity surrounds Chongui's fierce defence of the interests of his people. Canto 3 consists almost entirely of a long address by him to his chosen successor, dwelling in particular on the missionary influence in the Bay of Islands and elsewhere in the Pacific. The history of Pomare's subordination to the LMS in Tahiti becomes a cautionary tale. Hawaii, where Kamehameha kept the missionaries under close check, is the better model, permitting access to 'useful European discoveries without becoming a slave to their ridiculous institutions' (p. 158). Chongui's shrewd and well-informed account of LMS influence in Tahiti is said to be coloured by his 'wild imagination' (p. 330), but the nine pages of notes which follow rather confirm his secular anti-colonialist history. Their cumulative effect is to concede a good deal of the case that Chongui makes in the story. This shows again the complex relation between the different layers of the text, as well as its pan-Pacific interests and cultural relativism expressed in terms of shifting insider/outsider perspectives.

This latter is a feature throughout, and Chongui is its particular focus. His visit to London allows European culture to be seen through Maori eyes, and the categories of savage and civilized to be questioned. There was a long tradition of counter-histories of civility in eighteenth-century, particularly French, writing. In *The New Zealanders* the savage reverses the traditional order of travel and visits Europe to be confronted by the self-evident folly of European customs. A comparable example in English is Goldsmith's *The Citizen of the World*. Chongui is unimpressed by what he sees:

All that I really noticed was that that bizarre race of men, who have certainly outstripped us with regard to inventions and mechanical skills, have remained well below us when it comes to the attributes of spirit, soul and thought . . . they devote part of the night to pursuits or to games which are as ridiculous as they are futile, whereas their entire mornings are spent in a shameful sleep, of which nature disapproves . . . their time is so contrived that every moment of their lives is devoted to imaginary duties and puerile offices, and it leaves them no time to devote to noble reflections of the spirit and to sublime and profound meditations. (p. 163)

Set upon in a London street and pelted with mud and stones, Chongui remarks that it is these same 'uncivilized people . . . who boast of such marked superiority and treat us as barbarous and insolent' (p. 167). This is primitivism with a difference, uttered for once by a primitive rather than by an alienated cosmopolitan, but one who is determined to acquire European firepower to subjugate his own people and resist colonization.

Eventually Chongui's point of view is rejected, although dissonant notes continue to be heard. He returns home, curtails the power of the missionaries, and takes up arms against Moudi. His self-appointed role as protector of his people is challenged by Moudi, who argues that Chongui's cruelty will force the New Zealanders into becoming 'tributary peoples of the avid European' (p. 197). Total war is prevented by the intervention of 'the great Madden' (Samuel Marsden), the dominant figure of the early Australian and New Zealand missions. Chongui, trapped, makes peace. Moudi is formally converted, although 'Christian ethics seemed to . . . [him] scarcely to differ from that natural religion whose humane inspirations . . . [he] had followed until then' (p. 219). This derives from the influence of Balgueras, whose religious beliefs have never been made clear. Indeed, the tension between the Enlightenment values of Balgueras and the coercive moral code of the Protestant missionaries has been obscured throughout. There has, however, been enough criticism of missionary zealotry for the resolution to seem a sleight of hand. In fact it is undermined by a Post Scriptum, which functions rather as the notes have throughout the story, where we learn that Maori soon revert to their 'culpable practices'. Romance and fact separate out once more.

There is, however, a different kind of prospect opened up within the text. In Canto 2 Taniwa travels to Port Jackson and is amazed at the brave new world he discovers. He is even more amazed to learn that thirty years earlier there had been nothing but 'a vast, wild desert', and that the settlement was founded by convicts:

can you imagine a people which is powerful enough to create such a flourishing colony with nothing more than the rejects of its population? If these dregs of society are capable of producing such fine things and such impressive results, what a spectacle the English nation must present when seen in its own territory, in the bosom of civilized Europe! (p. 128)

This secular vision of a new Europe in the southern hemisphere overrides both Chongui's sour view of England and the fragile missionary ascendancy established at the end of the narrative. Within this vision the missionaries' main role is to assist the civilizing process rather than to establish Tahitian-style theocracies. Madden's elegant establishment at Parramatta, where Taniwa learns English, makes this plain. The notes underwrite Taniwa's awe. D'Urville remarks that 'even Europeans cannot help but admire the imposing spectacle and the magnificent view which the sight of that nascent city already presents' (p. 296), and he envisages a time when as one of the great ports of the world it 'will be peopled by a race similar to the Americans of the United States' (p. 297).

When d'Urville returned to the Pacific this colonialist vision of European civil society transplanted to the other side of the world was extended to include New Zealand:

If . . . Australia is destined to become the seat of a great empire, it is inconceivable that New Zealand should not follow . . . and her children, civilized and intermingled with the posterity of England, will themselves become a powerful and formidable people . . . Then these shores, at present without human habitation, except for a few isolated pas, will be alive with flourishing cities; these bays of unbroken silence, crossed occasionally by frail canoes, will be highways for ships of every type. And a few centuries hence, were it not that henceforth printing will record by its indestructible means the deeds and discoveries of modern times, future members of the Academy of New Zealand would not fail to question or at least to argue laboriously about the narratives of the earliest explorers, when they found them speaking of the wilderness, the lands, and the savages of their country.[34]

Aboriginals remain excluded from this purportedly inclusive vision of a hybridized European culture in the southern hemisphere. D'Urville's otherwise inclusive and optimistic colonialist vision, however, is based on an evolutionary theory of social development which his novel, in form and theme, has used to link European and Maori cultures. Just as classical civilization was the cradle of modern Europe, so too the scattered villages of New Zealand will be the source of a new antipodean European culture.

D'Urville's vision invites a post-colonial footnote. Only a few years later Macaulay was to imagine a time when 'some traveller from New Zealand shall . . . take his stand on a broken arch of London Bridge to sketch the ruins of St Paul's'.[35] Perhaps already implicit in d'Urville's picture, this vision of the decline and fall of Europe troubled other writers about the Pacific.

Later nineteenth-century French writing about the Pacific was to show little of d'Urville's interest in trying to construct indigenous points of view, give coherent expression to native resistance to colonization, or use indigenous people as the main protagonists. Segalen's *Les Immémoriaux* is an exception but its theme of cultural amnesia, the smothering of native memory by the European presence, is typically *fin de siècle*. As French influence in the South Pacific slowly consolidated, Francophone traveller-writers became less interested in the particularities of native lifeways. An obvious reason for this was the increasing westernization of indigenous cultures; there was less, as they saw it, to describe. Related to this, as Chris Bongie has argued, was the exhaustion of exoticism by the end of the century. With no more horizons to sail beyond, and confronted by a world entirely given over to modernity, the exotic became simply a matter of rewriting; it was 'an idea without a future'.[36] Bongie does not, however, always distinguish between the idea that Europe had effaced all difference and the more complex reality of French colonialism in the Pacific. He takes the intention for the deed, assuming too readily that the world was entirely given over to modernity. Exoticist nostalgia for a vanished Eden should not be taken at face value.

There were other, historically particular reasons for the self-preoccupied nature of this later writing. The French presence in the Pacific was predominantly naval and missionary.[37] Compared with Britain and Germany the French lacked significant commercial interests in central Oceania, and even within their own spheres of influence trade was dominated by other powers. This meant that French settlement was slow. As late as 1887 French nationals living in Tahiti were outnumbered by other Europeans and Americans. There was little enthusiasm in Paris for putting together an Oceanic empire until the 1880s, when most unclaimed islands were being taken over as protectorates by European powers or the United States. Although the Marquesas had been annexed and a protectorate established over Tahiti in the early 1840s, it was another forty years before Tahiti was annexed and the Leeward Islands brought under direct French control. New Caledonia was an important penal colony and mining centre for the French, but control was slow to spread to other islands of this group. Convicts apart, French settlement before the end of the century was thin, even though France was the second most important colonial power in the South Pacific.

This had important consequences for French traveller-writers later in the century. It meant that the Navy was central not only in patrolling the ocean and defending French interests, but also in the production of exotic images for home consumption. The two best-known traveller-writers of the period, Pierre Loti and Victor Segalen, were both Navy officers. New Caledonia, where convicts worked in the nickel mines, was ignored. Tahiti continued to be exoticized in terms which took little account of the social reality of a culture divided between settlers and natives, British and French, Catholic and Protestant, traders and missionaries, with growing hostility to a Chinese population brought in to work on the cotton plantations but which by the 1880s was forming a successful entrepreneurial class.[38] Most nineteenth-century French writing was oblivious to this.

In being so it fits neatly Said's description of French orientalism and the contrast he draws with its British counterpart. British literary pilgrims to the orient, he argues, treated the region as an imperial domain and a material possession. The French, on the other hand, felt no such sovereign presence and expressed an acute sense of loss in terms of memories, ruins and secrets. He explains this in terms of the British eclipse of French power in the Near and Far East in the nineteenth century.[39] In the Pacific, however, where the French had not been dispossessed, we find a similar structure of feeling. Perhaps this was a displaced expression of imperial loss. That French power in the region was based on the mobility of its Navy rather than on a settled population of government officials, plantation owners, traders and shop-keepers also seems to have freed its traveller-writers to indulge in a fleeting exoticism influenced by the orientalist writing of Chateaubriand and Nerval. Certainly the exotic tradition of representing the Pacific stemming from Bougainville's landfall at Tahiti persisted longer in French than in Anglo-American writing. Loti's *Le Mariage de Loti* needs to be read within this particular history of the French presence and interest in Oceania.

By the late nineteenth century the Pacific offered the makings of a career. In Europe and the United States the expanding periodical press provided a market for exotic journalism from remote places. Pierre Loti's first published work was of this kind. In 1871 as a junior officer on the Admiral's flagship in the Pacific, the *Flore*, he visited Easter Island from where he sent back illustrated descriptions to French periodicals such as *L'Illustration* and *Le Tour du Monde*. Easter Island, for Loti, was 'a world of phantoms . . . These men I now saw were the last debris of their mysterious race.' One of his sketches was of the French removing some of the giant monoliths which dominate the island. Loti showed these roped figures lurching forward across ground strewn with fallen idols.[40] Consciously or not, this drew on a long tradition of visual representation of these figures going back to Hodges and the many engravings of his work which illustrated successive nineteenth-century editions of Cook's *Voyages*.[41] Loti recycled these images to suggest a dead or dying culture, and modernized the picture by showing Europeans raiding the tomb.

France was mildly interested in Easter Island. French missionaries on the Island had requested the establishment of a protectorate, and one of the reasons for the *Flore*'s visit was to report on its possibilities.[42] Another was to purloin a monolith for the Jardin des Plantes museum in Paris.[43] This episode encapsulates the role of the French Navy in the Pacific as a defender of national interests, looter of artifacts, provisioner of museums and generator of exotic images for metropolitan consumption. Imperialism and exoticism, material and imaginative appropriation, were hand in glove.

Le Mariage de Loti derives from the seventy-three days Pierre Loti spent on Tahiti in 1872 and is based on notes from his *journal intime*, on articles which appeared in *L'Illustration*, and on letters he sent home. It was not composed until 1878–9, and first appeared in serial form in *La Nouvelle Revue* early in 1880. From the beginning it was a great success. Shops sold Rarahu ribbons (after its Tahitian heroine), and the book went through many editions, also winning belated success for Loti's first novel, the orientalist *Aziyadé*. Its reputation endured, and in 1898 Reynaldo Hahn made it into a musical, *L'Île du Rêve – Idylle Polynésienne en trois actes*.[44]

Puccini then used Loti's *Madame Chrysanthème* (1887) as the basis for his opera *Madame Butterfly* (1904).

Le Mariage de Loti originated in Loti's memory of his dead brother Gustave, a naval surgeon, who had stayed in Tahiti in 1859 and written seductively of it to his much younger brother. It was also fed by a childhood reading diet of Chateaubriand. It opens with the narrator's arrival in Tahiti and his reluctance to go ashore and perhaps destroy the land of dreams spun for him by his brother's sketches.[45] Initial disappointment ('spirit crushed and . . . fancy cheated') is followed by his rebirth into a new world vividly contrasted with the Europe he has left. As dreams are realized, Europe is forgotten. The narrator is rebaptized as Loti and his former self dissolves for the term of his island existence. He meets Rarahu, a fourteen-year-old child of nature, and they live together in a reprise of his brother's time with his Tahitian lover, Taimaha. This dream-like sense of recurrence and *déjà vu* establishes the enveloping narcissism of the text. In search of time lost on an island seen as out of time, Loti goes looking for Taimaha in the hope that there might be children from his brother's Tahitian marriage. The quest is fruitless, Loti sails away to become his former self, and Rarahu dies romantically of tuberculosis.

Loti's picture of Tahiti is very familiar:

In Oceania toil is a thing unknown. The forests spontaneously produce all that is needed for the support of these unforeseeing races; the fruit of the bread-tree, and wild bananas grow for all the world to pluck, and suffice for their need. The years glide over the Tahitians in utter idleness and perpetual dreaming, and these grown-up children could never conceive that in our grand Europe there should be so many people wearing out their lives in earning their daily bread.[46]

The prelapsarian dispensation from labour, constant surplus, a timeless world of play and the reflex comparison with industrial capitalist Europe are routine. Polynesian culture is yet again feminized and eroticized, with water play and oiling of the body the activities on to which more explicit sexuality is displaced. Loti stares deeply into himself and creates a dream world from the tropes and stereotypes of Euro-American Pacific discourse and French orientalism. Chateaubriand's 'je parle éternellement de moi'[47] becomes 'Tahiti, c'est moi.' *Le Mariage de Loti* is the most narcissistically appropriative of all Pacific texts. Even here, however, the waters of the pool are muddied. Looking into the heart of light Loti finds silence, melancholy, futility and death.

First there is a snake in the grass found polluting the charm of the bathing pool, under the guava trees, where Rarahu and Loti meet. This 'horrible thing' is 'an old Chinaman, quite naked . . . washing his ugly yellow body in the clear waters of our bath' (pp. 43–4). Tsin Lee is a predatory merchant who uses his showy merchandise as lure and bribe. Loti rescues Rarahu and expels Tsin from their paradise, but the text's horror of this particular kind of miscegenation resurfaces later when the attention paid by another ageing Chinaman to a little boy Loti believes might be his brother's son suggests 'a horrible fear' (p. 172). The casual racism of the text is striking. Elsewhere Loti recalls a 'prank' when he and a shipmate used the cover of dark in a Chinese theatre in San Francisco to tie together the pig-tails of those sitting in front of them (pp. 153–4). There was a campaign against the Chinese in Tahiti from the 1870s, including proposals for segregation, repatriation and the denial of business licences.[48] Loti's text exploits this through its recurring contrast between the ease and beauty of Tahitian culture and the corruption and ugliness of the Chinese traders. The only Europeans in the text, and apart from Loti they have only walk-on roles, are all naval officers transitorily associated with the native court of Queen Pomare. Apart from the Chinese presence, the reality of colonial settlement is elided.

A further disturbance in the clear waters of Tahiti is the monstrous figure of Pomare's eldest son, Tamatoa, who, when mad with drink, 'cut throats without rhyme or reason . . . [committing] atrocities beyond all imagining' (p. 51). This Herculean savage has been locked away for many years although he is rumoured to roam the palace gardens at night. Loti unwittingly shares a room with him one night: 'He was a stranger of supernatural height and build; with one hand he could have crushed a man like glass. He had huge square cannibal jaws; his big head was savage and grim, his eyes, half shut, had a look of wandering melancholy' (p. 52). He treats Loti with great solicitude but some time later slips his guards, murders a woman and two children at the Protestant mission, and follows this with 'a series of sanguinary horrors' (p. 54). Tamatoa is 'the last savage', a lurid reminder of a vanished world in which, according to Loti's fevered imagination, natives fed on missionaries. This monstrous throwback is also a figure of pathos, however, later seen cradling his daughter, the young dying Pomare, while she mourns the death of her pet song-bird and contemplates its empty cage. Native life is either sickly or monstrous; both forms are doomed. The island is silent and effectively dead.

The sadness in Tamatoa's face is found wherever Loti's gaze falls. The tranquillity and silence of Tahiti repeatedly modulate into an 'immeasurable solitude' (p. 33), which goes beyond charm into melancholy and approaches a kind of existential terror in which the immensity of the Pacific overwhelms all sense of purpose and meaning. There are many set pieces on the 'weird sadness' of Oceania (p. 55), its 'heart-broken sounds of nature' (p. 176) and its people 'living in immobility and contemplation, gently dying out under the touch of civilized nations' (p. 95). One culminating moment of this mood is when Loti and Rarahu journey into the highlands and contemplate the immense panorama of ocean and scattered islands 'inhabited by a mysterious race destined soon to perish'. As it darkens, the stars flickering in the 'immense void' of the night sky seem to become the equivalent of the pinprick islands of the Pacific. Then the stars are lost altogether as darkness rolls down from the mountain above them, a moment of total extinction prefiguring the inevitable fate of Polynesian peoples (pp. 108–12).

When nature speaks in this way, culture is powerless to resist. Pomare is old and her successor, the young princess, is dying. When Loti visits the Marquesas, Queen Vaekehu is on the point of death. All the queens of Polynesia are dying. Rarahu, doomed to abandonment, ruin and death, is explicitly 'a sad and pathetic personification of the Polynesian race as it gradually dies out under contact with our civilization and our vices, soon to be no more than a memory in the history of Oceania' (p. 132). The whole work is an elegy in which the lingering death of a culture lends it a peculiar charm. In this it is different from the French orientalist writing analysed by Said in which the orient is resuscitated by western influence. In the French discourse of the Pacific there is no hint of the colonizer reviving a dead world; rather, there is a tragic celebration of a dying one. Said quotes from Chateaubriand travelling in Judea and making the arid desert speak. Loti, too, speaks for the silence of Tahiti, but whereas in Chateaubriand the land speaks of the future and of God, in Loti the ocean speaks only of annihilation. Unlike Judea, this oceanic world has not heard the voice of the eternal.[49] There is an underlying similarity, of course. For both Chateaubriand and Loti what matters about the orient or the Pacific is what it permits them to realize and experience. But these very different areas of the world permit rather different things to be realized.

Loti departs into a restless, purposeless existence. Rarahu becomes that familiar nineteenth-century figure the fallen woman, forlorn, promiscuous and tubercular, eventually returning to her native Borabora to die. The European existential hero survives, his quest unfulfilled. The native woman dies and in doing so confirms her destiny. Rarahu's death becomes Loti's tragedy. The Pacific, unable to redeem Europe, has no reason to survive. Although Europe continues to prosper it becomes the real victim of colonialism, guiltily tantalized by a vision of beauty and otherness it can never possess but must always destroy. Loti's romantic fatalism ensures that the European presence in the Pacific can be understood only in terms of fatal impact, and then converts this impact into a European rather than a Polynesian tragedy.

Throughout *Le Mariage de Loti* Rarahu, Tahiti and indeed the whole South Pacific perform as Loti requires them to; narcissistic appropriation is complete. This culminates in Loti's nightmare, which concludes the text. He comes ashore at Borabora in the strange morning light of a huge pale sun: 'so pale that it might have been for a sign from heaven announcing to man the end of the ages – a sinister meteor, heralding final chaos – a huge, dead sun' (p. 216). The dead and naked body of Rarahu is stretched out on a bed of pandanus. As Loti bends over the 'childlike body shrouded in her long black hair', Rarahu laughs 'the soulless laugh of the Toupapahous' and the sun goes out (p. 216). Once again the Pacific does service for European anxieties of degeneration and extinction. We have already seen this particular version of the anxiety in Stevenson. London's nightmare of still-incurable leprosy being shipped back from the colonies to Europe is a different expression of a similar fear. Daniel Pick has noted the flood of French works on national *dégénérescence* in the troubled world of the Third Republic, and the pervasive use of a medical model to image this decline.[50] Although there are different national inflections the idea of degeneration and extinction is common to all three writers. In each case it starts with Polynesian cultures but in a movement reminiscent of 'In Memoriam', where contemplation of the extinction of one 'type' leads directly to the thought of the extinction of all, the end of the Polynesian world is elaborated into a nightmare vision of the death of all cultures, underwritten now by physics and biology rather than by geology and palaeontology.

The naval connection persisted. During the Franco-Prussian War third-class seaman Gauguin and trainee midshipman Loti served in sister corvettes under the same admiral. At the end of the war Loti sailed for South America and the Pacific; Gauguin joined the Bourse.[51] Twenty years later, however, as he wrote in the Appendix of the original manuscript of *Noa Noa*: 'I found I had to fall back on warships to get to Tahiti [and] to travel to the neighbouring islands where I planned to study.'[52] On his second visit to Tahiti in 1895 Gauguin accompanied the governor and his party on a tour of the Leeward Islands in a French battleship, witnessing the annexation of Huahine and resistance to the same on Raiatea.[53] Two years later the naval vessel sent to complete the takeover of the outer islands returned to France with news of annexation successfully completed and a consignment of Gauguin's canvases, one of them *Te rerioa* (The Dream).[54] Exoticism and imperialism were again fellow-travellers.

Le Mariage de Loti played a part in Gauguin's decision to go to Tahiti. He knew the book and was an avid reader of the literary equivalent of the Salon Orientaliste painting he despised.[55] His intended companion for a venture to Madagascar, Emile Bernard, read Loti's novel too and suggested they go to Tahiti instead. Bernard had also read a promotional handbook, *Les Etablissements français de l'Océanie*, produced by the Ministry of the Colonies, which itself drew on *Le Mariage de Loti*.[56] There were obvious if superficial similarities between that novel and *Noa Noa*, and Gauguin's paintings were often understood and domesticated in terms of a Lotiesque sense of the exotic. Gauguin later worked hard to distance himself from Loti, and in his last prose work *Avant et Après* (the English title is *The Intimate Journals*) made repeated disparaging asides about Loti's exoticism and 'innumerable adjectives'.[57]

Gauguin's writing, and *Noa Noa* in particular, has usually been read as if it were a supplement to Loti. Gauguin's latest biographer Sweetman, for example, describes its author as a 'bragging paedophile with his child-bride and his White explorer mentality'.[58] This is unusually crude (and opportunistic) but it makes explicit a widely shared unease. In looking closely at the texts of *Noa Noa* I shall argue that such a view takes the narrator entirely at face value and ignores the way in which the attempt to recreate himself as 'a savage' is repeatedly ironized. First, however, a summary of its complicated textual history must be attempted.

The genesis of *Noa Noa* remains unclear. Sweetman claims that Gauguin started planning the book before leaving Tahiti for Paris in 1893, and that it is 'likely' (that open door for biographers) he had also conceived a story in which, following Loti, he would have 'a Tahitian child-bride'.[59] On his own evidence this seems unlikely, or at least impossible to establish. These early jottings, if they ever existed, are lost.[60] Wadley is on firmer ground when he argues that *Noa Noa* 'was born out of the doubts and certainties which accompanied his reunion with Europe'.[61] Whatever might already have been in Gauguin's mind, *Noa Noa* was written in Paris looking south. It is a reflective sifting rather than a direct transcription of experience. From the beginning it was to be a collaborative work with the Symbolist poet Charles Morice, who had written the foreword for the catalogue of the Paris exhibition of Gauguin's early Tahitian paintings. Part of the idea must have been to provide an explanatory context for the startlingly new work that Gauguin exhibited. It was always intended, however, to be more than an apologia on the lines, say, of the Preface to *Lyrical Ballads*. It is not clear, though, where Sweetman gets the idea that during the exhibition Morice came up with a scheme for 'something as startling as *Le Mariage de Loti* . . . a work of art and a best-seller'.[62] On the evidence of the text(s), Loti's work helped Gauguin to know what to avoid.

The collaboration with Morice was intended to exemplify the text's main contrast between savage and civilized life. Gauguin explained this in a letter defending Morice from the charge of having damaged the text:

It occurred to me that I could bring out the character of 'savages' more clearly by comparing it to our own. It seemed an original idea for me to write with a primitive simplicity, side-by-side with the style of a cultured man – Morice . . . not being a professional writer myself, I thought it might tell us a little about the relative value of the two – the naive clumsy savage or the corrupted product of civilization.[63]

Morice's poetry was to be played off against Gauguin's prose, with illustrations to heighten the contrast. Almost from the beginning, however, Morice had an editing as well as a contributing role, and the intended contrast became blurred.

The collaboration resulted in three principal and distinct versions of the text as well as several fragments. There is the Draft Manuscript of 1893, some of it incomplete or in note form, which Gauguin handed to Morice to work on and embellish. Closely associated with this manuscript are three tales which Gauguin wrote soon after for Morice to fit into the text where he thought appropriate. Secondly, there is the Louvre Manuscript, a large exercise book into which in 1895 Gauguin copied out Morice's reworked version of the Draft MS just before quitting Paris for Tahiti the second time. This had pages left blank for his own woodblock prints and Morice's unfinished material. He took the exercise book back to Tahiti where he later added jottings on art and related matters under the heading *Diverses Choses*, and selections of drawings and prints he thought appropriate to the text.[64]

From the time of Gauguin's return to Tahiti, therefore, the collaboration came unstuck, with divergent texts resulting. In Gauguin's case this meant the filled-out Louvre MS and some fragments he published in the Tahitian paper *Les Guêpes*. In Morice's it meant excerpts in *La Revue Blanche* in 1897, and more significantly, the La Plume edition published in 1901 under the names of both authors. This alone incorporated full texts by Gauguin and Morice. However, although Gauguin obviously approved Morice's earlier work which he copied into the Louvre MS, he saw neither the new material that Morice completed after 1895 nor the continued editing of his text. It is almost certain that he never saw the published La Plume edition at all. By the same token, Morice had no access to Gauguin's embellished Louvre MS which was returned to France after the painter's death, first published in 1924, and presented to the Louvre in the following year.

As Wadley has noted, public knowledge of *Noa Noa* moved successively back from the 'final' form of the book in which both authors' texts were combined (La Plume), to an intermediate stage in which Gauguin's text was edited by Morice (Louvre MS), to Gauguin's first draft, virtually untouched by Morice, and only published for the first time in 1954 (Draft MS). This largely accidental publishing history has left the impression that Morice's participation has been pared away to reveal an 'authentic' ur-text.[65] This is somewhat misleading. Although Morice's poems seem dated, and his attempts to refine Gauguin's prose muffle the intended contrast between Europe and its other, the text was conceived and executed as a collaborative work. Removing all trace of Morice does not fulfil some originating intention; nor, however, can the La Plume edition or the Louvre MS be regarded as in any way definitive. My own interest is primarily in the Draft MS, but because it is Gauguin's original text rather than because it is the least adulterated version of *Noa Noa*.

Gauguin's self-image as a 'savage' had a long history. The self-aggrandizing fantasy of having Inca blood in his veins, and the unconscious irony of trying to decolonize himself in a French colony, are too obvious to labour. His writing is full of announcements of having shed his European carapace, as in a letter to his wife several years before departing for Tahiti: 'There are two sides to my nature, the Indian and the sensitive. The sensitive has disappeared so that the Indian can move forward with conviction.'[66] *Noa Noa* keeps repeating: 'I became, each day, a little more savage' (p. 23); 'civilization leaves me bit by bit' (p. 28); 'feeling myself thenceforward a different man, a Maori' (p. 28), while remaining acutely aware of his failure to effect such a transformation, and of his continued apartness from the life he seeks. Against the grain of its own assertions the text keeps dramatizing the way in which Gauguin's civilized attributes impede the attempt to become 'a Maori'. Conversion scenes, from which he emerges transformed and rejuvenated, need constantly to be re-enacted, as if the text remains unconvinced by its own assertions.

This is most apparent in the area where Gauguin has come to be most reviled, his relations with women. Whatever the biographical truth, in *Noa Noa* he is repeatedly hesitant, even intimidated, in his relations with young Tahitian women. The young women of Mataiea, where he first lives after leaving Papeete, 'look at you with such . . . utterly fearless dignity, that I was really intimidated' (p. 16). Living alone, he remains troubled by these 'calm-eyed young women': 'I wanted them to be willing to be taken without a word: taken brutally. In a way a longing to rape. The old men said to me, speaking of one of them: "Mau tera [take this one]." I was timid and dared not resign myself to the effort' (p. 23). In the Louvre MS the desire to rape has been sublimated into the more predictable sentiment that the women wish to be raped, and given a Lawrentian explanation: 'All have the secret desire for violence, because this act of authority on the part of the male leaves to the woman-will its full share of irresponsibility.'[67.] A major difference between the Draft MS and succeeding versions is the addition of sententious reflections of this kind.

When he first meets and arranges his 'marriage' with the thirteen-year-old Tehamana (Tehura in later versions), far from it being an encounter between 'a bragging paedophile and his child-bride', Gauguin is nervous of her 'independent pride . . . [and] serenity', hesitant about signing the contract, and sharply aware that her 'mocking, though tender, lip showed clearly that the danger was for me, not for her' (p. 33). Settled together back at Mataiea, he is made uneasy by his 'melancholy . . . ironic [and] impenetrable' wife who seems to know him like 'an open book' (p. 35).

This unease is given extended treatment in the tunny-fishing scene which concludes *Noa Noa*. In each version of the text this scene leads on directly to Gauguin's departure for France. He accompanies the native men on a deep-sea fishing expedition. At first the fishing goes badly and it is only when it comes to Gauguin's turn to cast that the fish start to bite. The huge tunny caught by him leads to a change in luck: 'A second time we were fortunate: decidedly the Frenchman brought luck. They all shouted joyously that I was a fine fellow, and I, full of pride, did not say no' (p. 40). But his pride is pricked when he discovers why his catches also provoked laughter and whispers. His fish have been hooked by their lower jaw, which means infidelity at home while the fisherman is at work. Far from being a sign of prowess, his tunny fish are the mark of the cuckold. Once more the claim to be 'a Maori' has dissolved. On returning home he confronts Tehamana with the evidence of the fish and accuses her of having a lover. Denying the charge, she prays for protection and then asks him to beat her. Gauguin is moved by this (he 'almost' prays himself) and quite unable to strike her. Throughout the episode he is strung out between native superstition and western scepticism, between conflicting sexual and moral codes, and is compelled yet again to recognize the unsettling otherness of the culture he is trying to embrace. This uneasiness is muted in later drafts of *Noa Noa* as Tehura's act of prayer transforms the atmosphere so that 'I felt that something sublime had risen up between us', and Gauguin actually joins her in prayer.[68]

Morice's text suppresses some of the awkwardness and discomfort of Gauguin's heterosexual relations in the Draft MS, and conventionalizes its narratives by providing resolutions of the kind described above. It also tones down Gauguin's text. The story of Princess Vaitua, for example, which Morice incorporated into an early section of *Noa Noa*, originally described her stretched out beside Gauguin on his sick-bed, drinking absinthe: 'Her naked feet caressed the wooden bedpost like the tongue of a tiger around a skull' (pp. 49, 52). Morice rewrote Gauguin's strikingly lascivious simile as: 'Her feet with a mechanical gesture continually caress the wood of the foot-end.'[69]

Heterosexual scenes in *Noa Noa* are, typically, muted and uneasy. The homosexual temptation scene with the woodcutter, named Totefa in later versions, is by contrast spectacular. Gauguin and the young man journey into the mountains to find a rosewood tree for a sculpture. They follow a rough path through dense vegetation up a cleft in the mountains, both men naked except for a loin-cloth, axe in hand. Gauguin, behind, contrasts his own age, civilized vices and lost illusions with the natural grace, beauty and 'sexlessness' of the young man from whom a perfect fragrance (*noa noa*) seems to emanate. He feels 'the awakening of evil', a 'weariness of the male role', and a desire to become 'the weak being who loves and obeys' (p. 25). Ideas and feelings of purity, androgyny, role reversal and lust mix uneasily. Whether these are rapidly succeeding states or a single compound one, the mood is singularly unstable. Gauguin draws close, 'without fear of laws ... temples throbbing' (p. 28). Then the figure turns, revealing himself not as an 'hermaphrodite' but as a young man with 'innocent eyes'. Gauguin is calmed (or stalled) and cools off in a nearby stream. In keeping with the Lawrentian flux of the scene, however, he then thrusts his way into the surrounding thicket and attacks the rosewood tree, bloodying his hands as he 'sates his brutality' in its destruction, singing in time with the noise of his axe; 'Cut down by the foot the whole forest [of desires]' (p. 28). This is the climactic, but not the last, of several conversion scenes which leave Gauguin feeling able to declare he is now 'a Maori'. Its resolution is no more stable than the shifting states within the scene itself, which leave it unclear whether the attack on the rosewood tree is the final stage of exorcising evil or a celebration of having already done so. In the later versions of *Noa Noa* Morice attempted to tidy up some of this ambiguity and deleted the remark about 'weariness of the male role', thereby organizing the fevered confusion of the original into something more ordered and less interesting.

Gauguin nevertheless uses homosexuality as an image of the evil of civilization and is clearly fighting something within himself which he feels to be corrupt. This might be sexual lust per se, but it cannot be an accident that homosexuality signifies the contaminating influence of civilization. Gauguin himself had been dubbed *taata vahine* (man-woman) on arrival at Papeete because of his shoulder-length salt-and-pepper hair. The local population seem to have taken him for a *mahu*, a recognized and accepted male transvestite figure within Tahitian society.[70] Gauguin was aware of the Tahitians' normative attitude to homosexuality, and it is surprising that it should be used as a sign of corruption in *Noa Noa*. The implication seems to be that homosexuality is corrupt in European but not Tahitian terms, and it therefore becomes another sign of difference between western and Polynesian cultures.

The young woodcutter, however, is not homosexual but 'sexless', which means genderless rather than asexual. The passage describing him in the Draft MS has a boxed note alongside, part of which reads: 'The androgynous aspect of the savage, the slight difference of sex among animals' (p. 74). When elaborated in the Louvre MS this becomes a short disquisition on how gender difference is less accentuated in warm savage societies than in cold European ones. In Europe woman has been remodelled into something physically and psychologically artificial, with obvious consequences for man; hence the burden of 'the male role'.[71] In Tahiti Gauguin found evidence for his already formed conviction of the exaggerated difference between the sexes in western cultures. A fascination with ambivalence is apparent in much of his Tahitian painting, from the 'soft-masculine' quality of his female figures with their solid arms, heavy thighs and muscular calves to the unequivocally feminized man of a late work, *Marquesan Man in a Red Cape* (also known as *The Enchanter* and *The Sorcerer of Hiva Oa*) which Sweetman describes as a painting of a *mahu*.[72]

This recurring theme of androgyny can mean different things

within different frames. In *Noa Noa* the multiform young wood-cutter, when in hermaphrodite guise, has moved beyond desire. This, in turn, excites Gauguin's desire, which is both an urge to corrupt such natural innocence and a yearning to share its freedom. The momentary vision of androgyny offers a glimpse of the resolution of other divisions, cultural as well as gender, which *Noa Noa* seeks. At the same time, however, that divide cannot be bridged without destroying the integrity and innocence sought. Homosexuality therefore becomes a figure for sexuality in general, which the scene as a whole seeks to be liberated from. This, of course, is a radical realignment of the traditional associa-tion of Polynesians with sex, and an interesting example of how a late nineteenth-century European interest in trans-sexuality is read back into Tahitian culture. The *mahu* had previously roused horror or bewilderment; suddenly there was a determinate place for such a figure in western representation of the Pacific.

The single biggest change between the Draft MS of *Noa Noa* and succeeding versions was the addition of many pages of material on Tahitian cosmology, myth and ancient culture, derived almost entirely from Moerenhout's *Voyage aux îles du Grand Océan* (1837). In the Draft MS Gauguin and Tehamana discuss the origin of the stars, and Tehamana recounts the Tahitian legend of Roua and his offspring. In the Louvre MS this becomes a nightly conversation in which Tehura gives a complete course in Tahitian theology. In doing so, the Polynesian woman is once more constructed as the repository of ancient knowledge:

Perhaps the men, more directly affected by our conquest or beguiled by our civilization, have forgotten the old gods, but in the memory of the women they have kept a place of refuge for themselves. It is a touching spectacle which Tehura presents, when under my influence the old national divinities gradually reawaken in her memory and cast off the artificial veils in which the Protestant missionaries thought it necessary to shroud them.[73]

This use of the Polynesian woman as a cultural archive has a long history in western representations of the Pacific. For Gauguin it is also a useful narrative device, enabling him to translate textuality back into orality and thereby reinforce the cultural authenticity of the passage. To scoff at the unreality of a thirteen-year-old com-moner at this point in Tahitian history having access to such knowl-edge, as many commentators do, is reductive. Furthermore, in a passing gesture towards realism the narrator adds that Tehura's lessons are completed 'with the aid of a very ancient manuscript found in Polynesia',[74] another device but also a half-reference to Moerenhout.

Until now my discussion of Gauguin has stuck close to the texts. How do we place and theorize what he was doing in *Noa Noa* and his paintings? Solomon-Godeau situates him within a broad nine-teenth-century orientalist tradition which was parasitic on the colonialism it shadowed and underwrote.[75] Hers is a feminist Saidean critique laced with the confident generalizing and moral-izing of international colonial discourse theory. Its strength lies in its analysis of how art history has uncritically invested in the terms of Gauguin's own myth of primitivism to produce a discourse she names 'Gauguinism'. This discourse takes Gauguin entirely on his own terms, sees his life as a paradigm of the primitivist quest, and recycles myths of the feminine, the primitive and the other on which his work was based. Its weakness lies in its uncritical confla-tion of Gauguin with 'Gauguinism', and more generally in the way that the familiar orthodoxies of colonial discourse theory are dumped on Gauguin in Tahiti with little regard for historical particularities. Solomon-Godeau's general critique of modernist primitivism as a form of mythic speech which obscured the reality of social relations in colonized territories is well founded. But Gauguin's primitivism, unlike Loti's for example, is more nuanced and contradictory than a straightforward application of these ideas can accommodate.

Solomon-Godeau sketches a European tradition of repre-senting Polynesian culture as feminine, langorous and seductive, with the female Polynesian body as its recurring and over-determined metonym. These were the terms in which Tahiti was made available to Gauguin, together with its status as a French possession. High and popular cultural forms, literary as well as visual, circulated and recycled this image. Solomon-Godeau does not allow, however, that Gauguin might have done anything to change the terms of its representation. Evidence which might complicate the argument, his interest in androgyny for example, is ignored. Her own rather good description of his 'strangely joyless and claustral evocations' sits uneasily with the tradition in which Gauguin is unproblematically situated and with his sup-posed affinity with Loti.[76] When she remarks of Gauguin's nudes that there is 'something in their wooden stolidity, their massive langour, their zombielike presence that belies the fantasy they are summoned to represent', we must ask whose fantasy this is.[77] The logic of Solomon-Godeau's accurate description points to Gauguinism rather than to Gauguin.

The contradictions and difficulties in Gauguin's position, which we have seen him dramatize in *Noa Noa*, are produced as if discovered for the first time and then turned against the author who has made them available. And there is a lack of scruple in relegating Gauguin's remark about his desire to rape to 'the margin of the *Noa Noa* manuscript' – it is *in* the text – as if to suggest this is a secret which has been uncovered.[78] There is no masking of the desire for domination here, nor any myth of primitivist reciprocity. Quite the reverse, and colonial discourse analysis is left revealing what the text has already made explicit.

Solomon-Godeau assumes that Gauguin never moved beyond the Club Med images of Tahiti which drew him there initially, and that he remained a sex-tourist while hypocritically constructing himself as a savage. For good measure she also describes Gauguin's art of bricolage as plagiarism. This enables her to pull together the two elements in the charge Pissarro famously made against Gauguin: 'Gauguin is always poaching on someone's land; nowadays, he's pillaging the savages of Oceania.' Pissarro's accusation marks one pole of a debate which has revived in recent years. It is a serious one but hardly the last word on the subject.

Peter Brooks, in his essay on Gauguin in *Body Work*, offers a more nuanced account which criticizes Solomon-Godeau for minimizing the disruptive and interrogative force of Gauguin's figuration of Tahitian sexuality in western discourse.[79] Brooks sees Gauguin as reaching back to a pre-colonialist Enlightenment discourse on primitivism and radically revising the western canon of the female nude. Although Gauguin remained caught within the terms of colonialist and gendered discourse, Brooks continues, he reversed many of its values and redirected western attention to the body as a site of beauty, pleasure and value. Brooks offers persuasive readings of sections of *Noa Noa* and several of the better-known paintings, but in doing so comes very close to the Gauguinism that Solomon-Godeau has powerfully criticized. One aspect of this is his fixation on the female body. Brooks writes as if Gauguin painted nothing else, thereby minimizing his interest in androgyny and the gender ambiguity of much of his figure painting. Like Solomon-Godeau, he also moves too easily between *Noa Noa* and the paintings, while treating *Noa Noa* as if it is a single text.

Brooks argues that Gauguin moved beyond the hackneyed myth of Tahiti and the exotic from which his interest derived. He wants to return him to the French Enlightenment tradition of Bougainville and Diderot rather than emphasize colonialism as the context and condition of Gauguin's articulation of the primitive. He is on stronger ground than Solomon-Godeau in arguing that the initial encounter between Europe and Tahiti was not a simple act of colonial possession, and that the discursive framework within which this encounter was represented derived from Enlightenment philosophy and ethnology: 'Gauguin ... reaches back beyond the simpler forms of colonial domination, to participate ... in the earlier debate – that of Bougainville and Cook – about how the sexual body in Tahiti problematizes standard European versions of the body'.[80] While this avoids the grosser abuses of colonial discourse theory it collapses the 1890s back into the 1760s, elides the long history of encounter and representation of the years between, and posits too simple a distinction between the Enlightenment and late nineteenth-century colonialism. The former was imbricated with the latter, and the problematic relation of the Tahitian to the European body was at issue in late nineteenth-century colonialist discourse as well as in the Enlightenment.

Another consequence of this historical compression is Brooks' uncritical acceptance of the fatal-impact thesis. Diderot's prediction of the total destruction of Tahitian culture is said to have had a 'quite chilling accuracy', and Polynesian culture at the time of Gauguin's arrival to have been 'pretty well eradicated'.[81] To move seamlessly from Bougainville to Gauguin is to efface one hundred and thirty years of cultural interaction. This allows Brooks and Solomon-Godeau, from different points of view, to argue that Gauguin was obliged to invent something which had totally disappeared. In turn, this frees Solomon-Godeau to attack Gauguin for colonialist appropriation and Brooks to value him for his daring inventiveness.

The metaphor of reaching back is also misleading. This so-called earlier debate had remained alive although its terms had changed somewhat. By Gauguin's time gender instability and the androgynous body were at least as pressing as the older terms of the debate that Brooks refers to. His elision of the sexual and the female body prevents him from seeing this. Enlightenment representation of the female Tahitian body emphasized its sensuous *femininity*: 'nymphs' was the favoured term of description, and in Bougainville's famous account of one such nymph 'unveiling her charms' on the deck of the *Boudeuse* the form revealed was 'the celestial one of Venus'.[82] One hundred and thirty years later the terms of description were markedly different. Henry Adams wrote: 'The Polynesian woman seems to me too much like the Polynesian man; the difference is not great enough to admit of sentiment, only of physical divergence.'[83] Solomon-Godeau and Brooks both quote Segalen on the masculine physique of Tahitian women, and there is the evidence of so many of Gauguin's nudes.[84] Put bluntly, why does the Eve of *Te nave nave fenua* look more like a front-row forward in the Samoan rugby team than Webber's *Poedua*?[85]

These elisions and compressions affect the way that Brooks reads *Noa Noa*, which he describes as a 'vademecum for Gauguin's Tahitian paintings, attempting to control the way in which they are to be read through a narrative of shedding civilization, progressing back to primitivism, and becoming savage'.[86] I have already argued that the narrative of 'becoming a savage' in *Noa Noa* is less straightforward than this suggests, and the same is true of the relation between the text(s) and the painting. Brooks gives a lucid analysis of the episode with the woodcutter. He argues that although the androgynous body of the young man seems to offer Gauguin release from European categories of difference, the attraction he feels involves a recognition of his own bisexuality which places him in the role of a woman, and from which he must then retreat. This he does by cutting down the rosewood tree in an act of male bonding with the young woodcutter. The scene, therefore, becomes an allegory of the cultural need to maintain sexual difference, reasserting sexual polarities and centring cultural discourse firmly on the female body. Although Gauguin is interested in 'polymorphous bodiliness', the foregrounded body must be female even if it does break from western canons of representation by being less feminine. This allegory is reinforced by the immediately following scene in which Gauguin meets Tehamana and brings Bougainville's Arcadia to life again.

In terms of my earlier account of this scene, Brooks' elegant reading smooths Gauguin's narrative, exaggerates its resolution

10 John Webber, *Poedua*, 1777, oil.

11 Paul Gauguin, *Te nave nave fenua*, 1892, oil.

and simplifies its relation to what follows. The next fragment of
narrative is an inland journey to the centre of the island which
invites and resists comparison with a parallel scene in *Le Mariage
de Loti*. En route to the sacred summit of the island he comes upon
a young naked woman drinking from a spring in the rocks above
a pool. Sensing Gauguin's presence she cries out, dives into the

12 Paul Gauguin, *Le Sorcier d'Hiva Oa*, 1902, oil; also known as *Marquisien à la cape rouge*.

water and disappears. Peering into the water Gauguin sees only an enormous eel. This can be read as another stage in his progress towards Tehamana. Having overcome homosexual temptation Gauguin must now follow the eel-woman to the underwater cave of heterosexual fulfilment.

But there are complications. Gauguin was much less concerned with sequence than were later commentators on his text. Morice was given a free hand to insert Gauguin's additions and his own contributions where he thought fit. The abrupt juxtapositions of this fragmentary and plural text must be read against each other, backwards and forwards, rather than ironed out into a smooth linear narrative. And the scene itself is one of the most complex examples of Gauguin's interest in gender-blurring. The Draft MS reads: 'Reaching a detour – what I saw – Description of the picture of "Papa Moe"' (p. 32). The picture of 'Papa Moe' (Mysterious Water) has an interesting history. It derived from a well-known photograph by Charles Spitz whose work for French magazines such as *L'Illustration* contributed to the exotic myth of Tahiti current in France. In Spitz's photograph the figure drinking from the spring is a young man in a *pareu*. Gauguin incorporated this image into both *Noa Noa* and his well-known painting *Papa Moe* (1892). In the former he changed the young man into a young woman, while in the latter the figure is of uncertain gender, its long hair and lack of breasts suggesting the *mahu* of work discussed earlier.[87] The figure at the spring therefore, though always conforming to Spitz's original composition, is another of Gauguin's multiform, ambiguously gendered images.

When Gauguin finally makes it to Tehamana the narrative becomes more familiar than Brooks implies when he describes it as a reaching-back to Bougainville's Arcadia. This is also Melville's Arcadia and, much more recently, Loti's. In fact it is almost everyone's, and if Gauguin had merely recycled this narrative *Noa Noa* would have been less interesting than it is. The process whereby physical intimacy breaks down cultural impenetrability and wins access to the primitive is a familiar pattern which *Noa Noa* reproduces and complicates. The retrieval of the primitive is repeatedly stalled and never secure.

Brooks' discussion of Gauguin's new kind of figuration of the female form in *Noa Noa* and the paintings draws the sting of many of Solomon-Godeau's charges. The substitution of Eve for Venus, he argues, was an attempt to rescue eroticism from its connotations of sin and shame, to render the body as both sexual and innocent, and to challenge the western duality of body and soul. Again, however, his insistence on the foregrounding of the female body makes Gauguin more conventional and less interesting than he was. Brooks discusses *Deux Femmes tahitiennes*, for example, as if it is a single figure painting, lavishing his prose on the 'full, strong body . . . [and] . . . erotic beauty' of the central figure, 'Her face . . . neither soliciting nor refusing our gaze', while totally ignoring the other, hardly less central figure whose contrasting body disturbs the painting's title and whose gaze is averted.[88] Gauguin, in fact, painted very few single-figure canvases. Typically he set up contrasting or complicating relations between several figures. His single-figure paintings are mainly portraits done during his first stay on Tahiti.[89] Brooks' analysis takes no account of this, nor of the late *mahu* paintings *Marquesan Man in a Red Cape* and its companion *Bathers*.

Many of the writers discussed in this book have worked both within and against dominant traditions of representing the Pacific. Gauguin, I have been arguing, swam against the current as often as he went with it. Much of his work, however, remained caught within the elegiac tradition of representation which was so pronounced in the late nineteenth century. In the Louvre MS of *Noa Noa* there is a long section from Moerenhout on the Arioi who are seen by Gauguin as the hub of a powerful feudal state responsible for the 'most glorious period' in Tahitian history (p. 54). Their disappearance is an index of the decline and inevitable fall of Tahitian culture. Their practice of infanticide was 'a potent means of selection for the race', saving it from 'the malign influence of an exhausted blood' (p. 55). The sacrifice of all children save the first-born kept alive the pride and force of this now 'dying race'.[90]

The constant spectacle and the frequent return of death was [*sic*] finally an austere but vivifying doctrine. The warriors learned to despise pain, and the entire nation obtained from it an intense emotional benefit which preserved it from tropical enervation and the langour of perpetual idleness. It is a historic fact that from the day on which sacrifice was forbidden by law the Maoris began to decline and finally lost all their moral vitality and physical fruitfulness.[91]

This passage looks back to Melville and earlier in its belief that if the Polynesians had always been as they now were they could never have survived. The vitality of the Arioi rescued them from the climatic determinism of their oceanic world; the suppression of the Arioi by the missionaries was their death-knell.

The later texts of *Noa Noa* conclude that 'Tahiti will die, it will die never to rise again.' This very familiar idea of the inevitable extinction of Tahitian culture is far more prominently thematized in the Louvre than in the Draft MS, and brings Gauguin much closer to Loti. Although there was a tendency for Morice's editing and additions to move Gauguin's text towards Loti's, there is no reason to lay this one at Morice's door. The idea of 'the dying race' was axiomatic. Even here, however, there are significant differences from Loti. None of the versions of *Noa Noa* suggest that Gauguin's departure for France will result in Tehamana's death. The tragic passion of the native woman for her European lover, and its accompanying colonial allegory, have become very muted. And the paintings themselves, with all those powerful bodies, are not elegies. They look back at us in the way Tehamana is described as doing in *Noa Noa* with the opacity of Easter Island monoliths.

Unlike his written texts, Gauguin is absent from his paintings. A very late painting, however, *Contes barbares* (1902), has been discussed by Brooks as one in which the European *conteur* is contradictorily present, visible as a claw-footed brooding presence behind and apart from two female figures (though, again, one is less clearly gendered than the other) who look out from the canvas in a state of 'nirvanic absolute calm'.[92] The composition suggests the *conteur*'s exclusion from his creation, and his discordant figuration is analogous to Gauguin's desire for the young woodcutter in *Noa Noa*. These are dream narratives which can never be realized, and to which the subjects remain impervious or oblivious.

Gauguin's life and work in Tahiti and the Marquesas were a serious quest for affinity which repeatedly discovered difference. The attempt to overcome this difference took analogous forms in different areas of his work. In his painting he broke with the dominant neo-classical tradition of representing Polynesians as ancient Greeks, drawing on Christian, Buddhist, Hindu and Javanese forms and attempting to synthesize these with what he knew of Maori and Marquesan art.[93] His fascination with the figure of the androgyne was an attempt to explore and resolve sexual difference. And more broadly, he was increasingly drawn to a religious syncretism which had its sources in diffusionist ideas found in Moerenhout, in theosophy, and in related forms of the mystic and occult which were influential in Paris in the 1880s and 90s.[94] These attempts at overcoming division through different kinds of synthesis, often based on a supposed common root or origin behind apparent difference, constituted an evolving project, often improvised, which aimed to find coherence where there was none.

Bound to fail, culturally and philosophically, it nevertheless represented one of the most distinctive and complex responses by a European to the South Pacific, going far beyond the sentimental narcissism of Loti and his school, and radically revising the terms in which a French tradition stretching back to Bougainville had attempted to understand and represent Polynesian cultures.

Epilogue

We have no means to live.

> (Paul Theroux, *The Happy Isles of Oceania*)

One hundred years after Gauguin the island cultures of the South Pacific survive although in many cases their existence remains precarious, threatened by rising ocean levels, nuclear contamination and neo-colonial dependence on foreign aid. Many of the western views of the Pacific examined in this book have also survived. Geopolitically it continues to be seen as empty water. This was apparent in the French government's recent defence of its resumption of nuclear tests on Moruroa Atoll, and the British government's support for this policy. Implicit in the statements of both governments was a view of the South Pacific as an almost vacant ocean thinly populated by peoples who counted for very little. Oceania continues to be regarded as a space rather than a place.

The various traditions of cultural representation examined in this book have also persisted. Sylvia Townsend Warner's beautifully ironized version of this discourse, *Mr Fortune's Maggot* (1927), is a rare exception. For most of the twentieth century the Pacific has continued to be seen as exotic or debased. The interdependence of these superficially contrasting terms is made clear in Paul Theroux's *The Happy Isles of Oceania: Paddling the Pacific* (1992). Like Loti, Theroux is a wounded romantic in search of cure or distraction. He is a misanthropic rather than an enchanted traveller, however, because at the end of the twentieth century the exoticist dream of an aboriginal culture is utterly dead while still unable to be forgotten. For the romantic traveller the mixing of cultures is always contaminating. Hence the contradictory and self-defeating nature of the romantic quest in which the traveller is doomed to spoil whatever he touches. This has been deftly summarized in Candia McWilliam's Scottish and Pacific novel *Debatable Land* (1994). Once more we are back on Tahiti:

Logan was not prepared to look at the living confusion travel and cash had brought the town and to be amused by the mix of habits and cultures growing there, too stirred together to extricate, as hard as unravelling a tapestry on to spools of different-coloured rewound wool. A place that offered flying-fish pizza in a neon-lettered bar named Chang's Gaff, a meal for which one paid in francs before taking a bus to a neatly labelled site of human sacrifice, this could not amuse him. In such confusion he saw not energy but degeneration. He wanted a place to be like itself, or what was the point of going to it? His own part in the modification he did not see.

The romantic traveller is stuck with a static and essentialized idea of the cultures he attempts to exoticize. Plural, composite and inclusive concepts of identity are anathema, with no place for the polyglot island worlds described by Epeli Hau'ofa or by Derek Walcott in his Nobel lecture. In this, Theroux's late twentieth-century disgust is the direct descendant of Enlightenment and Romantic wonder, making explicit the disenchantment which always shadowed its rapture.

Theroux's text also replicates most of the tropes and stereotypes I have examined. Full of sour Melvillesque remarks about the dead hand of missionary influence on island cultures, it also repeats the whole catalogue of missionary complaints about Polynesians. They are indolent, unreliable, fickle, light-fingered, child-like and so on: 'a lazy sort of boredom . . . [is] the Oceanic malaise'.[1] Although history has refuted the idea of the inevitable extinction of Polynesian cultures Theroux retains it in modified form in his picture of these worlds as only half-alive, permanently sunk in placid inertia. No longer dying, they are nevertheless almost devoid of cultural energy.

Similar tropes can mean different things at different times and in changed contexts. In Theroux's case, however, and in this I see him as representative, their repetition is the mere recycling of a powerful tradition of written and visual representation which has directed his gaze and helped write his book for him. To avoid being taken over by this stubbornly enduring discourse a westerner writing about Oceania today would need to take account of its self-representation, of its indigenous writing, to see how this has both confronted and avoided the traditions which have determined much of what has been written about these island cultures. Theroux seems unaware of the existence of a Pacific literature in English which, like other post-colonial literatures, has challenged and replaced colonial traditions of representation (there does not yet seem to be a corresponding Pacific literature in French). As a result the Pacific voices heard in *The Happy Isles of Oceania* are all filtered through his own consciousness and reporting.

Pacific literature in English, possibly the newest of the world's new literatures, is an expression of cultural identity which challenges the idea that 'We have no means to live', as well as western ignorance and indifference to Pacific island states and romantic appropriation of the region. Benedict Anderson has argued that the novel has historically provided one of the means by which 'the imagined community' can be represented. It provides a culture with images of itself and allows individuals to visualize many others like themselves simultaneously connected through print language.[2] In this way the development of an indigenous Pacific literature has begun to play a material role in the efforts of small Pacific nations to resist being forced into the ranks of so-called MIRAB societies, those dependent on migration, remittance, aid and bureaucracy. It faces many difficulties, particularly in sustaining the social institutions of literature necessary for such a print culture. Pacific writers have depended heavily on New Zealand and Australian publishing houses, and their work has often been allowed to go out of print. A Pacific reading public is inevitably small and scattered. In the South Pacific there are very few bookshops outside Suva. Until now the publishing industry has denied most Pacific writers a fully international readership. Nevertheless, a substantial body of writing has been produced since the early 1970s centred on the two regional universities, the University of the South Pacific and the University of Papua New Guinea. Albert Wendt and Epeli Hau'ofa are the region's outstanding writers. Wendt's novels and stories are sombre and predominantly realist; Hau'ofa's mode is the comi-grotesque. Both, in very different ways, are concerned with problems of continuity and change in South Pacific societies. Many of their themes are familiar post-colonial ones, but they are embodied in distinctive forms and carried by voices which speak to a growing number of younger Pacific writers.

Although the European representations examined in this book will continue to affect the way in which Pacific writers represent themselves, the generation of writers represented by Wendt, Hau'ofa, Subramani, Konai Thaman and Raymond Pillai has discovered new islands to inhabit and oceans to explore.

Notes

1 INTRODUCTION

1 Glyn Williams, 'The Pacific: great unknown', in *The Mutiny on the Bounty 1789–1989* (London: National Maritime Museum, 1989), pp. 19–20.
2 J. G. A. Pocock, 'Deconstructing Europe', *London Review of Books*, vol. 13, 1991, no. 24.
3 Epeli Hau'ofa, 'Our sea of islands', in *A New Oceania: Rediscovering Our Sea of Islands* (Suva: University of the South Pacific, 1993), pp. 2–16.
4 R. G. Ward and J. W. Webb, *The Settlement of Polynesia* (Canberra: Australia National University Press, 1973), quoted in Hau'ofa, *A New Oceania*, p. 17.
5 J. C. Beaglehole, *The Life of Captain James Cook* (Stanford: Stanford University Press, 1974), pp. 107, 117–21.
6 J. C. Beaglehole, ed., *The Journals of Captain James Cook* (Hakluyt Society: Kraus repr., 1988), vol. II, part ii, p. 322.
7 Beaglehole, *The Life of Captain James Cook*, p. 132.
8 Nicholas Thomas, *Colonialism's Culture: Anthropology, Travel and Government* (Cambridge: Polity Press, 1994), p. 74.
9 Quoted in *ibid.*, p. 84.
10 *Ibid.*, pp. 73–101.
11 Anthony Pagden, *European Encounters with the New World: From Renaissance to Romanticism* (New Haven and London: Yale University Press, 1993), p. 148 and passim.
12 *Ibid.*, p. 21.
13 Robert J. C. Young, *Colonial Desire: Hybridity in Theory, Culture and Race* (London and New York: Routledge, 1995), pp. 64–5.
14 O. H. K. Spate, *Paradise Found and Lost* (London: Routledge, 1988), p. 200.
15 Thomas, *Colonialism's Culture*, pp. 101–2.
16 Pagden, *European Encounters with the New World*, p. 128.
17 See Roy Porter, 'The exotic as erotic: Captain Cook at Tahiti', in G. S. Rousseau and Roy Porter, eds., *Exoticism in the Enlightenment* (Manchester and New York: Manchester University Press, 1990), p. 123.

18 Henry Louis Gates Jr, 'Critical Fanonism', *Critical Inquiry*, vol. 17, Spring 1991, p. 462.

19 Young, *Colonial Desire*, pp. 164–5.

20 *Ibid.*, p. 163.

21 Thomas, *Colonialism's Culture*, p. 60.

22 Nicholas Thomas, *Entangled Objects: Exchange, Material Culture, and Colonialism in the Pacific* (Cambridge and London: Harvard University Press, 1991), p. 80.

23 David A. Chappell, 'Shipboard relations between Pacific island women and Euroamerican men 1767–1887', *Journal of Pacific History*, vol. 27, 1992, pp. 131, 141.

24 Thomas, *Entangled Objects*, pp. 108–9.

25 Aijaz Ahmad, *In Theory: Classes, Nations, Literatures* (London and New York: Verso, 1992), pp. 171–2.

26 O. H. K. Spate, '"South Sea" to "Pacific Ocean": a note on nomenclature', *Journal of Pacific History*, vol. 12, 1977, pp. 206, 209–11.

27 Pagden, *European Encounters with the New World*, pp. 96–100.

28 'Introduction', in Alex Calder, Jonathan Lamb, Bridget Orr, eds., *Voyages and Beaches: Europe and the Pacific 1769–1840* (Honolulu: University of Hawaii Press, forthcoming).

29 For discussion of these matters see Pagden, *European Encounters with the New World*, pp. 183–8; Thomas, *Colonialism's Culture*, pp. 158–60.

2 KILLING THE GOD: THE AFTERLIFE OF COOK'S DEATH

1 Michael E. Hoare, 'Two centuries' perception of James Cook: George Forster to Beaglehole', in Robin Fisher and Hugh Johnston, eds., *Captain James Cook and His Times* (London: Croom Helm; Vancouver: Douglas & McIntyre, 1979), p. 227. I shall follow the common practice of using 'Hawai'i' to refer to the island so-named, and 'Hawaii' to refer to the group.

2 *The Gentleman's Magazine*, January 1780, pp. 44–5.

3 Peter Hulme, *Colonial Encounters: Europe and the Native Caribbean 1492–1797* (London and New York: Routledge, 1992), p. 172.

4 O. H. K. Spate, *Paradise Found and Lost* (London: Routledge, 1988), pp. 148 and 357–8 n. 72.

5 J. C. Beaglehole, *The Life of Captain James Cook* (Stanford: Stanford University Press, 1992), p. 500n.

6 *The Gentleman's Magazine*, September 1780, p. 432.

7 *Ibid.*, June 1781, p. 284.

8 Mary Louise Pratt, *Imperial Eyes: Travel Writing and Transculturation* (London and New York: Routledge, 1992), p. 7.

9 Quoted in Gananath Obeyesekere, *The Apotheosis of Captain Cook: European Mythmaking in the Pacific* (Princeton and Hawaii: Princeton University Press and Bishop Museum Press, 1992), p. 126.

10 Lodowick C. Hartley, *William Cowper: Humanitarian* (Chapel Hill: University of North Carolina Press, 1938), p. 74.

11 J. C. Beaglehole, ed., *The Journals of Captain James Cook* (Hakluyt Society: Kraus repr., 1988), vol. III, part i, p. ccvi.

12 *The Gentleman's Magazine*, May 1781, p. 233.

13 Beaglehole, ed., *The Journals of Captain James Cook*, vol. III, part i, p. ccix.

14 Rudiger Joppien and Bernard Smith, *The Art of Captain Cook's Voyages* (New Haven: Yale University Press, 1985–8), vol. III, pp. 163, 164, 169; Beaglehole, *The Life of Captain James Cook*, p. 691.

15 Beaglehole, *The Life of Captain James Cook*, p. 692; and ed., *The Journals of Captain James Cook*, vol. III, part i, p. cciv.

16 For accounts of *Omai* see Bernard Smith, *European Vision and the South Pacific* (New Haven and London: Yale University Press, 1985), pp. 114–18; Rudiger Joppien, 'Philippe Jacques de Loutherbourg's pantomime *Omai: or a Trip round the World* and the artists of Captain Cook's voyages', in *Captain Cook and the South Pacific* (British Museum Yearbook 3, 1979), pp. 81–7; Obeyesekere, *The Apotheosis of Captain Cook*, pp. 129–30.

17 Joppien, 'Philippe Jacques de Loutherbourg's pantomime *Omai*', p. 81.

18 There are no miscegenation fears in *Omai*, which reverses the later pattern of the European male leaving his female Polynesian lover weeping on the beach.

19 The passages from *Omai* are quoted in Obeyesekere, *The Apotheosis of Captain Cook*, p. 130.

20 Roy Porter, 'The exotic as erotic: Captain Cook at Tahiti', in G. S. Rousseau and Roy Porter, eds., *Exoticism in the Enlightenment* (Manchester and New York: Manchester University Press, 1990), p. 123.

21 Hulme, *Colonial Encounters*, pp. 47, 64–5.

22 Charles Darwin, *Journal of Researches into the Geology and Natural History of the Various Countries Visited During the Voyage of H.M.S. Beagle Round the World* (London: Dent, 1908), ch. 18.

23 See Joppien, 'Philippe Jacques de Loutherbourg's pantomime *Omai*', pp. 89–90, 130–1 (plates) for a detailed comparison of these different versions.

24 David W. Forbes, *Encounters with Paradise: Views of Hawaii and Its People 1778–1941* (Honolulu: University of Hawaii Press and Honolulu Academy of Arts, 1992), p. 17.

25 Beaglehole, ed., *The Journals of Captain James Cook*, vol. III, part i, p. ccxii.

26 Joppien and Smith, *The Art of Captain Cook's Voyages*, vol. III, p. 221. See also Webber's *Cook Meeting Inhabitants of Van Dieman's Land* (1777), in Smith, *European Vision and the South Pacific*, p. 113.

27 Joppien and Smith, *The Art of Captain Cook's Voyages*, vol. III, p. 126.

28 Bernard Smith, 'Cook's posthumous reputation', in *Imagining the Pacific: In the Wake of the Cook Voyages* (New Haven and London: Yale University Press, 1992), p. 233.

29 Beaglehole, ed., *The Journals of Captain James Cook*, vol. III, part i, p. clii.

30 Smith, 'Cook's posthumous reputation', p. 233. Cleveley's brother had been a carpenter on *Resolution*.

31 *Ibid.*, pp. 232, 236–7.

32 Forbes, *Encounters with Paradise*, p. 19.

33 Spate, *Paradise Found and Lost*, p. 147. Subsequent page numbers in parentheses refer to A. Kippis, *A Narrative of the Voyages Round the World Performed by Captain James Cook* (London: Bickers & Son), 1878.

34 In Smith, 'Cook's posthumous reputation', p. 239.

35 *Ibid.*, p. 234.

36 K. R. Howe, *Where the Waves Fall* (Honolulu: University of Hawaii Press, 1988), pp. 165–7, 171–5.

37 William Ellis, *Narrative of a Tour Through Hawaii, or Owhyee* (London: H. Fisher, Son & P. Jackson, 1827), p. 117. Subsequent page numbers in parentheses refer to this work.

38 'The accuracy of his directions is such, that you may follow them with as much confidence as you travel the high roads of England': John Williams, *A Narrative of Missionary Enterprises in the South Sea Islands* (London: J. Snow, 1838), p. 481.

39 The American Oriental Society was founded in 1842 'to cultivate learning in Asiatic, African and Polynesian language, and in everything concerning the Orient': Edward Said, *Orientalism* (Penguin, 1985), p. 294.

40 James Jackson Jarves, *History of the Hawaiian or Sandwich Islands* (Boston: Tappan & Dennet, 1843), p. 118. Subsequent page numbers in parentheses refer to this work.

41 Hiram Bingham, *A Residence of Twenty-One Years in the Sandwich Islands* (repr. New York: Praeger, 1969), p. 35.

42 Obeyesekere, *The Apotheosis of Captain Cook*, pp. 154–63.

43 Spate, *Paradise Found and Lost*, pp. 147, 357 n. 69.

44 Herman Melville, *Omoo* (London and Boston: KPI, 1985), p. 121.

45 Herman Melville, *Typee* (London and Boston: KPI, 1985), pp. 257–8.

46 A. Grove Day, *Mark Twain's Letters from Hawaii* (London: Chatto & Windus, 1967), p. 215.

47 Robert Louis Stevenson, *In the South Seas*, in *The Works of Robert Louis Stevenson*, Pentland Edition (London: Cassell, 1907), vol. XVII, p. 50.

48 Bill Pearson, *Rifled Sanctuaries: Some Views of the Pacific Islands in Western Literature to 1900* (Auckland: Auckland University Press and Oxford University Press, 1984), p. 52.

49 William H. G. Kingston, *Captain Cook; His Life, Voyages and Discoveries* (London: Religious Tract Society, n.d. [1871]), p. 267. Subsequent page numbers in parentheses refer to this work.

50 Accounts like this won Cook inclusion in the list of those blasted by Wyndham Lewis, alongside the Bishop of London, C. B. Fry and Beecham (Pills, Opera, Thomas): see *Blast*, no.1, 1914, p. 21.

51 In Obeyesekere, *The Apotheosis of Captain Cook*, p. 225 n.62.

52 Smith, 'Cook's posthumous reputation', p. 240.

53 Deborah Bird Rose, *Hidden Histories: Black Stories from Victoria River Downs, Humbert River and Wave Hill Stations* (Canberra: Aboriginal Studies Press, 1991), pp. 15–18.

54 'A Little Boy Meets Captain Cook', *Te Ao Hou*, no. 52, September 1965, pp. 43–9.

55 Obeyesekere, *The Apotheosis of Captain Cook*, pp. 136–7.

56 Epeli Hau'ofa, 'Bopeep's Bells', in *Tales of the Tikongs* (Penguin, 1988), p. 75.

57 Beaglehole, ed., *The Journals of Captain James Cook*, vol. III, part ii, p. 1215.

58 Paul Carter, *The Road to Botany Bay* (London: Faber & Faber, 1987), p. xxi.

59 *Ibid.*, ch. 1 passim.

60 K. R. Howe's *Where the Waves Fall* sketches out such an approach. Lynne Withey's *Voyages of Discovery: Captain Cook and the Exploration of the Pacific* (London: Hutchinson, 1988) carries it through in more detail. Obeyesekere's *The Apotheosis of Captain Cook* attempts a radical deconstruction of Cook from a more developed and theorized post-colonial stance.

61 Sahlins' case was argued in *Historical Metaphors and Mythical Realities: Structure in the Early History of the Sandwich Island Kingdom* (Ann Arbor: University of Michigan Press, 1981) and *Islands of History* (London and New York: Tavistock Publications, 1987). These are now sub-sumed in his *How 'Natives' Think: About Captain Cook, for Example* (Chicago and London: University of Chicago Press, 1995), which also has a complete bibliography of Sahlins' writing on Cook.

62 Sahlins, *How 'Natives' Think*, p. 197. Subsequent page numbers in parentheses refer to this work.

63 Obeyesekere, *The Apotheosis of Captain Cook*, p. 82. This criticism of Sahlins' structuralism was made previously by Judith Binney in a review of *Islands of History*, *Journal of the Polynesian Society*, vol. 95, December 1986. I am grateful to her for correspondence on the Sahlins/Obeyesekere debate.

64 Beaglehole, *The Life of Captain James Cook*, p. 668.

65 *Ibid.*, p. 663.

66 Greg Dening, *Islands and Beaches: Discourse on a Silent Land, Marquesas 1774–1880* (Honolulu: University of Hawaii Press, 1980), p. 4.

67 *Ibid.*, p. 42.

68 Gayatri Chakravorty Spivak, 'Can the subaltern speak?', in Patrick Williams and Laura Chrisman, eds., *Colonial Discourse and Post-Colonial*

Theory: A Reader (Hemel Hempstead: Harvester Wheatsheaf, 1993), p. 93.
69 Anthony Pagden, *European Encounters with the New World* (New Haven and London: Yale University Press, 1993), ch. 2.

3 MUTINEERS AND BEACHCOMBERS

1 On beachcombers see Greg Dening, *Islands and Beaches: Discourse on a Silent Land, Marquesas 1774–1880* (Honolulu: University of Hawaii Press, 1980), ch. 4; also H. E. Maude, *Of Islands and Men: Studies in Pacific History* (Melbourne: Oxford University Press, 1968), ch. 4. Many of the general ideas about beachcombing in this chapter derive from Dening's work.
2 In Greg Dening, *Mr Bligh's Bad Language: Passion, Power and Theatre on the Bounty* (Cambridge: Cambridge University Press, 1992), p. 8.
3 Peter Hulme and Ludmilla Jordanova, eds., *The Enlightenment and Its Shadows* (London and New York: Routledge, 1990), p. 10.
4 In Sir John Barrow, *A Description of Pitcairn's Island and Its Inhabitants with an Authentic Account of the Mutiny of the Ship Bounty and of the Subsequent Fortunes of the Mutineers* (New York: A. L. Fowle, 1900; repr. of 1831 edn originally titled *The Eventful History of the Mutiny and Piratical Seizure of H.M.S. Bounty: Its Cause and Consequences*), p. 89.
5 Dening, *Mr Bligh's Bad Language*, p. 147.
6 For a succinct, even-handed account see O. H. K. Spate, *Paradise Found and Lost* (London: Routledge, 1988), pp. 166–73.
7 Gavin Kennedy, *Captain Bligh: the Man and his Mutinies* (London: Duckworth, 1989), pp. 45–6; Dening, *Mr Bligh's Bad Language*, pp. 62–3, 114.
8 Kennedy, *Captain Bligh*, p. 47.
9 This, however, seems unlikely. Dening is describing the visit of Captain Cox in 1789. The National Maritime Museum dates Zoffany's *Death of Captain Cook* as between 1789 and 1797. See also Charles Mitchell, 'Zoffany's *Death of Captain Cook*', *Burlington Magazine*, vol. 84, 1944, pp. 56–62 for the same dating. Even if the painting had been completed in 1789 it is most unlikely that a print would have been available to give to the Tahitians in the same year. Dening does not give a precise source for his story. Nor is it clear from where Bernard Smith derives his date for the painting of c. 1795; see *European Vision and the South Pacific* (New Haven and London: Yale University Press, 1985), p. 119.
10 See *ibid.*, pp. 81–2 for more detailed discussion of these and related aspects of life on the *Bounty*.
11 Dening, *Mr Bligh's Bad Language*, p. 85; Spate, *Paradise Found and Lost*, p. 168.
12 Barrow, *A Description of Pitcairn's Island*, p. 131.

13 Dening, *Mr Bligh's Bad Language*, p. 258.
14 In *ibid.*, p. 261.
15 Hawkesworth's *Voyages* was a compilation of different voyagers' accounts of the South Sea. On Hawkesworth, Banks and the pamphleteers see Smith, *European Vision and the South Pacific*, pp. 46–9; Neil Rennie, *Far-Fetched Facts: The Literature of Travel and the Idea of the South Seas* (Oxford: Clarendon Press, 1995), pp. 102–7.
16 Roy Porter, 'The exotic as erotic: Captain Cook at Tahiti', in G. S. Rousseau and Roy Porter, eds., *Exoticism in the Enlightenment* (Manchester and New York: Manchester University Press, 1990), p. 132.
17 On *tayo* see Herman Melville, *Omoo: Adventures in the South Seas* (London: KPI, 1985), ch. 40. On *aikane* see Robert J. Morris, '*Aikane*: accounts of Hawaiian same-sex relationships in the Journals of Captain Cook's third voyage (1776–80)', *Journal of Homosexuality*, vol. 19, no. 4, 1990, pp. 21–54. More generally on Pacific voyages and homosexuality see Lee Wallace, '"Too darn hot": sexual contact in the Sandwich Islands (Cook's third voyage)', paper presented at Australasian and Pacific Society for Eighteenth-century Studies Conference, 'Voyages and beaches: discovery and the Pacific 1700–1840', University of Auckland, August 1993.
18 Barrow, *A Description of Pitcairn's Island*, p. 131.
19 Dening, *Mr Bligh's Bad Language*, p. 35.
20 See Alfred Gell, *Wrapping in Images: Tattooing in Polynesia* (Oxford: Clarendon Press, 1993), pp. 285–6 for how motifs seen on visiting sailors were incorporated into Hawaiian tattoos in the early nineteenth century.
21 *Ibid.*, pp. 10, 305, 314.
22 Rev. Robert Thomson, *The Marquesas Islands: Their Description and Early History* (Hawaii: Institute for Polynesian Studies, repr. of 1841 edn, 1980), pp. 57–8.
23 Gell, *Wrapping in Images*, pp. 3, 305–6.
24 *Ibid.*, passim.
25 *Ibid.*, p. 36.
26 Dening, *Mr Bligh's Bad Language*, p. 35.
27 Dening, *Islands and Beaches*, pp. 112–13, 140–1.
28 Thomson, *The Marquesas Islands*, pp. 46, 73. Moana travelled back from England to Tahiti on Rev. John Williams' vessel the *Camden*; see p. 72.
29 Dening, *Mr Bligh's Bad Language*, pp. 147, 253.
30 M. K. Joseph, *Byron the Poet* (London: Victor Gollancz, 1964), p. 68.
31 John Martin, *An Account of the Natives of the Tonga Islands, compiled and arranged from the extensive communications of Mr William Mariner* (London: John Murray, 1817), vol. I, pp. 267–79. The songs at the beginning of Canto II are also derived from Mariner. Neuha was the

name of a Tongan chief, brother of King Finow (Finau), who adopted Mariner; his murder is recorded in ch. 5 of Mariner.

32 *Ibid.*, p. 274.

33 Dening, *Mr Bligh's Bad Language*, p. 321.

34 There was an extensive *Bounty* literature in the nineteenth century. Bligh's experiences were staged as *The Pirates, or the Calamities of Captain Bligh* within seven weeks of his return to England. 'A NEW ROMANTICK OPERATICK BALLET SPECTACLE, founded on the recent Discovery of a numerous Colony, formed by and descended from the Mutineers of the Bounty Frigate called Pitcairn's island' was staged at Drury Lane in 1816. Byron's 'The Island' became an Aqua Drama at Sadler's Wells in 1823. Popular theatre remained one of the main cultural forms through which the Pacific was represented in Britain; see Dening, *Mr Bligh's Bad Language*, pp. 299–303. There were also Pitcairn novels: Frederick Chamier's *Jack Adams the Mutineer* (1838), R. M. Ballantyne's *The Lonely Island* (1880), Louis Becke's *The Mutineer* (1898).

35 Robert Southey spoke for English liberals then and since: 'If the *Bounty* mutineers had not behaved so cruelly to their officers I should have been the last to condemn them': letter to G. C. Bedford, 21–2 November 1795, in Kenneth Curry, ed., *New Letters of Robert Southey* (New York: Columbia University Press, 1965), vol. I, p. 19.

36 Fletcher Christian was born in the Lake District and attended the same school as Wordsworth. He was six years older than Wordsworth and the families knew each other.

37 I shall follow Melville's spelling of 'Taipi' as 'Typee'.

38 Charles Roberts Anderson, *Melville in the South Seas* (New York and London: Columbia University Press, 1967), pp. 189–91.

39 Herman Melville, *Typee: A Peep at Polynesian Life* (Penguin, 1972), p. 65. Subsequent page numbers in parentheses refer to this edition.

40 Fayaway is the central figure of a sorority dedicated to self-beautification and pleasure. This would seem to be a feminized version of the *ka'ioi*, a Marquesan youth association which provided a social focus for young unmarried men and girls no longer socially dependent on parents. Robert C. Suggs, *Marquesan Sexual Behaviour* (London: Constable, 1966), p. 95 notes cognate girls' groups on Nukuhiva. *Ka'ioi* is etymologically equivalent to the Tahitian *Arioi*, with which it shared many features: see Gell, *Wrapping in Images*, pp. 200–4.

41 Rennie, *Far-Fetched Facts*, pp. 193, 195.

42 Melville, *Omoo*, p. 192.

43 See, for example, the scathing description of King Kamehameha III in Melville, *Typee*, p. 258: 'His "gracious majesty" is a fat, lazy negro-looking blockhead, with as little character as power. He has lost the noble traits of the barbarian, without acquiring the redeeming graces of a civilized being.'

44 William Ellis, *Polynesian Researches* (London: Fisher, Son & Jackson,

1830), vol. II, p. 25. The reference is to Romans I, 26–7: 'The men . . . gave up natural relations with women and were consumed with passion for one another, men committing shameless acts with men.'

45 Caleb Cain, 'Lovers of human flesh: homosexuality and cannibalism in Melville's novels', *American Literature*, vol. 66, no.1, 1994, pp. 32, 36, 45, 46. The relation of Queequeg and Ishmael in *Moby Dick* is a vivid example of this displacement.

46 Melville, *Omoo*, pp. 26–7.

47 Nigel Rigby, *A Sea of Islands: Tropes of Travel and Adventure in the Pacific 1846–1894* (PhD thesis, University of Kent at Canterbury, 1995), pp. 87–9.

48 It is, however, possible that Marnoo's tattoo derives from Ellis, *Polynesian Researches*, vol. II, p. 465 where there is a description of Tahitian tattooing incorporating coconut trees and other foliage.

49 Thomson, *The Marquesas Islands*, p. 24 notes that Marquesan females generally had a few lines tattooed on their lips.

50 Suggs, *Marquesan Sexual Behaviour*, pp. 88–91; Gell, *Wrapping in Images*, p. 266.

51 Gell, *Wrapping in Images*, p. 27.

52 T. Walter Herbert Jr, *Marquesan Encounters: Melville and the Meaning of Civilization* (Cambridge, Mass.: Harvard University Press, 1980), pp. 162–71 describes four distinct stages in Tommo's reactions to the Typee – attraction, horror, delight and perplexity. However, these and other reactions occur throughout the text rather than in a successive and patterned development.

4 MISSIONARY ENDEAVOURS

1 John Davies, *The History of the Tahitian Mission 1799–1830*, ed. C. W. Newbury (Hakluyt Society and Cambridge University Press, 1961), pp. xxviii–ix.

2 Richard Lovett, *The History of the London Missionary Society 1795–1895*, 2 vols. (London: Henry Froude, 1899), vol. I, p. 44. See *ibid.*, p. 127 for a full breakdown of occupational categories.

3 Niel Gunson, *Messengers of Grace: Evangelical Missionaries in the South Seas 1797–1860* (Melbourne: Oxford University Press, 1978), pp. 34–5.

4 G. Bicknell, Eimeo, to Mr Weston, Sherbourne, 12 August 1816, MS, Council for World Mission (CWM) Archives, School of Oriental and African Studies (SOAS), London, South Sea Letters 1796–1840, Box 2. Bicknell had three children; the eldest was four, another was due. He died in 1820 and his widow married John Davies in 1824; she died in 1826.

5 Davies, *The History of the Tahitian Mission*, p. 18.

6 *Ibid.*, p. 113.

7 The main sources for this paragraph are Davies, *The History of the Tahitian Mission*, pp. xxxii–xlviii, 327–39; K. R. Howe, *Where the Waves Fall: A New South Sea Islands History from First Settlement to Colonial Rule* (Honolulu: University of Hawaii Press, 1988), pp. 117–18.

8 John Williams, *A Narrative of Missionary Enterprises in the South Sea Islands* (London: J. Snow, 1838), p. 227n. records how the proceeds from sales to merchant ships were forwarded to London. In a two-to-three year period Williams sent £300 from his station on Raiatea; £27 was contributed in one year by the Raiatean children.

9 Lovett, *The History of the London Missionary Society*, vol. I, p. 227; Davies, *The History of the Tahitian Mission*, p. 205n.

10 W. Henry, Eimeo, to LMS Directors, London, 3 February 1825; Henry, Eimeo, to LMS Directors, 9 February 1826; CWM Archives, SOAS, South Sea Letters, Box 5.

11 Davies, *The History of the Tahitian Mission*, pp. 297–8, 304–9. Davies' history was written in the late 1820s but its publication was obstructed by the LMS. Davies resented their censorship and felt upstaged by Ellis' *Polynesian Researches* (1829).

12 Threlkeld, Raiatea, to LMS Directors, London, August/September 1819, CWM Archives, SOAS, South Sea Letters, Box 3. For correspondence among the missionaries see CWM Archives, Boxes 2 and 3: in particular, Raiatean brethren to Eimeo brethren, 3 December 1818; reply from Eimeo brethren, 14 December 1818; Darling, on behalf of Eimeo brethren to Raiatean brethren, 17 March 1819; Davies, Papeete, to Tahitian brethren, 19 March 1819.

13 Davies, Papeete, to LMS Directors, London, 24 February 1821, CWM Archives, SOAS, South Sea Letters, Box 3.

14 Threlkeld and Williams, Raiatea, to LMS Directors, London, 30 October 1818, CWM Archives, SOAS, South Sea Letters, Box 2.

15 Threlkeld and Williams, Raiatea, to LMS Directors, London, 5 September 1819 (postscript to letter dated 30 August), CWM Archives, SOAS, South Sea Letters, Box 3.

16 Threlkeld, Raiatea, to LMS Directors, London, 30 October 1818, CWM Archives, SOAS, South Sea Letters, Box 2.

17 Williams, Raiatea, to LMS Directors, London, 7 June 1820, CWM Archives, SOAS, South Sea Letters, Box 3. Williams is referring to Henry's daughter, whose miserable history is recounted in a letter of Platt's. Having 'gone to the bad' growing up in Tahiti, she was shipped to New South Wales where she married but left her husband for another man. Returning to Tahiti 'as the prodigal, as a penitent', she was sent to England, 'To live retired among a few religious people, where she will be away from the temptations of these islands'. Her allowance of £50 was to be supplemented by needlework. The Secretary to the LMS was to decide 'whether spiritual or medical advice be most needed': Platt, Eimeo, to Mr Hudson, Missionary

Rooms, London, 19 August 1822, CWM Archives, SOAS, South Sea Letters, Box 3. Platt does not name the daughter. I am not clear whether or not she is Nancy, the half-Tahitian daughter of one of the shipwrecked crew of the *Matilda* who was taken into the Henry family; see H. E. Maude, *Of Islands and Men: Studies in Pacific History* (Melbourne: Oxford University Press, 1968), p. 165.

18 Old Orsmond MS, in Davies, *The History of the Tahitian Mission*, p. 358.

19 Gunson, *Messengers of Grace*, pp. 159–60.

20 See letters in CWM Archives, SOAS, South Sea Letters: Ellis, Huahine, to LMS Directors, London, 4 August 1819, Box 3; Williams, Raiatea, to LMS Directors, London, 7 June 1820, Box 3; Barff, Bourne, Ellis, Orsmond, Threlkeld and Williams, Raiatea, to the visiting Deputation, 9 November 1822, Box 3.

21 Nott, Eimeo, to LMS Directors, London, 2 July 1817, CWM Archives, SOAS, South Sea Letters, Box 2.

22 'William Ellis', *Dictionary of National Biography* (repr. Oxford University Press, 1959–60), vol. VI, pp. 714–15.

23 Charles Darwin, *Journal of Researches into the Geology and Natural History of the Various Countries Visited during the Voyage of H.M.S. Beagle Round the World* (London: Dent, 1908), pp. 397–8.

24 I am indebted for the information on Collins to Professor Ira B. Nadel who is editing the text for Princeton University Press. On Melville's debt to Ellis see Neil Rennie, *Far-Fetched Facts: The Literature of Travel and the Idea of the South Seas* (Oxford: Clarendon Press, 1995), pp. 200–5.

25 Mary Louise Pratt, *Imperial Eyes: Travel Writing and Transculturation* (London and New York: Routledge, 1992), part I, passim.

26 *Ibid.*, pp. 27–8, 59, 63–4.

27 Aijaz Ahmad, *In Theory: Classes, Nations, Literatures* (London: Verso, 1992), p. 99.

28 Greg Dening, *Islands and Beaches: Discourse on a Silent Land* (Honolulu: University of Hawaii Press, 1980), p. 43.

29 Subsequent volume and page numbers in parentheses refer to William Ellis, *Polynesian Researches* (London: Fisher, Son & Jackson, 1830), 2 vols.

30 Christopher Herbert, *Culture and Anomie: Ethnographic Imagination in the Nineteenth Century* (Chicago: University of Chicago Press, 1991), ch. 3, passim.

31 Lovett, *The History of the London Missionary Society*, vol. I, p. 341. See also Rev. Robert Thomson, *The Marquesas Islands: Their Description and Early History* (Hawaii: Institute for Polynesian Studies, repr. of 1841 edn, 1980), pp. 60–1: 'Never shall I forget the withering effect . . . which our first contact with savage and heathen life produced – nor the deep disappointment when we landed upon Tahiti . . . I, like most read the works of Ellis, Williams, etc. The glowing picture had dazzled the imagination.'

32 Ellis had compared Maori tattooing to the stripe and colour of the Highlander's plaid (anticipating Stevenson), and described it as the coat of arms of the New Zealand aristocracy. The parallels are explicitly European but Ellis is trying to understand the social function of tattooing rather than anathematizing it as the devil's signature; *Polynesian Researches*, vol. I, pp. 30–1.

33 See Peter Hulme, *Colonial Encounters: Europe and the Native Caribbean* (London and New York: Routledge, 1992), chs. 1–3.

34 Nicholas Thomas, *Entangled Objects: Exchange, Material Culture, and Colonialism in the Pacific* (Cambridge, Mass., and London: Harvard University Press, 1991), p. 162.

35 Biographical details in this section come mainly from Gavan Daws, *A Dream of Islands* (New York and London: Norton, 1980), pp. 23–69.

36 To Maria Lewis, 6–8 November 1838, in Gordon S. Haight, ed., *The George Eliot Letters*, 7 vols. (London and New Haven: Oxford University Press and Yale University Press, 1954), vol. I, p. 12.

37 Subsequent page numbers in parentheses refer to Williams, *Missionary Enterprises*.

38 Thomas, *Entangled Objects*, pp. 151–6.

39 Williams, Raiatea, to LMS Directors, London, 7 June 1820, CWM Archives, SOAS, South Sea Letters, Box 3.

40 Samuel Smiles, *Self-Help* (London: John Murray, 1958), p. 244.

41 Williams criticized the Wesleyan missionaries on Tonga for adding Christian names to the Polynesian ones of those they baptized: 'There is a native dignity in the name itself, which is lost when thus associated': *Missionary Enterprises*, p. 307.

42 Williams, Raiatea, to Ellis, Ohau, 1 October 1823, CWM Archives, SOAS, South Sea Letters, Box 4. Williams writes: 'I should like much to have a very long paraparau raa with you.'

43 Nicholas Thomas, *Colonialism's Culture: Anthropology, Travel and Government* (Cambridge: Polity Press, 1994), pp. 128–35.

44 *Ibid.*, p. 142.

45 Gayatri Chakravorty Spivak, 'Can the subaltern speak?', in Patrick Williams and Laura Chrisman, eds., *Colonial Discourse and Post-Colonial Theory: A Reader* (Hemel Hempstead: Harvester Wheatsheaf, 1993), p. 94.

46 Mrs Ellis, *The Island Queen: A Poem* (London: John Snow, 1846), Book 8.

47 Daws, *A Dream of Islands*, pp. 66–8.

48 Smiles, *Self-Help*, p. 243.

49 Marshall Sahlins, *How 'Natives' Think: About Captain Cook, for Example* (Chicago and London: University of Chicago Press, 1995), p. 178 n. 28.

50 Davies, *The History of the Tahitian Mission*, pp. l–li.

51 Threlkeld and Williams, Raiatea, to LMS Directors, London, 30 October 1818, CWM Archives, SOAS, South Sea Letters, Box 2.

52 Lovett, *The History of the London Missionary Society*, vol. 1, p. 227.

53 Davies, *The History of the Tahitian Mission*, pp. 330–1.

54 Old Orsmond MS, in Davies, *The History of the Tahitian Mission*, p. 358.

55 *Ibid.*, pp. 351, 359. Orsmond was the most root-and-branch of the missionaries who arrived in 1817. His grand-daughter Teuira Henry (also grand-daughter of William Henry) recorded his house- and church-building methods: 'To supply materials he did not hesitate to fell the village breadfruit and coconut trees, as he felt that the bountiful food supply so near at hand contributed to idleness. In later years . . . he seems to have tempered his methods.' Teuira Henry, *Ancient Tahiti, Based on Material Recorded by J. M. Orsmond* (Honolulu: Bernice P. Bishop Museum Bulletin 48, 1928), p. vi.

56 Williams, on board the schooner *Endeavour*, to native missionaries setting out for Aitutake, 6 July 1823, CWM Archives, SOAS, South Sea Letters, Box 4. The Biblical reference is to Matthew 5, 14–16: 'Ye are the light of the world. A city that is set on a hill cannot be hid.'

57 Platt, Borabora, to LMS Directors, 4 November 1824, CWM Archives, SOAS, South Sea Letters, Box 4.

58 Lovett, *The History of the London Missionary Society*, vol. 1, p. 399.

59 Homi K. Bhabha, 'Of mimicry and man: the ambivalence of colonial discourse', and 'Signs taken for wonders: questions of ambivalence and authority under a tree outside Delhi, May 1817', in *The Location of Culture* (London and New York: Routledge, 1994), pp. 86, 121.

60 One serious challenge posed by syncretism was the Mamaia sect, a cult which emerged from within the LMS church on Tahiti in 1826 and spread to the Leeward Islands. It mixed Christian ritual with Tahitian custom, and came into open conflict with the Tahitian royal forces in the late 1820s. After this its influence was largely restricted to the Leeward island of Maupiti where there were no European missionaries. Penned back by this alliance of missionaries and indigenous elites, it later spread to Samoa where it is claimed to have helped prepare the way for the arrival of John Williams in 1830. The Mamaia sect plays a significant part in Segalen's *Les Immémoriaux*. See also Davies, *The History of the Tahitian Mission*, pp. 254–5; Howe, *Where the Waves Fall*, pp. 151, 235.

61 Old Orsmond MS, in Davies, *The History of the Tahitian Mission*, pp. 357–8.

62 Williams, Raiatea, to LMS Directors, London, 24 December 1824, CWM Archives, SOAS, South Sea Letters, Box 4. Parts of this letter are also quoted in Lovett, *The History of the London Missionary Society*, vol. 1, pp. 272–3.

63 Ellis, *Polynesian Researches*, vol. 11, pp. 435–6. The code established by the Wesleyan missionaries on Tonga in the 1840s was taken from the description of the Huahine code in Ellis' *Polynesian Researches*; Howe, *Where the Waves Fall*, p. 191.

64 Darling, Otaheite, to LMS Directors, London, 1 October 1823, CWM Archives, SOAS, South Sea Letters, Box 4.
65 Alfred Gell, *Wrapping in Images: Tattooing in Polynesia* (Oxford: Clarendon Press, 1993), p. 123.
66 Threlkeld and Williams, Raiatea, to LMS Directors, London, 24 March 1824, CWM Archives, SOAS, Box 4. The letter is in Threlkeld's hand.
67 Bicknell, Hayward, Henry, Nott, Tessier and Wilson, Eimeo, to LMS Directors, London, 2 July 1817, CWM Archives, SOAS, South Sea Letters, Box 2.
68 Thomas, *Entangled Objects*, p. 153.
69 Davies, *The History of the Tahitian Mission*, pp. 330–1.
70 Ellis, London, to Queen Pomare, Tahiti, 25 October 1834, Pacific MSS, Rhodes House Library, Oxford, ML MSS 24/1.

5 TRADE AND ADVENTURE

1 For a fuller discussion of this wider context see Douglas A. Lorimer, *Colour, Class and the Victorians: English Attitudes to the Negro in the Mid-Nineteenth Century* (Leicester: Leicester University Press, 1978), chs. 7, 8, 9; Robert J. C. Young, *Colonial Desire: Hybridity in Theory, Culture and Race* (London and New York: Routledge, 1995), pp. 119–21.
2 D. K. Fieldhouse, *Economics and Empire 1830–1914* (Ithaca: Cornell University Press, 1973), p. 456. These two paragraphs of summary come mainly from this work, pp. 224–45, 437–56.
3 In A. G. L. Shaw, ed., *Great Britain and the Colonies 1815–1865* (London: Methuen, 1970), p. 4.
4 *Ibid.*, p. 2.
5 B. Semmel, 'The philosophic radicals and colonialism', in Shaw, ed., *Great Britain and the Colonies*, p. 78.
6 In John S. Galbraith, 'Myths of the "Little England" era', in *ibid.*, p. 30.
7 John Gallagher and Ronald Robinson, 'The imperialism of free trade', in *ibid.*, pp. 158–9.
8 *Ibid.*, p. 146.
9 P. J. Cain and A. G. Hopkins, *British Imperialism: Innovation and Expansion 1688–1914* (London and New York: Longman, 1993), p. 236.
10 Captain Marryat, *Masterman Ready, or The Wreck of the Pacific* (London: Macmillan, 1841), p. 117.
11 Herman Merivale, *Lectures on Colonization and Colonies, Delivered before the University of Oxford in 1839, 40, 41* (London: Longman, 1861; repr. Augustus M. Kelley, 1967), p. vi. The quotation comes from Merivale's 1861 Preface.
12 R. K. Webb, *Harriet Martineau: A Victorian Radical* (London: Heinemann, 1960), pp. 339–40.

13 In *ibid.*, p. 344.

14 Harriet Martineau, *How to Observe: Morals and Manners* (London: Charles Knight, 1838), p. 27.

15 Harriet Martineau, *Dawn Island: A Tale* (Manchester: J. Gadsby, 1845), p. 22. Subsequent page numbers in parentheses refer to this work.

16 Patrick Brantlinger, *Rule of Darkness: British Literature and Imperialism* (Ithaca and London: Cornell University Press, 1988), p. 31.

17 Patrick Brantlinger, ' "Dying races": rationalizing genocide in the nineteenth century', in Jan Nederveen Pieterse and Bhikhu Parekh, eds., *The Decolonization of Imagination: Culture, Knowledge and Power* (London and New Jersey: Zed Books, 1995), p. 43.

18 *Ibid.*, p. 45.

19 Jules Verne, *The Floating Island* (London and New York: KPI, 1990), p. 269.

20 Martineau, *How to Observe*, p. 25.

21 Brantlinger, *Rule of Darkness*, p. 31.

22 See Nicholas Thomas, *Entangled Objects: Exchange, Material Culture, and Colonialism in the Pacific* (Cambridge, Mass., and London: Harvard University Press, 1991), ch. 3 for many of the general ideas used in the next two paragraphs.

23 In *ibid.*, p. 128.

24 Martineau, *How to Observe*, pp. 13, 22–3, 42.

25 Webb, *Harriet Martineau*, pp. 71–4, 285.

26 Idya or Iddeah is an ubiquitous name in writing about the Pacific. Mary Russell Mitford used it in *Christina*; it was shortly to be used by Wilkie Collins in 'Iolani' and by Melville in *Omoo*. It derives from Itia, wife of Pomare I.

27 See J. S. Bratton, *The Impact of Victorian Children's Fiction* (London: Croom Helm, 1981), ch. 4 for a detailed account of this history.

28 Joseph Bristow, *Empire Boys: Adventures in a Man's World* (London: HarperCollins, 1991), p. 60. See also Martin Green, 'The Robinson Crusoe story', in Jeffrey Richards, ed., *Imperialism and Juvenile Literature* (Manchester and New York: Manchester University Press, 1989), pp. 46–7.

29 In Richards, ed., 'Introduction', *Imperialism and Juvenile Literature*, p. 6. (The quotation is from Hughes' *Tom Brown at Oxford*.)

30 *Ibid.*, p. 6.

31 Bristow, *Empire Boys*, pp. 57–8.

32 Bratton, *The Impact of Victorian Children's Fiction*, pp. 102, 111.

33 Thomas Hughes, *Tom Brown's Schooldays* (Puffin Books, 1983), p. 172.

34 For this short section on Kingston see Bratton, *The Impact of Victorian Children's Fiction*, pp. 115–33.

35 Green, 'The Robinson Crusoe story', in Richards, ed., *Imperialism and Juvenile Literature*, p. 46.

36 *Ibid.*, p. 47.

37 R. M. Ballantyne, *The Coral Island* (Bristol: Purnell Books, 1985), p. 37. Subsequent page numbers in parentheses refer to this edition.

38 Eric Quayle, *Ballantyne the Brave: A Victorian Writer and His Family* (London: Rupert Hart-Davis, 1967), pp. 114–15.

39 See K. R. Howe, *Where the Waves Fall: A New South Sea Islands History from First Settlement to Colonial Rule* (Honolulu: University of Hawaii Press, 1988), p. 261. Other accounts of Cakobau's cruelty circulated in Charles Wilkes, *Narrative of the United States Exploring Expedition During the Years 1838, 1839, 1840, 1841, 1842* (1845), and 'A Lady' [Mary Davis Wallis], *Life in Feejee, or, Five Years Among the Cannibals* (1851).

40 John Williams, *A Narrative of Missionary Enterprises in the South Sea Islands* (London: J. Snow, 1838), p. 390.

41 *Ibid.*, p. 149.

42 *Ibid.*, pp. 119, 362–3.

43 *Ibid.*, pp. 21–4, 80, 166, 181.

44 *Ibid.*, p. 492.

45 R. M. Ballantyne, *Jarwin and Cuffy: A Tale* (London: Frederick Warne, n. d. [1878]), pp. 132–3.

46 Williams, *Missionary Enterprises*, pp. 144–50.

47 In John M. MacKenzie, 'Hunting and the natural world in juvenile literature', in Richards, ed., *Imperialism and Juvenile Literature*, p. 159.

48 J. A. Mangan, 'Noble specimens of manhood: schoolboy literature and the creation of a colonial chivalric code', in *ibid.*, pp. 173–94. Mangan concentrates on the late nineteenth and early twentieth centuries.

49 In MacKenzie, 'Hunting and the natural world in juvenile literature', p. 149.

50 Cain and Hopkins, *British Imperialism 1688–1914*, ch. 1 passim, pp. 98, 104, 122–3, 137–8.

51 *Ibid.*, p. 32.

52 *Ibid.*, p. 31.

53 *Ibid.*, p. 34.

54 *Ibid.*, pp. 45–6, 98.

55 Lorimer, *Colour, Class and the Victorians*, pp. 45, 112–13.

56 *Ibid.*, p. 161.

57 Quayle, *Ballantyne the Brave*, pp. 129–30.

58 Lorimer, *Colour, Class and the Victorians*, pp. 160–1, 200.

59 Robert Knox, *The Races of Men: A Philosophical Enquiry into the Influence of Race over the Destinies of Nations* (London: Henry Renshaw, 2nd. edn 1862), p. 21.

60 Knox's racial essentialism was so intense that he thought it impossible for 'Saxons' to survive in tropical climates. He also believed that physiological law made impossible the mixing of races ('Nature produces no mules', *The Races of Men*, p. 65), and that all races degener-

ate when cut off from their source. Colonialism, therefore, was a doomed project.

61 On mid-century race theories see Lorimer, *Colour, Class and the Victorians*, pp. 137–44; Young, *Colonial Desire*, pp. 118–21.

62 Merivale, *Lectures on Colonization and Colonies*, pp. 549, 551.

63 *Ibid.*, p. 493.

64 *Ibid.*, p. 538.

65 *Ibid.*, pp. 561–2.

66 See Lorimer, *Colour, Class and the Victorians*, pp. 148–9.

67 See, for example, Christopher Parker, 'Race and empire in the stories of R. M. Ballantyne', in Robert Giddings, ed., *Literature and Imperialism* (London: Macmillan, 1991), pp. 55–6.

68 Other nineteenth-century texts used the Pacific in this way. Samuel Butler's *Erewhon* (1872) and Anthony Trollope's *The Fixed Term* (1882) are conspicuous examples. They, however, use the Pacific merely as an empty space in which to locate their utopias and dystopias, and are hardly at all concerned with matters of race or empire. They could just as easily be set in any other 'empty' part of the map.

69 Merivale, *Lectures on Colonization and Colonies*, p. 489.

6 TAKING UP WITH KANAKAS: ROBERT LOUIS STEVENSON AND THE PACIFIC

1 Robert Irwin Hillier, *The South Seas Fiction of Robert Louis Stevenson* (New York: Peter Lang, 1989). Neil Rennie, *Far-Fetched Facts: The Literature of Travel and the Idea of the South Seas* (Oxford: Clarendon Press, 1995), p. 210 gives an outline of its story.

2 Eric Quayle, *Ballantyne the Brave: A Victorian Writer and His Family* (London: Rupert Hart-Davis, 1967), pp. 216–17; Frank McLynn, *Robert Louis Stevenson* (London: Pimlico, 1994), p. 28.

3 Letter to Mrs Sitwell, 22 June 1875, in Bradford A. Booth and Ernest Mehew, eds., *The Letters of Robert Louis Stevenson* (New Haven and London: Yale University Press, 1994–5), vol. II, p. 145. This visit left Stevenson 'sick with desire to go there; beautiful places, green for ever; perfect climate; perfect shapes of men and women, with red flowers in their hair; nothing to do but to study oratory and etiquette, sit in the sun, and pick up the fruits as they fall. Navigator's Island is the place; absolute balm for the weary.'

4 *In the South Seas*, in *The Works of Robert Louis Stevenson*, Pentland Edition (London: Cassell, 1907), vol. XVII, p. 11. Subsequent page numbers in parentheses refer to this text. *In the South Seas* was a compilation, edited and published by Sidney Colvin after Stevenson's death, of the letters he sent to American and British newspapers. These were derived from the journal Stevenson kept as he travelled. The text

exists in several different forms. Most exclude the Hawaiian section of his journey, which has been separately published; see n. 66.

5 Barry Menikoff, '"These problematic shores": Robert Louis Stevenson in the South Seas', in Simon Gatrell, ed., *The Ends of the Earth* (London and New Jersey: Ashfield Press, 1992), p. 154.

6 Anthony Pagden, *European Encounters with the New World* (New Haven and London: Yale University Press, 1993), pp. 25–6. The passage discussed is from Humboldt's *Kosmos* (1845).

7 Rennie, *Far-Fetched Facts*, pp. 203–4, 286 n. 42 traces this ubiquitous proverb back via Ellis' *Polynesian Researches* to Davies' account of his tour of Tahiti in 1816. He suggests that Melville was responsible for replacing 'hibiscus' with 'palm tree', but *Dawn Island*, written two years before *Omoo*, had already substituted 'forest tree' for 'hibiscus'.

8 *The Wrecker* (London: Heinemann, 1928), p. 4.

9 On Thomson see Crosbie Smith and M. Norton Wise, *Energy and Empire: A Biographical Study of Lord Kelvin* (Cambridge: Cambridge University Press, 1989). On the cultural influence of the idea of the cooling sun see Gillian Beer, *Open Fields: Science in Cultural Encounter* (Oxford: Clarendon Press, 1996), ch. 10.

10 'Darwin and the Origin of Species', in *Papers of Fleeming Jenkin*, ed. Sidney Colvin and J. A. Ewing, with a Memoir by Robert Louis Stevenson (London: Longmans, Green & Co., 1887), vol. I, pp. 215–63. Jenkin used Thomson's argument about the steady dissipation of the sun's energy to argue that the time necessary for Darwin's theory of the evolution of species had not been, and would not be, available: 'the sun will be too cold for our or Darwin's purposes before many millions of years – a long time, but far enough from countless ages; quite similarly past countless ages are inconceivable, inasmuch as the heat required by the sun to have allowed him to cool from time immemorial, would be such as to turn him into mere vapour, which would extend over the whole planetary system, and evaporate us entirely': *Papers of Fleeming Jenkin*, pp. 241–2. 'Darwin and the Origin of Species' was first published in the *North British Review*, June 1867.

11 McLynn, *Robert Louis Stevenson*, p. 37.

12 See Garrett Anderson, *'Hang Your Halo in the Hall': A History of the Savile Club* (London: The Savile Club, 1993), pp. 48–9.

13 These include Flaubert in *Bouvard and Pécuchet* (1881), the medical psychiatrist Henry Maudsley in *Body and Will* (1883), and H. G. Wells in *The Time Machine* (1894–5); see Daniel Pick, *Faces of Degeneration: A European Disorder, c. 1848–c. 1918* (Cambridge: Cambridge University Press, 1989), pp. 1, 160, 209.

14 Jenkin, 'Darwin and the Origin of Species', vol. I, p. 241.

15 Its population was estimated at between 50, 000 and 80,000 in 1798.

At the first census in 1887 it was 5,246; see Greg Dening, ed., *The Marquesan Journal of Edward Robarts 1797–1824* (Canberra: Australia National University Press, 1974), p. 18.

16 Quoted in Menikoff, '"These problematic shores": Robert Louis Stevenson in the South Seas', p. 146.

17 Letter to Colvin, early June 1889, in Booth and Mehew, eds., *The Letters of Robert Louis Stevenson*, vol. VI, p. 312.

18 *A Footnote to History: Eight Years of Trouble in Samoa*, in *The Works of Robert Louis Stevenson*, Pentland Edition (London: Cassell, 1907), vol. XVI, p. 33.

19 Letter to *The Times*, 10 February 1889, in Booth and Mehew, eds., *The Letters of Robert Louis Stevenson*, vol. VI, p. 252.

20 Letter to Edward L. Burlingame, late November 1891, in Booth and Mehew, eds., *The Letters of Robert Louis Stevenson*, vol. VII, pp. 195–6. In this letter to his New York publisher he describes the project as 'a history of nowhere in a corner . . . it is very likely no one would possibly wish to read it, but I wish to publish it'.

21 Letter to J. F. Hogan, 7 October 1894, in Booth and Mehew, eds., *The Letters of Robert Louis Stevenson*, vol. VIII, p. 376. This letter was later published in the *Daily Chronicle*, 18 March 1895.

22 Letter to *Pall Mall Gazette*, 4 September 1893, in *The Works of Robert Louis Stevenson*, vol. XVII, pp. 387–8.

23 Letter to *The Times*, 23 April 1894, in Booth and Mehew, eds., *The Letters of Robert Louis Stevenson*, vol. VIII, p. 275.

24 McLynn, *Robert Louis Stevenson*, p. 426.

25 Letter to Colvin, 24(?) June 1893, in Booth and Mehew, eds., *The Letters of Robert Louis Stevenson*, vol. VIII, pp. 119–20.

26 Fanny and Robert Louis Stevenson, *Our Samoan Adventure*, ed. Charles Neider (London: Weidenfeld & Nicolson, 1956), pp. 213–14.

27 *Ibid.*, pp. 219, 221.

28 McLynn, *Robert Louis Stevenson*, pp. 109, 120.

29 Letter to Austin Strong, c. 18 September 1892, in Booth and Mehew, eds., *The Letters of Robert Louis Stevenson*, vol. VII, p. 390 n. 4.

30 Letter to Colvin, 19 April 1891, in *ibid.*, vol. VII, p. 100.

31 See letter to *The Times*, 22 June 1892, in *ibid.*, vol. VII, p. 320.

32 Appendix to Sidney Colvin, ed., *Vailima Letters* (London: Methuen, 1895), p. 363.

33 Letter to Colvin, 7 November 1890, in Booth and Mehew, eds., *The Letters of Robert Louis Stevenson*, vol. VII, p. 27.

34 Letter to Colvin, 28 September 1891, in *ibid.*, vol. VII, p. 161.

35 See Barry Menikoff, *Robert Louis Stevenson and 'The Beach of Falesá': A Study in Victorian Publishing* (Edinburgh University Press, 1984), pp. 17–31.

36 'The Beach of Falesá', in Jenni Calder, ed., *Island Landfalls: Reflections*

from the South Seas (Edinburgh: Canongate, 1987), p. 162. Subsequent page numbers in parentheses refer to this edition.

37 Stevenson, *In the South Seas*, pp. 268–9. He also claimed in a letter to the novelist Mary Braddon that a novel of his own had been used instead of a Bible for a similar marriage on the same island; see Booth and Mehew, eds., *The Letters of Robert Louis Stevenson*, vol. VIII, p. 379.

38 Menikoff, *Robert Louis Stevenson and 'The Beach of Falesá'*, p. 57.

39 Katherine Bailey Linehan, 'Stevenson's complex social criticism in "The Beach of Falesá"', *English Literature in Transition*, vol. 3, no. 44, 1990, p. 415.

40 Letter to Colvin, 6 September 1891, in Booth and Mehew, eds., *The Letters of Robert Louis Stevenson*, vol. VII, p. 153.

41 Mary Louise Pratt, *Imperial Eyes: Travel Writing and Transculturation* (London: Routledge, 1992), pp. 92–7.

42 See Suzanne Romaine, *Pidgin and Creole Languages* (Oxford: Blackwell, 1988); Loreto Todd, *Modern English Pidgins and Creoles* (Oxford: Blackwell, 1984).

43 Pratt, *Imperial Eyes*, p. 100.

44 Linehan, 'Stevenson's complex social criticism in "The Beach of Falesá"', p. 414. Linehan is endorsing Menikoff.

45 Patrick Brantlinger, *Rule of Darkness: British Literature and Imperialism 1830–1914* (Ithaca and London: Cornell University Press, 1988), pp. 39–43.

46 Letter to Colvin, 17 May 1892, in Booth and Mehew, eds., *The Letters of Robert Louis Stevenson*, vol. VII, p. 282.

47 Elaine Showalter, *Sexual Anarchy: Gender and Culture at the Fin de Siècle* (London: Virago, 1992), p. 79.

48 *Ibid.*, pp. 81–3.

49 *Ibid.*, p. 129.

50 Brantlinger, *Rule of Darkness*, pp. 39–42.

51 Stevenson, *The Ebb-Tide*, in Jenni Calder, ed., *The Strange Case of Dr Jekyll and Mr Hyde and Other Stories* (Penguin Books, 1981), p. 173. Subsequent page numbers in parentheses refer to this edition. This novel began as a collaborative work with Lloyd Osbourne. For Stevenson's account of this collaboration see letter to Colvin, 23–4 August 1893, in Booth and Mehew, eds., *The Letters of Robert Louis Stevenson*, vol. VIII, p. 379.

52 R. M. Ballantyne, *Gascoyne the Sandal-Wood Trader: A Tale of the Pacific* (New York: John W. Lovell, n. d. [1864]), p. 238.

53 *The Wrecker*, p. 319.

54 McLynn, *Robert Louis Stevenson*, p. 467.

55 Stevenson, *In the South Seas*, pp. 313–16.

56 Letter to Colvin, 16 May 1893, in Booth and Mehew, eds., *The Letters of Robert Louis Stevenson*, vol. VIII, p. 68.

57 *The Ebb-Tide* also has a similar structure to Conrad's *Victory* (1915). In both novels an island recluse is visited by three adventurers seeking treasure. There is some correspondence between these two sets of four characters, and some thematic overlap in terms of each story's interest in violence and nihilism.

58 McLynn, *Robert Louis Stevenson*, p. 380.

59 Quoted in Booth and Mehew, eds., *The Letters of Robert Louis Stevenson*, vol. VII, pp. 2–3. Adams made less impression on Stevenson: 'I saw Mr. La Farge here, and another gentleman . . . name forgotten': letter to Edward L. Burlingame, 4 November 1890, *ibid.*, vol. VII, p. 33. La Farge, the American painter, was Adams' travelling companion.

60 Gavan Daws, *A Dream of Islands: Voyages of Self-Discovery in the South Seas* (New York and London: Norton, 1980), p. 176.

61 McLynn, *Robert Louis Stevenson*, pp. 455–6.

62 See *ibid*, pp. 434–5, 461 for an account of the correspondence between Stevenson and the Foreign Secretary Lord Rosebery on Stevenson's involvement in Samoan affairs.

63 See letters to Edmund Gosse, April 1891, and H. B. Baildon, October or November 1891, in Booth and Mehew, eds., *The Letters of Robert Louis Stevenson*, vol. VII, pp. 106, 187.

64 Letter to Charles Baxter, 11 August 1892, in Booth and Mehew, eds., *The Letters of Robert Louis Stevenson*, vol. VII, p. 350.

65 Letter to Andrew Chatto, August 1890, in Delancey Ferguson and Marshall Waingrow, eds., *Robert Louis Stevenson's Letters to Charles Baxter* (London and New Haven: Oxford University Press and Yale University Press, 1956), p. 272.

66 *Travels in Hawaii*, ed. A. Grove Day (Honolulu: University of Hawaii Press, 1973), pp. 9–10. This volume includes the Hawaiian section of Stevenson's Journal 'The Eight Islands' (see n. 4) as well as letters and poems from Hawaii.

67 Letter to Colvin, 17 January 1891, in Booth and Mehew, eds., *The Letters of Robert Louis Stevenson*, vol. VII, p. 77.

68 *Ibid.*, vol. VII, p. 95 n. 5.

69 H. J. Moors, *With Stevenson in Samoa* (Boston: Small, Maynard & Co., 1910), pp. 97–9.

70 Basil F. Kirtley, 'The devious genealogy of the "Bottle Imp" plot', *American Notes and Queries*, vol. 9, no.1, 1971, p. 69n.; Robert J. Hillier, 'Folklore and oral tradition in Stevenson's South Sea narrative poems and short stories', *Scottish Literary Journal*, vol. 14, no.2, 1987, p. 44.

71 John Charlot, 'The influence of Polynesian literature and thought on Robert Louis Stevenson', *Journal of Intercultural Studies*, vol. 14, 1987, p. 91.

72 *Ibid.*, p. 92 for meetings with Oskar Stuebel and F. Otto Sierich.

73 Hillier, 'Folklore and oral tradition in Stevenson's South Sea narrative poems and short stories', p. 35.

74 Booth and Mehew, eds., *The Letters of Robert Louis Stevenson*, vol. VII, p. 404 n. 2.
75 David Daiches, 'Stevenson and Scotland', in Jenni Calder, ed., *Stevenson and Victorian Scotland* (Edinburgh University Press, 1981), p. 26.
76 Peter Womack, *Improvement and Romance: Constructing the Myth of the Highlands* (London: Macmillan, 1989), pp. 96, 108–9.
77 Mark Williams, 'Literary constructions of oral culture', in Graham McGregor and Mark Williams, eds., *Dirty Silence: Aspects of Language and Literature in New Zealand* (Auckland: Oxford University Press, 1991), pp. 77–8.
78 See Ruth Finnegan, *Literacy and Orality: Studies in the Technology of Communication* (Oxford: Blackwell, 1988), ch. 5.
79 Janet Adam Smith, ed., *Robert Louis Stevenson: Collected Poems* (London: Rupert Hart-Davis, 1950), p. 493.
80 Charlot, 'The influence of Polynesian literature and thought on Robert Louis Stevenson', pp. 92–4. 'The House of Tembinoka' was particularly intended for Tembinok, with whom genealogy was a preoccupation.
81 *Ibid.*, pp. 94–5.
82 Kirtley, 'The devious genealogy of the "Bottle-Imp" plot', p. 67.
83 'The Isle of Voices', in Calder, ed., *Island Landfalls*, p. 158. Subsequent page numbers in parentheses refer to this edition.
84 For a genealogy of the enchantress who lives with her handmaidens on a lonely island see Marina Warner, 'Siren, hyphen; or, the maid beguiled: R. L. Stevenson's "The Beach at [sic] Falesá"', in Hena Maes-Jelinek, Gordon Collier, Geoffrey Davis, eds., *A Talent(ed) Digger: Creations, Cameos and Essays in Honour of Anna Rutherford* (Amsterdam: Rodopi, 1996), p. 214.
85 Letter to Colvin, 24 or 25 April 1894, in Booth and Mehew, eds., *The Letters of Robert Louis Stevenson*, vol. VIII, pp. 281–2.
86 Letter to Colvin, 6 October 1894, in *ibid.*, vol. VIII, p. 373.
87 Arthur Johnstone, *Recollections of Robert Louis Stevenson in the Pacific* (London: Chatto & Windus, 1905), p. 4.

7 SKIN AND BONES: JACK LONDON'S DISEASED PACIFIC

1 J. C. Beaglehole, *The Life of Captain James Cook* (Stanford: Stanford University Press, 1974), p. 678.
2 A common response to this was to blame a rival European nation for having introduced syphilis first. The Forsters went further, arguing that syphilis was probably indigenous: see O. H. K. Spate, *Paradise Found and Lost* (London: Routledge, 1988), p. 243.
3 The terminology for disfiguring ailments was often interchangeable. George Forster (J. R. Forster's son), for example, thought that syphilis in Tahiti was 'a kind of leprosy . . . such as the elephantiasis, which resembles the yaws': see Spate, *Paradise Lost and Found*, p. 243.

4 The main source of information about leprosy in Hawaii in the following paragraphs is Gavan Daws, *Holy Man: Father Damien of Molokai* (Honolulu: University of Hawaii Press, 1973), passim.

5 Susan Sontag, *Illness as Metaphor* (Penguin Books, 1987), pp. 62–5.

6 'An Open Letter to the Reverend Dr. Hyde of Honolulu', *The Works of Robert Louis Stevenson*, Pentland Edition (London: Cassell, 1907), vol. xv, pp. 350–66.

7 Stoddard visited the colony in 1869 and 1884. He published *The Lepers of Molokai* in 1886, and his *Diary of a Visit to Molokai in 1884* was edited and published in 1933. The story 'Joe of Lahaina' appeared in his *Summer Cruising in the South Seas* (1874); it associates leprosy with homosexuality. Stoddard was accompanied on his second visit by Dr Fitch, the physician who believed that leprosy was the fourth stage of syphilis.

8 Fanny Van de Grift Stevenson, 'The Half-White', *Scribner's Magazine*, vol. 9, January–June 1891.

9 For Stevenson's account of his visit to Molokai see 'The Eight Islands', in A. Grove Day, ed., *Travels in Hawaii: Robert Louis Stevenson* (Honolulu: University of Hawaii Press, 1973), pp. 46–70.

10 Letter to James Payn, 13 June 1889, in Day, ed., *Travels in Hawaii*, p. 143. Stevenson was actually quoting a resident of Molokai.

11 *Ibid.*, p. 84. Stevenson remained interested in the subject. An unpublished essay 'Talofa Togarewa' warned Samoans of the dangers of leprosy and of Hawaii as its source. In a letter to the editor of the missionary magazine for which the essay was presumably intended he also expressed interest in writing more about Molokai; see letter to Rev. Arthur E. Claxton (? Summer 1891), in Bradford A. Booth and Ernest Mehew, eds., *The Letters of Robert Louis Stevenson* (New Haven and London: Yale University Press, 1994–5), vol. VII, pp. 143–4.

12 Jack London, *The Cruise of the Snark: A Pacific Voyage* (London and New York: KPI, 1986), p. 99. Subsequent page numbers in parentheses refer to this edition.

13 Charmian Kittredge London, *Jack London and Hawaii* (London: Mills & Boon, 1918), p. 123.

14 *Ibid.*, p. 239.

15 Jack London, *Tales of the Pacific*, Andrew Sinclair, ed. (Penguin Books, 1989). Subsequent page numbers in parentheses refer to this edition.

16 Julia Kristeva, *Powers of Horror: An Essay on Abjection*, trans. Leon S. Roudiez (New York: Columbia University Press, 1986), pp. 3–4 and passim. There is a useful discussion of this work by Elizabeth Gross, 'The body of signification', in John Fletcher and Andrew Benjamin, eds., *Abjection, Melancholia and Love* (London: Routledge, 1990). I am grateful to Monica Turci for this reference.

17 This story, translated and introduced by Frances N. Frazier, was published in the *Hawaiian Journal of History*, vol. 21, 1987, pp. 1–41.

18 This sheriff, Louis Stolz (Lui in Pi'ilani's story), was the father of one

of London's crew on the voyage from California to Hawaii. The connection is not made in *The Cruise of the Snark*, where the younger Stolz figures in passing as Bert. It is spelled out, however, by Charmian Kittredge London who records that Oahu gossip had it that Stolz was the son of the leper of Kauai; see her *Jack London and Hawaii*, pp. 41–2.

19 Alfred Gell, *Wrapping in Images: Tattooing in Polynesia* (Oxford: Clarendon Press, 1993), passim. Part of Gell's argument derives from D. Anzieu, *The Skin Ego* (New Haven: Yale University Press, 1989).

20 Gell, *Wrapping in Images*, pp. 278–87.

21 Daniel Pick, *Faces of Degeneration: A European Disorder, c. 1848–c. 1918* (Cambridge: Cambridge University Press, 1989), pp. 20–1, 180.

22 *Ibid.*, pp. 37–42.

23 Martin Johnson, *Through the South Seas with Jack London* (London: T. Werner Laurie, n.d. [1914]), p. 295.

24 On London's ailments see Andrew Sinclair, *Jack: A Biography of Jack London* (London: Weidenfeld & Nicolson, 1978), pp. 150–4, 170–2.

25 London, *Tales of the Pacific*, pp. 210–11. Subsequent page numbers in parentheses refer to this edition.

26 According to Ellis, Cook's bones underwent a similar fate. When the religious processions associated with Lono were abandoned after Hawaii converted to Christianity, Cook's bones were probably hidden in a secret cave: *Narrative of a Tour Through Hawaii* (London: H. Fisher, Son & P. Jackson, 1827), pp. 117–22.

27 'My Hawaiian Aloha', in Charmian London, ed., *The New Hawaii* (London: Mills & Boon, 1923), p. 43. Subsequent page numbers in parentheses refer to this edition.

28 'The Red One', in *Jack London, Novels and Stories*, Donald Pizer, ed. (New York: Library of America, 1982). Subsequent page numbers in parentheses refer to this edition.

29 Beaglehole, *The Life of Captain James Cook*, p. 241.

30 Robert J. C. Young, *Colonial Desire: Hybridity in Theory, Culture and Race* (London and New York: Routledge, 1995), pp. 98,152.

31 Linda Nochlin, *The Body in Pieces: The Fragment as a Metaphor of Modernity* (London: Thames & Hudson, 1994).

32 *Ibid.*, pp. 16–18.

33 *Ibid.*, p. 16.

34 Pick, *Faces of Degeneration*, pp. 74ff.

35 Nochlin, *The Body in Pieces*, pp. 19–23.

8 THE FRENCH PACIFIC

1 Anne Salmond, *Two Worlds: First Meetings between Maori and Europeans 1642–1772* (Auckland: Viking, 1991), p. 376.

2 See John Dunmore, *French Explorers in the Pacific: I The Eighteenth Century* (Oxford: Clarendon Press, 1965), p. 182; Salmond, *Two Worlds*, p. 384.

3 Dunmore, *French Explorers in the Pacific*, vol. I, p. 178.

4 See Salmond, *Two Worlds*, p. 403 for Marion's habits of contact and observation.

5 *Ibid.*, pp. 382–95.

6 In Dunmore, *French Explorers in the Pacific*, vol. I, p. 185; also Salmond, *Two Worlds*, p. 388.

7 John Dunmore, *French Explorers in the Pacific: II The Nineteenth Century* (Oxford: Clarendon Press, 1969), pp. 254–5, 337–8.

8 Salmond, *Two Worlds*, pp. 427–8.

9 Dunmore, *French Explorers in the Pacific*, vol. I, pp. 4–7, 116–21.

10 *Ibid.*, vol. I, pp. 116–21; Salmond, *Two Worlds*, pp. 311–12.

11 Dunmore, *French Explorers in the Pacific*, vol. I, pp. 109–10; O. H. K. Spate, *Paradise Found and Lost* (London: Routledge, 1988), pp. 255–6.

12 See Spate, *Paradise Found and Lost*, ch. 11; Neil Rennie, *Far-Fetched Facts: The Literature of Travel and the Idea of the South Seas* (Oxford: Clarendon Press, 1995), chs. 4 and 5.

13 See Spate, *Paradise Found and Lost*, pp. 252–5 for the debate about Hawkesworth's revisions and intentions.

14 *Ibid.*, pp. 249–50.

15 In Dunmore, *French Explorers in the Pacific*, vol. I, p. 276.

16 In Spate, *Paradise Found and Lost*, pp. 262–3.

17 *Ibid.*, p. 263.

18 Dunmore, *French Explorers in the Pacific*, vol. II, p. 253.

19 Salmond, *Two Worlds*, pp. 309, 314, 356.

20 In Spate, *Paradise Found and Lost*, p. 261.

21 *Ibid.*, p. 260.

22 In Salmond, *Two Worlds*, p. 428.

23 See Dunmore, *French Explorers in the Pacific*, vol. I, pp. 257–64; Spate, *Paradise Found and Lost*, pp. 155–6.

24 This summary is from Dunmore, *French Explorers in the Pacific*, vol. II, pp. 49–50.

25 *Ibid.*, vol. II, pp. 230–1.

26 J. S. C. Dumont d'Urville, *The New Zealanders: A Story of Austral Lands*, trans. and ed. Carol Legge (Wellington: Victoria University Press, 1992). Subsequent page numbers in parentheses refer to *The New Zealanders*.

27 Introduction to d'Urville, *ibid.*, p. 14.

28 See Rennie, *Far-Fetched Facts*, ch. 3 for a fuller discussion of this, particularly in relation to Dampier, Defoe and Swift.

29 Anthony Pagden, *European Encounters with the New World* (New Haven and London: Yale University Press, 1993), chs. 1 and 2.

30 *Ibid.*, pp. 58–65.
31 See ch. 3, p. 83.
32 These details of d'Urville's stay come from Legge's Introduction to *The New Zealanders*.
33 Dunmore, *French Explorers in the Pacific*, vol. II, pp. 151–2, 281.
34 In *ibid.*, vol. II, p. 190.
35 T. B. Macaulay, 'Von Ranke', *Critical and Historical Essays* (London: Longman, 1862), vol. III, p. 101.
36 Chris Bongie, *Exotic Memories: Literature, Colonialism, and the Fin de Siècle* (Stanford: Stanford University Press, 1991), pp. 18–19.
37 The following historical paragraph is based on Robert Aldrich, *The French Presence in the South Pacific 1842–1940* (London: Macmillan, 1990), passim.
38 *Ibid.*, ch. 5.
39 Edward W. Said, *Orientalism* (Penguin Books, 1985), pp. 169–70.
40 Lesley Blanch, *Pierre Loti: Portrait of an Escapist* (London: Collins, 1983), p. 71.
41 Bernard Smith, *European Vision and the South Pacific*, 2nd edn (New Haven and London: Yale University Press, 1985), pp. 70–1; *Imagining the Pacific: In the Wake of the Cook Voyages* (New Haven and London: Yale University Press, 1992), p. 129.
42 Eventually, to France's irritation, it was annexed by Chile in 1888; Aldrich, *The French Presence in the South Pacific*, pp. 24, 32, 97.
43 Michael G. Lerner, *Pierre Loti* (New York: Twayne, 1974), p. 21.
44 Blanch, *Pierre Loti*, pp. 145, 240; Lerner, *Pierre Loti*, pp. 24–5.
45 Clive Wake, *The Novels of Pierre Loti* (The Hague: Mouton, 1974), pp. 67–8.
46 Pierre Loti, *Tahiti: The Marriage of Loti*, trans. Clara Bell (London and New York: KPI, 1986), p. 40. Subsequent page numbers in parentheses refer to *The Marriage of Loti*.
47 In Said, *Orientalism*, p. 171.
48 Aldrich, *The French Presence in the South Pacific*, p. 166.
49 Said, *Orientalism*, pp. 171–3.
50 Daniel Pick, *Faces of Degeneration: A European Disorder c. 1848 – c. 1918* (Cambridge: Cambridge University Press, 1989), pp. 74, 97–9.
51 David Sweetman, *Paul Gauguin: A Complete Life* (London: Hodder & Stoughton, 1995), pp. 41–63.
52 Nicholas Wadley, ed., *Noa Noa: Gauguin's Tahiti*, trans. Jonathan Griffin (Oxford: Phaidon, 1985), p. 72. Subsequent page numbers in parentheses refer to this edition of *Noa Noa*.
53 Sweetman, *Paul Gauguin*, pp. 421–2.
54 *Ibid.*, pp. 443–4.
55 *Ibid.*, p. 151.
56 *Ibid.*, pp. 250–1.
57 Paul Gauguin, *The Intimate Journals* (London: KPI, 1985), p. 105.

58 Sweetman, *Paul Gauguin*, p. 370.

59 *Ibid.*, pp. 346–7.

60 *Ibid.*, p. 369.

61 Wadley, ed., *Noa Noa*, p. 7.

62 Sweetman, *Paul Gauguin*, p. 366.

63 In Wadley, ed., *Noa Noa*, p. 105.

64 Sweetman, *Paul Gauguin*, pp. 406, 439, 490.

65 Wadley, ed., *Noa Noa*, pp. 8, 97.

66 In *ibid.*, p. 123.

67 Paul Gauguin, *Noa Noa: The Tahitian Journal*, trans. O. F. Theis (New York: Dover, 1985), p. 14.

68 *Ibid.*, pp. 63–4.

69 *Ibid.*, p. 6.

70 Sweetman, *Paul Gauguin*, pp. 274–5; Wadley, ed., *Noa Noa*, p. 74 n. 2.

71 Gauguin, *Noa Noa*, trans. Theis, p. 19.

72 See Jehanne Teilhet-Fisk, *Paradise Reviewed: An Interpretation of Gauguin's Polynesian Symbolism* (Ann Arbor: UMI Research Press, 1983), p. 40; Sweetman, *Paul Gauguin*, pp. 509–10.

73 Gauguin, *Noa Noa*, trans. Theis, p. 40.

74 *Ibid.*, p. 41.

75 Abigail Solomon-Godeau, 'Going native', *Art in America*, July 1989.

76 *Ibid.*, p. 7: 'to contemplate Gauguin's strangely joyless and claustral evocations of Tahiti and the Marquesas is to be, in the final instance, not at all far from Loti'.

77 *Ibid.*, p. 9.

78 *Ibid.*, p. 7.

79 Peter Brooks, *Body Work: Objects of Desire in Modern Narrative* (Cambridge and London: Harvard University Press, 1993).

80 *Ibid.*, p. 180.

81 *Ibid.*, pp. 169, 174.

82 In Brooks, *Body Work*, p. 166.

83 In Teilhet-Fisk, *Paradise Reviewed*, p. 40.

84 Solomon-Godeau, 'Going native', p. 6; Brooks, *Body Work*, pp. 308–9 n. 26.

85 Reproduced in Bernard Smith, *Imagining the Pacific*, p. 193.

86 Brooks, *Body Work*, p. 181.

87 Sweetman, *Paul Gauguin*, pp. 287, 342–3.

88 Brooks, *Body Work*, pp. 193–4.

89 I am grateful to Bronwen Nicholson for this point and other comments on the Gauguin section of this chapter. See also Bronwen Nicholson, ed., *Gauguin and Maori Art* (Auckland: Godwit Publishing and Auckland City Art Gallery, 1995).

90 Gauguin, *Noa Noa*, trans. Theis, pp. 54–5.

91 *Ibid.*, pp. 55–6.

92 Brooks, *Body Work*, p. 195.

93 Teilhet-Fisk, *Paradise Reviewed*, pp. 171–2.
94 *Ibid.*, pp. 41, 52, 171–2.

9 EPILOGUE

1 Paul Theroux, *The Happy Isles of Oceania: Paddling the Pacific* (Penguin Books, 1992), p. 465.
2 Benedict Anderson, *Imagined Communities: Reflections on the Origin and Spread of Nationalism*, rev. edn (London and New York: Verso, 1994), ch. 2.

Index

References to illustrations are given in *italic.*

Aboriginals (Australian), 48–9, 51, 217, 223, 227, 238
Aborigines, Society for the Protection of, 156
Adams, Henry, 185, 289n59
Adams, John (Jack), 79, 184
adventure stories, 18, 41–2, 51, 142–6, 148, 150, 177–8; *see also individual writers*
Aesop, *Fables*, 186
Ahmad, Aijaz, 11, 14, 106
aikane, 69, 275n17; *see also* androgyny; *mahu*
America:
  and Hawaii, 196, 216
  imperialism, 169–70, 229, 239
  missionaries, 42, 45, 52
  and Samoa, 169–70
American Board of Commissioners for Foreign Missions (ABCFM), 42, 44
American Civil War, 130
American Declaration of Independence, 132
American Oriental Society, 44, 272n39
Americans, Native, 156
amputation, 210–11, 217, 221–2
Anderson, Benedict, 267
Anderson, Charles Roberts, *Melville in the South Seas*, 84
androgyny, 251–3, 254, 255–7, 261, 263; *see also* homosexuality, transvestism
Anthropological Society, 156, 157
anti-conquest narratives, 105, 174–5; *see also* conquest narratives
Anti-Corn Law League, 18, 132, 135
Apemama, 183; *see also* Tembinok
Apotheosis of Captain Cook being Crowned by Britannia and Fame, The (painting), 31
Apotheosis of Cook, The (etching), 32, *33*

Arabian Nights, 187
Arioi cult, 80, 126, 262, 276n40
Arnold, Dr Thomas, 111, 143, 144
asthma, 207
Austen, Jane, 72
  works: *Mansfield Park*, 178
Australia, 13
  founding of, 16–17, 47, 61, 229
  imperialism, 131
  representations of, 237–8
  see also Aboriginals

Balfour, Graham, 170
Ballantyne, Robert Michael, 42, 135, 145, 155, 157–9, 171
  works: *The Coral Island*, 18, 117, 135, 142, 145–52, 158, 160; *Gascoyne the Sandal-Wood Trader*, 158, 181; *The Gorilla Hunters*, 150–1, 152; *Jarwin and Cuffy*, 148; *The Young Fur Traders*, 142, 146
Banks, Sir Joseph, 69, 70, 217, 226, 232
Barrow, Sir John, *The Eventful History of the Mutiny . . . of HMS Bounty*, 69
Beach-la-Mar (Beach de Mar), 162, 172, 175
beachcombers, 17, 63–5, 70, 72, 84–5, 89–90, 91, 208–9
  beachcomber narratives, 73
  Fr. Damien, 197
  R. L. Stevenson, 180–1, 185
  see also degeneration, cultural
Beaglehole, J. C., 7, 49, 51, 54, 64
  death and deification of Cook, 25, 29, 36, 37, 55, 56
Beinecke Collection (Yale), 187
Bentham, Jeremy, 133
  works: *Emancipate Your Colonies*, 132
Berlin Conference (1889), 169, 171, 174

297